Joe
Tumulty

and the Wilson Era

WILSON AND TUMULTY IN THE WHITE HOUSE.
PHOTOGRAPH BY EDMONSTON.

Joe
Tumulty

and the Wilson Era

With a New Preface by the Author

By JOHN M. BLUM

ARCHON BOOKS
1969

SBN: 208 00736 9
Library of Congress Catalog Card Number: 69-15787
Printed in the United States of America

FREDERICO MERK

MAGISTRO ARTIBUS HISTORIAE

ATQUE ANNALIUM DISCIPLINA PRAECIPUO

QUI MIHI PRINCEPS

ET AD SUSCIPIENDAM ET AD INGREDIENDAM

RATIONEM HORUM STUDIORUM

EXSTITIT

FOREWORD TO THE 1969 EDITION

THIS IS NOW an old, young book—young in the sense that it reflects some of the transitory identifications and uncertainties of a youthful author; old in the sense that the author and the world, including the special world of history, have changed a good deal in the years since the book was first published. It appears in this new printing exactly as it first appeared, though as the author I would now alter it in various ways if a new edition rather than a new printing were appropriate.

There are a few errors: a double setting of a line within the quotation on p. 101, and misspellings of two names—they should read Assistant Secretary of War Crowell (now Cromwell) on p. 144, and Walker (not Walter) Vick on p. 111 and elsewhere in Chapter VIII. There are, too, sundry lapses in prose that reveal themselves without further comment here. More important, there are some questionable judgments. Arthur S. Link has long since persuaded me that my treatment of Vick in Chapter VIII was too harsh, and of James M. Sullivan and his sponsors, too generous. My own re-reading of the book suggests to me that I should have been more charitable toward Colonel E. M. House and Mrs. Edith B. Wilson. Even though I still consider them to have been petty in their dealings with Joe Tumulty, I recognize now that their own personal anxieties, however misplaced, were the normal anxieties of men and women in circumstances like theirs and produced the ordinary consequences, doubtless unpleasant but surely forgiveable.

More significant, were I to rewrite this book I would elaborate on certain themes already explicit in the text. Tumulty and his political associates from St. Peter's College, for one thing, represented an emerging rather than an established group within the middle class. They had aspirations and ideals similar to those of the more patrician progressives whom George Mowry and Richard Hofstadter have characterized so well. Yet they also had roots in and identifications with blue collar Americans whose role within the progressive movement needs more study. Progressivism in New Jersey depended not the least on Tumulty and his counterparts, but also on men of socially prominent families and on the temporary political convenience of city machines and their regular constituents. Those factors and others accounted for Wilson's victory in 1910, which this book treats rather too cryptically on p. 24. So, too, the election of 1918, which marked the end of the national influence of the progressive spirit, deserves more analysis than it receives on pp. 166–68. Tumulty's own increasing conservatism during the last years of Wilson's administration, of biographical interest to be sure, had a larger importance symbolically. He typified the national temper more than this book indicates, and he turned toward the right for psychological and intellectual reasons that are clear enough in this narrative but pertinent also beyond his personal experience. I find, then, to put the matter another way, that I am satisfied with summary views such as those on pp. 66–67 or pp. 256–259, but I regret that I did not extend my reflections better to cover the environment within which Tumulty lived and worked.

Still, the book as it stands gets at the essence of Tumulty's career. By intuition rather than by training, he was a premier practitioner of public relations, a function little understood during his years in office but nevertheless pertinent to the governing of men, then and later. Most important, this is a book about the politics of the ward and the politics of the palace as both relate to the politics and government of the United States. That relationship made a difference, for better or for worse, in the destinies of the nation and of the world. Further, the patterns of politics, in ward and palace alike, continue to make a difference and continue to follow the contours that Tumulty knew so well.

This new foreword should end with an explanation of one deliberate omission in the text. When the book was first published, Joseph P. Tumulty was very ill. I did not choose to violate the privacy of that illness by discussing it. Death came later, to a man who had had great joy in life and given much happiness to others, on April 8, 1954.

JOHN MORTON BLUM
YALE UNIVERSITY

November, 1968

FOREWORD

JOSEPH PATRICK TUMULTY was the only man close to Woodrow Wilson throughout Wilson's political career. The exigencies of politics brought them together and held them together. Trained in the wards of Jersey City and the legislature of New Jersey, Tumulty was interested and competent in those areas of politics where Wilson was bored and clumsy. Tumulty's frankness made him a useful counselor. His influence extended beyond exclusively political matters. As a Secretary, while implementing Wilson's policies, he frequently stamped them with his own ideas. A trusted adviser and capable agent, he was also a loyal friend.

The focus of this biography is on Tumulty's public career. A study of his public career, continually related to American politics at every level from the precinct to the White House, helps to explain many of the controversies of Wilson's administrations. It also reveals much of Tumulty's character and that of his chief. Concentrating, as it does, on Tumulty, it is confined largely to those issues, preponderantly political, with which he was concerned. This precludes a full picture of Wilson, his associates, or his times. To such a picture, however, this biography is intended to contribute. Only with further analyses of the men and issues of the time — if then — will an exact measurement of Tumulty's rôle be possible, but it is already abundantly clear that he played a significant one.

In pursuing this study I have benefited from the help of a great many people. The quality of my work, in regard both to thought and to prose, has been improved measurably by the incisive suggestions of Professor Frederick Merk. Professors Oscar Handlin and Arthur S. Link also benefited the entire manuscript with their generous advice and criticism. Mr. Craig Wylie of Houghton Mifflin often helped me to balance the human equations. Miss Sylvia Rice contributed her talented care to improving the proof. For all errors of fact or interpretation that remain I am, of course, solely responsible.

Miss Katharine Brand, custodian of the manuscripts which I investigated at the Library of Congress, gave me the valuable assistance she has given other students of the Wilson period. I profited not only from her thorough knowledge of source materials but also from her nice understanding of Wilson and his times. Her colleagues in the Manuscripts Division, the late Russell G. Pruden, custodian of the E. M. House Collection at Yale, and the late Nora Cordingley, custodian of the Theodore Roosevelt Collection at Harvard, also facilitated my research. The excerpts, by President-Emeritus Charles Seymour of Yale, of the House Diary aided my exploration of that source. Doubleday & Company, Inc., has kindly permitted me to reproduce substantial passages from the text of and the letters in *Woodrow Wilson as I Know Him* by Joseph P. Tumulty. For financial assistance I am grateful to the Department of History and the Committee on General Fellowships at Harvard University.

This project would have been impossible without the co-operation of Joseph P. Tumulty, Jr. He gave me unrestricted access to his father's papers, availed me of every facility of his office, answered my questions, and assisted my searches without regard to his personal convenience. Warren F. Johnson, for many years secretary to the Tumultys, father and son, led me through the documents he has carefully arranged. In spite of their intimate interest in my subject, neither has asked me to revise any comment or conclusion. For their patience and generosity I am deeply indebted.

My greatest debt I can neither adequately acknowledge nor properly describe. Much of the research for and all of the writing of this book took place over five years in those hours which should belong to a man's family. My absence imposed a continuing burden on my wife of which she has never complained. This was but her smallest contribution toward creating an environment in which writing was always possible because living, for us and our children, was always enjoyable. Without that, I believe, I would have written nothing at all.

JOHN M. BLUM

Cambridge, 1951

CONTENTS

Joe
Tumulty

and the Wilson Era

CHAPTER I

A Political Apprenticeship

PERCHED in the large elms and sycamores on the Capitol grounds, clusters of men and boys overlooked the undemonstrative crowd that gathered on March 4, 1913, to witness the inauguration of Woodrow Wilson. That impressive ceremony seemed from first to last too long, often as dull as the overcast sky. The new President himself was twice dwarfed, at his left by the smiling bulk of his predecessor, William Howard Taft, at his right by the commanding popularity of his Secretary of State, William Jennings Bryan. Yet Wilson dominated the day. Before beginning his address he underlined the theme of his campaign. Observing the crowd herded back from the rostrum, he ordered: "Let the people come forward." [1] The address underscored the austere outlook of its Scotch Presbyterian author. "This is not a day of triumph; it is a day of dedication," Wilson concluded. ". . . Men's hopes call upon us to say what we will do. Who shall live up to the great trust? Who dares fail to try? I summon all honest men, all patriotic, all forward-looking men, to my side. God helping me, I will not fail them, if they will but counsel and sustain me!" [2]

The two-mile yell that greeted the new President along Pennsylvania Avenue sustained him for the while. Those assembled there cared more, perhaps, for the occasion than for the man, but they doubtless felt his dedication.

Some on the avenue, however, were less enthusiastic. Social

Washington resented Wilson's cancellation of the inaugural ball. Diplomatic Washington was disquieted by his appointment as Secretary of State of Bryan, whose shirt-sleeve past promised a change from the proprieties of the outgoing Secretary, the urbane Pittsburgh millionaire, Philander Chase Knox. Bryan, substituting grape juice for champagne at receptions, soon kept the promise. Political Washington fretted, the Republicans and Bull Moosers in the bitterness of division and defeat, the Democratic factions in the uncertainties of office-hunger. Marching in the inaugural parade, the braves of Tammany Hall found the weather no chiller than Wilson's passive review.

Near Wilson stood members of his successful political team who, rewarded for their work in the campaign, now entered office with him. Bryan at long last had an executive position, albeit not the one he had so arduously sought. William Gibbs McAdoo, able, ambitious builder of the Hudson Tube and buttress of the Democratic National Committee, had received the Treasury portfolio. The Navy's new civilian chief, Josephus Daniels, long a Bryan Democrat, had left his Raleigh newspaper for a military task which received his earnest attention but never his sympathy. Albert Sidney Burleson, former Texas Congressman, brought his measured political talent to the Post Office Department. For these men the length of Pennsylvania Avenue, where celebrants then marched, posed a continuing problem. The two miles of boulevard between the Capitol and the White House, depending on their leadership and the responsiveness of their fellow Democrats in Congress, could seem two yards or twice two hundred leagues.

Of the political team, he who had served Wilson longest and was to serve him most intimately was conspicuously absent from the Capitol rostrum and the reviewing stand. While his chief swore the oath of office, Joseph Patrick Tumulty, Secretary to the President, at the White House end of Pennsylvania Avenue took over the executive offices for Wilson and the Democratic Party. Here the day was as warm and friendly as the blond, stocky, conservatively dressed young man in charge. The few newspapermen there then and later valued most the good-natured frankness mirrored in his smiling eyes. "You boys are great personages in public affairs,"

PHILIP TUMULTY, SECOND FROM RIGHT.

GRADUATING CLASS, ST. PETER'S COLLEGE, 1899. TUMULTY SECOND FROM RIGHT, STANDING.

Tumulty told them that March afternoon, "and in Washington I will look after the publicity of this administration myself." [3] For eight years he did. For eight years he also soothed the office hunters Wilson ruffled, shortened the flexible gap of Pennsylvania Avenue, counseled and sustained his chief.

Gregarious, volatile, compassionate, Tumulty, an Irish-Catholic politician schooled in the wards of Jersey City, was Wilson's natural political complement. Having helped make Wilson President, Tumulty for a characteristic reason missed the pageantry of the inauguration. His youngest child was ill. At the executive offices, where he had work to do, he could keep in touch with his troubled wife. Furthermore, he laughingly but honestly explained to the press, he disliked wearing a silk hat. Characteristic also was his first official act. After entering his new quarters and greeting the staff, Tumulty called Jersey City on the telephone and exuberantly announced: "Well, Dad, I'm in the White House." [4]

1. Youth in the Horseshoe

As the Hudson River approaches the sea, the beauty of its valley fades where the bluff Palisades on the west bank recede and finally disappear into an unlovely marsh between the Hudson and the Hackensack. Here lies Hudson County, New Jersey, of which the central area, across the river from Manhattan, is Jersey City. In the southern part of the city, divided by the freight tracks of the Pennsylvania Railroad, a dreary slum houses the least fortunate of a largely impoverished citizenry. The slum consists of the Second and Fifth Wards whose boundaries delineate a horseshoe, from which the region takes its popular name. In a gerrymander designed to group together the Democratic immigrants then populating the area, the Republican legislature in 1871 sketched this derisive pattern of luckless misery. [5]

During the decades after the Civil War willow trees still bloomed in the Horseshoe, and small boys drove cows and pigs on Railroad

Avenue alongside the Pennsylvania's tracks. The section was less run down, less commercial than it is today, but the slum was already there. The predominantly Irish-American population struggled with the vicissitudes of modern city life shoulder-to-shoulder with other recent arrivals who had emigrated from Germany and Italy. Their squalid bailiwick housed forty saloons. When their "Dutch" neighbors were not waging local civil war against the "Glans," innumerable internecine brawls, wakes, weddings, fires, and political rallies relieved the monotonous poverty of the Horseshoe's Irish.

Wayne Street runs one block away from and parallel to Railroad Avenue in the heart of the Fifth Ward. Number 260 Wayne Street was a plain, two-story, frame building. Philip Tumulty's grocery store faced the street on the ground floor. Behind and above the store his family lived. There, on May 5, 1879, while the willows still bloomed, Joseph Patrick Tumulty was born, the fifth son, the seventh child of Philip and Alicia Feehan Tumulty.

The neighborhood promised little for Philip Tumulty's children. It was their good fortune, however, that their parents refused to surrender to the handicaps of their surroundings. The melting pot had quickly absorbed the Tumultys who demonstrated that happy facility of the Irish to adapt themselves to American life with a minimum of effort and a maximum of contribution. John Tumulty, Joseph's grandfather, had led his family from Cavan County, to seek the opportunities of the New World. He became a railroad gang foreman, working his way out to Illinois before he died. His sons, Philip and Patrick, remained in Jersey City and, when the Civil War began, rallied to the colors of their adopted land. After the war Patrick joined the United States Cavalry in the West, later became a Pony Express rider, cultivated long, curly hair, a flowing mustache, and a neat goatee, and in time brought a wind of western romance back to his brother's home in the Horseshoe.

Philip enlisted as a private in the Seventh New Jersey Infantry. His regiment hurried to join Hooker at the Peninsula. During the Wilderness campaign Philip was shot in the right leg. After his wound healed, he was mustered out, resuming civilian life in Jersey City in December of 1862, firm in his determination to succeed. For a time he served a happy but unfruitful apprenticeship in the iron foundry of William Blackmore. Then he met and married Alicia Feehan, a pretty colleen, and established the grocery store at 260 Wayne Street.

Alicia was the mainspring of Philip Tumulty's progress. Although unlettered, she was wise in the ways of the world. Her guidance and common sense, her faith in her God and in the promise of the future, and her loving kindness immeasurably eased the struggle against the slums. She bore eleven children of whom nine survived infancy. Her tireless hands moved ceaselessly to feed, to clothe, and to clean. Her wisdom figured large in family decisions. She found her reward in the increasing prosperity of her husband and children, and even more in their deep and unflagging devotion.

Philip Tumulty rose gradually. Hard work and careful planning enabled him to branch out from the grocery store to contracting, house-moving, and finally investments in real estate, the foundation of what became a modest fortune. Not very long after Joseph was born, Philip moved his family next door to 262 Wayne Street where a basement evidenced his increased affluence. Shortly thereafter the Tumultys moved again, to 251 Railroad Avenue, directly behind their former houses. Alicia directed her husband to knock down part of the fence between the abutting back yards and carry the furniture through the gap instead of hiring a wagon to move it around the block. The new home represented another social advance for it had both a basement and a piazza. In this house Joe Tumulty lived during most of his childhood.

It was a busy time. Philip Tumulty could afford a parochial school education for his sons, and Joe attended St. Bride's Academy and then St. Bridget's School. His was the normal primary and secondary education of a Catholic boy. The high precepts and stern moral code of the Jesuits were imprinted on his mind. Besides English grammar and literature he studied elocution, geography, algebra, French, Latin, and Greek. After school he often walked home with Mary Byrne and stopped to watch her father, Patrick, at work in his carpenter shop. Patrick Byrne helped the boy build a miniature house-moving rig, and Joe whiled away countless hours moving miniature buildings along imaginary streets. For another project he one day enlisted the services of his little brother, Felix.

Together they constructed a scaffolding to "paint" the back fence. Lacking paint, the boys industriously applied water, moving the scaffolding to finish the job. When Joe found that half the fence had dried by the time he reached the end, he doggedly replaced the scaffolding and began again.

From his earliest boyhood, however, he was most fascinated by the many occasions when his father permitted him to share the consuming avocation of his own adult life, politics. With the consent and assistance of the local machine, the Wayne Street grocer twice campaigned successfully for the State Assembly. His store lay deep in the "Bloody Angle" of Jersey City politics, where Philip Tumulty established himself as the leader of an informal, independent caucus of Irish Democrats. Almost every evening they seated themselves on barrels and boxes before the round-bottomed, white-clay stove and around the plain, old-fashioned counters of the store. "No matter how far back my memory turns," Joe Tumulty wrote, "I cannot recall when I did not hear politics discussed — not ward politics only, but frequently the politics of the nation and the world. In that grocery store, from the lips of the plainest folk who came there, were carried on serious discussions of the tariff, the money question, [and] our foreign relations. . . ." [6]

"Politics," he told a reporter, "had me years before I could vote. We used to have a lot of good scraps in those days. One election night I remember — this was before direct primaries of course — my eldest brother Philip, who was an athlete, led the rest of us shrimps over to a stable where the gang had a ballot box, the gang, we knew, intending to manipulate the returns back in the stable. But Philip went in at the gang leader and grabbed him around the legs. And we all waded in and punched right and left. And we grabbed the ballot box and ran to police headquarters with it and had the vote counted there correctly."

Joe Tumulty could not vote then, but he could and did parade. "I was a great little parader," he recalled. "One night I paraded through pretty nearly every big street in northeastern Jersey. I walked beside the carriage in which my father was riding with Jimmy Norton. My father wore a high hat that night and it made an awful hit with me. And I remember how all the time I wasn't admiring my father's high hat I was looking at Jimmy Norton, who was in the New Jersey lower house then, and thinking what a grand thing it would be to be in the legislature." [7]

To play an active part in politics was Joe Tumulty's burning desire. Advised by his father that he must start at the bottom, doing political chores, he joined the Fifth Ward Democratic Club, and in time was elected financial secretary. He helped raise funds, distribute literature, and get out the vote. Within the organization he espoused candidates and learned to accept defeat without rancor. He made his first speeches and first felt the pulse of a sympathetic audience.

On one occasion, a few nights before an election, observing one of the club members intently tabulating figures, Tumulty asked what he was doing. "I am writing the returns," he was informed.[8] This was not extraordinary in Jersey City, for Robert Davis, boss of the Democracy and patron of the local ward clubs, was a master of machine techniques. Davis' black suit, bowler hat, and neck-line shirt symbolized machine politics in Jersey City. An Irish immigrant, genial, calculating, but kindly, dominant in the Hudson County organization since 1890, Davis exchanged floaters and repeaters with the Tammany and Brooklyn machines across the river; cultivated his own electorate with handouts, summer picnics, and the hospitality of the Robert Davis Association; subsidized and befriended parish priests, rabbis, and ministers; and protected Jersey City's saloonkeepers in return for their unfailing assistance at election time. He financed these activities with funds supplied by E. F. C. Young, the local utilities magnate, whose reward was immunity from interference by the candidates Davis sponsored.[9]

Obscured by Davis' careful arrangements, the social problems of the community nevertheless cried for political solution. The power and success of the machine taught Tumulty to accept party regularity as a fundamental tenet, but the squalor and poverty of the Horseshoe pleaded also the need for enlightened statesmanship. The large immigrant families barely subsisted on average wages of a dollar or two a day.[10] Charitable Alicia Tumulty frequently distributed baskets of groceries to her less fortunate neighbors. Her son read the ghastly accounts of the Homestead Strike with "passionate resentment." [11] Later he and his fellows joined the fierce crusade against the "cross of gold." In the summer and autumn of 1896 the religion of the Horseshoe ceased to be Catholicism and became Bryanism When the Peerless Leader, accompanied by his wife and Bob Davis, drove through Jersey City, crowds lined the streets and the Tumulty boys added to the bedlam by exploding the firecrackers they had saved for the occasion.

It was on that memorable day that Joe Tumulty, with all the intensity of his seventeen years, first addressed a large audience. Family, friends, and neighbors listened proudly as the young orator delivered his carefully prepared speech, replete with the flowery phrases, the studied peroration typical of the period.[12] The intricacies of the money problem were beyond the grasp of the boy, but he tried to develop what he considered the "great moral issue" of the campaign — "the attempt by eastern financial interests to dominate the Government of the United States." [13]

The voices of social protest that sounded the cause of the Great Commoner were not stilled by his defeat. In New Jersey they echoed louder and louder in the years after 1896. A host of the courageous men who led the battle against special privileges for corporations in the state came from the Horseshoe where they daily encountered the evils they fought. Henry George provided them with a gospel and program, and along with the others Joe Tumulty read and reread *Progress and Poverty*.

It was in his home ward that Joe Tumulty first faced the dilemma of reconciling party regularity with the fight for social improvement. In the very year that Bryan met his initial defeat, Mark M. Fagan began his astonishing political career. Fagan was a poor Irish undertaker whose object in life was to improve the lot of his neighbors. In 1896 the Republican leaders of Jersey City, seeking a strong progressive candidate to combat the silver forces of the Democracy, persuaded him to run for Freeholder from the Fifth Ward. The Democratic incumbent, Phil McGovern, a distant relative of the Tumultys, was beholden to the status quo. He had grown careless in office, spending more and more time at gatherings of uptown leaders and less and less attending to his apparently unbreakable fences in the traditionally Democratic Fifth. Fagan conducted a careful campaign, personally approaching every voter, promising to bring honesty to the hopelessly corrupt Board of Free-holders, and developing remarkable strength among the Italians who came to idolize "Marka da Fage." His personal charm, his earnest deliberation, and the temporary support of the Catholic clergy combined to accomplish his unprecedented election. During the campaign, Philip and Joe Tumulty maintained an attitude of cautious neutrality. Privately they urged that nothing be done to help McGovern, but publicly neither challenged the authority of the organization. Two years later, in spite of Fagan's commendable record of service, they aided McGovern, who had meanwhile rebuilt his fences, in his successful campaign for re-election.[14]

With a growing group of Republican allies, however, Mark Fagan continued his crusade in city and state for many years after 1898. Tumulty fought him at every election, but within the Democracy he joined the ranks of young Irish reformers whose ends were no less lofty than those of their Republican counterparts.

To a remarkable degree this vanguard of Democratic liberalism was recruited from the alumni of St. Peter's College, a tiny Jesuit institution on Grand Street in Jersey City, where Tumulty matriculated in 1895. In the years in which he was an undergraduate student body never exceeded fifty. Hamills and Sullivans, Cahills, Donahues, Mulligans, Dolans, McCoys, and O'Briens abounded. Recipients of at least seven of the eight degrees conferred in 1899 were of Irish parentage.[15]

The Ratio Studiorum had been adapted for the late nineteenth century and incorporated in St. Peter's curriculum where English literature, rhetoric, and composition, elocution, history, political science, philosophy, and especially the classics were emphasized. Tumulty found the work difficult, but by diligent application he kept well up in his class. He developed a familiarity with and taste for English drama that was to last his life through. From Cicero and Demosthenes he learned the techniques of classical oratory; and from Plato and Thucydides the humanistic democracy of classical philosophy. He excelled in public speaking, winning the gold medal for elocution at his graduation. But as is so often the case, he doubtless learned most from his fellow students. These included George

Cutley, later Tumulty's law partner, Mark A. Sullivan, for years Tumulty's most intimate political ally, and James A. Hamill, future Democratic Congressman. To a man this group found the transition easy from the responsible morality of the Jesuits to the responsible, moral liberalism of the New Freedom.

For the aspiring politician of 1899 law was the most attractive profession. After receiving his bachelor's degree, Tumulty, then in his twenty-first year, began his legal training as a clerk in the Jersey City firm of Bedle, McGee, and Bedle. This old and noteworthy firm had been established by Joseph D. Bedle, sometime governor of New Jersey and justice in the state Supreme Court. In an era in which the foundations for a legal career were laid during a clerkship, Bedle, McGee, and Bedle produced scores of successful lawyers. Joseph D. Bedle's political and legal ability was equally enjoyed by Gilbert Collins, in whose offices Tumulty completed his apprenticeship. In Bedle and Collins Tumulty found patrons whose wide experience, broad outlook, and good sense furnished endless lessons in the lore of statescraft as well as law, the stuff of his intended career.

In 1902 Tumulty was admitted to the bar. The following year he married his former schoolmate and childhood sweetheart, pretty, vivacious Mary Catherine Byrne. The newlyweds established themselves at 395 York Street in the better part of the Fifth Ward, next door to the new home of Philip Tumulty. Their adjoining houses boasted the only paved section in a clay-street area. There the Tumulty family began to grow. The first child, Mary, was born in 1904 and two years later Joseph P. Tumulty, Jr., arrived. Grace Catherine, Alice, and Philip followed in less than a decade. In 1904 Tumulty contracted a legal partnership with his college contemporary and political ally, George E. Cutley. Their profitable practice was based largely on real estate business for the growing Italian population of the Fifth Ward. Tumulty soon learned to speak Italian, a valuable political as well as legal asset. Through his own connections and those of his father, Tumulty also had considerable influence in Jersey City police courts where he defended alike those who could afford lucrative fees and those who depended on his warm charity to resolve their difficulties with the law.

Tumulty's growing family and law practice did not smother his interest in politics. He remained active in the Fifth Ward Club, acquiring more knowledge of the ways of politicians, favorably impressing the local leaders as a speaker and worker, meeting more people and gaining their confidence as a thoughtful, helpful, friendly young man.

Politics in Jersey City were moving in new directions. Mark Fagan, who after his defeat for re-election as Freeholder in 1898 was elected Mayor in 1901, and his brilliant adviser, George L. Record, embarked on a program of reform that soon agitated all of New Jersey. To finance their plans for social improvement, they sought state authority to increase assessments and taxes on corporation and railroad properties and utility franchises, thus threatening the hoary privileges of the financial sponsors of both of New Jersey's powerful political machines.[16] While Fagan and Record successfully challenged their local Republican organization Tumulty joined those Democrats agitating for new leadership. Boss Bob Davis, disapproving, prevented Tumulty's election as president of the ward club. "Joe," the boss lamented, "I could make you Mayor of New Jersey City if you'd only behave." [17]

Danger soon provoked Davis to modify his standards of political behavior. The success of the liberal Hudson County Republicans on the one hand, and the animosity of the Democratic state boss, James Smith, Jr.,* of Essex County, on the other, forced Davis to make his peace with the young rebels. They were, after all, in spite of their agitation, tested regulars, safe on the pressing issue of local option, and like Davis himself, unfriendly to Smith. If some of their ideas were potentially dangerous, they were also immediately effective at the polls. Consequently in 1906 Davis permitted Joe Tumulty to run for the Assembly in the "Fighting Fifth."

The New Jersey campaigns of 1906 were hard fought, for the legislature elected would name a United States Senator. The Old Guard in both parties, victorious in the primaries, offered slates of

---

* Ex-Senator James Smith, Jr., was as large as Davis was little, as suave as Davis was crude. The outstanding organization Democrat in the state, Jim Smith based his power on the Newark machine which his son-in-law ran. Smith and Davis had long been cautiously antagonistic.

seemingly docile, mostly obscure legislative candidates who ran on platforms of platitudinous progressivism. Commenting on the situation in Hudson County, one metropolitan reporter suggested that Davis had publicly supported Grover Cleveland as his choice for the United States Senate "in order to give dignity to his Assembly ticket, something for which it is not especially marked." [18]

Tumulty and his colleagues, however, were not disturbed by the barbs of the New York press. Personally popular among the electorate, they conducted a vigorous street-corner campaign, capitalizing on division in the Republican ranks and on the appetites of Hudson County's immigrant population who recognized the Democracy as the protector of the saloon. With his fellow Democratic candidates for the Assembly, Tumulty was swept into office with a plurality of twenty thousand votes. Their party surprisingly emerged with a small majority in the Assembly, and in Jersey City every contested office fell to one of Davis' men.[19]

Tumulty was elated by his victory. The boy who had paraded with awe beside Assemblyman Jimmy Norton was now himself an Assemblyman. For twenty-seven years Joe Tumulty had been preparing to put his political finesse to the test. Eagerly he turned his steps to Trenton.

2. Tenderloin Statesmanship

The problems which confronted Tumulty in the Assembly grew out of the political situation in New Jersey. Nowhere was the need for reform more evident. The Pennsylvania Railroad, the Prudential Insurance Company, the Public Service Corporation and other railroads, banks, and holding companies controlled the machinery of government through the subservient organizations of both major parties. The immigrant populations of the cities, the politically apathetic commuters, the cumbersome, inefficient constitution, and the regional jealousy of the small, rural counties provided a fertile field for the manipulations of the flourishing corporation-machine alliance. Lincoln Steffens observed that New Jersey had become "a veritable tenderloin State." [20]

By 1907, however, New Jersey had begun to feel the impact of the progressive ideas which swept the country during Theodore Roosevelt's Administration. While Mark Fagan and George L. Record set the pace in Hudson County, in neighboring Essex the suburban population, aroused by the muckrakers and attracted by the prospect of increased revenues for local improvements without higher personal taxes, rallied to the cause of reform. The early objectives of the progressive program in New Jersey, the so-called "New Idea," were the assessment and taxation of railroad and utility properties at full local rates, the limitation of utility franchises, and the popular election of United States Senators. Achieving partial success in the first two of these, the proponents of the New Idea, Democrats and Republicans alike, expanded their program to include effective state regulation of railroads and utilities and their rates, municipal ownership of certain utilities, stringent controls on corporation capitalization and practices, definition and protection of the rights of labor, and such instruments of political democracy as the direct primary, the reformed ballot, the initiative and referendum, and comprehensive civil service.[21] These newer objectives preoccupied New Jersey progressives in both parties during the years in which Tumulty held office.

Tumulty and his fellows from Hudson County continually maintained a precarious balance between fidelity to Boss Davis and to reform. Shortly after the election the Hudson delegation, led by Assemblymen-elect Tumulty and Baker, in a prolonged caucus contest resolutely opposed Jim Smith's candidate for Speaker of the Assembly. At one point Tumulty himself was the favorite of the younger men. In the end, however, one of Smith's puppets carried the caucus.[22]

A second skirmish redressed the score. For five weeks after the legislature convened in January 1907, a struggle over the election of a United States Senator dominated its proceedings. The Republicans held a small majority in the combined houses where the contest would be decided; while they squabbled among themselves the Democrats also divided over the candidates for their endorsement.

James Smith, Jr., an ex-Senator himself, had chosen Woodrow Wilson as the candidate of the Democratic Old Guard. Colonel George Harvey, already grooming Wilson, then president of Princeton, for the White House, had enlisted the assistance of Smith who was impressed equally by Wilson's national reputation as an educator and by his safely conservative statements on public policy. Wilson's chief Democratic rival was one of his college classmates, Colonel Edwin A. Stevens who, in a vigorous campaign as the avowed opponent of the Smith régime, had enlisted the support of the liberals in his party and of the Davis machine. Until Stevens by repeated explanations and entreaties persuaded Wilson to withdraw, Tumulty led the fight against the Princeton president in the legislature, and in a strong anti-Wilson speech, formally placed Stevens in nomination. By the time the Republicans had reached a compromise and ensured their victory, the Democratic rebels had forced Smith to accept James A. Martine, the most articulate Bryan Democrat in the state, as their party's candidate.[23]

Out of allegiance to Davis and distaste for legislated morality Tumulty, during the session, opposed attempts to enforce the Sunday closing law or to curb saloons in other ways,[24] but his other activities as a freshman legislator were independent of his relation to the Jersey City machine. A sponsor of the program adopted by the Hudson caucus, which conformed to the objectives of the New Idea, he joined liberal leaders in both parties who in 1907 championed a long list of reforms. He introduced four ill-fated bills, drawn up with the approval of William Jennings Bryan, providing for the initiative and referendum in state and municipal affairs. With Assemblymen Alexander and Mark A. Sullivan, his old college friend, he led a futile fight for a civil service commission. He voted for laws forbidding insurance companies to make campaign contributions, extending direct primaries to state legislators and municipal and county officials, and establishing a non-binding preferential primary for the office of United States Senator.[25]

Tumulty's interest lay even more in social than political democracy. He supported laws to restrict child labor in mercantile establishments and to establish night schools for adult immigrants.

Tumulty and Sullivan were two of the group who pushed through the Assembly a bill establishing a powerful elective commission to regulate railroads and utilities. The conservative Senate defeated this measure, but some degree of victory was salvaged by securing the creation of an appointive commission with mild supervisory power over the railroads, a first step toward more complete control.[26]

Tumulty's most celebrated work in the legislature demonstrated the affinity of purpose between liberals in both parties. The Republicans, Fagan and Record, had been hamstrung in their efforts to control corporate malpractice in Jersey City by the refusal of the Attorney General to give his consent to pressing test cases involving the franchises and property of local corporations. McCarter, the Attorney General, was also the lawyer for two interested railroads and through his family had other business connections. With this in mind, Tumulty introduced a bill to raise the pay of the Attorney General and at the same time prohibit him from private practice, but the Senate buried it in committee. A more vital part of the assault on McCarter was Tumulty's bill divesting the Attorney General of power to block such prosecutions as Fagan and Record contemplated. This bill, however, in spite of Tumulty's grandiloquence in its behalf, failed to reach a third reading in the Assembly.[27]

On the last evening of the session, several of the successful measures already described were still pending when Speaker Lethbridge, seeking to prevent their enactment, announced adjournment *sine die*. Tumulty jumped from his seat and ran down the aisle, loudly protesting and even threatening physical violence. His vigorous attitude sparked the other liberals to similar vociferous dissent, and Lethbridge, bowing to the storm, permitted the calendar to be cleared.[28]

Progressives in both parties, encouraged by their achievements in 1907, found the next three years disappointing. In vain they sought a clearer mandate from the voters. The governor in that period, John Franklin Fort, a middle-of-the-road Republican, was an earnest but colorless man whose tolerant conservatism permitted him to lend only occasional, often ineffectual support to reform measures.

His party controlled the legislature, but Republican liberals *
worked less with their own party than with such Democrats as
Tumulty and Sullivan.

Tumulty easily won his successive campaigns for re-election, but
the liberals made little headway within the Democracy. The Davis-
liberal alliance suffered a characteristic defeat in the presidential
contest of 1908. At the state convention Smith's conservative forces,
brushing off the vituperative assaults of Tumulty and his fellows
from Hudson, pledged the Jersey delegation to support Judge
George Gray for the Democratic presidential nomination. When
Bryan won at the National Convention in Denver, several prominent conservative Democrats deserted to Taft.[29]

Within the legislature Tumulty continued to devote much time
to measures designed to bring New Jersey abreast of the rapid
social and industrial developments of the twentieth century. He
introduced various road bills and worked for legislation to improve
municipal judicial and administrative practices. He sought authorization for enlarged fire departments and improved procedures for
fire insurance, for more efficient control of water supplies, for the
regulation of cold-storage warehouses, for the construction of elec-
trified rapid-transit facilities, for restrictions on the sale of small
explosives, and for the use of interpreters and written interrogations
in those courts where immigrants found language a barrier to
justice.[30]

Such bills, showing Tumulty's awareness of the day-by-day concerns of his neighbors, were not incompatible with measures dear to
Boss Davis. Davis gave the Hudson liberals relatively free rein, but
in return he demanded and received their co-operation on the
liquor question and on the distribution of political largess. The
construction of highways, bridges, subways, water mains, and municipal buildings afforded a broad field for exploitation, and Tumulty
and his fellow liberals supported their share of "boodle" measures.[31]

---

* Two important liberal Republicans were Everett Colby, Senator from
Essex, perhaps the most renowned New Idea leader in the state, and his
lieutenant in the Assembly, William P. Martin, also from Essex. Robert La
Follette once called Colby "the soldier of the New Redemption."

They did so, however, with the comfortable foreknowledge that Governor Fort would interpose his veto.

Tumulty expended most of his energy on the program of the New Idea. He enjoyed a few triumphs. He and his Republican colleague, William P. Martin, assisted by Governor Fort's executive patronage, forced through a comprehensive civil service law in 1908. The following year the Governor's threat of an extra session induced the Assembly to provide for the nomination of county committeemen by direct primaries. For this device to democratize party machinery Tumulty had delivered a cogent, ringing address.[32] He was less vocal but equally effective in supporting several labor laws.

On other issues, particularly those affecting corporations, reform was moribund. Tumulty, Mark A. Sullivan, and Martin gave special attention to the growing demand, increasingly resisted by the Old Guard, for a commission with rate-making powers to regulate the railroads and utilities. Attacking the published opinions of Grover Cleveland and Woodrow Wilson against such a measure before the Assembly in 1908, Tumulty relied equally on Supreme Court opinions, economic statistics, and angry eloquence. Such tactics neither then nor later carried the bill, but gradually they helped rouse public opinion. In 1909 both parties promised action.[33]

The utilities issue overshadowed the session of 1910. The Old Guard, controlling the victorious Republican Party, gestured toward its campaign promise. Their bill, providing for an appointive commission with only investigatory powers, included utilities within the jurisdiction of the commission but otherwise represented little advance over the old railroad board. The lack of adequate provisions for enforcement and of any control over rates belied Governor Fort's endorsement of the measure as the answer to progressive demands. Tumulty, in principle opposed to the bill, recognized also the political potentialities of the issue. At the Democratic legislative caucus he admonished his colleagues to stand firmly for a strong measure. The obduracy of the conservative Republicans, he predicted, would make possible the election of a Democratic governor that fall. The caucus adopted his view. In the Assembly Sullivan and Tumulty, with the approval of the New Idea Republicans, condemned the conservative proposal.[34] Before it passed and became law, Tumulty stated his own and his party's position. Deploring the absence of a rate-making clause, he described the bill as a triumph for the corporations and a breach of faith with the people. "If it takes the Republican Party three years in which to put on the statute books a fake statute, how long, in all patience, will it take the party to pass a real public utilities bill?" he asked. "The time is coming when the people of New Jersey will rise in their might and smite the men who have broken their pledges." [35]

With the enactment of the utilities bill the session of 1910, the last session of Fort's administration, came to its end. Incomplete as were the achievements of the liberals, they constituted some progress over the conditions against which Fagan had first rebelled. More important than the statutory results were the growing bipartisan support for the principles of the New Idea, and the education of the public in its objectives.

As a leader of the insurgents Tumulty added four terms of rich experience in the Assembly to the groundwork of his formative years. He emerged with a reputation for distinguished and courageous work. Governor Fort, although a Republican, described Tumulty and the other young Hudson liberals as "the hope of the country." [36] The crusading Jersey City *Journal* vigorously supported his campaigns for re-election. His constituents rewarded him with overwhelming majorities. His colleagues applauded his tactical skill and his candid, fiery oratory. His party endorsed him for Speaker in 1910. The habit of regularity remained strong, but with broadening vision Tumulty became increasingly impatient with his obligations to the organization.

By 1910 another term in the Assembly was unthinkable. He had outgrown the office. Because of his growing family and the demands of his law practice he could no longer afford it. He enjoyed a minor mayoralty boom, but Bob Davis still withheld that office.[37] Thus even as he reached full political maturity Tumulty contemplated retiring from the arena, at least temporarily.[38] The possibility of a Democratic victory in the coming election, however, incited a bitter struggle for the gubernatorial nomination. Loyal to the principles of the New Idea then threatened by a new alliance of Smith and Davis, loving politics and loving battle, Tumulty soon plunged into the thick of that contest.

CHAPTER II

Enter Woodrow Wilson

1. The Election of 1910

IN 1910, for the first time in a generation, James Smith, Jr., and Robert Davis merged their forces for a single purpose, the nomination of Woodrow Wilson for Governor of New Jersey. Colonel George Harvey had persuaded Smith that the conservative college president would be a stalwart candidate who could be catapulted from Trenton to Washington. Smith dreamed of Democratic victory in New Jersey, of his own return to the Senate, and of national power as the Warwick of the Democracy. Weary of the long years of Republican hegemony, threatened in Hudson by the rivalry of H. Otto Wittpenn, the Mayor of Jersey City, who aspired to the governorship; and guaranteed a fair share of spoils, Bob Davis readily aligned himself with Smith. Wilson was no longer happy at Princeton. Although he refused to campaign actively for the nomination, he assured the bosses that, if elected, he would not fight the existing organization, and with their support he announced his willingness to accept.

The progressive Democrats considered Wilson merely a respectable tool for his corrupt sponsors. Throughout the state they marshaled their strength to defeat him. Several influential editors publicized their cause. Mayor Wittpenn announced his candidacy on a comprehensive reform platform. Joe Tumulty, Mark A. Sullivan, and other Hudson liberals previously affiliated with Davis rejected Wittpenn, but at a conference in the Lawyers' Club in

New York they pledged their support to the quietly progressive George S. Silzer of Middlesex County.

Davis attempted to break up the opposition. He argued with Tumulty that if Wilson were nominated the party could count on a larger campaign fund. When Tumulty asked him if he thought Wilson would make a good governor, Davis characteristically replied: "How the hell do I know whether he'll make a good governor? He will make a good candidate and that is the only thing that interests me." [1] Tumulty, unpersuaded, intensified his activities for Silzer, but Davis blocked his election as a delegate to the convention with such effective stratagems that "epitaph writers were busy disposing . . . of all that was mortal" of his political career.[2]

Tumulty attended the convention as an unenthusiastic balcony spectator. The organization permitted the progressives to frame a strong platform that mollified their antagonism and also provided excellent campaign propaganda, but a vociferous liberal demonstration could not prevent Wilson's nomination on the first ballot. Seeking some palliative for the bitterness of defeat, Tumulty left the gallery and wandered to the rear of the hall. Judge John W. Wescott, a leader of the frustrated opposition, stalked angrily out the door, and Tumulty might have followed him had not the clerk of the convention shouted above the bedlam in stentorian tones that Wilson had just received word of his nomination and was on his way to Trenton to address the delegates. Curiosity prompted Tumulty to push his way through the crowd of inebriated celebrants and strong-armed ward heelers to the bandstand, where he stood waiting for a first glimpse of the new standard bearer.

When Woodrow Wilson walked onto the stage of the Taylor Opera House, he launched the most exciting campaign New Jersey had seen in many years. Contrary to the suppositions of his opponents, Wilson had never been a tool of Smith. He had welcomed organization support but espoused no organization principles. Determined to win the election as well as the nomination, he had prepared a speech of acceptance calculated to please those who had fought him. For Wilson this was an honest as well as expedient plan, for he sincerely believed in the moralistic liberalism his address announced. Well phrased, forcefully spoken, contrasting sharply with what had been expected, his speech of acceptance struck a responsive chord in the minds and hearts of the delegates. Asserting that he had not solicited the nomination, he announced that, pledged to no one, he sought only to serve the people in the battle against privilege which the platform described. His earnest eloquence moved some of his more emotional and less sober audience to tears. Even the bitterest liberals were favorably impressed by the quality of the address and its uncompromising espousal of progressive principles.[3] By the time the nominee finished talking, Tumulty had succumbed to the infectious enthusiasm. He threw his arms around Dan Fellows Platt and said: "Dan — this is one of the happiest days of my life: — the Wisconsin Railroad law! — the best in the country: — if Wilson stands for legislation of that calibre — Jim Smith will find he has a 'lemon'!" [4]

Wilson's stirring speech of acceptance helped persuade Tumulty to assist in the gubernatorial campaign. He was moved also by other considerations. Ambitious for a judicial appointment, Tumulty, with the other liberal Democrats, reaffirmed his regularity.[5] For similar reasons liberal Republicans supported Vivian M. Lewis, their machine-dictated candidate who ran on almost the same platform as did Wilson.

Tumulty soon met Wilson. The candidate's initial campaign speech, at Jersey City, was vague and platitudinous. Depressed, Tumulty advised him thereafter to deal with such specific issues as the regulation of public utilities and the need for an employers' liability law. Similarly advised by others, Wilson made more definite attacks on the status quo.[6] His speeches, untheatrical and barren of invective, still failed, however, to appeal to the "mechanics' class" of Bryan Democrats. Tumulty was chosen to overcome this deficiency. In late September, at West Hoboken, he was holding the attention of a meeting until Wilson could get there. Good-natured, peppery, young and energetic, Tumulty combined pointed political remarks with Irish dialect stories to the delight of his listeners. The audience was so enthralled that when the candidate arrived they failed to notice his entrance. Wilson, who had previously been little aware of Tumulty, was now impressed. Immediately after the meeting, he asked Tumulty to join him in his campaign tour. Tumulty of course accepted.[7]

On the stump Tumulty's frequent appearances evoked much acclaim. A former chairman of the Democratic Publicity Committee of New York City wrote Wilson: "After you left Mr. Tumulty delivered an address so valuable to the campaign that I think it would be very much in your interests to have him make the opening address at every one of your meetings . . . to take advantage of Tumulty's eloquence and clear knowledge of affairs." [8]   Since Wilson's high-minded idealism, academic dignity, and lack of first-hand experience ill fitted him for the polemics which arouse political gatherings, Tumulty attended to that essential matter. He never descended to the bedroom, barroom prevarications that had highlighted other New Jersey campaigns, but he hammered away at the records of the Republican candidates, emphasizing the discrepancies between Lewis' current demands and his votes as a member of the legislature. Typical of Tumulty's work was his Hackettstown speech. Only a few minutes after Wilson had told a gathering at a neighboring town that it was not the candidate but the Republican Party he opposed, Tumulty launched a tirade against Lewis. At Plainfield, Phillipsburgh, Hackettstown, Lakewood, and Hoboken, Tumulty's speeches merited separate reporting by New York or Philadelphia newspapers, a rare compliment for an auxiliary speaker in New Jersey.[9]

Helpful as these speeches were, they constituted a relatively insignificant factor in the campaign. Even Wilson's addresses were not decisive. Rehearsing the basic proposals of New Jersey progressivism, he differed from Lewis primarily in that he promised to lead rather than follow the legislature. Wilson's forceful reply to George L. Record in an epistolary debate on the issues of the campaign provoked some New Idea Republicans to desert Lewis; [10] Wilson's Princeton background, attractive to the suburban middle class, helped the whole Democratic ticket, but the party enjoyed impersonal advantages of more conclusive importance. Smith's son-in-law, James Nugent,* the Democratic State Chairman, capitalizing on the co-operation between Smith and Davis, perfected the Demo-

---

* Nugent lacked his father-in-law's urbanity. A veteran organization Democrat, he was more like Bob Davis than Smith, but he was less efficient than Davis. Yet the three, "Jim-Jim" and "Little Bob," when working together as they were in 1910, made an effective Democratic triumvirate.

cratic organization. The Republicans, on the other hand, already
suffered from the mounting antagonism between Roosevelt and Taft
adherents and from national indignation over the high cost of living,
the Payne-Aldrich tariff, and unpopular tactics of "Uncle Joe"
Cannon, the Republican Speaker of the House of Representatives.

A final advantage of the Democracy was the issue which Tumulty
and Sullivan had anticipated in their resistance to the insipid Republican railroad and utilities law of the previous legislative session.
The New Jersey railroads raised their commutation fares twenty
per cent late in the summer of 1910. Throughout the suburbs,
leagues of indignant commuters demanded a strong commission with
power to restore the lower rates. Both parties promised action, but
only the Democrats could "point with pride" to their past record.
Tumulty's prediction that the Republican law would make possible
the election of a Democratic governor was borne out by the heavy
suburban vote, considered crucial by the New York *Tribune*, which
was for Wilson in 1910 and never again.[11]

Wilson carried New Jersey with the second largest plurality in
the history of the state. In his wake the Democrats captured the
Assembly and won five of seven Congressional seats. The huge
Hudson County vote, a tribute to Davis' skill, and the abnormal
suburban support would alone have provided the margin of victory.
With gains in every county, the scope of the Democratic majority
startled the nation. Throughout the country, editors contemplated
Wilson's availability as a presidential candidate.[12] If his administration proved as impressive as his election, the Wilson boom would
be hard to stop. But with the eyes of the country upon him, Wilson
found himself in the midst of a crisis which threatened to cost him
either his large liberal following or his organization support.

2. *"New Jersey Made Over"*

The Democrats had won enough seats in the legislature to determine the choice of a United States Senator to succeed the Republican
incumbent. James Smith, Jr., the only living Democratic ex-Sen-

ator, considered himself heir-apparent. Before the campaign he had given Wilson reason to believe he would not be a candidate. He had also refused to register for the preferential primary authorized by the law of 1907. After the election, however, noting that that primary was not compulsory, Smith made known his ambition. The progressives rebelled at this. Two of their number had forced James A. Martine into the primary which he easily won. Although Martine was something of a buffoon, his liberal record and the issue of popular selection of United States Senators intensified the progressives' normal antagonism to Smith. Both sides warned Wilson of the damage they could do to his gubernatorial term and presidential aspirations. The progressives emphasized the principle at stake. Smith, aided by some of Wilson's Princeton friends who doubted Martine's capacity for office, reminded the governor-elect of the importance of party backing.

At this critical juncture Tumulty entered the foreground. All of his sympathies lay with Martine. After that candidate had frightened his mentors by giving some disconcerting interviews to the press, James Kerney and William St. John, two newspapermen who were interested in his election, persuaded Martine to let Tumulty manage his campaign and do his talking for him.[13] Unaware of this development, Wilson paid a surprise visit to Tumulty's office in Jersey City late in November. Never had a more distinguished visitor called there. Yet Tumulty, accustomed to political conferences, was doubtless unflustered. And Wilson, too, must have felt at home, for the law office he visited was not unlike that he himself had once had in Georgia. There was nothing pretentious in Tumulty's suite of rooms, no shiny fixtures, no battery of secretaries. The anteroom was designed to put at ease the poor folk of Jersey City who came as clients.

While Wilson and Tumulty talked in the inner office, Felix Tumulty, excited over the unexpected call, fidgeted with the tangled cord of a half-drawn, green window shade in the anteroom. He need not have worried about his brother's judgment. The governor-elect had practically decided to support Martine, but he wanted to know what to expect from the Hudson delegation and he wanted the benefit of Tumulty's political insight which he had come to respect during the campaign. The fight for Martine, Tumulty informed Wilson, would be made. With Wilson's assistance, he predicted, it would be won. "You cannot afford not to fight," he advised, for leadership on the senatorial issue would be "the first step to the Presidency." [14]

Tumulty himself managed the Hudson situation. He took Wilson to visit Bob Davis, then dying of cancer. Although Wilson could not persuade Davis to break his pledge to support Smith, his obvious determination impressed the boss. Later Tumulty reported that "the impending storm" in Hudson was causing Davis to waver. That storm Tumulty, at Wilson's suggestion, had helped to brew. After talking at length with Davis and the Hudson legislators-elect, he felt sure that, if Wilson "could find the time to confer with the whole delegation," a majority would support Martine.[15] Wilson therefore invited the Hudson group to Princeton where they all promised their assistance.[16]

Shortly before this temporary victory Tumulty had become even more intimately involved in the senatorial fight. At the suggestion of James Kerney, editor of the Trenton *Evening Times*, Governor Fort had recommended to Wilson that he appoint Tumulty his personal secretary. Wilson was delighted with the idea. He realized that he needed a close adviser with an intimate knowledge of New Jersey affairs and he considered Tumulty one of the ablest young Democrats in the state. At first Tumulty hesitated because of the meager salary, but prodded by his brother Felix, his father, and his liberal friends, and recognizing the opportunity for enlarged political influence and service to reform, he agreed to accept. The Martine forces rejoiced that their candidate's manager was now the Governor's personal aide.[17]

Tumulty needed his new prestige. Three days after conferring with the Hudson delegation, Wilson, unable to get Smith to withdraw, announced his support of Martine. At once Smith began to fight. He held Bob Davis to his pledge and together they set out, with threats and promises, to repair and keep the allegiance of the legislature. Among those who succumbed were several from Hudson who had previously declared for Martine.[18] Smith also relied upon a whispering campaign calculated to win the large Irish-Catholic vote by capitalizing on Wilson's Presbyterian background.[19]

Tumulty supervised the counterattack. With Sullivan and Harry V. Osborne, a Martine manager in Essex County, he urged Wilson to take the stump at public meetings in Jersey City and Newark. These focused state and national attention on the contest.[20] At Jersey City, before an enthusiastic audience, Tumulty introduced his chief as "a man with a great soul." Wilson's well-received address there included a reference to Tumulty and his friends as "men who illustrate in their lives and conduct not only public morality but the teachings of the great church of which they are members." [21] Tumulty was more ruthless in appealing to the Irish. Recalling a speech Smith had made, while in the Senate, arguing for closer relations between the United States and Great Britain, he had a friend, "a fine, clean-cut Irishman, who stood high in the ranks of the Clan-na-Gael," write letters to the press, especially the Irish press, setting forth Smith's views on England. Very soon Irish societies throughout New Jersey issued resolutions condemning the boss for his advocacy of the much detested "Anglo-Saxon Alliance." [22]

The patronage at the governor's disposal gave Tumulty a most convincing weapon. There is no record of promises made, but Democratic leaders on whom Smith had counted, lined up for Martine. Robert Hudspeth, New Jersey's Democratic National Committeeman, a power in Hudson County and an old friend of Smith, was one who disappointed him. Years later Hudspeth referred pointedly to Tumulty's skill in handling politicians.[23] This talent served Tumulty well after the death of Bob Davis on January 9, 1911. His death precipitated a scramble for control of the Hudson machine. James Hennessy, who temporarily inherited Davis' mantle, was one of the many contestants for dominion in Hudson who needed gubernatorial patronage. Bringing seven decisive votes with him, Hennessy swung over to Martine after talking with Wilson and Tumulty on the eve of the senatorial election.[24]

Hennessy's decision assured Martine's victory. To the people of New Jersey and the nation, however, Wilson emerged as the hero. At the same time, the rough-and-tumble campaign alienated the regular Democratic machine. Wilson had gained prestige but split his party. In the face of this split, in order to retain his growing stature as a presidential candidate, the Governor had to drive the program of reform he had promised through the legislature. Governor and Secretary turned at once to this problem in practical politics.

Wilson's achievement was complete. In the first four months of 1911 he succeeded in getting legislative approval of the laws that had been the objectives of reformers for a decade. These included a primary and election law, a corrupt-practices act, the creation of a strong public utilities commission with rate-making power, and an employers' liability law. For these measures Wilson used effectively private conferences, public speeches, and personal charm. Equally important was the work of his associates in both parties, men such as George L. Record who drew up much of the legislation and lobbied in its behalf, and particularly Tumulty whose practical liberalism justified his appointment.

Tumulty's task was formidable, for Nugent, as Democratic State Chairman, labored ceaselessly to obstruct legislation that restricted his tactics and regulated his financial backers. Career politicians in the legislature could not ignore the Organization which would continue to function after Wilson passed from the scene. Tumulty controlled the only counterweight, patronage, which Wilson, repulsed by that area of politics, had assigned to him. Assisted by Kerney, Hudspeth, and E. E. Grosscup, a South Jersey Democrat soon to succeed Nugent as State Chairman, Tumulty distributed offices both to deserving progressives and to those whose support, whatever their convictions, was essential to Wilson's program.[25] During the first test of power at the session, Nugent accused Wilson to his face of using patronage to buy votes. The irate Governor banished him from his office. Nugent departed shouting that Wilson was no gentleman. Wilson replied that Nugent was no judge.

Although Wilson was unwilling to recognize it, there was some substance in Nugent's political charge. Tumulty wisely withheld a complete list of appointments until the last day of the session in order that doubtful legislators might not be disappointed before the Governor's program had been completed. Preliminary lists, however, including rewards for Grosscup, Martine, Record, and Sullivan, indicated that the faithful would not be forgotten.[26]

Early in May Wilson signed the last of the reform laws. His campaign promises were fulfilled. But there were dark clouds ahead. In satisfying the state's appetite for reform, Wilson deprived himself and his party of any telling campaign issues. He also completely estranged Smith and Nugent. The Governor set out to tour the West as a celebrated candidate for the presidential nomination, but Tumulty faced continuing political problems in New Jersey that arose out of Wilson's success.

CHAPTER III

Joe Tumulty's Master Plan

1. The Phalanx Formed

NEW JERSEY, although a small state, is a state of sharp contrasts. Princeton and Jersey City, only a few hours distant by railroad, are a world apart. Wilson and Tumulty in 1911 brought them closer together. The Governor continued to live in Princeton, at the Inn there, where his family preserved their long-time customs. There they saw Wilson's former academic colleagues, his devoted old students, occasionally his classmates. There of an evening the Governor, Mrs. Wilson, and their three grown daughters gathered, as they had for years, around the piano for a family sing. Life in Princeton was subdued, removed, relaxing. During his daily drives from the college town to Trenton Wilson found the countryside also relaxing. He enjoyed Trenton less. At the state capitol the corridors buzzed with legislators, lobbyists, job hunters, reporters. The visitors at his office were more demanding, less genteel, less patient than had been students, faculty, or, for the most part, alumni and trustees at Princeton. Often Wilson, by his own admission, let his mind wander to reminiscences of simpler ivy days or the quiet of Wordsworth's English countryside. When this occurred, it fell to Tumulty to bring the Governor's mind back. Tumulty, when he could leave Trenton, traveled to his home on the edge of the Horseshoe. There awaited him the politician-lawyers he had worked with for years, men whose interests were bound up with the problems he could not leave in his office. There of an evening he could rarely find time to relax and enjoy his family. His were the political-social obligations of a governor's secretary — dinners with the Friendly Sons of St. Patrick, rallies at ward clubs, meetings at the Robert Davis Association, where an official "greeting" from the Governor, a joke, an exhortation for the party were always in order. During his train rides from Jersey City to Trenton he saw less of the countryside, what there was of it, than of the legislators from Hudson and Essex who rode with him. Their minds never wandered from politics. Even when Wilson toured the country, he lived less intimately with politics than did Tumulty.

On occasion Tumulty went to Princeton to see his chief on business. In time his visits became personal, too. The Wilson family liked the new Secretary. Mrs. Wilson and the girls, for whom politics and politicians were a new experience, found that they could learn much from him. He was, furthermore, good company — jovial, sympathetic, energetic. They discovered that this professional politician was, after all, a person, with likes and dislikes, with worries about children, with a taste for the theater, a familiarity with literature and history, with irrepressible charm. If they had not suspected it before, they learned now that the people of Jersey City, like the people of Princeton, bled when they were cut.

Tumulty, in turn, enjoyed the Wilsons. His response to their warm family circle, like their response to him, forged his loyalty to Wilson, already growing in their professional relationship. When Tumulty accepted the position of secretary to Wilson, he knew that his duties would be political rather than clerical. He further understood that his chief's primary interest was not in the governorship but the presidential nomination. As Wilson associated himself convincingly with the progressive movement in New Jersey, Tumulty became increasingly devoted to the Governor's larger ambition. Contact with a cultured man of broad vision, lofty purpose, and deep integrity stimulated Tumulty's political thinking and capacity. As their close association became personal as well as official, Wilson responded to Tumulty's enthusiasm and loyalty with the affectionate warmth that lay below his public reserve and austerity. The differences in their ages, backgrounds, and social positions constrained them from addressing each other by their Christian names, but Tumulty's habitual "Governor" frequently evoked a fond "my dear boy" in reply. Their deepening friendship came to resemble that of father and son.

Tumulty was even closer to Ellen Axson Wilson, the Governor's charming wife. He found her not only a better politician than her husband but a sympathetic confidante with whom he discussed everything. Her maternal spirit helped fill the void he had felt since the death of his mother. On her part, Ellen Wilson enjoyed Tumulty's effervescent humor and youthful intensity and recognized the value of his experience and advice to her husband. Under these conditions Tumulty came to identify Wilson's aspirations with national well-being, devoting himself with ardent fealty to the Governor's prenomination campaign in the state and the nation.

Tumulty's responsibilities were confined largely to the familiar territory of New Jersey and particularly Hudson County. He had foreseen that the liberal course he urged upon Wilson would propel Smith and Nugent into angry opposition, and that this opposition would threaten Wilson's control of New Jersey's vote in the presidential primary and election. As a candidate Wilson had to demonstrate his ability to carry his home state. Furthermore, Tumulty's rôle in Martine's campaign for the Senate the year before, and his battle for reform, made his own political future contingent upon the destruction of Smith's power. As soon as possible, therefore, Tumulty began to build a new organization committed to Wilson, his program, and his election.

Tumulty's initial efforts were closely connected to the legislative session. The men who could be won to the progressive policies formed a logical nucleus for further group action. The new laws themselves were of immediate importance, for they forbade many of the devices that urban bosses had employed to control elections, cut off much of their income, and established a new primary and convention system which divested the bosses of their traditional authority over the determination of candidates and platforms. Thus these laws, increasing the chances of a new and relatively penniless organization to win New Jersey, provided an opportunity for a disciplined group of experienced liberals.

Progressive Democrats responded spontaneously to Wilson's

leadership. Democrats who were mere bandwagon tacticians inclined toward the Governor after his success gave him prestige and popularity. Their allegiance depended on effective use of patronage. Almost without exception New Jersey's poorly paid legislators and county officials aspired to some judicial or administrative office that provided a good salary or useful prestige. This was the type of patronage, desired by middle-class lawyer-politicians, that Tumulty dispensed.

Tumulty and James Kerney, his willing assistant, adopted a compromise policy. They endeavored to choose men who would be a credit to Wilson, who had rendered party service, and who would not be offensive to local organizations. Frequently the "exigencies of the situation" forced them to overlook the intrinsic merits of a candidate in order to strengthen Wilson's forces.[1] This political necessity caused Wilson to complain after his administration was over that his record would have been better had there been no offices to fill.[2] On the other hand, Harry E. Alexander, the editor of the Trenton *True American*, who considered the support of Tammany Hall essential for Wilson's nomination, complained to the Governor that Tumulty and Kerney were impeding the preconvention campaign and alienating machine leaders in New York by ignoring the demands of important organization men in New Jersey.[3] Tumulty's patronage policy, however, accorded with the needs and beliefs of the majority of the politicians affected and helped to combine progressive and hard-shell Democrats into a co-operative team.

The first problem facing Wilson's political managers when the legislature adjourned in 1911 concerned the Democratic State Committee. To ensure New Jersey for Wilson in the National Convention, his followers had to control that body of county leaders. But the Chairman, the officer who alone had authority to convene the committee and who was its most important member, was James Nugent. Gradually the Wilson strategists won his committee from him. By the end of July his majority had become questionable. Nugent then sealed his own doom. During the annual encampment of the State Guard, he proposed a toast to Woodrow Wilson, "an ingrate and a liar." Guardsmen and politicians alike were shocked. Nugent, legend has it, drank alone. Tumulty, Wilson, and William

F. McCombs, Wilson's national campaign manager, immediately arranged to use this incident to oust Nugent and elevate E. E. Grosscup, Tumulty's ally in the legislative session, to the chairmanship.[4]

The deposition of Nugent, accomplished with the assistance of Democratic leaders in South Jersey, left one area in doubt. To ensure the nomination of liberal state candidates in 1911 and of a pro-Wilson delegation to the Baltimore Convention in 1912, the Wilson forces had to dominate at least part of the populous northern section of the state. In Essex County the Woodrow Wilson League strove in vain to overcome the Smith-Nugent organization.[5] In Hudson, however, prospects for victory were brighter. There Tumulty concentrated his efforts.

For the keystone of his master plan to hold New Jersey for Wilson, Tumulty turned homeward. Hudson had furnished a significant proportion of Wilson's plurality in 1910. A stronghold of the Democracy, it sent the largest single delegation to the Assembly. Tumulty had more friends and knew more about politics in Hudson than anywhere else. And after the death of Bob Davis politics in the county were wide open.

If Tumulty could capture the Davis machine and with it the county, he could provide Wilson and Wilson's candidates with a formidable vote in any state election. His chances to do so were excellent. The traditional enmity of the Davis Democrats to Smith, persisting in spite of their temporary co-operation in 1910, provided a useful psychological lever. Tumulty was one of the best-known young men in the county. As an Assembly candidate he had usually led his ticket. He had long-standing, close connections with the machine leaders. At the time of Davis' death, Tumulty, as manager of Martine's campaign, was working at cross purposes with most of Davis' henchmen, but many of the more liberal, younger men had joined him. His power and prestige as their head was enhanced by his position as dispenser of patronage. The conversion of Hennessy, chairman of the Hudson Democratic Committee, to the Martine cause had already indicated Tumulty's new strength.

Tumulty, however, was only one of many politicians interested in control of the county. Congressman Eugene F. Kinkead, chair-

The Mature Washington Lawyer.

The Young New Jersey Lawyer.

Judge Mark A. Sullivan (standing),
Vice-Chancellor Griffen of New Jersey,
and Tumulty.

Rear Admiral Cary Grayson, Tumulty, and
Bernard Baruch on the White House Steps.

man of the Robert Davis Association, and a group of bosses known as the "Big Five" who represented every municipality in the county, worked together to strengthen and perpetuate their power. Mayor Otto Wittpenn, opposing the "Big Five," nursed large ambitions of his own. Through his control of city patronage he could reach the voters more directly than could any of his rivals. In his stronghold in the Second Ward, Frank Hague, the ablest ward boss in Hudson, juggled his allegiance, patiently awaiting the propitious moment to extend his dominion. Far away from the rough and tumble of the wards Judge Robert S. Hudspeth, vice-chairman of the Democratic National Committee, represented the interests of the wealthier, conservative Democrats who benefited from machine policies without soiling themselves with machine practices. To one of these determined contestants the mantle of Davis was bound to pass.[6]

Tumulty, while realizing the necessity of reaching an agreement with some other leader, rejected two. Hudspeth, lacking any personal following, was unsatisfactory. The Judge soon found Tumulty's door closed to him. Indignantly he observed that he had been "dropped" from the Wilson movement.[7] Wittpenn, whose camp Hague had joined, had long been an opponent of Tumulty's Hudson friends. His ambitions, furthermore, collided with Tumulty's desire to succeed Davis himself. Hopeful that, while serving Wilson, he could assure his own permanent influence in Jersey City, Tumulty ignored the Mayor.

With the remaining faction, that of Kinkead and the "Big Five," Tumulty reached an agreement. The terms of their arrangement were quickly obvious. Kinkead and his fellows announced their support of Tumulty's friend, Mark A. Sullivan, for Mayor.[8] In Sullivan's primary campaign Tumulty played a major rôle, distributing state patronage, as the New York *Tribune* reported, so that "it figures large in Hudson County." [9] Wittpenn, Sullivan's opponent, accused Tumulty of trying to become the new boss.[10] Kinkead, however, did not stop with local matters. He saw to it that the old Davis machine and the Hudson Democratic Committee endorsed Wilson for the Presidency. At the annual chowder and marching party of the Robert Davis Association, at which Tumulty represented his chief, a potpourri of hard-shell politicians and progressives roared approval when Kinkead referred to Wilson as the next occupant of the White House.[11] The Governor, in return, to the horror of the liberal Jersey City *Journal*, endorsed for re-election three Hudson Assemblymen, allies of Kinkead, who had consistently opposed the reform program.[12]

Wilson, however, cautiously avoided the Jersey City mayoralty contest. Between the personal qualifications of Wittpenn and Sullivan there was little to choose. Both had good and bad sponsors; both promised to support Wilson. In spite of Tumulty's urging, therefore, his chief remained neutral. This was a wise decision, for, relying on the power at his disposal as Mayor, Wittpenn won the primary.[13]

Tumulty then faced a personal crisis. The defeat of his closest friend ended their chance to control Hudson together. For the time being, that was Wittpenn's domain. Tumulty could have joined the guerrilla resistance to the Mayor that continued after the primary. Had he done so, he would have committed himself to the process by which Frank Hague ultimately rose to power. This he did not do. Instead, he modified his master plan to exclude personal ambition. Linking himself irrevocably to Wilson's future, he set out to win every receptive leader to the Governor's side. Wilson's neutrality permitted this change in tactics. Henceforth Tumulty's policy rested on co-operation from without instead of contest within his home county. With this change Wittpenn became his effective ally and serenity reigned in Hudson.[14]

The Wilsonians lost some ground in the state elections of November 1911. The reversion of the suburbs to their traditional standard and the apostasy of Smith and Nugent helped the Republicans regain control of the legislature. There were, however, hopeful omens. The Democracy elected seventeen county sheriffs, polled a plurality of the total vote cast for Assemblymen, and carried Hudson by a landslide.[15] In the months remaining before the presidential primary and election these gains could be solidified. Smith, irreconcilable, was isolated in Essex. And Wilson's managers had a firm base of power in the State Committee, the Governor's patronage, and Tumulty's developing rapport with the Hudson factions. Tumulty, after Sullivan's defeat, successfully followed that old American axiom admonishing the politician to conciliate those he can and to isolate those he cannot conciliate.

2. The Battle Won

In 1912 Woodrow Wilson assumed a leading rôle in the national political drama. Throughout the year he was too involved in the presidential contest to have the time or inclination to devote more than cursory attention to affairs in New Jersey. Gone was the leadership that had inspired the legislature in 1911. In dealing with the Republican houses and in meeting local political problems the Governor's advisers were left largely to their own devices. Tumulty and William P. Martin briefed Wilson on the legislation that came to his desk.[16] Tumulty, Grosscup, and Hudspeth wrestled with the incessant demands for patronage. In addition to these duties, Tumulty found himself, as one of Wilson's most intimate counselors, drawn more and more onto the national political stage.

The legislative session, except for an unimportant impeachment trial, was dull and unproductive.[17] Just one important issue arose. Both parties, honoring their platforms, sponsored measures to eliminate grade crossings. The Democratic version called for gradual elimination through the agency of the Public Utilities Commission. The Republican bill, passed to embarrass Wilson by a coalition of Republicans and Smith Democrats, established a schedule of improvements so demanding that many of the state's railroads could not have met it without going into bankruptcy.[18] If the Governor signed the bill, he would condone confiscatory legislation and alienate further the property interests which were beginning to fear his candidacy. If he rejected the bill, he would seem to renege on a campaign promise and antagonize the anti-railroad progressives of New Jersey and the nation.

Exponents of these alternative courses brought considerable pressure to bear on Wilson. Tumulty, thinking of the nominating convention only a few months away, feared that a veto would enable

Smith to paint a lurid picture of Wilson as the protector of the rail-roads. He urged his chief to sign the bill, but Wilson, convinced that it was unjust and impracticable, returned it to the legislature with a ringing message of disapproval.[19] His veto did not prove to be a telling factor in the presidential campaign.

Tumulty's caution in the grade-crossing matter reflected his concern about the efficacy of his political plan, for, in spite of their reverses, Smith and Nugent had refused to give up. Their opposition, along with adverse developments elsewhere, caused Tumulty to refer always to the first months of 1912 as "the dark days." In that period he took care that patronage allocations should serve to bolster the Governor's organization. He helped persuade Wilson to appoint Vice-Chancellor Edwin R. Walker of Hudson County Chancellor * of the state. Walker was not only an able lawyer without corporation affiliations but also an old friend and political ally of Tumulty. He returned the favor by heeding Tumulty's requests in assigning clerkships in his demesne.[20] The office of Secretary of State was also vacant. If Wilson was to control the delegation to Baltimore from New Jersey's Third District, he needed the support of David S. Crater of Monmouth and George S. Silzer of Middlesex, both of whom aspired to the position. Wittpenn showed a marked preference for Crater who exerted more influence in Monmouth than did Silzer in Middlesex. Crater got the job. Silzer was appeased by an appointment as prosecutor of the pleas in his home county.[21] In Essex County the politicians who had jeopardized their future by opposing the Smith-Nugent machine were generously rewarded. In south and central Jersey, leading Wilsonians received desirable judicial and administrative positions.[22] These men could be relied upon to show their gratitude. Tumulty himself was appointed Clerk of the Supreme Court, a position that would be especially welcome if Wilson should fail to win the nomination or election. He continued to serve as the Governor's secretary.[23]

Tumulty also used patronage to balance accounts on local option. Wilson had written a letter to the temperance people indicating his

* The Chancellor was the ranking judge in New Jersey's chancery court, the final court of appeal in one of the two parallel judicial systems then existing in the state.

approval of local option as a moral issue, but insisting that it was not a political issue. Even this mild comment was distasteful to the liquor interests. Their feelings were assuaged when a New Brunswick saloonkeeper, the head of the liquor lobby, was made a tax commissioner; an ex-barman was placed in the Chancery Clerk's office; and a Paterson brewer was designated as a candidate-at-large for the Democratic National Convention on the Wilson ticket.[24]

Tumulty, Grosscup, and Hudspeth directed the presidential primary campaign so adroitly that Smith and Nugent were obviously beaten in every county but Essex and Hudson. Essex was as surely theirs as the state was Wilson's, but Hudson was problematic, for Smith had found a valuable ally in Frank Hague who had deserted Wittpenn.[25] Hague's control of the Second Ward and of the patronage of the Street and Water Commission made Smith once again a formidable foe.

To forestall this new combination Tumulty juggled offices deftly. Wittpenn's candidate, Job H. Lippincott, who was also a close friend of Tumulty, received the office of Assistant Secretary of State. As President of Jersey City's Police Board, Lippincott could help to provide protection against Hague's small-time gangsters at the polls. The leader * of an independent Jersey City faction was designated a delegate-at-large on the Wilson primary ticket and one of his associates was made a deputy clerk under Chancellor Walker.[26]

Two months before primary day politics in Hudson had reached the boiling point. The Republicans and Smith Democrats in the legislature strengthened Hague's hand by passing a law over Wilson's veto which divested Wittpenn of any control over the Street and Water Commission. Hague promptly began replacing pro-Wilson laborers with pro-Smith laborers. Wittpenn pursued a retaliatory policy in the City Hall Commission which he dominated.[27] Hague, adopting Smith's old stratagem, used the county committee meetings to air charges that Wilson was inimical to all immigrants, especially Catholics. Tumulty answered by circulating a list of the many Irish and Italian Democrats whom Wilson had appointed to

* This was Nicholas P. Wedin, who later, in 1917, helped Tumulty in New York City political affairs.

office.[28] At street-corner gatherings both sides resorted to recriminations beside which even the bitterness of the Taft-Roosevelt contest paled. Tumulty, in his final stumping effort in the Horseshoe, drew on every rhetorical device. He exhorted his audiences to reject an opposition to Wilson "founded on the petty spite and revenge — the spleen of one man . . . Smith." He excoriated Smith for a lifetime of connivance with the railroads and corporations, pointing, by way of contrast, to the labor legislation Wilson had supported. The charge that Wilson was a "religious bigot" he labeled "a contemptible lie." [29] In the last week of the campaign, just before Wilson spoke in Jersey City, Tumulty issued a statement accusing those in Hague's camp of opposing the Governor simply because they were disappointed office seekers — a charge which came close to the mark.[30]

The results of the primary demonstrated the greater efficiency of the Wilson organization. Only in Essex did the Governor lose. Elsewhere he swept the state, in some places by a majority of ten to one. All three Hudson districts went to Wilson.[31] Tumulty's master plan had prevailed. Except for the four Essex members, the New Jersey delegation left for Baltimore pledged to Woodrow Wilson. The Governor, characteristically, closed his eyes to the methods by which this delegation had been won. He must have understood, but he disliked to admit, the immediacy of political allegiances. For Wilson friendly delegations were always manifestations of the voice of the people. Tumulty could not afford so to delude himself. Eventually, he knew, he would have to pick up the loose ends of New Jersey politics, but for the time being his attention was riveted on the nominating convention and on national Democratic affairs with which he had already become familiar.

CHAPTER IV

Broader Horizons

1. Baltimore

COLONEL GEORGE HARVEY, the most ardent and influential of Wilson's first boomers, exercised a certain perverse capacity for political manipulation in behalf of a strange series of candidates. He sponsored Alton B. Parker in 1904, Wilson in 1912, and Warren G. Harding in 1920. Harvey chose these men because he felt they were safely conservative. To their cause he gave the support of the magazines he edited (in Wilson's day *Harper's Weekly*), and for them he procured funds from his many Wall Street friends and associates. Ambitious, calculating, vindictive, Harvey loved the rôle of king maker. To his everlasting anger, in 1912 he calculated wrong. Like the other conservative men who started the Wilson boom, Harvey misjudged the temper of the times. The nation simply was not in a conservative mood. He misjudged also the temper of his candidate. Wilson was far from radical, but as he experienced public life, he became an apostle of reforms which seemed radical to Harvey. Furthermore, Wilson, an ambitious and discerning man, sensing the temper of the time, conformed. By the end of 1911 his ideas and his friends had become, by the contemporary standards, distinctly liberal. His attacks on the "money-trust" shocked Harvey. Instead of turning for advice to Harvey, "Marse Henry" Watterson, the querulous editor of the Louisville *Courier-Journal,* and their comfortable allies in Manhattan's wealthy Southern Club, Wilson turned to new friends such as Colonel Edward M. House, the suave Texan who had adopted him, and Dudley Field Malone, an anti-Tammany, Irish-American Democrat, associated in New York politics with Franklin D. Roosevelt. The base of Wilson's potential support moved from the Bourbon South and moneyed East to the agrarian West and reform East. Harvey was puzzled and displeased.

To Wilson's campaign and to his gradual reorientation Tumulty contributed continuing impetus. In New Jersey he helped to force the shift to the left. In the national arena he was less influential, by no means a "President maker," but always active, and, while considerate of conservative support, definitely of liberal views. He was one of the first to urge the Governor to show himself to the country and to recommend the organization of a national Wilson movement. Although he never accompanied Wilson on his tours, behind the scenes at the Wilson-for-President office in New York City he handled many of the "intimate personal" details that Wilson was reluctant to entrust to William F. McCombs, his official manager. At Trenton he screened the Governor's mail, keeping up to date on the developments of the prenomination campaign.[1] Tumulty regarded the assistance of Bryan and his faction in the party as essential to Wilson's cause, and he respected Bryan's power and principles, but he recognized the importance of keeping the allegiance of Harvey and Watterson. He was therefore distressed to learn of the frigid conversation between Wilson and Harvey that precipitated their estrangement. In December 1911, Wilson blandly told Harvey that the support of *Harper's Weekly* was damaging his cause. He requested the Colonel to remove the Wilson-for-President flier on the magazine's masthead. Harvey, still proud, in spite of Wilson's changed views, that he had "discovered" him, was shocked. He complied, but never forgave. No king maker meekly relinquishes his place next to the throne. Realizing that Harvey would be offended by Wilson's offhand remarks and that the Governor would be accused again, as in the case of Jim Smith, of ingratitude to a political friend, Tumulty helped persuade his chief to write a public letter to Harvey apologizing for his manners. The letter failed to placate the Colonel, but Tumulty continued to make conciliatory overtures to Harvey and the equally offended Watterson.[2]

Distressed by the Harvey episode, Tumulty none the less rejoiced at Wilson's substantial gains among liberals. Neither Wilson nor Tumulty could persuade testy old Senator R. F. Pettigrew of South Dakota to join their forces,[3] but Pettigrew was of little importance compared to Bryan. Throughout 1911 Wilson's friends cultivated Bryan assiduously. When the Great Commoner came to New Jersey, Ellen Wilson arranged a family dinner in his honor. This homey affair was so obviously pleasurable to Bryan that Tumulty cheerfully observed that Mrs. Wilson had nominated her husband.[4]

Just before the Jackson Day Dinner of 1912, however, Wilson's lieutenants, assembled in Washington for the Democratic love-feast, were thrown into a panic. The Governor's enemies published a letter he had written to Adrian H. Joline in 1907 expressing the desire that something might be done to knock Bryan into a "cocked hat." Wilson, embarrassed and confused, telegraphed Tumulty to join him in Washington at once. When Tumulty arrived, he found the Governor's brain trust trying to decide how to soothe Bryan. While Josephus Daniels, long a Bryanite, was conferring with Bryan to this end, William F. McCombs advised Wilson to write an apologetic letter assuring the Silver Orator that he had long since changed his mind. This was characteristic of McCombs, a weak, southern-born Wall Streeter who mistakenly fancied himself as a Thurlow Weed. Tumulty convinced Wilson that Bryan would consider a letter such as McCombs suggested insincere. Largely on this advice Wilson rejected the proposal, instead paying a "handsome tribute" to Bryan in his after-dinner speech. Meanwhile Bryan's initial anger had cooled. He realized that Wilson's conservative opponents were also his own. Pleased by the Governor's speech, he threw his arm over Wilson's shoulder in a gesture of continued friendship.[5]

Bryan's support again became an issue just before the Baltimore Convention. Resisting a movement to make Judge Alton B. Parker temporary chairman, Bryan sent identical wires to Wilson, Champ Clark, and several favorite sons asking each to express his preference for a progressive keynoter. Seeking the favor of all factions, Clark equivocated in his reply. McCombs, who was working frantically to line up Tammany for Wilson, urged the Governor to do the same. Wilson preferred to stand with Bryan, but believed that McCombs, then on the job at Baltimore, had reason for the opposite counsel. He also felt that no candidate should attempt to dictate to the convention. Mrs. Wilson and Tumulty, however, argued that Bryan's essential allegiance could be ensured only by a favorable response. Their advice sustained Wilson's preference. His telegram to Bryan left no doubt that he was the one candidate who stood adamantly on the progressive side. This was a bold and wise stroke, for Bryan had decided not to tolerate a conservative selection. The Great Commoner was further gratified when Wilson, again influenced by Tumulty, agreed to support Ollie James, an able parliamentarian, popular orator, and friend of Bryan, for permanent chairman.[6]

The Baltimore Convention was one of the most exciting and bitterly contested in the history of the Democratic Party. At various crucial moments on the floor "Alfalfa Bill" Murray and William Jennings Bryan, agrarian radicals, lent their invaluable support to Wilson. Behind the scenes Thomas Taggart and Roger Sullivan, organization leaders from Indiana and Illinois, rendered similar services.[7] As in New Jersey, the national Wilson movement rested on the combined strength of the progressives attracted by Wilson's liberal stand and the old-line politicians enlisted by the astute trading of his managers.

While the convention met, Tumulty was with the Governor at Sea Girt, New Jersey. From friendly reporters and Wilson's floor managers in Baltimore he received complete details over private telegraph and telephone lines. The constant tension permitted him no relaxation. He walked miles each day between the telegraph booth and the Governor's living room.

Tumulty's disposition accurately mirrored Wilson's chances. He timed every demonstration, suffered through each second of the sixty-five minutes accorded to Speaker of the House, Champ Clark, and breathed freely again only after seventy-five minutes elapsed before Wilson's followers ceased their cheers and parades. He rarely slept. Often when there was no news at night he sat outside with Wilson's oldest daughter, immersed in discussion of the Governor's progress or peering blankly into space. So intense was his feeling that Wilson, who remained relatively calm throughout the ordeal, tried to revive his natural sense of humor by teasing him good-naturedly.

On the tenth ballot Charles F. Murphy, Tammany's chief, swung New York into the Clark column, expecting to stampede the convention. It was a bad moment for the Wilsonians at Baltimore and Sea Girt. Tumulty paled visibly when he heard the news. By skillful bargaining and firm discipline, however, Wilson's managers held off the stampede. But the next morning, McCombs, always nervous, and obsessed with the idea that Tammany's vote was decisive, telephoned Wilson to suggest that he withdraw his name. Wilson agreed and began to plan a vacation in England. Tumulty pleaded with the Governor to keep fighting, insisting that there was latent strength that would come to his side as soon as it became obvious that Clark could not command a two-thirds vote. William G. McAdoo, second in command of the Wilson forces at Baltimore, telephoned indignantly to urge Wilson to overlook McCombs' hysteria and to assure the Governor that his nomination was inevitable. Their exhortations, confirming his own inclinations, prompted Wilson to retract his directions to McCombs.[8]

Murphy's action frightened Bryan who thus far had voted, with the rest of the Nebraska delegation, for Clark. Now suspecting some sort of a deal between his Tammany foes and Clark, preferring Wilson to Clark in any case, and perhaps himself ambitious to profit from a deadlock, the Great Commoner withdrew Nebraska's vote from Clark and informed the delegates, in resounding tones, that he would condone no candidate whom Tammany supported. Shortly thereafter the convention adjourned over Sunday. Wilson's managers used this time to seal their agreements with Taggart, Sullivan, and other powerful state leaders. A flood of telegrams from all over the country applauded Bryan's stand. McCombs, however, made a last effort to win Tammany. He telephoned Wilson asking him to promise that, if nominated and elected, he would not appoint Bryan Secretary of State. Wilson refused to commit himself. McCombs' message, Eleanor Wilson observed, bred "murder in Tumulty's eyes." [9]

On the second ballot on Monday Tom Taggart switched Indiana's vote from Thomas Riley Marshall to Wilson. As other states followed Indiana's lead, Wilson passed Clark for the first time. The reporters at Sea Girt dashed from their tents to Wilson's porch with the news. Thereafter Tumulty was confident. On the forty-third ballot, on Tuesday, Roger Sullivan delivered Illinois to Wilson. On the forty-sixth ballot Oscar Underwood's managers gave up and Wilson was nominated. As soon as the wires carried the news to Sea Girt, Tumulty rushed out of the house, waving toward a clump of trees. Out marched a brass band blaring "Hail to the Chief." Wilson laughingly asked if Tumulty had ordered the musicians to slink away in case of defeat.[10]

The "dark days" were over. Theodore Roosevelt's Bull Moose practically assured Democratic victory. For the rest of his life Tumulty was to feel indebted to the tireless men in New Jersey and the nation who had made possible Wilson's triumph at Baltimore.

2. The 1912 Campaign

After Wilson's nomination national politics occupied more and more of Tumulty's time. As secretary to a presidential candidate he could not be too tactful. Many of the Democratic politicians who flocked to New Jersey to confer with their standard bearer also talked at length with Tumulty. Wilson's mail called for even more attention. The letters of congratulation and advice which flooded the office had to be answered. Tumulty, Charles L. Swem, Wilson's personal stenographer, and Warren F. Johnson, a New Jersey clerk who was to become Tumulty's secretary, devised over twenty form letters to satisfy almost any correspondent. There were special types to be sent to New Jersey well-wishers, to college men, to Princeton men, to the Governor's classmates, to Republicans who favored Wilson, to newspaper editors, and to Democratic clubs. Other forms ·dealt with invitations to speak, requests for interviews, and Cabinet recommendations.[11] Tumulty screened all the incoming mail. When a form would not do, he eased Wilson's load by summarizing the question at hand and suggesting a reply. Typical of his routing slips was one that read: "Attached is a letter from a Doctor in Maryland who aided in the primary fights and now finds fault with the prominence that has been given to certain men in Maryland who were not your firm friends in the 'dark days.' Write him a pleasant letter." [12]

By handling the Governor's mail and conversing with his visitors Tumulty accumulated a vast amount of national political information, all of which he recorded for future use in a little black book. He gave particular consideration to conditions in New York State where Wilson's managers feared that Tammany would slash the ticket. Murphy and his henchmen, disgruntled over the beating they had received at Baltimore, resented Wilson's postconvention coolness. Tumulty sought to mitigate their hostility by arguing the party's cause to his personal friends in the organization. During his years of service to Bob Davis he had met many leaders of the New York and Brooklyn machines. Other New York politicians were introduced by McAdoo, Senator James O'Gorman, and Dudley Field Malone, O'Gorman's capable son-in-law. Through these men Tumulty mollified Tammany's antagonism. News of his success soon reached Wilson in a letter from John B. Stanchfield, a Wigwam favorite who had fought the Governor at Baltimore. ". . . I had a very interesting chat with your attractive secretary about certain confidential matters, and have conveyed the information imparted by him to me to the proper party, and you need have no anxiety as to the situation in New York. The organization is a unit for you, and I have great hope that you will carry the state. . . ." *[13]

Tumulty's charm, tact, and good humor made a striking impression on the newspapermen who covered Wilson's headquarters in New Jersey. Press relations were of particular importance to a candidate in the days before the radio or cinema. To balance Wilson's frigid antipathy to reporters, Tumulty extended himself to please them. Long before the Baltimore Convention he had made many friends. During the convention one of the newspapermen stationed at Sea Girt for the first time referred to him in a dispatch

---

* Tumulty's good work in placating Tammany was undone by Wilson in August and September, see Link.

as plain "Joe Tumulty," an indication that the reporters felt completely at home.[14] After the nomination Tumulty gave a dinner for Wilson and the press. This affair and Tumulty's frequent news conferences thereafter helped to present Wilson and his program to the electorate through sympathetic commentaries.[15]

In spite of his multifarious duties in the national campaign, Tumulty had to devote most of his energy to the New Jersey salient. James Smith, Jr., had voted against Wilson to the bitter end at Baltimore. After the convention he refused to visit the nominee. Assuming that Wilson's career in New Jersey was almost over and that Wilson's interest in state affairs had flagged, Smith reorganized his forces and announced his intention to run for the Democratic senatorial nomination. He still ruled Essex with a firm hand, and in Hudson he had persuaded Nicholas P. Wedin to join Hague in opposition to the Wittpenn-Wilson group.[16]

The senatorial primary was complicated by the candidacies of three of Wilson's supporters: John W. Wescott, William C. Gebhardt, and Congressman William Hughes. If they all remained in the contest, Smith would probably win because of a division in the progressive vote. Wilson warned them that only one could run, but he refused to choose among them. Gebhardt withdrew. Wescott and Hughes agreed to submit their claims to the National Democratic Headquarters, and on the recommendation of O'Gorman, McAdoo, and Daniels, Hughes was selected as the progressive candidate.[17] Tumulty, delighted that Hughes, an old friend, was chosen, counted on the Congressman's popularity with labor and immigrant groups to dull the impact of Smith's usual charges against Wilson.

Nevertheless Tumulty was worried about Hudson where Hague was rapidly gaining strength. Neither Tumulty nor Hudspeth could give the county his full attention. Wilson was preoccupied with the national scene and tired of the incessant squabbles in Jersey City. Reluctantly, however, he finally agreed to address a meeting there. Tumulty attributed victory to the Governor's speech.[18] At least it raised the tone of a rough-and-tumble primary at which Nugent went down fighting, arrested on five separate charges growing out of altercations at the polls. In every county but Essex Wilson's candidates survived primary day. Hughes' majority was so large that Smith retired forever from active politics.[19]

Winning the presidential election was considerably easier than winning the senatorial primary. Except for Smith who came out for Roosevelt, the Democrats stood firmly behind Wilson. The opposition in New Jersey, as in the nation, was hopelessly divided. Wilson's comfortable plurality would have been a minority had the Taft and Roosevelt votes been combined. The Democrats captured both houses of the New Jersey legislature just as they won control of Congress, but their total vote in New Jersey was less than that of 1908, to say nothing of 1910.[20]

Theodore Roosevelt pushed Tumulty's master plan over the top. Nevertheless the plan had succeeded 'and the skillful politics of Wilson's advisers had permitted the Governor to benefit from Republican schism. Tumulty's rôle in Wilson's campaign had not escaped notice. From faraway Wisconsin Joseph E. Davies wrote with a sympathetic understanding of Tumulty's point of view:

> . . . You have had a hard time of it for the last two years; but it must be a matter of tremendous gratification to you to know that you have been of service . . . to the great man, to whom we both owe fealty and affection. . . . That the Governor has the largest measure of appreciation of you and what you have done during these trying months, I feel confident, and in that fact, you must feel great additional compensation.[21]

It was singularly appropriate that Wilson received the first definite news of his election as President of the United States from Tumulty.[22]

3. Last Days in New Jersey

Wilson continued to serve as Governor of New Jersey until the week of his inauguration as President. He did so in order to help to round out reform in the state and to postpone the impending party battle over the choice of his successor. His larger interest, which Tumulty shared, was in national affairs. Consequently neither man evidenced the zeal and determination that had characterized the fruitful legislative session of 1911, but their final efforts reflected the rancor which had developed in state politics.

The New Jersey Democratic platform of 1912 advocated three measures dear to the hearts of progressives: regulation of corporations, revision of the jury system, and amendment of the constitution to establish a more balanced representation. To ensure the success of this program the liberals sought to guide the work of the Assembly by supporting Charles O'Connor Hennessy for Speaker. Many in the legislature who had co-operated with Wilson, however, were anxious to appease Nugent for his strength would tend to increase after the Governor had gone to Washington. The progressives, therefore, anticipated troublesome resistance from their tenacious rivals.

Before the Democratic caucus met, Wilson had gone to Bermuda for a much-needed vacation, leaving Tumulty in charge of state affairs. Tumulty's initial reports confidently predicted that the Governor's friends would dominate the legislature. His letters pleased Wilson who replied that he would be mortified if Hennessy were defeated. Tumulty, however, discovered too late that his opponents had constructed impregnable defenses and that some of the men on whom he had counted had deserted the field. The day of the caucus was among the most miserable of his life. In an acrimonious atmosphere which generated both verbal and physical contests Hennessy was beaten. Tumulty at once wrote Wilson, explaining the cause of the setback. The Governor, with characteristic understanding, replied approving and applauding his Secretary's rôle.[23]

After the session began the progressives scored some measure of revenge. Tumulty's expeditious use of patronage and Wittpenn's peremptory intervention obtained senatorial approval for their candidate for State Treasurer.[24] The same devices helped Wilson climax his constructive achievements in New Jersey by forcing the enactment of seven bills, known as the Seven Sisters, which regulated corporation capitalization and practices, established comprehensive safeguards against restraint of trade, and made offending corporation officials liable to criminal prosecution. The rest of the liberal program, however, faltered. Nugent delayed action on constitutional revision and jury reform until after Wilson, no longer governor, had lost most of his power in New Jersey.[25]

Wilson and Tumulty were busier with plans for the presidential years than with state problems. Among the first of the appointments Wilson announced was that of Tumulty as his personal secretary. The President-elect reached this decision only after much debate. There was considerable opposition to Tumulty. McCombs, who disliked him, suggested Walter W. Vick, a New Jersey Wilsonian, in his place.[26] A host of anti-Catholics opened fire on Tumulty. Harry E. Alexander had complained that Tumulty diverted an excessive amount of patronage to his fellow religionists. Tom Watson expressed the bigotry of those Southern anti-Catholics who ranted about the Jesuitical menace and predicted that Tumulty would reveal vital state secrets to the Vatican. Wilson's mail was filled with such warnings. One self-styled "Patriotic American" even wrote one of Wilson's daughters about the dangers inherent in Tumulty's Catholicism.[27] Personal and religious opposition made little impression on Wilson, but he was inclined to agree with those who argued that Tumulty was inexperienced in national affairs and engrossed with the mechanisms of small politics.[28]

Various favorable factors, however, far outweighed these considerations. The reporters, to whom Tumulty had further endeared himself by participating in their jokes on Wilson, were on his side. They realized how much he wanted to accompany his chief to Washington. Oswald Garrison Villard's New York *Evening Post*, Wilson's favorite newspaper, carried a special article on the duties and importance of the Secretary of the President, especially with regard to press relations. After Tumulty's appointment was announced, the *Post*, as if to say "I told you so," outdid other papers in extolling it.[29]

Of greater importance was the support of Colonel Edward M. House, to whom Wilson was turning more and more for advice. House by 1912 had become Wilson's most intimate counselor. A feline man, House purred advice. In disposition rather feminine, but not effeminate, he was a wonderful listener. He had an excellent mind — quick, sure, penetrating. While devoid of ambition for office, he sought and ably filled the rôle of Wilson's ex-officio prime minister. His contributions to policy-making were great; his ability to deal alike with local politicians and European diplomats proved indispensable; above all, he gave Wilson the intelligent, sympathetic, personal support that earned for him the President's frequent "dear friend." House could see no objection to a Catholic Secretary to the President. He found Tumulty bright, quick, honest, courageous, and outspoken. To Wilson's complaint that Tumulty's vision was too narrow, House replied that his political instinct would be an essential asset. Like House, William Gibbs McAdoo, also in Wilson's confidence, concluded that Tumulty was the best man for the job.[30]

Actually Wilson had seriously considered no other candidate. He was extremely fond of Tumulty, recognized his devotion, depended on his information, and appreciated his services. He realized that Tumulty had grown in stature in their years together and was capable of growing more. He disliked change. And Mrs. Wilson was eager to have Tumulty appointed.[31] Before making his decision public, Wilson rather casually asked Tumulty if he would continue as his secretary. Tumulty managed a restrained affirmative, left the Governor's office, closed the door, and only then vented his unbounded joy. "Charley," he cried to the lone reporter sitting in the anteroom, "I've got it!"[32]

Immediately after the appointment was announced, congratulatory letters began to arrive. President Taft's secretary, Charles D. Hilles, to whom Tumulty had been introduced by Colonel Harvey, expressed his pleasure and offered his assistance. "The duties are arduous and confining," he wrote, "but the reward is commensurate, for in no position in the gift of the President is there greater opportunity to render a real service to one's chief. . . ."[33] McKee Barclay of the Baltimore *Sun* sent his best wishes. "By the way," he concluded, "don't you know that it is going to be hard to call *him* anything but 'Governor.' I hate to think of having to change and I believe that I will stick to the old title if he will let me. . . ."[34] To Barclay and Tumulty and the other friends of New Jersey days, Wilson remained always the "Governor."

Of all the congratulatory letters, Tumulty was perhaps most pleased by one from William Jennings Bryan, his boyhood hero. Tumulty had been present at luncheon at the Hotel Sterling in Trenton when Wilson formally offered Bryan the position of Secretary of State and Bryan accepted. No decision of the President-elect stirred up more controversy. While the friends and enemies of the Great Commoner had deluged Wilson with letters, Tumulty had warmly advocated the appointment, arguing that Bryan had earned it by his years of party leadership and his services at the convention and in the campaign.[35]

In the conferences over the choice of the other cabinet officers Tumulty's voice was frequently heard. He urged that Brandeis be made Attorney General, but Wilson found it advisable to delay his recognition of that great Boston lawyer. The appointments of Daniels, Burleson, Redfield, and McAdoo were all endorsed by Tumulty.* One selection was entirely his doing. On March 1 the War portfolio was still vacant. Tumulty told Wilson that he was anxious to see a New Jersey man placed in the cabinet, suggesting Lindley M. Garrison, vice-chancellor of the state. Wilson had never met Garrison, but he offered him the position the next day.[36]

On March 3, 1913, Tumulty entrained for Washington to begin a new phase of his life. Wilson's inauguration was only a day away. Many milestones had been passed since the hot and hectic afternoon in the Taylor Opera House when Tumulty had cheered his chief's first political address. Wilson had found New Jersey still the "tenderloin of America." When he left, it was in the van of progressive states. In a sense he had reaped the harvest of the seeds others had planted, but he had worked hard to gather the crop. Although his reforms were not original, Wilson had been audacious, persistent, and sincere.

Wilson's reforms would have been unattainable without the practical politics to which Tumulty attended, just as New Jersey's support for Wilson as a presidential candidate would have been impossible without them. Tumulty's politics, never dainty, were

---

* Josephus Daniels, Secretary of the Navy; Albert S. Burleson, Postmaster General; William C. Redfield, Secretary of Commerce; William G. McAdoo, Secretary of the Treasury.

both essential and successful. They were by no means extraordinary. Incorporating the lessons Tumulty had learned from Bob Davis, they suited the unlovely tactics employed by Wilson's opponents. Tumulty's methods were simply the indispensable weapons of a political realist.

As his train rolled across New Jersey toward Washington, Tumulty could reflect with satisfaction on the achievements of the past three years. He could also view the future with eager anticipation. There would be friends in the capital — Jim Kerney, Bob Norton, Dave Lawrence and others of the press; Billy Hughes, Ollie James, Tom Pence, and other Democratic leaders in and out of Congress. In the Cabinet were Garrison, a fellow citizen of Jersey City; Bryan, an acquaintance of long years; and McAdoo, Redfield, and Daniels, all of whom Tumulty knew casually. His tasks would be larger, but therefore more interesting. If the challenge was greater, success would be more rewarding. It was a long way from the Horseshoe to the executive offices of the President of the United States, but Tumulty was confident that he had earned his position and would be equal to it.

CHAPTER V

Daily Routine

WASHINGTON in 1913, while no longer the muddy village of Lincoln's day, was still more a sleepy southern town than the granite and marble metropolis of today. Only the climate has remained constant, and impossible — damp-cold, penetrating in winter; steaming-hot, enervating, at worst sickening in summer. Then as now, the city was romantically beautiful in the early spring, but it was an unhappy location for the seat of government. Where the imposing buildings of the government agencies now stand along Constitution Avenue, there was in 1913 little but swampy, rough land, scattered with rickety buildings. Just to the north, Pennsylvania Avenue, the axis between the White House and the Capitol, although known to the local people as "*The* Avenue*,*" was an enormously wide, unattractive street lined largely by dilapidated residences and grimy stores.

Clattering streetcars swayed through Washington with more competition from balky horses than from the few automobiles. The hub of the fashionable district, Dupont Circle, not yet a traffic hazard, was an easy walk from the shops on F Street. Georgetown remained a distinct, typically southern town, and Chevy Chase, now a teeming dormitory of government workers, was a sparsely settled rural suburb.

To the city's permanent, voteless inhabitants, the administrations that came and went were a passing show, only rarely taken seriously as a part of life. In the eyes of the élite of Potomac society, still living in the shadowy tradition of the post-Civil War decades, the government worker, elected or appointed, remained somewhat disreputable, a notch, perhaps, above the tradesman. A few exceptions — the judiciary, the diplomats, the occasional Senator who had been in service for a generation — were received in fashionable parlors; even they, to their good fortune, were not subjected to the rigors of the cocktail party, then happily uninvented.

The First World War was to impel in the District of Columbia great changes: the beginnings of the construction that has made Constitution Avenue a street of palaces; of the search for experts who have since lent to government the dignity, or at least the prestige, of collegiate Gothic and financial Gotham; of the scramble for "contacts" which has generated among tireless seekers of influence a tiresome, tinny social whirl. But the war was four years away when Wilson took office.

The Wilsons found sleepy Washington agreeable. A southern family, they were at once at home in the provincial southern atmosphere. Local "Jim Crow" ordinances seemed as natural to them as did the soft drawl of clerks who dispensed yard goods to the girls. Never accustomed to the pace or diversions of urban life, they did not miss them. They were quickly busy. Mrs. Wilson, quiet, warm, efficient, gave endless hours to slum-clearance and settlement-house work. Margaret, the oldest daughter, setting a precedent for a later day, went on the concert stage. The two younger girls lost themselves in romance: Jessie soon married Francis Sayre, an able academician; Eleanor later married William Gibbs McAdoo who seemed, to his critics, to be relying on matrimony as well as the patronage of the Treasury to further his career. Wilson himself, immersed in his office, must have found his life and surroundings somehow familiar. He had become accustomed, after all, while president of Princeton, to the limitations on privacy that presidencies impose. And to be in the South was to be in his native land.

For Tumulty and his family, however, Washington was a novel experience, a vast change from industrial Jersey City, a disheartening distance from the friends and recreations familiar for a lifetime.

But they were, fortunately, all young enough to find pleasure in the novel, and they adapted quickly to their new environment. The weight of official business never changed Tumulty's paternal habits. He always enjoyed getting home, joking with his elder children and romping with the babies. He and his wife avoided the official social whirl of the capital. His modest salary permitted no lavish entertainment. Their domestic duties and their preference for hearthside leisure impelled them to decline most of their many invitations to dinners, receptions, and evenings-at-home.[1] So little did Tumulty appear at Washington functions, so little was he mentioned or photographed with groups of elegant celebrities, that as late as October 1913, a sightseeing bus driver failed to recognize him among his passengers. Even in 1915 the Indianapolis police refused to admit him to one of Wilson's meetings until a friendly reporter verified his identity.[2]

The Tumultys, however, were by no means recluses; they were inveterate theatergoers, and their friends were always welcomed warmly at their house. Ellen Axson Wilson and her daughters made frequent informal visits to the Tumulty nursery, and little Miss Mary Tumulty, "with the dignity of a princess," went with her mother to return the First Lady's calls. Mary idolized Jessie Wilson, especially after "Miss Jessie" invited her to her dazzling wedding.[3] The elder Tumultys almost always accepted formal invitations from the President and members of the Cabinet, and Tumulty frequently accompanied Wilson to an Army-Navy football game or Washington's opening American League baseball game. On very special occasions, however, like his thirty-sixth birthday, Tumulty journeyed from the Potomac to the Hackensack to celebrate with old friends in familiar surroundings.[4]

The companions of his youth remained faithful. When Mrs. Tumulty underwent an operation, Joseph D. Bedle, James A. Hamill, and Mark A. Sullivan were the first to send letters of sympathy.[5] Meanwhile Tumulty was making new friends. Across La Fayette Square and a couple of blocks east from the White House stood the grand hostelry of the capital, the old Shoreham Hotel. In its heavily decorated main dining room whispering waiters daily served official Washington. There Tumulty's luncheon table was a popular rendezvous for his intimates among newspapermen, politicians, and theatrical people.[6] There also Tumulty helped organize the "Common Counsel Club" to bring together Democrats of liberal views for an exchange of information and the promotion of progressive principles.[7]

His family circle, old cronies and new, and formal and informal social activities relieved the strain of onerous official duties during the entire period of Tumulty's incumbency. Before assuming his tasks he had also eased his load by severing all his legal connections. Lacking time to practice law, he refused to accept the remuneration that could have been his had he permitted his name to remain on the door of his old offices. The partnership of Tumulty and Cutley was dissolved. Scrupulously careful to make it clear that they were no longer associated, Tumulty urged Cutley to decline any retainers from clients who hoped to capitalize on his government position.[8]

Tumulty took his oath of office on the morning of March fifth in the presence of fifty of his friends.[9] A few moments later he was at his desk, immersed in what has been called Washington's hardest job.[10] He was the personal assistant to the President of the United States, expected to advise his chief on patronage, politics, and public policy, and directly responsible for supervising the executive office and for establishing contacts with Congress and the public, including the press.

Of these duties the routine of the office was least demanding. As in other departments of the government, the real work fell to permanent undersecretaries. Their overseer was Rudolph Forster, a taciturn, efficient man who had served many Presidents. Assisting Forster were Thomas Brahany, his second in command, a head correspondence clerk, a head letter clerk, the chief of the telegraph and telephone systems, and a corps of stenographers and filing clerks. Charles L. Swem continued as Wilson's stenographer and Warren F. Johnson served as Tumulty's personal secretary.[11]

Tumulty, therefore, had little to do with the details of his office. Although he screened a significant proportion of the mail, much of this could be disposed of by such form replies as he had used at Trenton. Even a well-known figure such as Simon Wolf, the prominent Jewish leader, received routine responses from Tumulty to his letters to Wilson.[12] Where a more personal answer was needed, Tumulty abided by the simple rule of never writing a letter that would not stand publicity.[13] His burdens decreased at the time of the Mexican crisis when Wilson rearranged the mail system for security purposes. As successive foreign difficulties arose, more and more correspondence was routed directly to the President's personal file, and with the coming of war Wilson secreted his most important documents in a locked drawer of his own desk.[14]

Tumulty's office was next to Wilson's on the ground floor of the executive office building which was in the west wing of the White House. He could come and go as he chose, but the President preferred to do business in writing. Tumulty therefore submitted his most significant suggestions in memoranda to which Wilson often appended a simple "Okeh" * or "No." Tumulty alone enjoyed free access to his chief. In Trenton Wilson had kept an open door, but the tremendous duties of the Presidency forced him to seclude himself as much as possible. All callers had to reach him through Tumulty. The red rug in Tumulty's office was worn thin by the thousands who carried their hopes and their troubles to the highest authority in the land. Fortunately Tumulty had a remarkable capacity for dealing with people. To ascertain their mission he insisted that every caller know what he wanted, and state it honestly and succinctly. Daily he disposed of endless demanding, inquisitive, and discursive visitors.[15]

Those who arrived with legitimate business often could be cared for without disturbing Wilson. Oswald Garrison Villard, Samuel Gompers, and Lincoln Steffens recalled conferences with Tumulty on important matters of state before passing his desk. Only when he could not solve their problems himself did he refer them to his chief.[16] Many callers were given introductory notes to department heads who could satisfy their requests. This was especially true of patronage hunters whom Wilson refused to see. A special class of visitors, often preoccupied with patronage, were the Congressmen

---

* Wilson always used "Okeh," which he considered an expression of Indian origin. Characteristically, he rejected "O.K.," which, Mencken has shown, derived from the political history of the Democratic Party in the days of Martin Van Buren, "old Kinderhook."

who constantly sought the President's assistance on matters of mutual interest. Only those who had appointments were admitted at once. Others were satisfied by a conference with Tumulty or by an exchange of letters. On Tumulty's recommendation Wilson eventually allotted three hours a week to Congressional callers who did not need a lengthy audience, but aggrieved and hostile legislators continued to appear unannounced. A reporter who frequented the outer office observed that it required Tumulty's consummate tact to send them back to the Hill in an improved frame of mind.[17]

Wilson early formed the habit of fleeing his offices for a restful weekend on the Presidential yacht *Mayflower* or a vacation in the country. Tumulty remained behind as he had at Trenton. Only four months after the Inauguration Wilson went to Cornish, New Hampshire, to escape the summer heat of the capital. During his absence Mrs. J. Borden Harriman and Tumulty initiated steps to forestall a threatening strike by the railroad brotherhoods.[18] Later in his first administration the President sojourned in Pass Christian, Mississippi, and in December 1915, took time off for a wedding trip. On these occasions Tumulty acted as a buffer from afar, assuming unusual responsibilities that prepared him for his troublesome last years in office.

Supervising routine and guarding the President's door were generally dull pursuits, but Tumulty relished his other, more significant duties. Wilson's closest journalist friend found the President "totally deficient in the art of advertising . . . aloof from all the points of public contact . . . never [offering] . . . to explain himself or his attitude on any issue." [19] Tumulty made up this deficiency. He was the President's interpreter of public opinion, his guide to mass psychology. Wilson sent most of his speeches and many of his state papers to Tumulty for approval and revision. Tumulty changed a word or a sentence to make a meaning clearer or more expedient. Frequently he eliminated or added significant portions, deleting or inserting whole paragraphs or pages. "When it is specially important that I be understood," Wilson told Ida M. Tarbell, "I try . . . [a speech] on Tumulty, who has a very extraordinary appreciation of how a thing will 'get over the footlights.' He is the most valuable audience I have." [20]

Tumulty devoted endless hours to analyzing American sentiment. With no public opinion polls to aid him, he had to rely on his reading and private sources of information. Every day his staff clipped the leading newspapers and magazines from all over the country, arranged the clippings topically, and pasted them on long sheets of yellow paper. Each evening Tumulty took this "Yellow Journal" home, studied it carefully, evaluated the importance of every item, and, when appropriate, wrote memoranda based on his findings to Wilson or to a responsible department head.[21] "Tumulty . . . reads everything," Wilson informed Ray Stannard Baker.[22]

Tumulty also relied on his political scouts. Typical were the observations on the encouraging effects of Wilson's preparedness tour in 1916 which were submitted by the Democratic National Committeeman from Kansas and the Postmaster at St. Louis. Personal friends were helpful. Villard reported discontent among Negroes over McAdoo's segregation policy. David Lawrence sent his expert opinion on political conditions in the Far West. Mark Sullivan, the journalist, assured Tumulty that the uproar in the Senate and press over Bryan's lecturing tours was devoid of influence among the electorate.[23]

Armed with such information, aware of every nuance in editorial opinion, Tumulty followed each fluctuation in popular political thinking with uncanny accuracy. Count von Bernstorff, the German Ambassador, observed that Wilson was guided by public opinion of which Tumulty supplied a correct interpretation.[24] Edward N. Hurley, the Chicago politician who became Chairman of the Shipping Board, called Tumulty the "Weather-vane" of the Administration. "With his quick faculties of perception," Hurley wrote, "he easily was able to sense the sentiment of the country. . . . He seemed to understand the state of mind of the people. . . ."[25]

Intent as he was on interpreting public opinion, Tumulty was even more concerned with forming it. He was the first Secretary to have a flair for public relations.[26] He knew how to exploit the news value of a heartrending pardon case. He understood the use of headlines. He was a great stage manager, skilled at building up interest by provocative hints and a mysterious aura of forthcoming secrets. He appreciated the efficacy of little favors, cigars, football tickets, hotel reservations, and succulent luncheons in winning the good will of the writers, actors, and public figures whose voices the electorate heard with eager interest. He did these things graciously and well, for he was genuinely fond of people and people liked him. Few could resist his Irish good humor, his generosity, and his sympathetic sentimentality.[27]

The force of public opinion was one of Wilson's main weapons. The President believed in "pitiless publicity" for official business, trusting the people to decide wisely when they knew the facts. For this the press was the natural medium. Tumulty's most important publicity work, therefore, involved his press relations, the business of meeting reporters and securing their favor, a technique which he had begun to develop in New Jersey.

Wilson made this task difficult. Although his speeches impressed even the newspapermen, the President was rigid, unbending, a poor source of copy, a cold and unfriendly informant. He was shy and sensitive, jealous of his privacy. Published rumors about his daughters' engagements irritated him. He became infuriated when unscrupulous editors circulated apocryphal stories about his private life. The reporters covering Washington in 1913 were largely of the school trained in police courts and at murder trials. There were exceptions, like Cobb and Lawrence and Seibold, but for the most part Wilson could neither understand nor get along with the newspapermen. Feeling that most journals were hostile to him, he returned this hostility.[28] At the suggestion of several of his advisers, he instituted biweekly news conferences, but he made it clear that he was accessible primarily through his Secretary. His press conferences were not successful. He considered the journalistic barrage of questions undignified, welcoming the excuse of overwork and the need for security growing out of diplomatic crises to abandon the sessions. More and more he left his press relations to Tumulty.[29]

Tumulty delighted in this assignment. Unlike Wilson, he understood newspapermen and enjoyed their company. Early in February of 1913 he had prepared the ground by a special trip to Washington with James Kerney for the express purpose of meeting the White House correspondents;[30] and after the Inauguration, his friendly attitude was immediately effective. "It delights my soul

to see how well you have won the good graces of the correspondents . . . " an informed observer wrote. "Few men, who have been
appointed to this position have won the encomiums which have
been heaped upon you. . . . Keep up the good work!" [31] Tumulty
found his morning press conferences "delightful interludes in a
busy day." [32] While being interviewed he was cautiously formal,
but when the interview was over he was jovial and easygoing. He
knew when to be reticent, when to be enlightening. He made it a
practice to give out the names of callers at the White House and,
when possible, the nature of their business. He promptly made
public policies and appointments, once they had been decided upon.
He played no favorites. Rarely did a reporter receive exclusive information regarding an official act. [33]

Tumulty, unwilling to pamper the press, absolutely refused to
appeal for support to Hearst. [34] He had James Kerney discipline a
Trenton *Times* reporter who persistently misquoted him. [35] When
the newspapermen ran into difficulties, however, Tumulty helped
them. Secretary Bryan, claiming that the reporters at the State
Department had affronted his dignity and menaced security, in 1915
expressed a desire to exclude them from the premises. After Villard
and Lawrence stated the case for their colleagues, the President
turned to Tumulty for a solution. Tumulty agreed that Bryan had
cause for irritation, but he persuaded Wilson that the contemplated
exile of the correspondents was unwise. [36]

Tumulty protected inadvertently indiscreet reporters, such as
those on the New York *Herald* which in 1915 carried a ludicrous
story that Wilson had broken with House over the recognition of
Carranza. The President, furious, denied access to the White House
to the responsible correspondent, and wrote the *Herald* editor
demanding that the offender be discharged. He was unmoved by an
apologetic explanation that the copy had been filed for rejection
and printed in error. The newspapermen, stunned by the President's personal intervention against an earnest, impecunious colleague, looked to Tumulty for redress. Tumulty, as angry as
Wilson, for there was talk that he had inspired the story out of
jealousy of House, nevertheless realized that his chief's action was
petty and unpopular. He heard the case of the head of the *Herald's*

Washington bureau sympathetically. When he was convinced that publication had occurred by mistake, he urged Wilson to abandon his request that the reporter be fired. After others supported this counsel, Wilson's temper cooled; the *Herald* representative kept his job; and shortly thereafter Tumulty readmitted him to his morning conferences.[37]

By supplying them with complete information in a friendly manner and by interceding when they were in trouble, Tumulty earned the gratitude of the newspapermen, who responded with favorable accounts of Wilson, his program, and his purposes. Tumulty saw to it that the President expressed his appreciation. "Marse Henry" Watterson of the Louisville *Courier-Journal*, Fred Essary of the Baltimore *Sun*, and Matt Ely of the Hoboken *Observer* were among those who received friendly letters from Wilson which Tumulty had inspired. When the wife of Richard Oulahan, the pro-Wilson correspondent of the New York *Times*, died, Tumulty sent flowers in the President's name and urged his chief to write a "generous" reply to Oulahan's note of thanks. Often Tumulty himself praised Wilson's journalistic supporters or congratulated them when they received promotions.[38]

These policies were effective and rewarding. Tumulty soon numbered dozens of reporters among his most loyal friends. During and after his tenure they rallied to his side in times of stress, and they invariably invited him to their Gridiron Club dinners where they teased him affectionately in their humorous skits. In one of these Tumulty was made to explain why Wilson attended a different church every Sunday. The Republican press had suggested, not without reason, that the President had been advised to cultivate as many congregations as possible. The Gridiron Club, however, put another answer in Tumulty's mouth. Wilson's reason, the thespian Tumulty said, was to help the Administration's economy program, for it was cheaper to move than to pay rent on a pew.[39]

Wilson's inadequacies in public relations were overbalanced. When the President was away from the capital, Cary Grayson, his companion and personal physician, followed Tumulty's advice in dealing with the reporters.[40] Their news needs were filled as never before. The resulting publicity was invaluable in gaining public approval for Wilson's policies. Charles L. Swem, Villard, Lawrence, and Fred Essary considered this Tumulty's foremost contribution to Wilson's success.[41]

When he stepped into the executive offices, Tumulty was, fortunately for Wilson, adept in both the science and the art of politics. In its scientific aspects politics involves only an understanding of relatively simple mechanisms and a willingness to use them. Power input and power output cannot be measured in political science as they can in a machine, but the relation of patronage and organization to campaigns and legislation is sufficiently important and sufficiently defined to permit no successful politician to ignore them. Whereas Wilson preferred to ignore, or at least to slight, political mechanics, Tumulty delighted in tinkering. On the whole he tinkered effectively.

Tumulty's continuing, deft contributions to the political process on the organization level were, however, probably less important to Wilson than was his proficiency in political art which is, essentially, human relations. In this area Tumulty performed intuitively with magnificent success. Wilson, on the other hand, often failed. The President inspired loyalty and admiration, but rarely devotion. When he chose, he could be amusing. He was never funny. He sought to serve humanity, but he loved few human beings. Tumulty, in those respects, was Wilson's antithesis. Boundlessly compassionate, generous to a fault, he gave freely his time, his sympathy, and his money whether or not politics was involved. His charity was natural, completely unconceptualized. Tumulty could be uproariously funny. George M. Cohan, a great comedian, his close friend, delighted in the comedies Tumulty performed in the privacy of his drawing room. The reporters and politicians with whom Tumulty swapped stories in the late afternoon at his office during the nineteen twenties enjoyed his Coolidge yarns as much as they enjoyed his bootleg whiskey. Tumulty's humor, generosity, and warmth, clear in his every act, endeared him to professional as well as to private friends.

A lovable man and an effective politician, Tumulty also demonstrated other qualities essential to success. He was scrupulously honest. Conscientious, diligent, he worked perhaps too long and too hard. His letters, almost without exception confined to the problem at hand, although often verbose were, in context, the letters of a man who did not relax at his desk. Nevertheless, even when rushed, Tumulty was courteous and patient. Although excitable and capable of strong emotions, he did not easily lose his temper, and he never lost it in public. Ambitious, self-confident, proud but not arrogant, Tumulty carefully prepared himself-for his duties by reading widely in American history, by observing more-experienced men at work, by listening to anyone who had something of importance to say. Wilson, after 1912, read little and listened impatiently.

Hollywood, in its version of Wilson's life, pictured Tumulty badly. In true life he did not flutter, nor did he dress like a carnival barker. His clothing, in fact, was meticulously neat and conservative. This restraint in dress was revealing. Tumulty enjoyed good food and good liquor. As he reached middle age he grew mildly stout. But he neither ate nor drank in excess. In large degree a self-made man, Tumulty was self-controlled.

Tumulty's political thinking was consistent with his personality. His middle-class liberalism, like that of the great majority of his contemporaries, was meliorative. He once candidly and accurately described himself to Colonel House as a conservative progressive. Accepting without reservation, but also without complacency, the institutions of democratic capitalism, he sought only, to the best of his understanding, to adjust them to the changing conditions of American life. Unlike many Wilsonians, he reached his conclusions on policy without reference to any sharply articulated theory of government. He had read and enjoyed Henry George, heard and applauded Bryan; he followed, assisted, worshiped Wilson. His religious training and beliefs gave him a sharp sense of injustice and a strong moral conscience. But fundamentally Tumulty's economics and political economy were unsophisticated and empirical. He accepted the expressions of Wilsonian liberalism because those expressions defined a program which seemed to him applicable to what he knew and felt from experience. He had seen poverty, filth, corruption. Later, from afar, but with a discerning mind, he knew war. Instinctively he attacked them. He knew little of finance, nothing of business cycles. For his task he rarely had to. By 1912 his sympathies, like Wilson's, were typically middle class. Neither man fully understood the then developing problems and policies of "big labor." Their countrymen for the most part shared this deficiency.

Resting, as it did, on experience interpreted with compassion, Tumulty's thinking nurtured his remarkable capacity for growth. From 1906 to 1921 he gradually assumed positions of more and more responsibility until, toward the end, when only forty, he was in fact the assistant President of the United States. Throughout those years he dealt with issues of increasing size and significance. To each, as it arose, he brought not only energy and willingness, but also intelligence, and sometimes wisdom. For his duties, official and unofficial, Tumulty was well equipped. Fascinated by politics, devoted to his chief, fond of people, willing to work and to learn, he loved life. Wilson's Secretary had to be such a man.

For eight years Tumulty knew no relief from his obligations as administrator of the executive offices, shield of the President, and White House manager of press and public relations. No matter how concerned he was with the problems he faced as an adviser to Wilson, these routine duties demanded continual attention. From the moment he arrived at his office before eight o'clock in the morning until he left after five in the afternoon, later at home in the evening, and six and often seven days a week, his time belonged to Wilson and to the people and the representatives of the people who came to Wilson on official or personal business. Tumulty was the last man to carry this load alone. Today his duties are divided among almost a dozen men. He served longer and under more trying conditions than had Lamont, Cortelyou, or Loeb, his illustrious predecessors. At times he was doubtless less efficient as an administrator than an older, more experienced man would have been,[42] but it is greatly to his credit that he did so much so well. His capacity for hard work and his solid, often extraordinary achievements, moreover, can be appreciated fully only in the light of his extensive ex-officio activities in Democratic politics and as an adviser on the Administration's domestic and foreign policies.

CHAPTER VI

Political Manager

1. The National Scene

WILSON was a minority President whose election had depended largely on the unusual presence of a third strong candidate. His real strength and the nature of his mandate were nebulous quantities. Although the Democrats controlled Congress, after sixteen years of Republican rule they were unaccustomed to governing. They were by no means a unified group. The personal rancors of the Baltimore Convention dissipated slowly and incompletely. Within each state rival factions viewed the vast patronage of the federal government jealously and greedily. And on Capitol Hill the traditional Southern Democrats, the Bryanites, and the representatives of the urban machines had few constructive legislative ideas in common.

Three of Wilson's earliest objectives aggravated the instability within the party. Tariff reduction, for which the President called a special session of Congress, involved the establishment of sugar and wool schedules, the pampered children of southern and western Democrats. Currency reform, debated at the same special session, pitted Bryan and his Congressional stewards against the conservative group led by Carter Glass and McAdoo. And Wilson's insistence that Congress repeal the law exempting American shipping from paying tolls for the use of the Panama Canal raised the hoary question of our relations with Great Britain, for the British had long argued that this repeal was mandatory under the terms of the Hay-

Pauncefote Treaty. Wilson's demand, widely interpreted as truckling to England, frightened those Democrats who equated the party's future with the continued allegiance of the Irish-Americans.[1]

Nevertheless, in keeping with his theories of government, and on the advice of Burleson and Daniels, Wilson decided to work through his party rather than to attempt to construct a progressive coalition. The implementation of this decision called for the recognition of each important Democratic faction in the assignment of political largess. This worrisome task fell largely to Postmaster General Burleson, Secretaries Bryan and McAdoo, and Tumulty.[2]

From his first day in office Tumulty applied himself to the legislative and political problems that confronted the new administration. The very nature of his position brought him into intimate contact not only with the President but also with members of the Cabinet and Congress and with national and local party leaders. He was constantly apprised of all aspects of Administration policy and frequently consulted in its formation. It was his business to be accessible, to hear complaints and to prescribe remedies.

Tumulty's place in the echelon of command was broadly defined. It depended on his informal but close relationship with Wilson and on the central location of his office. He could undertake as little or as much as his own inclinations and those of the President dictated. The first eighteen months of his tenure he devoted primarily to adjusting himself to his new duties, to conciliating personal differences among the party's prima donnas, and to local political problems. As these tasks consumed less time and as he gained experience in national affairs, he gave increasing thought to policy-making, but in the initial legislative battles his part was relatively minor.

Executive tactics in behalf of the tariff bill devolved largely on Burleson and Bryan.[3] Their influence, Wilson's resolute leadership, and the parliamentary skill of the Democratic House and Senate leaders effected the prompt enactment of the Underwood-Simmons Law, the first real reduction of the tariff since the Civil War. It passed almost before Tumulty was at home in Washington.

On the next problem before Congress, the banking and currency issue, Tumulty brought into play his resources as a mediator. His contribution, while small, was characteristic and not insignificant. For years the country had suffered from the inelastic currency and credit imposed by the limitations of the national banking system. Neither the government nor private bankers could deal adequately with seasonal and cyclical needs for expansion and contraction of credit. This condition, aggravating economic crises and precipitating brokers' panics, had provoked, in large part, persistent demands by agrarian and debtor groups for inflation and by financiers for a central banking system. Over proposals to remedy the situation the Democratic Party, like the nation itself, was divided on sectional and economic lines. Wilson at first accepted the legislation, sponsored by Carter Glass, which, incorporating the general desires of the financial community, gave a larger influence to the bankers than to the government in the Federal Reserve system it created. Bryan, his long-held convictions challenged, vigorously opposed the Glass Bill, making its passage improbable. The Secretary of State even contemplated resigning from the Cabinet. This would have weakened seriously the still fledgling Administration. Wilson, worried, requested Tumulty to intercede. After hearing Bryan's argument, Tumulty agreed that the bill should be amended to provide that the entire Federal Reserve Board be appointed by the President and the Federal Reserve notes be obligations of the government. He reported favorably to Wilson and helped arrange the conferences at which the measure was revised in accordance with Bryan's views.[4] The resulting Democratic unity assured the success of the amended Federal Reserve Act, perhaps the greatest achievement of Wilson's first term.

Tumulty's zeal for the success of the Administration made him wary of the Panama tolls issue. He urged Wilson to avoid that troublesome question so as not to endanger party harmony on domestic affairs. Convinced of the righteousness of his position, however, Wilson persisted in his course, leaving it to Tumulty and Burleson to buttress the Administration's wavering Congressional forces. In the Senate, O'Gorman of New York, Martine of New Jersey, and Reed of Missouri, aggrieved over patronage and fearful of the disapproval of their Irish and German constituents, led the Democratic deserters. Martine doubtless recalled that he and

Tumulty had profited in 1910 by the reputedly pro-British stand of James Smith, Jr. In the House of Representatives rebellion was rife. Speaker Clark, Majority Leader Underwood, and Finance Committee Chairman Fitzgerald fought the President's measure. Undeterred by the prestige of the opposition leaders, Burleson disciplined their lesser colleagues with his club of patronage. Tumulty plotted strategy with Senators James and Hughes and Representatives Adamson, Palmer, and Covington.[5] He successfully undermined Martine's influence with most of the New Jersey delegation to the lower house. Typical was the case of his boyhood friend, James Hamill of Jersey City. Irish himself and representing a predominately Irish district, "Jimmie" Hamill risked his political life by supporting Wilson's proposal. Unexpected votes such as his carried the measure through Congress. Tumulty and Burleson rewarded Hamill by arranging for the construction of a branch post office in his district, a project that enhanced his prestige and provided jobs for his constituents. Tumulty also persuaded the local New Jersey press to support Hamill's successful candidacy for renomination and re-election.[6]

While Wilson's first Congress was compiling its remarkable record of achievement, Tumulty was striving to halt the feuds among leading Democrats. He was instrumental in arranging a public meeting, their first since Baltimore, between Champ Clark and Bryan.[7] Before the election of 1914 he welcomed Colonels Harvey and Watterson back in the Wilson fold. When Ellen Wilson died, "Marse Henry" wrote a beautiful editorial about her and sent Wilson a kind letter of condolence inviting a renewal of their friendship. Watterson's genuine sympathy helped Tumulty persuade Wilson to forgive and forget.[8]

Tumulty had remained on speaking terms with George Harvey. Certain that many Americans misunderstood Wilson's treatment of his original mentor, Tumulty begged the President to take steps to resume their old relationship. Harvey's vitriolic pen caused Wilson to abandon his first plan to patch up their differences, but in September of 1914 the Colonel changed his tune, urging support for the President and his party in the coming elections. Tumulty called

Wilson's attention to Harvey's article. Shortly thereafter he visited Harvey and escorted him to a conference with the President. Within the next week Harvey sent Tumulty suggestions for campaign tactics and propaganda, and Tumulty's grateful reply invited the Colonel to participate in forthcoming Democratic councils of war.[9]

Tumulty's indefatigable peacemaking did not extend to the most deeply offended of the early Wilsonians, William F. McCombs. McCombs' frail health and emotional instability destroyed his usefulness during the campaign of 1912.[10] The appointment of his archfoe, McAdoo, as Secretary of the Treasury, a position he coveted, embittered him permanently. Wilson offered him the French Ambassadorship, but McCombs suspected, not without reason, that this was a device to get him out of the country and away from his chairmanship of the National Committee. After vacillating for months, he finally declined.[11] His primary grievance was political. He wanted to direct party policy and "supervise the distribution of patronage throughout the United States." [12] As he found his voice increasingly ignored, he grew more and more vindictive.

To a great degree McCombs directed his animosity against Tumulty and his friends, for they assumed most of the power and responsibility McCombs expected as Chairman of the National Committee. The Committee had established permanent headquarters in Washington for the first time in the party's history in 1913. This office was to work in close co-operation with the Democratic Congressional Campaign Committee. The titular chairman of the headquarters group was Representative A. Mitchell Palmer, but the guiding genius of the organization was Thomas J. Pence of North Carolina, a newspaperman of versatile talents as a propagandist and money raiser.[13]

As early as June of 1913 Pence began to prepare for the election of 1914. Several evenings a week the tacticians who determined campaign policies conferred in Pence's small apartment above a Chinese laundry on New York Avenue near Fourteenth Street. In constant attendance at this Democratic nerve center were Pence, Tumulty, and Senators Ollie James and Billie Hughes. They were a colorful group: James, a huge Kentuckian with a shining bald head and coarse features, a veteran Bryan Democrat, like his leader a florid speaker; Pence, almost as tall as James, but physically and mentally more lithe, a master of political invective and innuendo in print, but in conversation terse, dry; Hughes, an Irish immigrant, a self-made lawyer, long the champion of labor, unsophisticated on the surface, but of them all the only economist and probably the most radical politically; Tumulty, the smallest by far in body, the youngest and, in spite of his career, the least experienced of the quartet, but the closest to the source of political favors and the most sympathetic to Wilson's views. As the occasion required, the four were joined by such "division superintendents" as Roger Sullivan of Illinois, Thomas Taggart of Indiana, and John T. McGraw of West Virginia.[14]

Tumulty was their link to the White House, to Wilson's ear, and to executive patronage. He and Pence shared the *de facto* chairmanship of the National Committee until Pence died and McCombs resigned. Since Tumulty's "Yellow Journal" amply demonstrated the efficacy of Pence's propaganda, Tumulty left that function and money-raising to his colleague while he gave his extraofficial attention to the distribution of patronage. A little black looseleaf notebook served as his encyclopedia of politics. Therein he compiled data on every state in the Union, balancing the salaries of the major offices allotted to sons of each state against the contributions from that state to national funds.[15]

The pages of the "Black Book" revealed the backstage strategists of the Democracy. Tumulty chose his counselors carefully, adjusting his course to fit local conditions. Dudley Field Malone and Colonel Edward M. House furnished a large portion of the important information. Congressmen, National Committeemen, and State Chairmen, for whom Tumulty's office was a mecca, unburdened themselves freely and frankly. Their collective advice directed Tumulty to the platoon leaders who had legitimate claims to federal offices.

As Secretary to the President Tumulty acted in the apparently traditional position of arbiter of patronage for the District of Columbia. Often he could place one of the worthy in a small post there. His influence in the determination of other appointments frequently transcended that of Wilson's old friends and Cabinet officers. The

President required the Cabinet members to include a case history with each of their important recommendations. These diplomas of regularity and availability, along with lists of lesser choices, almost invariably cleared through Tumulty's desk before reaching his chief. Tumulty's detailed information with regard to applicants and vacancies enabled him to submit timely requests to department heads. His accessibility to Wilson permitted him to interpose opportune objections. Thus armed, on occasion, such as in the case of appointing a Postmaster in Newark, New Jersey, and a Collector of Internal Revenue in Connecticut, he successfully raided the extensive preserves even of Burleson and McAdoo.[16]

Only rarely did personal considerations temper Tumulty's advice on patronage. Like Wilson, he frowned on nepotism, keeping his family out of the picture as much as possible. On the other hand, his sympathy for the problems of the very poor motivated him to devote generous attention to finding menial jobs for the unfortunates of the Horseshoe, and his concern about press relations led him to direct a few desirable billets to newspapermen or their relatives.[17] Generally, however, he abided by his lifelong practice of taking the middle road between incorrigible professional politicians and amateur reformers. This policy had proved effectual in constructing Wilson's prenomination organization. It conformed to the political necessities posed by Wilson's decision to work within the party. As a corollary, Tumulty agreed to the recognition not only of the President's preconvention friends but also of his "whilom enemies." In this policy Burleson and Bryan heartily concurred. Early evidence of their efforts lay in the appointments of two Clark leaders and two Underwood leaders to distinguished judicial and diplomatic posts.[18]

2. Local Salients

The "Black Book" contained quantitative evidence of Tumulty's regional activity. Except for Kentucky and to a small degree Maryland and Virginia, the politics of the South were not his domain, and entries under the southern states were sparse. Nor, for the most part, was Tumulty personally concerned with the trans-Mississippi West. He did not ignore that section, but his major interest rested in the East and Middle West, the heavily populated areas that controlled the largest electoral vote and presented political patterns resembling that of his home state.

Particularly in New Jersey, New York, Massachusetts, and Illinois Tumulty intervened not only as an umpire for patronage but also as an Administration adviser on local political affairs. His constant objective was to strengthen the Democracy in those states by policies similar to those he had used in New Jersey. His favored agents were organization men who were willing to support Wilson and his measures either directly or through their representatives in Congress. By 1914 the rationale behind this course became apparent to the President, who recognized that the votes of the regulars had made his reforms possible. Wilson, however, used professional politicians without any real appreciation of their services.[19] In his efforts to form pro-Wilson Democratic forces, Tumulty enjoyed only occasional co-operation from his chief. He was further embarrassed by opposition to his plans from both the impenitent machine elements and the uncompromising liberals. These groups had their own avenues to federal patronage. As a result the political strength of the Administration, particularly in Illinois and New York, was frequently employed at cross purposes.

Conditions in New Jersey did not permit Tumulty to relax his vigilance there when he left Trenton. The legislature was still considering Wilson's plan to revise the system of drawing grand juries so as to eliminate their control by the machine-dominated sheriffs. Nugent's strength in the Assembly and the factionalism resulting from the gubernatorial aspirations of Mayor Wittpenn and Acting Governor James Fielder blocked the bill. Fielder, an undistinguished Hudson regular, had adopted Wilson's program as his own. Wittpenn, on the other hand, impeded the chances for jury reform by supporting a plan to settle the issue by referendum, a device favored also by Nugent and Hague. Wilson asked the Mayor to change his views. Publicly and privately Tumulty warned him to do so. Wittpenn's response was halfhearted, but Fielder, encouraged, at Wilson's suggestion called a special session of the legislature for jury reform. To aid the cause Wilson spoke in Newark and Jersey City. While the President was there, he and Tumulty conferred with representatives of all the state factions on the issue. Preoccupied with national affairs, the President agreed to an ineffective compromise measure to which his former allies were decidedly cool. Nevertheless Tumulty, mustering his forces for the last time, expedited its enactment. Lamely, Wilson claimed victory. Even the claim vanished when the courts found the act unconstitutional.[20]

Wilson and Tumulty were losing command of New Jersey's political destiny. Gradually the state, and especially the Democratic Party in the state, were reverting to pattern. The action of the White House in the gubernatorial campaign delayed this reversion, but to protect the party Tumulty and Wilson again lowered their standards. For a time Tumulty was boomed for governor. His friends described him as Wilson's logical heir whose election would guarantee the President's continued participation in state affairs. But Tumulty lacked any personal organization. Furthermore, he felt that he could do more constructive work in Washington. His emphatic declaration that he was not available left either Fielder or Wittpenn as the candidate on whom liberals could unite to defeat Nugent's choice in the primary.[21]

Although Fielder, never entirely reliable, was making peace overtures to Nugent, Tumulty preferred him to Wittpenn.[22] Fielder's Hudson supporters were Tumulty's former allies. Fielder's course in the jury matter closely followed Wilson's. And from a practical point of view Fielder was stronger, for in the first election under a newly adopted commission government plan in Jersey City, Frank Hague had routed Wittpenn. Tumulty canvassed various county leaders throughout New Jersey who reported unanimously that even with White House assistance Wittpenn could no longer win the primary.[23] Tumulty, therefore, quietly set the political stage for Wilson's endorsement of Fielder. At the President's request, Wittpenn withdrew from the race.[24]

Tumulty next aided Fielder's election. Although ex-Governor Stokes, the Republican candidate, had little appeal, Everett Colby, running as a Bull Mooser, initially enjoyed considerable favor

among influential editors who disliked Fielder's rapport with
Nugent. To remove this obstacle Tumulty warned Fielder to read
Nugent out of the party.[25] After the Governor reluctantly com-
plied, Tumulty persuaded the editors of the Newark *News*, Trenton
Times, and Philadelphia *Record*, somewhat against their wills, to
lend their support to the Democratic candidate.[26]

After Fielder's election, Tumulty set out to weld the party together for united action in state affairs and in the Congressional elections of 1914. He helped to engineer the appointment of Wittpenn
as Naval Officer of the Port of New York and of Congressman
Walter I. McCoy, one of Nugent's lieutenants, as an Associate
Justice on the Supreme Court of the District of Columbia. Before
the jury act was declared unconstitutional he directed Chancellor
Walker's choice of tentative jury commissioners with a view to
appeasing all factions.[27] Fielder, however, made it clear that he
resented any interference from Washington. Thus informed, busy
elsewhere, and discouraged by the precipitate decline of progressive
sentiment in his homeland, Tumulty gradually turned his back on
the tenderloin state.[28] In the interest of party amity he rejected the
urgent pleas of George Record and Mark Fagan to give battle to
Hague in Jersey City.[29] He refrained from public comment on conditions in Trenton. He wrote Burleson less frequently about the
allocation of New Jersey's postmasterships. Not until Republican
resurgence induced Democratic leaders to invite his assistance did
Tumulty resume his participation in New Jersey's local affairs.[30]

His inactivity, however, never extended to the state's Congressional elections. Even in 1913 he was primarily concerned with
preparing the way for the choice of pro-Wilson candidates. In the
spring of 1914 he labored in behalf of the unsuccessful Democratic
aspirant for a seat that had been vacated in a normally Republican
district. That fall he influenced his friends among the state's newspapermen to support candidates who had assisted the President, and
he persuaded Wilson to endorse personally two Congressmen whose
re-elections were in doubt.[31] Fielder understood that in these contests Democratic policy was to emanate from Washington. The
Governor had no cause for complaints, for, as in Fielder's own case,
Tumulty upheld members of the organization whose devotion to

the New Freedom was a matter of party regularity rather than of strong progressive principles.

Events in New York caused Tumulty even more pain than those in New Jersey. The Administration could not avoid involvement in the everlasting contest between Tammany Hall and the reformers. Influenced by McAdoo, House, and Malone, Wilson early demonstrated his antagonism to Boss Murphy of Tammany in filling the office of Collector of the Port of New York, the most politically desirable position in the state. The protests of James O'Gorman, Tammany's senatorial guardian, persuaded Wilson to abandon his first choice, but he substituted John Purroy Mitchel, a declared enemy of the machine. The President made his decision with full knowledge that Mitchel would soon resign to become the reform candidate for Mayor in 1913. Tammany naturally considered the appointment an open declaration of war.[32]

When Mitchel resigned to begin his successful campaign, Wilson selected Dudley Field Malone, who was every bit as antagonistic to Tammany, as his successor. This was a clever move, for Senator O'Gorman could not very well oppose the appointment of his rebellious son-in-law. Indeed, Wilson's decision to satisfy Malone's long-standing ambition for the office probably helped to persuade O'Gorman to support the Federal Reserve Bill which he had previously opposed.[33]

With Mitchel and Malone in control of the vast patronage of their offices, Murphy had reason to worry but not to surrender. He demonstrated his enduring power by engineering the impeachment and removal from office of Governor Sulzer. Meanwhile, his deputies sought succor in Washington.[34] They discovered in Tumulty an interested listener who feared that, unless drastic steps were taken, the Republicans would sweep New York in 1914. After Sulzer's removal Tumulty saw no chance for the reformers to unseat Tammany. Privately even Dudley Field Malone admitted the impossibility of success.[35] Furthermore, Tumulty doubted the sincerity of purpose among progressive leaders. Mitchel's close affiliation with the "silk stocking" element in Manhattan belied his liberal label. Malone appeared to work more for McAdoo than Wilson, and McAdoo's intentions were extremely suspicious. His former law partner, Stuart Gibboney, injudiciously revealed that the primary purpose of the Secretary of the Treasury was to procure personal strength for a presidential nomination in 1916 or 1920.[36]

At the same time, Tumulty found the organization willing to make concessions. McCombs, Martin Glynn, the new governor, and State Chairman William Church Osborn were working with regulars amenable to liberal ideas. Their advances apparently made Murphy and Boss McCooey of Brooklyn willing to adopt pro-Wilson candidates in their organizations in return for a share of patronage and a guarantee of Administration neutrality in local affairs.[37] William Jennings Bryan befriended Glynn, whose newspapers warmly supported Wilson's policies.[38] These factors demonstrated the expediency of a compromise. As the New York primaries approached, Tumulty threw his influence behind Glynn and Ambassador James W. Gerard, the Tammany candidate for the United States Senate whose record was happily unassailable.

The Malone-McAdoo group, supporting John W. Hennessy for Governor and Franklin D. Roosevelt, then Assistant Secretary of the Navy, for the Senate, competed with Tumulty for Wilson's assistance. They beleaguered House with requests for help, but, uncertain about Wilson's opinions, the Colonel confined his assistance largely to the privacy of his correspondence and diary where he scolded Tumulty regularly.[39] While Malone in vain implored Wilson to build up liberal strength for the future by the use of patronage,[40] Tumulty procured patronage for the pending elections. He influenced the choice of Thomas B. Rush, a wealthy Tammanyite of good repute, as Surveyor of the Port of New York, an office normally under the aegis of both McAdoo and Malone.[41] He welcomed unexpected support from Attorney General McReynolds who, at odds with McAdoo, selected Gerard's campaign manager * as Marshal of a New York district.[42] Burleson tried to appease both factions, but, sympathetic with Tumulty's purpose, he concurred in Tumulty's choice of one of McCooey's district leaders † as Postmaster of Brooklyn.[43]

Wilson himself dealt the Hennessy and Roosevelt campaigns

* Thomas N. McCarthy.
† James W. Kelly.

their final blows. Either his political caution, his disinclination to enter local disputes, his distrust of McAdoo, or his respect for Tumulty's advice induced the President to silence Malone, an able and persuasive orator. Because of his office, the press interpreted Malone's incessant attacks on Glynn as representative of White House sentiment. Wilson, however, explained that Malone spoke only for himself. Later, just before Malone planned to embark on a lengthy stumping tour for Hennessy, the President instructed him to refrain from any further comment.[44] This command, patronage favors, and Murphy's control of the New York City election boards ensured victory for Glynn and Gerard in the primaries.[45]

The Democracy faced the election, however, handicapped by continuing enmities. With the Republicans again united, this condition troubled the President and his agents. Colonel House, Wilson's confidential peacemaker in New York in 1914, set to work at once, with Tumulty's assistance, to improve the situation. Partly on Tumulty's advice, Glynn won the approval of Wilson by preventing the selection of McCombs, whom Murphy favored, as State Chairman. House conferred with Mitchel and Glynn, found their rapport promising, and approved Wilson's plan to send the Governor a personal letter of endorsement. Although Hennessy bolted, Wilson, prodded by Tumulty, insisted that McAdoo support the ticket. Malone did this without orders. His co-operation Tumulty encouraged and repaid by opposing the introduction in the House of Representatives of a resolution condemning Malone's conduct of office.[46] Tumulty also prepared the Democratic reply to a Republican anti-Catholic whispering campaign directed against various Democratic candidates. A few days before the election, the President signed a message Tumulty had written calling on the people of New York to vote as Americans and not as sectarians, a last-minute appeal for Glynn.[47]

With the exceptions of Hennessy and his negligible following, and of the ultra-machine elements who sponsored the resolution against Malone, the New York Democracy was united behind an acceptable, regular ticket. Less than a year after the disputes over the Collectorship, the Mayoralty, and the removal of Sulzer, and only a few weeks after a bitter primary, Tumulty and House, themselves only recently rivals, had restored sufficient concord to permit the party to make a strong fight for Congressional seats.

In Massachusetts a unique singleness of purpose among Wilson's advisers eased Tumulty's burdens. House, McAdoo, and Malone worked with Tumulty to enable favored local leaders to reorganize the chaotic Bay State Democracy. While Tumulty and House consulted Josiah Quincy, Malone reconnoitered throughout Massachusetts to discover the best approach to political conditions in the state.[48] Ultimately Tumulty pursued the systematic course delineated by Malone. He ignored Governor Foss and Mayor Fitzgerald of Boston, the former because of his self-centered political irregularity, the latter because of his infamous record. In allotting patronage Tumulty first interrogated the Democratic Congressmen, especially James M. Curley, with regard to positions to be filled in their districts, and then consulted with National Committeeman Coughlin for the sake of formality, with State Chairman Thomas P. Riley to ascertain the practical effects of prospective appointments on the party's organization, and with Lieutenant Governor David I. Walsh for an "honest and fearless" opinion.[49]

Through these channels Tumulty, McAdoo and House chose the Collector of the Port of Boston. Although Walsh had insisted that the Administration recognize only party regulars and not the "high brow" element, in return for various favors he agreed to the appointment of Edmund Billings, a wealthy anti-Fitzgerald Democrat who enjoyed the support of Curley, Quincy, and the Boston business interests. The selection of Billings set off a fierce controversy that raged during the campaign of 1913. Fitzgerald ordered his representatives in Congress to voice their protests. Cardinal Archbishop O'Connell called the appointment offensive to the Catholic Church. And the Massachusetts Democratic State Convention threatened to withhold approval of the national administration unless Billings' name were withdrawn.[50]

Worried by such manifestations of disorder and by Walsh's questionable record on the railroad issue, House urged Tumulty to come to New England to assist Walsh in the gubernatorial race. Tumulty, however, remained in Washington, confident of the outcome. Pursuant to his advice and McAdoo's, Wilson stood firmly behind

Billings. Thanks to irreparable cleavages in Republican ranks, to Curley's growing Boston machine, and to federal assistance in patronage, Walsh and the entire Democratic slate of state officers swept Massachusetts.[51] The *via media* between Foss and Fitzgerald, reform and reaction, had proved to be smoothly paved.

During the next year Tumulty continued to side with Walsh, Riley, and Curley. This policy contributed to the decline of Fitzgerald's power in Boston and helped to prepare the Democracy to face the reunited Republicans in the state and Congressional elections of 1914.

The concord among Administration leaders in regard to Massachusetts was painfully lacking in Illinois. There Roger Sullivan, the conservative state boss, struggled against an unnatural, fluctuating alliance of liberal Democrats with the factions led by United States Senator James Hamilton Lewis, Governor Dunne, and Mayor Harrison, the spokesman of William Randolph Hearst and the leader of the Chicago machine. Each of these groups had powerful allies in Washington. William Jennings Bryan and the Assistant Secretary of Agriculture, Carl Vrooman, a native of Illinois, supported the liberals and thus, indirectly, Harrison and Hearst.[52] Malone and Tumulty befriended Boss Sullivan. Tumulty liked Sullivan personally, felt indebted to him for his assistance at Baltimore, and considered him a man of his word who would support Wilson's program in spite of any theoretical disagreements. Nevertheless, in the interest of harmony, Tumulty drew up a plan for the apportionment of Illinois patronage which gave equal recognition to Sullivan, Dunne, Harrison and Lewis, and incidentally took care of the Polish-Americans, Irish-Americans and other powerful hyphenate groups. This arrangement hurt Sullivan, for the combined rewards of his rivals far outweighed his own.[53]

Illinois factionalism came to a head in the senatorial primary of 1914. The leading candidates were Sullivan, Congressman Lawrence B. Stringer, who laid claim to the adherence of Democratic liberals, and Carl Vrooman, who ran under the banner of an apocryphal "Wilson-Bryan League." Each sought Wilson's support, but the President would not intervene and Tumulty imitated his chief's neutrality. Bryan, however, consulted with all of Sullivan's opponents, partially succeeded in uniting them behind Stringer, and pleaded their cause before the Illinois electorate.[54] Nevertheless Sullivan's disciplined organization won the primary handily.

Vrooman, Harrison, Lewis, and Dunne refused to accept the verdict of the party's rank and file. Vrooman bolted, joining Democratic Senator Robert Owen of Oklahoma, a faithful Bryanite, in an active campaign in behalf of the Bull Moose senatorial candidate. The others undermined Sullivan by their calculated inactivity.[55] These Democratic defections made almost inevitable the re-election of the Republican incumbent, Lawrence Y. Sherman, a consistent opponent of Wilson's policies.

Sullivan and his lieutenants concluded that his only chance lay in obtaining a strong endorsement from the President. Several leading Democratic businessmen from Chicago and Congressman Henry T. Rainey of Illinois urged Tumulty to procure an unequivocal statement from his chief. Tumulty was thoroughly sympathetic to their request. Out of personal gratitude and in the interests of the party's strength in the Senate he did not see how Wilson could fail to comply.[56] At first Wilson agreed to an exchange of letters between himself and Rainey. Rainey drafted the letter endorsing Sullivan which the President was to sign. But while Rainey impatiently awaited an official copy for use in the campaign, Wilson changed his mind. He yielded to the pressure of Illinois liberals and prohibitionists who implored him to give no assistance to Sullivan because of his conservative record, unseemly reputation, and overt affiliation with liquor interests.[57]

Tumulty and Burleson were appalled at Wilson's reversal. Burleson tried to salvage the situation by announcing in Peoria that Wilson favored Sullivan, but liberal Democrats continued to desert to the Bull Moose, and Lewis, Dunne, and Harrison remained inactive.[58] Rainey and Sullivan considered the lack of an endorsement from the President a fatal blow. Without Wilson's help, Tumulty's influence had been insufficient to overcome the personal bitterness and intransigent opposition that confronted Sullivan within his own party. In Illinois the path down the middle of the road was dangerously narrow and crooked.

3. The First Test

Tumulty's participation in affairs in New Jersey, New York, Massachusetts, and Illinois did not preclude a broader concern for the campaign of 1914 as a whole. From the beginning of that year he advised Wilson to direct his appeal to every interest in America. He considered harmony among the economic groups in the country as important to national welfare as factional amity to the Democratic Party. When J. P. Morgan, George F. Baker, and other financial leaders announced their intention to withdraw from the directorships of many corporations they controlled, Tumulty interpreted the action simply as an "act of good faith . . . an impressive assurance that the great financial interests are as ready to come into agreement with the government and work in harmony with it *as the government is to come into agreement with them*. . . ." [59]

The President accepted this attitude toward the Morgan announcement as his own. In his annual message in December, 1913, he stated that antagonism between business and government was at an end. Although in the same speech he recommended the program which the Clayton Antitrust Law and the Federal Trade Commission Law ultimately enacted, his words elicited a "truly remarkable chorus of approval" from conservatives as well as liberals.[60] The applause scarcely indicated a willingness on the part of financial and industrial interests to forego their normal Republicanism, but Wilson could hopefully anticipate their increasing co-operation in day-to-day business activities.

The implementation of Wilson's message, providing, as it did, both an agency and a yardstick for the control of corporations, completed the first phase of the New Freedom. Concurrently with the progress of Wilson's reforms through Congress, his political overseers were accelerating the muster of shock troops for the autumn. Probably after consultation with Pence and Frank Doremus, Chairman of the Congressional Campaign Committee, Tumulty submitted a memorandum designed to collate these separate functions and the developing diplomatic crises, and to establish the nature of the President's activity in the pending election. His "Programme for the Fall Campaign" suggested the timing and the texts of the President's speeches, rehearsing Democratic accomplishments at home and abroad, and defining Democratic plans for the future.[61]

This was the first of Tumulty's important papers that Wilson accepted almost without reservation. Only the details of the procedure Tumulty outlined were altered. The various meetings and addresses gave way to an exchange of letters between Wilson and Doremus, and a long letter from Wilson to Oscar Underwood calling for the election of a Democratic Congress. These were published and widely circulated. To a remarkable degree they incorporated not only the ideas but also the exact phraseology that Tumulty had proposed.[62] Indeed, Wilson altered his first draft of the Underwood letter in accordance with Tumulty's further suggestions which iterated and emphasized the text of his "Programme for the Fall Campaign." [63] Tumulty himself prepared and released an essay supplementing the President's public letters. Appropriately entitled "Democratic Solidarity," it exuded pride in the party's achievement and confidence in the party's future, and eulogized Wilson as a man and as a President.[64]

Besides taking an active part in various intra-state contests and composing the basic documents for the campaign of 1914, Tumulty prompted Wilson to send personal endorsements to candidates throughout the country who needed special presidential approval to overcome Republican strength in their districts. Both Tumulty and Burleson accurately predicted the dimensions of the Democratic victory. Although their majorities were reduced, the Democrats retained control of both houses of Congress. The collapse of the Progressive Party worked to the advantage of the Republicans, but the Democratic vote nevertheless increased over that of 1912 and maintained its relation to the total vote in spite of a reduced registration in the solid South.[65]

The over-all returns constituted a national endorsement of Wilson's program, but in the states of Tumulty's primary interest the weakness of the Bull Moose, the basic hostility of business interests, and various uncemented Democratic cleavages contributed to Republican resurgence. Wilson's coolness toward Sullivan assured Sherman's re-election in Illinois where Democrats did well in other Congressional contests. In Massachusetts Walsh retained the governorship by a small margin, but four Congressional districts reverted to their normal Republicanism. New Jersey and New York evidenced a similar pattern. The upstate vote in New York unseated Glynn and defeated Gerard. The Democracy, however, retained a large delegation from the Empire State and saved several Jersey seats.[66] Tumulty's policies were not so much a failure as a partial success. Had he been less active, Democratic factionalism could have produced even less successful results.

Tumulty was not discouraged by the results of the election. He drew up a memorandum for the President's information pointing out where the lack of federal patronage had resulted in "weak points in the armor." [67] He wrote his close friends that the western returns, particularly in California, showed "a new field of conquest" for the Democracy in 1916.[68] The astute, optimistic analysis which he sent James Kerney dealt intimately with the entire national scene. Satisfied but not complacent, Tumulty predicted that the next two years would "demonstrate the virtue and effectiveness" of laws Wilson had sponsored. As for the present, he concluded, "the only thing that I can exclaim . . . is 'God rules and the Democratic Party still lives.' " [69]

One aspect of the election returns worried Tumulty, however. The European war had unsettled business and financial conditions, and the vote in the East suggested that businessmen lacked confidence in the Democratic program. Yet this very vote made Wilson hesitate to reassure them. Tumulty, therefore, hastened to persuade his chief of the necessity for a conciliatory temper for the sake of national well-being. Soon after the election he sent the President a draft for the pending state-of-the-union message. Elaborating on the theme that "we are all in the same boat," Tumulty pointed to the common interest of all classes in America in the continued prosperity of the railroads, then threatened financially by European investors liquidating their stocks and bonds.[70]

Although Wilson incorporated the bulk of this document in a public letter to Secretary of the Treasury McAdoo,[71] Tumulty was still not satisfied. The President, pursuant to the advice of Colonel House, had decided not to mention business in his message to Congress. Convinced that House was wrong, Tumulty addressed a last-minute appeal to his chief. Warning Wilson that the public would interpret silence as an indication that further business legislation was pending, Tumulty urged him to encourage business and to dispel doubts by stating clearly that his program had been completed.[72]

Again Wilson followed his secretary's advice.[73] The President's message to Congress on December eighth wrote a finale to Tumulty's concern for the election of 1914 and its attendant problems. The healing potions which he had brewed diligently for almost two years characterized his initial venture in national statesmanship. His political efforts were helpful in the re-election of a Democratic Congress; his advice influenced the nature of Wilson's plans for that Congress. These achievements were significant corollaries to the more permanent and penetrating accomplishments of the New Freedom.

But Tumulty could not pause to exult. Even before his initial triumphs, and with increasing frequency thereafter, conditions at home and abroad jeopardized the harmony that was his predominant objective for the Democracy and the nation. And a threefold nemesis of bigotry, jealousy, and death threatened his dearest ambitions for himself.

CHAPTER VII

The Klan and the Hyphen

1. Mexico

THOSE who enter public life in America subject themselves to the cruel tradition that opens family, faith, and fortune to exploitation in the vendettas of partisan politics. Tumulty was no exception to this rule. He was a deeply religious man whose Catholicism gave him peace and moral purpose. Among his close friends were many priests whose disinterested altruism, like his own, knew no racial or party lines. He was ever tolerant of all beliefs. But religious bigots vilified him sometimes because of his faith and sometimes because of his exclusively personal feeling for his faith. Tumulty, proud of his Irish antecedents, hoped for the day when Ireland might be independent. He was intimate with "dear old 'Tay-Pay' O'Connor," a journalistic apostle of Home Rule. But American descendants of English immigrants sneered at his forebears and their aspirations, and violent American Sinn Feiners damned his patriotic forbearance and objective first concern for the interests of the United States. Tumulty's creed in public life was strictly that of country and party, but his private beliefs and his firm adherence to that public dogma exposed him to the bitter hostility of extremists on all sides.

Tumulty appreciated the political implications of the Catholic and Irish questions in America. He warned his chief of the inevitable antagonism that Irish-Americans would feel against the Panama tolls repeal. He advised the President to demonstrate his friendship for the Church by attending Thanksgiving Mass at St. Patrick's in Washington. He defended Wilson against false charges of disrespect toward Cardinal Gibbons.[1]

On the other hand, strictly secular considerations motivated Tumulty to advise the appointments of various Catholics in the face of stormy protests from future members of the Ku Klux Klan.* In two cases in particular his political objectives unfortunately aroused religious feelings. Martin J. Wade, the Democratic National Committeeman from Iowa, aspired to a vacancy in the southern district court in that state. Because of Wade's qualifications and his faithful support of Wilson, both Burleson and Tumulty endorsed him. But Wade was a Catholic, and the American Protective Association therefore fought his appointment, unjustifiably accusing Tumulty of favoring a co-religionist.[2] A more violent controversy arose over the selection of John F. Sinnott as Postmaster in Newark, New Jersey. Tumulty supported Sinnott because, as a regular Democrat who had rebelled against the Nugent machine, he had labored for Wilson in the "dark days." Furthermore, his son was the Washington correspondent of the Newark *Evening News*. Both New Jersey Senators endorsed Sinnott. When his name was sent to the Senate for confirmation, however, the spokesman of his principal rival for office deliberately misquoted Tumulty in order to picture him as preferring Sinnott because he was a Catholic. No one at any time questioned Sinnott's fitness for office or loyalty to Wilson. Instead, the opposition, inventing a sectarian issue, made Tumulty's religion a political football.[3]

Habitual anti-Romanists, attacking Tumulty without any provocation, described him as an insidious intermediary through whom the Pope sought to dominate Wilson. Senator John Sharp Williams of Mississippi, a lovable statesman of the old school, ridiculed such imputations. He assured Tom Watson that Tumulty was not a papal spy.[4] To a constituent who predicted a repetition of the Spanish Inquisition under Tumulty's direction, Williams replied

---

* The Klan of the post-Civil War period, dedicated to white supremacy, had long since died. During World War I, however, a new Klan was founded. It exploited the prejudices against Negroes, Jews, Catholics, and foreigners on which the American Protective Association had long fed.

that no such danger need be feared. He forwarded his correspondence to Wilson with the facetious comment that ". . . if you and Tumulty want to start an Inquisition, I hope you will make it either French, Dutch, or Italian, for the adjective 'Spanish' in connection with an inquisition, has a pretty bad sort of meaning. . . ." In an equally jovial vein Williams wrote Tumulty that he never knew a man "with as innocent a face as you have who was possessed with as fiendish and felonious designs." [5]

Wilson himself came to Tumulty's defense. Various misled evangelists, including the editor of the *Protestant Magazine*, claimed that Tumulty prevented any communication relating to the Catholic Church from reaching the President. Wilson denied this allegation, admonishing Tumulty's accusers to reconsider their views.[6] A more publicized remonstrance emanated from *Life*. A Protestant missionary asked the editor whether Tumulty was not using his knowledge and power for Rome. "Tumulty," the editor replied, "will use what he knows for Wilson, Tumulty, the Democratic party and the people of the United States. . . . If Tumulty goes to confession he will merely confess for Tumulty, not for Wilson. . . . Do you really suppose, brother, that chaps like Tumulty want the Pope to govern the earth. . . ? Go chase yourself, dear man; nothing of the kind. . . ." [7] Wilson echoed these sentiments with a hearty "Amen." [8]

Priestly dictation failed to cause Tumulty to deviate from his political principles as dismally as did threats of reprisals from the American Protective Association. Constantly embroiled in the partisan and sectarian altercations over American policy in Mexico, he warmly approved Wilson's decisions in the successive diplomatic crises with the régimes of Victoriano Huerta and Venustiano Carranza. Huerta he rightly considered the apostle of reaction; Carranza he saw as the agent of necessary progress in Mexico. He recognized that the turmoil, bloodshed, and destruction of property south of the border was a part of the violence which attends social revolutions. Except when the American flag, American lives, or American territory was involved, he agreed with Wilson that Mexico deserved patience and understanding from the United States. And he persisted in these views in spite of the insistent protests of Catholic prelates that the American government intercede in behalf of Huerta or against Carranza to protect the dignity and property of the Church.

Huerta's hopelessly reactionary government early demonstrated hostility toward the United States. His local officials at Tampico, without provocation, early in 1914 arrested a shore party of uniformed American sailors. The American demand that he salute the flag by way of reparation Huerta refused to obey. Wilson then asked permission to use force. Before Congress acted, the President learned that a German merchant ship was about to land arms for Huerta at Vera Cruz.

Tumulty took part in the telephone conference with Bryan, Daniels, and Wilson in which the President decided to send marines into Vera Cruz to prevent this landing. He applauded the strategy as a dangerous but essential move to frustrate Huerta and uphold national honor.[9] He was equally pleased, however, with Wilson's acceptance of the offer of Argentina, Brazil, and Chile to mediate in the troubled affairs in Mexico.

By the time the mediators' deliberations resulted in the withdrawal of American troops, Carranza had established a precarious supremacy over other factional leaders. His accession introduced a period of high revolutionary fever as angry mobs unleashed their fury at the symbols of their discontent, the propertied interests and the Catholic Church. In the United States, Carranza and his followers were blamed both for their share in this violence and their inability to prevent mob attacks. In December of 1914, in an article in the New York *Times*, Theodore Roosevelt condemned Wilson for his Mexican policy, particularly for removing the troops from Vera Cruz before the apology the President had demanded had been received. Roosevelt exploited religious feeling in this country by quoting affidavits which claimed that the sanctity of the Catholic Church had been violated.[10] Catholic opinion already opposed Carranza. The *America*, a Catholic magazine, had reported alleged outrages in incendiary tones.[11] Catholic conferences had passed resolutions demanding official intervention. And Wilson had found it necessary to assure James Cardinal Gibbons that he was powerless to relieve the sad conditions by any word or message until passions in Mexico should have subsided. This refusal to resort to arms doubtless cost the Democrats many Catholic votes in 1914. After Roosevelt's attack, at the insistence of Dudley Field Malone, Wilson had Bryan write Father Francis C. Kelley, the president of the Church Extension Society, in an effort to explain again that the President had done his utmost, within the limits of his developing policy of Pan-Americanizing the Monroe Doctrine, to protect the Church in Mexico.[12]

The letter to Father Kelley, however, had no discernible effect on Catholic opinion as voiced by the *America*. When the United States government in October 1915, recognized Carranza, then accepted by a Pan-American conference as the *de facto* ruler of Mexico, the offensive acerbity of that publication reached a new high. The *America* described Carranza as a villain, destroyer, liar, and murderer. Inferentially these editorial sentiments seemed also to be directed toward Wilson.[13]

As the ranking Catholic in the Administration, Tumulty sprang to his chief's defense. His faith in Wilson and the righteousness of his policy, and his understanding of Mexico's troubles transcended any immediate considerations of political expediency. To James J. McGuire he wrote a public letter, setting forth the Administration's position. Tumulty intended to demolish the charges the *America* had made, not to mollify sectarian prejudice. Never did he more clearly demonstrate his secular approach to national affairs. He reminded his correspondents of the chaos that accompanies revolution and war, and of the complications of the ecclesiastical issue in Mexico. He maintained that official records disclosed no instance of the alleged dastardly crimes against nuns. He rehearsed the case for the recognition of Carranza. Finally, he advised sympathetic counsel instead of rancorous recrimination as the needful and merciful attitude toward a neighbor faced with the problems of reconstruction and reunion.[14]

Father R. H. Tierney, the editor of *America*, Monsignor Kelley, and Bishop Nilan of Connecticut hastened to reply. They questioned Tumulty's veracity, reproaching him for permitting partisanship to blind him to conditions in Mexico.[15] Tierney had publicized stories of the violations of nuns. "Some men," he wrote, obviously referring to Tumulty, "who seem to think that they are baptized politicians, not Christians, are declaring that . . . I have not the facts. These people . . . fear the facts. . . . The situation in Mexico . . . is . . . just plain hell. . . ." [16]

Tierney's words cut Tumulty deeply. He was no less devout than he had ever been. His refusal to permit his religion to affect his political thinking was typical of thousands of American Catholics. Yet because of his outspoken defense of the Administration he had been accused practically of paganism. Ironically, while Tumulty was silent, a Methodist editor best phrased his rebuttal: "When Mr. Tumulty became secretary to President Wilson some perhaps oversensitive anti-Romanists were quick to discover a Papist plot. . . . However, in withstanding the severest pressure from Romanist ecclesiastics in the matter of the recognition of Carranza in Mexico, even publicly discrediting charges against Carranza vouched by Roman Catholic priests in the United States . . . Tumulty has demonstrated that a Catholic layman can be the most independent sort of a patriot. . . ." [17] President Wilson characterized this article as a "deserved tribute." [18]

Neither Tierney's aspersions on his faith nor repeated warnings that the Catholic vote would desert the Democracy in 1916 changed Tumulty's views toward Mexico. But his attitude of sympathetic understanding fled before the machinations of Pancho Villa. Of the many chieftains who opposed Carranza, Villa was the strongest and most sanguinary. His forces in Northern Mexico courted popular favor by provocative sallies against American property and citizens. On March 9, 1916, they crossed the border, pillaged and burned Columbus, New Mexico, and murdered nine townspeople as well as eight American soldiers. Carranza, powerless to stop such raids, nevertheless firmly opposed permitting American troops to enter Mexico to punish Villa. Congress and the people demanded his capture. Although Wilson declared that Villa would be restrained, he hesitated to offend Carranza by ordering the army to cross the border. Tumulty, out of patience with "watchful waiting," beseeched the President to act even if it meant war.[19] With the approval of Congress, Wilson sent Brigadier General John J. Pershing after Villa. In June, after American soldiers engaged in that futile pursuit had been captured and imprisoned by Carranza, Tumulty implored both Wilson and Robert Lansing, then Secretary of State, to issue a peremptory ultimatum calling for their release.[20] Three times he telephoned Lansing, urging "immediate action." [21] Recognizing this as a popular, legitimate sentiment, Wilson sent the ultimatum which Carranza wisely honored.

Tumulty's bellicose indignation in 1916 received no publicity. His letter to McGuire, on the other hand, continued to rankle many Catholic prelates. Months after the ultimatum to Carranza, Father H. McMahon portrayed Tumulty as a Catholic in public life who had betrayed the Church.[22]

2. Neutrality

Just as Tumulty's stand on Mexico alienated extremists in his Church, so did his convictions with regard to American neutrality and the European war antagonize the extremists among his fellow Irish-Americans. In the latter case, however, operating almost exclusively behind the scenes, he was less subject to personal attacks. Furthermore, his first difference with Wilson would have pleased the Sinn Feiners had they known about it. In the autumn of 1914 he protested to the President that the Republicans were capitalizing on his patience toward England's blockade. Wilson replied with irritation that Britain was fighting our fight and he would not press her further.[23] Loyally accepting this view, Tumulty for some time silently subscribed to his chief's doctrines of neutrality.

It is now difficult to recapture the state of American opinion at the time of the outbreak of the First World War. Uninformed about European affairs, unacquainted with the conditions of modern warfare, the American people thought in terms of their long-time isolation and traditional definitions of neutral rights and duties, not in terms of global conflict. Sentimentally, most Americans, including Wilson and his advisers, from the beginning favored England and France. A vocal minority, however, preferred Germany. In and out of the government, the overwhelming sentiment was initially against American involvement.

Wilson, subduing his emotions, tried to be neutral. He also committed the government to protecting America's neutral rights as they were then interpreted. These positions were irreconcilable. The Western Powers, controlling the sea, blockaded Germany and her allies. Only the Western Powers could benefit from American shipments of noncontraband materials, many of them essential to a war effort, which international law as then defined permitted. Only the Western Powers, therefore, had reason to negotiate loans in the United States for the payment of those materials. While Wilson again and again protested against the practices of the British blockade, he at the same time contended that shipments of noncontraband were legal and he permitted private American loans to the Allies. Germany's only retaliatory weapon was the submarine, then an effective new device of warfare. Submarines could not warn vessels they were about to torpedo, especially armed vessels, or remove passengers, without forfeiting their tactical advantage. Consequently submarine tactics violated the age-old procedures of belligerent commerce destroyers, taking lives in that process, including, ultimately, the lives of Americans on whose traditional right to travel on belligerent ships Wilson insisted. The President warned Germany in February 1915, a few months after the war had begun, that he would hold her to "strict accountability" for any American lives or property injured or destroyed by her submarines in her counter-blockade of the British Isles. Since the Allies consistently ignored our demands, however, Germany could not be expected to honor them. As "strict accountability" was defined in the crucible of maritime war, the United States moved toward belligerency.

Had Wilson reversed his views he would, in fact, have sided with Germany. His position as it emerged in fact assisted the Allies. There were personal and popular emotional reasons for this alignment. There was precedent in international law for it. The developments of the decades since the "neutrality" of 1914–17 sustain the basic wisdom of Wilson's course. Before the period of neutrality ended he had been driven to the conclusion that aggressors must be punished. Yet during that time the President reached each painful decision along the road to war only after an effort to preserve neutrality as he understood it, and always without a clear conception of the larger meaning of his commitments in the changing pattern of world affairs. Some of his advisers, like Walter Hines Page, Ambassador to Britain, pretending little neutrality, openly sponsored England's cause. Others, however, like Tumulty, groped as did Wilson for answers to the insoluble problems posed by their simultaneous desires for noninvolvement, for the protection of American rights and American honor, and for Allied victory. For Tumulty each crisis was also a problem in public opinion, and in each his reactions, his growing anger toward the Germans, his gradual, wavering, unwilling movement toward a will to fight, reflected that opinion.

On the seventh of May, 1915, the people of the United States were shocked by the news of the sinking of the *Lusitania*. German torpedoes had already killed American citizens on the *Gulflight*. Germany's bold warning, the tremendous loss of life — of men, women, and children — the whole tragic drama of the *Lusitania* sinking aroused the nation to a frenzy of anger. While few, mostly pro-Germans or pacifists, remained cool and cautious, the majority of Americans probably did not want war. Tumulty's initial wrath and thirst for retribution, however, approached that of Theodore Roosevelt and Secretary of War Garrison. Foreseeing that Wilson's celebrated expression, "too proud to fight," which the President planned to use in a speech at Philadelphia, would be misconstrued, he begged his chief to delete that phrase. Wilson refused. The furor that followed the address confirmed Tumulty's analysis of American opinion and strengthened his resolve to influence his chief to take an unequivocal stand against Germany.[24]

Tumulty contended that Germany must be forced to apologize. He urged that an ultimatum be sent warning that no repetition of such a flagrant offense to American honor would be tolerated. Wilson, however, contemplating war with horror, adopted the conciliatory course which Bryan urged. Like Tumulty, Wilson was deaf to the argument of the Secretary of State that Americans had no right to travel on the ships of belligerent powers. But unlike Tumulty, Wilson accepted Bryan's plea that, for the sake of peace, the United States should abide by the principles of Bryan's treaties for a "cooling off" period and arbitration. The President planned to accompany the publication of a strong note to Germany with the release of a statement to the press expressing confidence that the "cooling off" principle would permit a peaceful settlement.[25] This was the so-called "postscript" of which Henry Cabot Lodge made a campaign issue in 1916. The Senator was correct in declaring that Wilson had intended to temper his note. Wilson stretched the truth by resting a denial of Lodge's charge on errors in the Senator's details.[26]

The statement to the press on the "cooling off" treaties, largely because of Tumulty's protests, was never released. When Robert Lansing, then Counselor of the State Department, and Secretary of War Garrison informed him of the President's decision to modify the note to Germany, Tumulty was appalled. Going at once to Wilson, he analyzed the dangers in Bryan's plan. He predicted that the American people would "raise a terrible howl" and charge the President with "double-dealing." He argued that Germany would conclude that the United States would not fight for her rights. At first Wilson insisted that Bryan, a wise politician, was a competent judge of public opinion. Burleson, who had been summoned, believed that the "postscript" was not really so bad. But Tumulty persisted. Wilson finally assented to suppress the statement. "White as a ghost," Tumulty joined Garrison at the Shoreham dining room. "I have just had the worst half hour of my life," he told the Secretary of War, and he related the details of the interview with Wilson. With great relief Garrison commented: "You should receive a medal of honor for this day's work." [27]

Wilson's *Lusitania* notes satisfied the great center segment of American opinion. But the jingoes would have preferred a more warlike course, and German- and Irish-Americans denounced the notes to Germany as excessively strong. Secretary Bryan concurred in this latter view. He advised Wilson as a counterbalance to address a note to England protesting against her violations of neutral rights. When the President refused, Bryan concluded that he had no course but to resign from the Cabinet.[28]

Although his interference in the "postscript" affair had precipitated Bryan's decision, Tumulty was as sorry as was Wilson to see the Great Commoner go. The President had learned to respect Bryan's loyalty, sincerity, and ability. Tumulty had been a Bryan enthusiast for twenty years. Their differences in Washington had not dampened his admiration and affection. Except possibly for Garrison, he had no closer friend in the Cabinet. When Bryan departed Tumulty publicly expressed the deep regrets of the Administration. He wrote the Great Commoner a personal letter reminding him that he had looked up to him "as the great leader of the people," assuring him of his heartfelt veneration and continued "profound admiration," and commending him for his "tireless . . . co-operation with the President." [29]

Tumulty approved of Wilson's selection of Robert Lansing to succeed Bryan as Secretary of State. Although Lansing was patently an Anglophile, Tumulty had concurred in his views on the "postscript" and admired his skill in press relations.[30] As negotiations over the *Lusitania* affair proceeded, Tumulty applauded the insistence of Wilson and Lansing that Germany had to modify her submarine tactics to recognize the unalterable rights of a neutral. He considered America's self-respect contingent upon the observation of that doctrine.[31]

Still, Tumulty was not consciously unneutral. After the sinking of the *Hesperian* by a German submarine in September of 1915, while the country was agog over spy rumors, he declared to Wilson that when all the facts were available they would show no lack of good faith on the part of Germany. He opposed any diplomatic rupture, considering a clearer definition of the German position adequate. Earlier that summer he had adopted Bryan's position, recommending to Wilson that he demand that Great Britain recognize America's commercial rights on the high seas. In February and again in May of 1916 he pressed Lansing for similar action.[32]

Neither the abuse of professional Irish-Americans nor the inertia of Democratic isolationists swayed Tumulty. After Bryan's resignation and during the progress of the *Lusitania* negotiations, the *Irish World*, an organ of American Sinn Fein opinion, increased its crescendo of denunciation.[33] Tumulty ignored it. In February of 1916 Democratic Congressional leaders rebelled openly against the

WILLIAM GIBBS McADOO AND
TUMULTY, 1914.

TUMULTY AND SENATOR OLLIE M. JAMES
OF KENTUCKY.

TUMULTY IN THE 1916 PRESIDENTIAL CAMPAIGN.
CARTOON BY CLIFFORD KENNEDY BERRYMAN,
FROM THE WASHINGTON *Evening Star*.

President's policies. Tumulty's immediate reaction was to counter-attack.

Resolutions introduced by Representative McLemore and Senator Gore forbade travel by American citizens on the armed vessels of belligerents. In keeping with Bryan's theories, they were designed to eliminate the danger of a war resulting from further loss of American life. But negotiations were already in progress by which the State Department hoped to persuade the Western Powers to disarm merchantmen in return for a German promise to regulate submarine tactics. Like Wilson, Tumulty considered the Gore and McLemore resolutions dangerous obstacles to the successful prosecution of the diplomatic program. Furthermore, he resented any Congressional challenge to Wilson's leadership. He advised the President to restate his position emphatically in letters to Senator Stone and Representative Flood, the chairmen of the Congressional committees on foreign affairs, and to force a vote on the restrictive resolutions.[34] His counsel fortified Wilson's determination. The President wrote Stone, incorporating many of Tumulty's words, and shortly thereafter precipitated a vote by which the resolutions were tabled. Choosing to interpret this as an Administration victory, Tumulty vented his exuberance in a letter to the editor of the Jersey City *Journal* in which he boldly stigmatized the attitude of the Irish in Hudson County.[35]

3. Preparedness

After the sinking of the *Sussex* in March 1916, and the American protest that followed, the Germans promised to abandon unrestricted submarine warfare, provided that Britain "observe the rules of international law." This pledge afforded a breathing spell during which Wilson labored for peace, but from the time of the *Lusitania* affair and even after the *Sussex* pledge, the possibility of war increased. Once he realized that war was imminent, Tumulty became an advocate of preparedness. He had adopted Wilson's theories of international law and morality, but unlike his chief he grasped their immediate military and political implications.

Agitation for preparedness began with the outbreak of war in Europe. Garrison had been advocating reorganization of the army from the time he took his office. To his voice were added those of Theodore Roosevelt, Republican Congressman A. P. Gardner of Massachusetts, Democratic Senator G. E. Chamberlain of Oregon, General Leonard Wood, Elihu Root, Henry Stimson and the members of the National Security League. Wilson, however, expressed complacent satisfaction with the army and navy in his message to Congress of December 1914.[36] Tumulty, by his silence on the subject, indicated his agreement, but the doctrine of "strict accountability" and the *Lusitania* incident brought him to his senses. Implicit in the phrase was the possibility of a war which Garrison quickly convinced Tumulty the United States was in no condition to fight. Furthermore, Tumulty sensed that the American people were becoming dubious about Wilson's leadership on diplomatic and military affairs.

During the critical summer of 1915, while Wilson was vacationing in Cornish, New Hampshire, Tumulty wrote his chief importuning the need for a program of military expansion. He argued that the Republicans had but two issues for 1916: the tariff and national defense. He advised an expression of willingness to adjust tariff schedules to meet the changes in economic conditions wrought by the war. The question of national defense he considered paramount. In so far as public opinion would condone them, he adopted Garrison's views in a memorandum to Wilson:

. . . We must have a sane, reasonable, and practicable programme. This programme must have in it the ingredients that will call forth the hearty, enthusiastic support of, first, the Cabinet (particularly the Secretary of War); second, the leaders of the party in the Senate and House; third, the rank file of Congress; fourth, the Army and the Navy; and last but not least, the great body of the American people.

The successful carrying through of this programme will test the leadership of the President to the last degree. Just on the eve of the campaign of 1916, it will be accepted by the country as the final test of his leadership, and will be of incalculable *psychological* importance to the party. . . . Any trivial mistake will be magnified. . . . It will be the ultimate test of our party's power to govern the nation. . . .

Of one thing I am certain, that the whole country wishes effective preparedness and will ruthlessly cast aside any man or party who stands in the way of the carrying out of this programme.

I realize that there is one thing that may cause the Democratic leaders to hesitate about pushing this programme, and that is the opportunity they fear will be given to Mr. Bryan "to play" this issue as an effective means of getting back into popular favor. This ought not to daunt us in the least. I do not fear it. *In fact, were I coldly to consider this, I would invite opposition of this kind.*

Therefore, the necessity of having a programme to which the Secretary of War will give his hearty support. For let it be remembered at the present time, he has the ear of the country and any programme suggested by the President with which he would not agree, would be looked upon with suspicion would not agree, would be looked upon with suspicion throughout the country. (I say this with the deepest regret.) . . .

To push a programme with which the Secretary of War was at variance, the leaders of both Houses not in agreement with, and about which the country was indifferent, would be more than disastrous. It would be pitiful. . . . [37]

Advised along similar lines by Colonel House, Wilson set out to win public support for national armament. Congress was slow to recognize America's military needs, partly because Wilson took so long to begin his appeal. Not until November did he make his first address on preparedness. Tumulty helped write that speech. Wilson had intended to say that the nation did not want a great standing army and did not need one. Tumulty made this statement more flexible and more adaptable to Garrison's views on the necessity of increasing the regular army by mobilizing, if necessary by conscription, a substantial reserve. He suggested the peroration and inserted several paragraphs asking nonpartisan support for a policy designed to protect America's rights.[38]

Late in November Tumulty returned to his theme of the previous summer with new vigor. The resistance of German- and Irish-Americans, by propaganda and even sabotage, to Wilson's diplomatic policies and preparedness ideas had aroused him. He felt that the people demanded firmness. While the President was writing his message to Congress, Tumulty sent him a pressing memorandum:

> . . . I do not like to alarm you but there is no mistaking the fact that the country is dissatisfied with our seeming indifference toward the propaganda initiated by our hyphenated friends. The country every day reads of the efforts of these hyphenated Americans to destroy manufacturing plants, to poison and control public opinion in every way, and is astounded at the seeming indifference of the Administration toward these efforts to undermine us and injure our people.
>
> The Lusitania affair is again referred to and the demand for speedy reparation is growing by the hour. The Ancona affair is another cause for irritation. In my opinion, it is all leading to one idea, — that this Administration, for some reason, is lacking in *aggressive assertiveness.* Congress will soon be in session and then the propaganda of our Republican friends to destroy us will be started anew.
>
> It seems to me that the time has come for *action,* and ACTION and MORE ACTION all along the line. . . .
>
> Your message should be a clarion call to the Nation; a defi to those Americans who would challenge the very sovereignty of America and engage in movements and attacks which strike at her very heart.
>
> When I spoke to you the other day about legislation to cover the acts of those who are destroying manufacturing plants, you thought it would not be wise to include in your Message a recommendation for such legislation. I do not agree with you in this matter. There ought to be a ringing paragraph with reference to the necessity for legislation which will prevent things of this kind from happening in the future. . . .[39]

Tumulty, delighted that Wilson followed his advice, nevertheless found more to criticize in the draft of his chief's message. He felt that the President had weakened his plea for defense measures by overemphasizing the merchant marine program which had been advanced earlier as a peacetime proposition. In order to avoid charges of using national defense as an excuse to promote a partisan policy, he recommended that the section on the merchant marine be divorced from the section on the army and navy. Wilson again altered his message and much of his phraseology in accordance with Tumulty's ideas.[40]

Tumulty next persuaded the President to take the issue to the people. While Congress delayed, the Republicans made political capital of Democratic inaction. Tumulty, believing that only a direct appeal would arouse public opinion sufficiently to move Congress, once again composed a forceful note. Reminding Wilson of his advice at the time of the Smith-Martine affair in New Jersey, he insisted that, as on that occasion, the "great bulk of the people" were looking for leadership. They did not wish to follow Bryan and were reluctant to follow Roosevelt, "except in sheer desperation," but, Tumulty declared, "the impression abroad in the country is that we are drifting." If an unfortunate incident should arise with Mexico or Germany, he pointed out, an appeal for national defense would seem anticlimactic. Therefore he urged that the "psychological" moment had come for an emphatic statement from Wilson on the related questions of foreign affairs and preparedness.[41]

Wilson was at last convinced. Garrison's contemplated resignation in protest against continuing inactivity underscored Tumulty's concern. The President embarked, in January 1916, on a speaking tour which carried him from New York City as far west as Kansas. Tumulty planned the itinerary and accompanied his chief. Although the tour was advertised as nonpolitical, Tumulty consulted Democratic leaders at every stop, gathering information on local attitudes and reactions to the preparedness program.[42] It was on this trip that Wilson, shaking off what remained of the Bryanesque philosophy of military weakness, spoke out for a navy second to none.

In spite of his increasingly forceful attitude, however, the President found his Secretary of War still on the verge of resigning.

Tumulty's hope for a program of national defense on which Congress and Cabinet could unite proved impossible of fulfillment. Garrison considered a large, standing army a *sine qua non*. Congressional leaders, frightened by the specter of a standing army, advocated expansion through the more traditional agency of the National Guard. This latter course was the only program that stood a chance of enactment. Wilson therefore rejected Garrison's advice.

When Garrison had first written Wilson of his disdain for Congressional opinion on military matters, Tumulty helped the President prepare a reply. He pointed out that the Secretary of War had admitted that there was a perfectly legitimate field for debate on how to increase American forces. He advised Wilson to emphasize the fact that he was waiting to see whether Chairman Hay of the House Committee on Military Affairs could not produce a plan as good, if not better, than the one proposed by Garrison. "The President," Tumulty wrote, "is just as much interested in the defense programme as the Secretary of War or anybody else but he has been embarrassed by the unyielding attitude of those who have had to do with it. . . ." He suggested that Wilson express his confidence in Hay and assure Garrison that he would accept no unsatisfactory solution, that he would, if necessary, appeal to the country.[43]

The President's reply to Garrison rested on the arguments Tumulty had set forth.[44] The preparedness tour buttressed those arguments. But a few weeks later Garrison, disturbed also by Wilson's Mexican policy, made the Clarke Amendment favoring American withdrawal from the Philippines the occasion of his resignation. Nevertheless, he and Tumulty remained on good terms. Tumulty missed him as he missed Bryan, for their successors were never as sympathetic as these friends had been.

Although Garrison's departure temporarily aggravated the dissensions within the Democratic Party which came to a head in the Gore-McLemore Resolutions,* ultimately it enabled Wilson to work more closely with Congress. Tumulty saw to it that Wilson appeared at the head of preparedness parades.[45] In co-operation with Wilson and Newton D. Baker, Garrison's successor, Congressional

* See p. 99.

leaders formulated and enacted a program of national defense which stilled most of the President's critics. Before the campaign of 1916 began, the Republicans could no longer claim preparedness as their own.

4. Shillelaghs

The hostility of unregenerate German- and Irish-Americans to Wilson's diplomatic and military policies confronted Democratic leaders at the Convention of 1916. Nevertheless Tumulty, the editor of the Milwaukee *Journal*, and Frank Polk, the Counselor of the State Department, agreed that there should be no truckling to the hyphen.[46] Senator Paul O. Husting of Wisconsin, where the population included a large proportion of German-Americans, drafted a plank on that issue. His central idea was to accept the challenge of the German-American Alliance and define the issue as "being between those who stand for America and those who stand for some other country first."[47] Tumulty welcomed Husting's plan. He urged Wilson to write an open letter to Newton D. Baker, then the Chairman of the Committee on Resolutions, reiterating his principles of neutrality "in no uncertain terms" and thereby defying those who sought to "debase our politics through the creation of the German vote in the United States as a power."[48] Secretary of the Interior Franklin K. Lane supported this view,[49] and with Wilson's assent the plank on the hyphen vote was adopted substantially as Husting had recommended. The platform also applauded Wilson's policies toward Mexico and Europe.

The Convention of 1916 had barely adjourned when Tumulty began to receive worried reports on the party's position from Democratic battalion leaders. James M. Cox of Ohio forwarded a letter from a Democratic Catholic politician who warned that the "poison" originating in the Catholic press had provoked priests in Ohio, Illinois and Wisconsin to treat Wilson unfairly.[50] From Indiana came tales of a German Catholic priest who had slandered the President from the pulpit. A representative of the Brooklyn Democracy sounded the alarm there.[51] Tumulty received the most comprehensive analysis from the Reverend Edward Flannery. Beyond a doubt, Flannery wrote, the Irish-Catholic vote in New York, New Jersey, Delaware, Indiana, Connecticut, Montana, and Massachusetts had been alienated by Wilson's foreign policies. Flannery suggested that the remedy lay in winning over the Catholic press, especially the *Gaelic American*, the organ of the Clan-na-Gael, which had criticized Wilson scurrilously. He advised Tumulty to silence Daniel Cohalan, the owner of that paper, through Charles Murphy, Cohalan's intimate friend. Flannery believed that Tom Taggart, the leading clansman in Indiana, would control the vote there, but he saw no hope for New Jersey and he predicted that Monsignor Kelley would upset the Democrats in Illinois. He included in his letter a distinct demand that a Catholic be appointed to the commission which was to deal with Mexican affairs.[52]

Tumulty rode the storm. He denied the rumors that Wilson had insulted a Cardinal, an Archbishop, and a papal legate, and he again distributed widely a list of the Catholics whom the President had appointed to office,[53] but he studiously ignored the crafty, unscrupulous Cohalan. When no Catholic was named to the Mexican Commission, Father Flannery switched his allegiance, informing Tumulty that he would use all of his influence to defeat Wilson.[54]

Catholic lay societies and publicists intensified their campaign of vituperation. *The Catholic News Bulletin* announced itself for the Republican presidential candidate, Charles Evans Hughes. The *Irish World* painted Wilson as almost an anti-Christ.[55] After the Republican victory in Maine, Jeremiah O'Leary, an organizer of the movement against the President, sent Wilson an offensive letter predicting his defeat. Tumulty applauded his chief's sharp reply which invited O'Leary and all "disloyal Americans" to vote against him.[56] If Hughes did not cultivate this group, at least he never repulsed it. The movement did not extend, however, to the Catholic clergy. Father M. D. Collins of Jackson, Missouri, after canvassing the situation all over the United States, reported that the great majority of priests were favorable to Wilson and what they regarded as his sincere efforts for peace.[57]

Tumulty considered it good politics to underline the Administration's Americanism by rejecting the support of all those who blatantly opposed Wilson's foreign policies, but he had no desire, particularly in a campaign year, to antagonize the Irish needlessly. He was deeply distressed, therefore, by the events attending the execution of Sir Roger Casement. With German assistance, Casement had led an abortive invasion of Ireland which coincided with the Easter Rebellion of 1916. He was captured by the British, imprisoned, and tried and convicted for treason. There was no doubt of his guilt in British eyes, for as a subject of the crown he had openly aided the enemy. The Irish, however, both in Ireland and America, idolized Sir Roger as a daring, patriotic leader in their struggle for national independence.[58]

Casement's sister retained Michael Francis Doyle, a Philadelphia lawyer who had long been friendly with Bryan, to defend her brother. Largely working through Tumulty, Doyle sought official assistance first in the trial and then for a commutation of the death sentence. Lansing refused, explaining that the State Department could not intervene in a case exclusively concerning a foreign government and its own citizen, but Polk assured Tumulty that the American Embassy in London had been instructed to give Doyle all proper aid. Since Ambassador Page was pressing Lansing to decline to take any action for Casement, Tumulty appreciated the futility of such instructions.[59]

Late in June, after Casement's conviction, eight Congressmen petitioned Wilson to use his good offices for clemency. Tumulty put them off with the evasive reply that the President would take up the matter with the State Department.[60] Meanwhile the *Irish World* was constructing a hero's legend around Sir Roger and Tumulty was becoming increasingly uncomfortable. In an effort to win Wilson's co-operation, he arranged an audience with the President for Franz H. Krebs, a newspaperman thoroughly conversant with the affair. Krebs departed with the feeling that Wilson had listened sympathetically to his description of Casement's humanitarian work in the Congo and consequent frail health.[61] Perhaps Tumulty felt that Wilson had been convinced. Early in July he showed his chief a letter from Doyle which asserted that John Redmond, a leader of the Irish moderates, and Lord Northcliffe, influential publisher of the London *Times*, thought that a personal word from Wilson to the British Prime Minister or Foreign Secretary would help Casement. But the President told Tumulty that such action on his part would be both inexcusable and embarrassing.[62] Wilson was equally deaf to an appeal from the Knights of St. Patrick which invoked the precedent of Jefferson's intercession on behalf of Lafayette.[63] Tumulty had failed to change Wilson's views, but as usual he accepted his chief's final decision.

In the meantime Casement's fate received attention from the United States Senate. With the election campaign in progress, the Senators took occasion, by voicing their sympathy for a loyal son of Eire, to woo the Irish vote. On July twenty-ninth, four days before Casement's scheduled execution, they passed a resolution requesting the President to transmit their hope that the British Government would exercise clemency. The resolution reached the executive offices on the day it was passed, but the State Department did not receive a copy until the day before the execution. Because of the process of coding and the difference in time, the cable forwarding the resolution did not reach the British Foreign Office until after Sir Roger had gone to the gallows.[64]

Irish-American indignation over the delay knew no bounds. Since Tumulty had little to do with office routine, the time lost in the executive offices was probably not his fault, but as the responsible official he found himself in an unenviable position. Senator James D. Phelan of California, the sponsor of the resolution, James J. McGuire, Executive Chairman of the Irish Friends of Freedom, and Michael F. Doyle peremptorily demanded an explanation. Casement's sister contended that had the resolution been presented in time, her brother's life would have been spared. Tumulty appealed to Polk and Lansing for a rejoinder from the State Department. They hesitated, however, to extricate him from a predicament for which they felt no liability.[65]

By the first week in September Tumulty was desperate. Informing Lansing that anti-Administration organs all over the country were stressing the matter, he begged the Secretary of State to attest officially "in diplomatic language" that Page had apprised the

British Government of the attitude of the large body of Americans who desired clemency for Casement.[66] It was early October, however, before Polk rescued Tumulty. He stated definitely that the night before Casement was executed the British Ambassador read Polk a letter from his government stating that, after considering the Casement case and the Senate Resolution, the Cabinet had concluded that it could not grant clemency. Fortunately for Tumulty, the British Ambassador had transmitted the resolution unofficially.[67]

With Polk's assistance, Tumulty composed a letter to Doyle invalidating the claims of Casement's sister.[68] Explaining that the resolution had been received, he set forth the reasons why the request had been rejected. He incorporated statements made on the floor of the Senate by Phelan and Hughes, both Irish-Americans but both also worried Democrats, expressing their satisfaction with the efforts of the United States Government.[69] Doyle replied that the explanation "set at rest for all time the allegation that our Government was remiss. . . ."[70] Jeremiah O'Leary, Daniel Cohalan, and others of their ilk were beyond appeasement long before the Easter Rebellion or the apotheosis of Sir Roger, but Polk's intercession resolved the embarrassments attending the Casement affair in time to placate less hysterical Irish-Americans before election day.

By October of 1916 Tumulty had demonstrated that neither his religion nor his antecedents determined his conclusions on domestic or foreign affairs. His loyalty to Wilson, his nationalism, and his instinct for politics governed his views. But neither the Klan nor the Hyphen had permitted him peace. He had persevered in his convictions at the expense of his personal happiness. The constant cross-fire, moreover, had almost persuaded Wilson that his secretary was no longer useful. The jealous malice of Tumulty's personal and political rivals deepened this impression. For during the years that religious bigotry and nationalistic prejudice infested his privacy and complicated his public duties, the schemes and the gossip of Tumulty's enemies were depriving him of the confidence of his chief.

CHAPTER VIII

Stratagems and Spoils

1. "Deserving Democrats"

IN THE intense competition of politics, even the consummate tacticians make enemies. There can be only one policy for each problem, one appointment for each office, and disappointment breeds displeasure. Inevitably, therefore, Tumulty's methods and objectives antagonized influential Democrats of differing opinions and purposes. McCombs and his friends resented their loss of control in the National Committee; House, Malone, and Frank Polk bewailed Tumulty's course in New York. These men retaliated by misconstruing his actions and exploiting his errors in an effort to undermine his influence with Wilson. When their attacks were open, the Republicans cheerfully capitalized on the resulting unfavorable publicity. And to the general discomfort of the Democracy, the Republicans themselves assaulted Tumulty's reputation. The total effect was embarrassing. But the bulk of the charges against Tumulty proved to be based on spiteful fabrications, and even where true, largely to stigmatize others than him. Nevertheless they upset his equanimity, reduced his influence, and very nearly cost him his position.

The background of the first public scandal in which Tumulty's name was involved lay in the machinations of American spoilsmen in the turbulent Republic of San Domingo. Theodore Roosevelt had sent the marines to quell the constant disturbances there. Through an American Receiver of Customs the Republic's finances were reconstructed and her foreign creditors appeased. But during the Taft Administration the cycle of meaningless revolutions recommenced, and the National City Bank stirred up the muddied waters of Caribbean finance in floating a new Dominican loan. Consequently Wilson inherited a Dominican problem, and within a year, dollar diplomacy, banana politics, and Democratic patronage combined to produce a tangled pattern of inefficiency and corruption.

Tumulty quickly discovered that minor diplomatic posts were no more sacrosanct and no less solicited than were appointments under Jersey City's Street and Water Commission. For the offices of Minister and Receiver of Customs in San Domingo he had no candidates of his own, but his old friend, Congressman James Hamill, persuaded him to endorse for Minister James Mark Sullivan, a New York City Democrat, lawyer, and sometime prize-fight promoter. Besides Hamill, Senator James O'Gorman of New York, Homer Cummings of Connecticut, and Judge John G. Gray of Delaware urged that Sullivan's efficient campaigning among Catholic voters in 1912 be recognized.[1] After a perfunctory inquiry, Secretary Bryan satisfied himself that Sullivan was not affiliated with any interested individuals or institutions in San Domingo. Bryan therefore joined forces with Tumulty, and in spite of the political objections of McAdoo, Sullivan received the appointment.[2]

Tumulty also played a part in the selection of the Receiver. Walter W. Vick of New Jersey sought that post. Vick, an original Wilson man, had labored long and well in New Jersey and parts of the South. Among his sponsors were William F. McCombs, Colonel House, Dan Fellows Platt, Joseph E. Davies, and Homer Cummings. Tumulty knew that Vick had been McCombs' candidate for the position of Secretary to the President, but, appreciating the extent of Vick's services, he added his voice to those in Vick's favor. Secretary Garrison, who had cognizance over the Receivership, put through the appointment without comment.[3]

The New York *Times* characterized Vick's selection as a strictly political move, deploring the action especially because San Domingo was in the throes of civil war.[4] The *Times*' complaint was well founded. Eight days after Vick was appointed, Bryan wrote him requesting information as to what positions were available as re-

wards for "deserving Democrats." [5] Tumulty, Sullivan, and Vick
co-operated to make San Domingo a repository for New Jersey
worthies recommended by Senator Hughes, Congressmen Bremner
and Hamill, and Chancellor Walker.[6]

Tumulty and Bryan, Vick and Sullivan were violating none of
the political mores. To keep an organization going, loyal party
members had to be rewarded. Patronage was hard to find and the
rules of civil service did not extend to San Domingo. The distribution of spoils was a regular, even necessary, activity at which
Tumulty and Bryan were adept and about which they had no
compunctions. Neither man, however, wished to advertise his
actions.

Unfortunately Minister Sullivan's behavior bred publicity. The
principal rival of the National City Bank in San Domingo was the
Banco Nacional, an unreliable institution represented, in the United
States, by William C. Beer. Long friendly with Sullivan, Beer gave
impetus to the movement for his appointment as Minister, using
Hamill, and, indirectly, Tumulty as his innocent agents. Sullivan,
in turn, used his official influence for Beer's bank, a policy which
incidentally reflected Bryan's distaste for the National City Bank.
Sullivan's cousin, Timothy Sullivan, a builder, received timely financial assistance from the *Banco Nacional* and a suspiciously large
share of contracts from the Dominican Government which owed its
existence in part to the Minister's support. Sullivan, furthermore,
proved totally inept as a diplomatist. He climaxed his indiscretions
by cultivating the personal enmity of his American associate,
Receiver Vick.[7]

Bryan and Tumulty began to suspect the full implications of
Sullivan's appointment in December of 1913 when Walter Vick
visited Tumulty in Washington with stories of Sullivan's suspicious
relations with the *Banco Nacional.* Tumulty then instructed Vick
to advise Sullivan to be more circumspect. About the same time
Bryan learned, probably from Vick, of Timothy Sullivan's loans
and contracts. Although the Minister assured Bryan that his cousin
had arrived without invitation and was about to leave, Bryan doubtless was concerned about the financial assistance the *Banco Nacional*
had rendered the wandering contractor.[8]

While Vick was in the United States, he also reported to his old friend, William F. McCombs. They saw the possibilities of using Dominican affairs to injure Bryan and Tumulty, against both of whom McCombs bore grudges.[9] Possibly Vick still hoped to get Tumulty's position, for he was dissatisfied with the Receivership and unwilling to take his wife back to the tropical climate which had sapped her strength.[10] Furthermore, although his conduct with regard to patronage was no different from Sullivan's, he not only resented the Minister's interference with the funds of the Receivership, but also genuinely feared Sullivan's inadequacies. Doubtless Vick's ambition and indignation became entwined.

After Vick returned to San Domingo, he began unjustly to suspect Tumulty and Bryan of protecting Sullivan. He wrote Tumulty and House, charging Sullivan with malfeasance in office, asserting that Bryan was conniving in Sullivan's allegedly dishonest schemes, and insisting that Sullivan be dismissed. When Wilson refused to act without evidence, Vick tendered his own resignation, which the President reluctantly accepted. Wilson sent a commission under John Franklin Fort to investigate conditions in San Domingo. Fort's findings did not substantiate Vick's charges. But after the *Banco Nacional* went into receivership, Vick apparently resolved to have his way at any cost. He used a newspaperman to take his story to Colonel House. House's report alarmed Wilson, who quickly assured Vick that he respected his integrity. Shortly thereafter the President directed Bryan to appoint James D. Phelan of California to investigate the entire matter.[11]

Phelan's public hearings made front page news. Vick, his own star witness, presented the letter Bryan had written requesting jobs for "deserving Democrats," but he did not rehearse his own rôle in implementing that request. He put the worst possible interpretation on Sullivan's relation with the *Banco Nacional* and with Timothy Sullivan. And he attempted, at every opportunity, to involve Hamill and Tumulty.[12]

Preparing for such trouble, Tumulty had accumulated a vast amount of information on Vick's questionable personal and financial dealings both in the United States and San Domingo.[13] To Tumulty's credit, he did not retaliate by publicizing these facts.

Except for an explanation of Vick's ambition to be Secretary to the President, Tumulty limited his defense to conclusive proof that he had no connection with the financial rivalries and manipulations in the Republic, and that he had not even met Sullivan until Hamill introduced them. Bryan candidly asserted that he considered his patronage policies perfectly legitimate. Both Tumulty and Bryan were patently guiltless of dishonesty in any form.[14]

But the Democratic Party in general and Vick and Sullivan in particular lost prestige as the hearings progressed. Sullivan, as Phelan concluded, was "not a proper person to hold the position" that he held.[15] He had no recourse but to resign. Nor did the hearings reflect any credit on Vick as a person or as a representative of the government. The Republicans were delighted. Henry Cabot Lodge gleefully sent for a complete report of the Democratic recitals of Democratic iniquities.[16]

Tumulty never forgave Vick. Tumulty's error, and Bryan's, had been carelessness in endorsing Vick and Sullivan too hastily. Vick's fault was deliberate. He had violated the first political commandment, loyalty to one's party. Tumulty explained the bitterness he felt to Charles O'Connor Hennessy:

> . . . If you could understand how loyally I stood by Vick when his appointment as receiver was under consideration, . . . you would appreciate how deeply aggrieved I was to know that he lent himself to a campaign, the only object of which was to injure me and the Democratic Party in a most grievous way.
>
> Of all the treatment I have received from friend or enemy while I have been in politics, his treatment of me has been the most base and contemptible. . . .[17]

Wilson's attitude intensified Tumulty's distress. The President's conscience was uneasy. He had tacitly condoned Sullivan's appointment although he had known from the beginning that it was strictly political. Initially he had even agreed with Sullivan's financial policies.[18] He redeemed himself in part by reappointing Taft's Minister to San Domingo. But Wilson had been mortified by the publication of those intimate political details which he preferred always to ignore or forget. Apparently holding Tumulty responsible for failing to dissolve the party's troubles before the situation gave rise to unfavorable publicity, he showed his pique by giving Vick an audience over Tumulty's protest.[19] Regardless of Tumulty's innocence or culpability in the Dominican affair, he had lost favor in the eyes of his chief.

2. "A Political Cabal"

Even before Vick broadcast his exaggerated stories, more subtle antagonists had jostled Tumulty's tranquillity. Dissatisfied with the Secretary's policies and jealous of his intimacy with Wilson, Colonel House and his friends berated Tumulty in their conversations with each other and eventually with the President. Speaking privately to the Colonel, Dudley Malone, with New York in mind, called Tumulty politically timid. McAdoo, perhaps now closer to Wilson by virtue of his marriage to the President's daughter, Eleanor, declared to House that Tumulty was vindictive. Admiral Cary Grayson, Wilson's personal physician, maintained that Tumulty divulged confidential information and fomented trouble within the Administration. House recorded their comments in his diary with many of his own, describing Tumulty as egotistic, narrow, unrefined, indiscreet, and reactionary.[20]

These acid assessments mirrored the prejudices of the self-appointed judges better than the character of their victim. If Tumulty's policies were unwise, as House's circle thought they were, his motives were at least as unimpeachable as theirs. Nor were his views necessarily unsound. House assailed Tumulty's opinion on railroad matters without advancing any more practicable theory.[21] The revealer of state secrets proved to be not Tumulty but an unsuspected Cabinet member.[22] Tumulty's sin lay in prevailing over his accusers. Political differences and disappointments warped their accuracy and understanding. Indiscretion, vindictiveness, and egotism resided in their very charges.

While indulging in this backbiting, House carefully preserved his cordial relations with Tumulty who never guessed the Colonel's real feelings. Tumulty told him confidentially that he had thought of resigning because of the difficulties of supporting his family on his meager salary. House knew that Tumulty had no intention of leaving his position, but to test Wilson's sentiments, the Colonel relayed the information. He found the President upset at the idea.[23] House therefore continued to confine his criticisms to his diary until the accidents of death and courtship combined to make the time for attacking Tumulty more propitious.

In August of 1914 Wilson lost his most faithful, most gentle, most devoted ally when, after a long illness, Ellen Axson Wilson died. To all who knew her, her passing was a calamity. The President's grief was boundless. Except for her family, no one mourned her more than did Tumulty. She had always understood him and usually supported him. He waited heartbroken outside her door while she lay dying. He never had a better friend.

In the months following Ellen Wilson's death, Tumulty observed the dejection of the lonely master of the White House. Vainly he sought some palliative. But Wilson's life was incomplete. Only a woman could begin to fill the void a woman had left. Providentially for Wilson, through Grayson he met Edith Bolling Galt. She was a handsome, charming widow, a descendant of Pocahontas, an interesting conversationalist, sympathetic listener, and gay companion. Wilson learned to laugh again. In time he proposed, and she accepted. She became a loyal and devoted wife who, putting her husband's health and happiness above all else, helped him face the trials and responsibilities of world crisis.

The advent of Mrs. Galt, however, destroyed the rapport between Wilson and his Secretary. Perhaps because both she and Tumulty were so deeply interested in Wilson's welfare, each failed to understand fully the importance of the other. Tumulty did not appreciate how badly and how immediately Wilson needed a woman at his side. Tumulty's conservative moral training made him frown upon a second marriage so soon after the end of a first. Anticipating a similar reaction on the part of the general public, he feared it would injure Wilson in 1916. He therefore urged the President to postpone his wedding until after the election. Wilson not only refused, but also told his fiancée what Tumulty had advised.[24] This revelation inevitably opened a gulf between Tumulty and Edith Wilson, making her receptive to the objections which House and Grayson, who had encouraged her marriage, advanced against Tumulty. He never had an opportunity to answer or to explain.

According to his unvarying creed, Tumulty accepted Wilson's decision to announce the engagement without further argument. He presented the news to the press in a most sympathetic way, attempting to minimize the impact by releasing at the same time another important story on the President's support of woman suffrage in New Jersey.[25] The next day he accompanied Wilson and Mrs. Galt to New York and dined with them at the home of Colonel House. He and his wife attended the wedding and sent luggage, a tasteful gift.[26] But the damage done by his expressed objections to the time of the wedding could never be repaired. Edith Bolling Wilson became a protagonist in the conspiracy to unseat him.

Meanwhile the failure of the Democrats to carry New York in the election of 1914 had permitted House and Malone to retrieve control of Administration politics in the Empire State. During a long controversy over the New York City Postmastership Tumulty was conspicuously silent. In the shifting political kaleidoscope, McAdoo joined Tumulty as a sponsor of ex-Governor Martin Glynn and helped secure Glynn's selection as temporary chairman of the National Convention in 1916, but for the most part both Tumulty and McAdoo left New York alone.[27] In November of 1915 Tumulty refused even to try to help a friend get a political job in New York, observing with accuracy that he had no influence there.[28]

By the end of 1915 Tumulty was more weary and depressed than resentful. Vick's perverse charges and Wilson's hurried courtship had upset him; the Republicans had made decisive gains, especially in the Northeast; the Mexican situation was intensifying religious bigotry; and the battles over neutrality and preparedness were threatening. But his troubles were still multiplying. Shortly after the turn of the year Tom Pence, Tumulty's closest ally, became fatally ill.

While Pence lay fighting for his life, McCombs' resignation as

National Chairman was being arranged, and the struggle for control of the Committee had begun. The first skirmish was over the choice of a new director of publicity. Tumulty and Fred Lynch of Minnesota succeeded in having Fred Steckman, Pence's assistant, installed temporarily, but House and Robert Woolley, one of the Colonel's political agents, set out to remove him in favor of one of their group. The friction between Woolley and Tumulty, impeding plans for the Jefferson Day Dinner, increased House's determination to destroy Tumulty's influence.[29] Mrs. Wilson, in complete agreement, told the Colonel that she had decided that Tumulty and Josephus Daniels had to go. Daniels probably fell into disfavor because of his initial opposition to the proposed promotion of Cary Grayson to an admiralcy over the heads of senior medical officers. House undertook to get rid of Daniels, while Mrs. Wilson gave her attention to Tumulty's dismissal.[30]

Tumulty's authority waned rapidly as the Convention approached. He had foreseen the efficacy of a peace slogan for the campaign and had made various suggestions for the platform,[31] but Wilson, prodded by House and Mrs. Wilson, looked elsewhere for advice. Tumulty's ideas carried little weight except on the hyphenate issue. Shortly before the Convention met he was embarrassed by confusion in the New Jersey contingent. Judge Wescott and Governor Fielder both wanted to place Wilson's name before the delegates. The President had decided to let Wescott renominate him, but Fielder thought he had been chosen when State Chairman Grosscup misunderstood Tumulty's instructions. Before Tumulty could rectify it, the newspapers reported Fielder's misapprehension, perturbing the President by the consequent necessity for an explanation.[32] Since New Jersey politicians and reporters were under Tumulty's aegis, he fell heir to Wilson's irritation.

The personnel and policies of the reconstituted National Committee reflected the ascendancy of House's coterie. Largely through the Colonel's influence, Vance C. McCormick was selected as National Chairman. He quickly chose Robert Woolley as his director of publicity. Daniel C. Roper, Hugh Wallace, and other friends of House received various key positions.[33] Tumulty was particularly upset by Woolley's program. First in anger and then in desperation,

Tumulty fought to save the system of publicity which Pence had instituted and Steckman had continued. McAdoo, Lane, and Burleson supported his views. But McCormick and Woolley went their own way. In spite of the protests of Steckman and Tumulty, Woolley discontinued the Democratic *Bulletin*, Pence's most useful propaganda device. And even Wilson's doubts failed to prevent Woolley from moving the publicity bureau from Washington to New York while Congress was still in session.[34]

Out of loyalty to Wilson and the party, Tumulty swallowed his pride. For three years he had striven to accomplish Wilson's re-election, and no consideration, personal or otherwise, outweighed this objective. Less than two weeks after Woolley's appointment Tumulty sent him suggestions for campaign tactics. He helped McCormick investigate means to hold the Irish vote. He advocated the passage of the Adamson Act, establishing an eight-hour day for railroad labor, and worked with A. M. Palmer to ensure a large labor turnout to counterbalance any loss of strength in the business community.[35] But this co-operation failed to win McCormick's friendship or regain Wilson's confidence. The President rejected all but one of Tumulty's campaign proposals, using that only partially and mechanically.[36] Especially after the Casement affair, Tumulty found his chief cold and unresponsive.

The hostility of the Democrats who controlled the party's destiny in 1916 did not affect Tumulty's political judgment. He appreciated the skill of their campaign tactics, especially Woolley's success in dealing with labor questions.[37] As early as 1914 Tumulty had envisioned Democratic victory through strength in the West. From the first he felt that Hughes would be a poor campaigner. The reports he received sustained his optimism. On the eve of the election, with a politician's typical overstatement, he predicted a sweeping victory for Wilson.[38]

Election night was melodramatic. The President was at Shadow Lawn, New Jersey, his Secretary at nearby Asbury Park. As the returns came in Tumulty needed every bit of his confidence. Hughes raced to an early lead. The Democratic New York *World* conceded defeat. But the huge Republican majorities in New York, New Jersey, Illinois, and New England did not unsettle Tumulty.

Even as the Republicans began prematurely to rejoice, the evidence to sustain Tumulty's continual, emphatic predictions of victory began to trickle in. Democratic strength appeared west of the Mississippi. By two in the morning the Far West began to report. Tumulty then informed the anxious tabulators and weary newspapermen that Hughes' lead would shortly be overturned. The atmosphere in his office brightened. As normally Republican states were counted under the Democratic banner, the suppressed excitement grew. Not until after sunrise would anyone go out for breakfast.[39]

All that day Tumulty and his staff remained at their posts, receiving and analyzing the reports from the critical states in the Far West and exchanging information with headquarters in New York City. Wilson, after sleeping most of the night, had gone to play golf before assurance of his re-election arrived. Tumulty rejoiced in the victory, certain in his mind and heart that America was safest with his chief at the helm. To the press he interpreted the returns as a popular declaration "not for a provincial but for a great America" and predicted a period of national prosperity.[40]

Tumulty's only personal wish was to remain as Wilson's Secretary. He sought no advancement, carefully scotching the rumors that he was destined for a Cabinet post.[41] Actually these stories had no foundation in fact, but the report that Tumulty was to be appointed to the Board of General Appraisers was sound.[42] Wilson had decided to remove him. Tumulty's political mishaps, the constant pressure of anti-Catholic spokesmen, and the arguments of House, McCormick, and Mrs. Wilson had convinced the President that Tumulty's work was unsatisfactory and his presence politically dangerous. House had even canvassed the field for a replacement, concluding, after consulting McCormick, that Daniel C. Roper was the man for the job. Wilson accepted this decision.[43] To remove Tumulty from Washington, but with a pretense of concern for Tumulty's financial well-being, the President requested his resignation and offered him the appraisership.

Tumulty was dumbfounded. For several days his future remained undecided. At Wilson's request Burleson twice took up the matter with him, although the Postmaster General could not understand just what had happened.[44] Mrs. Wilson asked the President to compel Tumulty to leave. When the President refused to force the issue, House reminded him once more of the disadvantages of having a Catholic Secretary.[45] Three days later, obviously still shocked, Tumulty wrote Wilson, refusing any office but that which he held and offering to resign if the President so desired. His letter bared his heart:

> I have thought over most carefully, and with a full realization of the kindness of your motives, all that you have said to me. There is no doubt in my mind that you believe I would improve my condition by accepting the appraisership.
>
> After deep reflection, however, I have decided that I cannot accept the appraisership; nor do I feel that I should embarrass you by accepting any other office. I had hoped with all my heart that I might remain in close association with you; that I might be permitted to continue as your Secretary, a position which gave me the fullest opportunity to serve you and the country. To think of leaving you at this time when the fruits of our long fight have been realized wounds me more deeply than I can tell you.
>
> I dread the misconstruction that will be placed upon my departure and its reflection upon my loyalty which hitherto had been unquestioned, for I know, as you probably do not, that rumors have been flying thick and fast in the past few months as to the imminence of my removal and even as to the identity of my successor. But despite these regrets, I feel that I can not do otherwise than leave you, if you really wish it.
>
> You can not know what this means to me and to mine. I am grateful for having been associated so closely with so great a man. I am heart-sick that the end should be like this.[46]

The day after writing this letter Tumulty informed four intimate friends, Warren Johnson, Charles Swem, David Lawrence, and Ray T. Baker,* of what had transpired. Suspecting foul play, they

---

* Ray T. Baker, a California Democrat, not Ray Stannard Baker, the journalist, essayist, and biographer of Wilson.

decided to investigate. David Lawrence, assuming the onerous task
of spokesman, asked the President to explain his decision. Lawrence
concluded that "a prejudice based on a political cabal and upon
impressions which were wholly unjust" had warped Wilson's mind.
For forty-five minutes he argued with the President, pointing out
that no one who realized what Tumulty had accomplished would
be able to understand why he had been forced to resign. Finally
Wilson yielded. He sent for Tumulty and took him back again as
his Secretary.[47]

The reports of these events reached House too late for further
action on his part. Grayson suspected what was afoot, but Frank
Polk informed House that Tumulty would resign. Laboring under
this misconception, House, with a touch of compassion, confided to
his diary that Tumulty had many good qualities, but that the President would show lamentable weakness if he permitted him to stay.
Wilson had already committed himself to do just that! As late as
January of 1917 Mrs. Wilson and House still hoped Tumulty would
leave in March, but that was out of the question. In spite of the
tremendous odds in their favor, their careful plot had failed.[48]

Unhappily David Lawrence could not restore the old friendship
between President and Secretary. Wilson never again trusted
Tumulty as he had before their troubles began. Tumulty's wounds
healed, but the scars must have remained. His letter revealed a
pathos rare in politics. Wilson was not without some reciprocal
sentiment, for he had refused to force Tumulty out; had even taken
him back against the wishes of his wife. Both men, however, had
sacrificed self-respect in agreeing to continue a relationship which
had been strained almost beyond endurance. And although the
irritants in that relationship had been checked, they had not been
removed.

3. The "Leak" Investigation

The tensions within the President's official family had scarcely
begun to subside when a partisan attempt to invest normal specu-
lative activity with an aura of political indecency disconcerted
those closest to Wilson. During the so-called "leak" investigation

of 1917,[49] Republicans inside and outside of Congress accused Tumulty and McAdoo, R. W. Bolling, Wilson's brother-in-law, and Bernard Baruch, an affluent subscriber to the Democratic campaign fund, of profiting in stock market transactions by virtue of inside information of government plans. A protracted Congressional examination of these charges served primarily as a sounding board for partisan effusions and empty gossip, ending with the complete exoneration of the men whose reputations had been defiled.

The background of the incident lay in the European war and its effect on American business and on Wall Street. December of 1916 found the war at a temporary stalemate, with the Germans occupying an advantageous military position. Wilson had been contemplating a note to both sides to attempt to initiate armistice proceedings. On December twelfth the President and the American people were startled by the news of a speech by German Chancellor von Bethmann-Hollweg which made cautious peace overtures to the Allies. Several days later Baron Sonnino of Italy commented in a way which left the door for negotiations slightly ajar, and David Lloyd George, British Prime Minister, while superficially spurning the German proposal, stated that his government awaited full details of the offer. These developments, fully reported in the American press, induced many competent observers to believe that peace was in sight.

On December eighteenth Wilson dispatched the peace note on which he had been working. Addressing the neutral and warring powers of Europe, the President called for an exchange of views by the belligerents as a preliminary to peace, expressed his willingness to take the initiative therein, and called attention to the intimate interest in the war of the United States, a neutral whose position might become intolerable.

Although Wilson guarded the contents of his note carefully, the intuition of veteran reporters penetrated his secrecy. Only Lansing, Polk, and a few confidential clerks in the State Department had seen the message.[50] Fearing an inadvertent slip by Tumulty in a press conference, the President had given his Secretary no hint of his intentions. But the newspapers on the eighteenth, nineteenth, and twentieth circulated rumors of Wilson's action.

At his morning press conference on the twentieth, Lansing told the reporters that he would have an important announcement that afternoon, but he requested that this be not divulged until the announcement was made. That afternoon he released Wilson's note. The following day Lansing issued an explanatory statement so phrased that it led some to believe that the United States was close to war with Germany. Privately the Secretary of State hinted at some mysterious reason for creating this feeling, but he dispelled the misapprehension with a second statement later in the day.[51]

The rumors about Wilson's note, Lansing's release of the note, and Lansing's statements were all well reported. The afternoon papers on the twentieth carried the full note. At 2.05 P.M. the Dow-Jones ticker told Wall Street what was coming. It later developed that the confidence of Lansing's morning press conference had been violated. As a matter of fact, informed newspapermen and even intelligent newspaper readers who were cognizant of European developments and familiar with the Administration's attitude toward the war could readily make a fairly accurate guess of what was in the air even before Lansing's confidential revelation.

The condition of American business and finance necessitated the secrecy for which Wilson strove and put a premium on the ability of newspapermen and stock brokers to guess correctly. The United States was enjoying a prosperity born largely of the orders for war materials being filled for the Western Powers. This boom was reflected in Wall Street by a market which experienced analysts considered dangerously bullish. A cessation of war would immediately affect American industry, and, in the sensitive, overextended market, could precipitate a bad crash, especially in the "war babies" like steel. Similarly, the entrance of the United States into the war would depress the market because of the uncertainties of such a new position. The speech of von Bethmann-Hollweg, the rumors of Wilson's note, Lansing's release of the note, and Lansing's misleading interpretive statement had precisely that panicking effect.

On December 13, after von Bethmann-Hollweg's speech had been reported, wise speculators began to sell short, especially in steel. The peace note rumors of the eighteenth increased such selling. While the rumors persisted, the market continued to drop. The twentieth, the day Wilson's note was released to the press, and the twenty-first, the day of Lansing's statements, saw the bottom of the bearish trend. The very next day prices began to rise again. During the bearish period, however, those operators who had been selling short realized immense quick profits. The overextended market had reacted violently to the diplomatic developments in an uncertain world.

Stocks had hardly recovered before two unprincipled men, Thomas W. Lawson and William R. Wood, attempted to distort the nature of this market for their own selfish and partisan ends. An ex-speculator turned muckraker, Lawson was a New England Republican with an insatiable penchant for publicity. Wood was a Republican Congressman from Indiana, more interested in bespattering the recently victorious Democrats than in verifying the statements he incautiously repeated.

Lawson publicized the story that he had information on a peace note "leak" involving government officials. After interrogating him, Congressman Henry of the House Rules Committee described Lawson's story as a "mirage," but Theodore Roosevelt, once again in the Republican fold and a candidate for the nomination in 1920, announced that he intended to force an investigation of the "leak." In the meantime Wood had introduced a resolution in the House calling for an investigation to ascertain whether government officials or their families had profited during the market's collapse by inside information on the peace note. During the initial debate on Wood's resolution, Republican Congressman William S. Bennett of New York charged that Baruch, then a member of the Council on National Defense, had done just that. The House directed the Rules Committee to report in ten days on whether an investigation was necessary.

Lawson appeared as the star witness, but he refused to divulge any names, claiming only that Congressman Henry was the source of his information. Representative Wood was less bashful. He accused Tumulty of advising Baruch at the Biltmore Hotel in New York City that the peace note was forthcoming. He charged further that R. W. Bolling and his brokerage firm had capitalized on similar information. As evidence he introduced a letter from one "A. Curtis." But Wood could not identify "A. Curtis," had never even heard of him until the letter suddenly appeared. His mysterious informer remains to this day unidentified.

Tumulty and Bolling categorically denied Wood's charges. Incensed by Wood's statement, Tumulty, white-hot, told the press that Wood would have to retract his accusation. He soon realized that this was easier to say than to manage. Testifying before the Congressional Committee, Tumulty was more controlled. In a hurry to return to his desk, and aware of the futility of angry vehemence, he spoke quickly and briefly. Nevertheless, he closed his rebuttal with a ringing demand for an apology which he never received. His denial was fortified by his testimony that he had not known the note was in preparation, a fact attested to by Wilson himself. Had the investigators been aware of Tumulty's close escape from the oblivion of the appraisership shortly before the peace note episode, they would have needed no such assurance.

While Wood's accusations were still ringing in the ears of the public, Lawson let it be known that he would reveal definite names if Congress would authorize a committee of investigation. In the debate over this proposition acrimonious partisanship ran rampant. The Republicans accused the Democrats of blocking an inquiry to cover members of their party. The Democrats accused the Republicans of deliberate mendacity. The House finally referred the Wood Resolution back to the Rules Committee, voted the Committee additional powers, and authorized the employment of an attorney to assist in the investigation. For this task Sherman L. Whipple of Boston, an able lawyer of national reputation, was hired. Before he finished, Whipple interrogated accused and accusers, and even checked the books of leading Wall Street brokerage houses for the bearish period.

Wood's charges had been so flimsy that the case for the accusers rested on Lawson whose appearance as a witness was sensational. His testimony implicated Lansing, McAdoo, McAdoo's brother, McAdoo's former law partner, Baruch, Paul Warburg of the Federal Reserve Board, Bolling, and Tumulty. These men all denied the charges, but Tumulty did not rest there. While Lansing, with studied indifference, ignored the investigation, while McAdoo confined himself to angry oaths,[52] Tumulty began a search of his own.

Lawson had stated that one Mrs. Ruth Thomason Visconti had

informed him that Tumulty had "received his bit" for divulging information through a newspaperman to interested parties. A week earlier this Mrs. Visconti had telephoned Tumulty, threatening to supply Wood with incriminating evidence against him. In the presence of various government officials, Tumulty replied that she could tell Wood anything she wished.[53] Actually Mrs. Visconti had nothing to say that could have withstood Whipple's examination. But Tumulty, with the assistance of David Lawrence, took the precaution of gathering data on her undependability.

William J. Burns, employed to investigate Mrs. Visconti for Tumulty and Lawrence, assigned several detectives to the case. Their reports read like fiction. Mrs. Visconti's path crisscrossed those of naïve government girls, Latin-American millionaires, and Bulgarian spies. Erroneously blaming Tumulty for her failure a few years earlier to secure a good government job, she sought out Lawson and Wood to offer them a baseless story about Tumulty and the "leak." [54] As Burns' men scrutinized Mrs. Visconti's past, Tumulty foresaw how ridiculous Lawson's whole testimony would appear. He never needed to define her character publicly.

While Tumulty and Lawrence were privately checking Lawson's sources, Whipple was exposing the emptiness of his charges. A series of witnesses substantiated the innocence of Tumulty, McAdoo, Bolling, and Lansing. Baruch told the Committee candidly that he was a speculator, that he had sold short during the market break, and that he had realized large profits, but insisted that he neither needed nor had any inside information. He had begun to sell short after the Bethmann-Hollweg speech, sensing that the peace overtures would depress the overinflated market. He had continued to do so until shortly before Wilson's note was released, but he had begun to cover a day before that release. It was easily established that he had not met Tumulty at the Biltmore or anywhere else during the entire period of his operations. Furthermore, Baruch's books proved that he had stopped selling too soon, that he had begun to cover before the worst break. He had even missed the 2.05 P.M. report on the Dow-Jones ticker! Baruch was justly proud of his facility in speculation. Had he had any inside information, he could have increased his profits considerably.

Before Tumulty, Baruch, and the others were completely cleared, the real nature of the "leak" was discovered. Two indiscreet reporters, contrary to Lansing's expressed desire, had informed various brokerage firms of the forthcoming announcement, the nature of which they guessed. No government official had been involved. The newspapermen were receiving retainers for this type of service, a standard practice of many journalists and brokers. Tumulty later assured the editor of the paper for which one of the men worked that the reporter would continue to be acceptable as a White House correspondent.[55]

The specific testimony of several witnesses, including the guilty newspapermen, exonerated those whom Lawson had accused. The iniquity of Lawson's fabrications became painfully apparent when Mrs. Visconti took the stand. Her unreliability was not fully exposed, but she was forced to admit that her incriminating account, presented by Lawson as fact, was based on an exaggerated version of a garbled story of an adolescent girl. Before the investigation closed, New York financiers further discredited Lawson and Wood. Beyond the shadow of a doubt, the market would have broken had there been no "leak." And the "leak," such as it was, emanated from and aided no government employee.

The whole affair left a bad taste. David Lawrence observed that apparently the only sin the Republicans sought to reveal was that Baruch had gambled and won. Henceforth, he opined, no contributor to Wilson's campaign fund would be permitted to speculate and profit. Editorial comment noted that malicious and misdirected partisanship forced Congress to injure its own reputation by assigning a House Committee to a task resulting only in the release of false and scandalous gossip, always plentiful in Washington.

The private papers of the accused men revealed the needless heartache to which they were subjected. James Smith, Jr., Robert Woolley, William Randolph Hearst, and even Colonel House were among the many who sent expressions of sympathy to Tumulty.[56] With time, however, Tumulty recovered his natural good humor. While the investigation was still in progress, he wrote a friend who had suggested he buy some stocks. "Please do not tempt me to deal in stocks of any kind . . ." he began. "Were I to, . . . that suave but persistent Mr. Whipple . . . would be after me with a sharp stick.

I might even get into the editorial columns of the Wall Street Journal, and in that case my Jersey City friends would throw up their hands in horror and admit I was beyond redemption. No, I cannot invest now in anything, even though Andrew Carnegie, John D. Rockefeller and J. Pierpont Morgan should guarantee it. . . . Besides, I haven't any money." [57]

By the time Whipple had finished his work, Tumulty had had his full share of personal troubles. No error in his judgment, no mistake in the running of his office justified the grief created by Tom Watson, Father Tierney, Michael Francis Doyle, Walter Vick, Colonel House, Lawson, and Wood. Politics abjure gentility. As an experienced politician Tumulty expected no quarter, but he could hardly have predicted the magnitude of the punishment he received for practicing his profession.

Tumulty had no opportunity, however, to become preoccupied with adversity. While Whipple was still at work, the United States was rejecting neutrality for belligerency. The problems of the nation obscured those of every individual. The coming of war dwarfed all other news. And the war altered Tumulty's duties and responsibilities, his relations with the President, the press, the whole government, and the party.

CHAPTER IX

The Great War

1. End of Neutrality

LATE in the afternoon of January 31, 1917, Tumulty brought Wilson the Associated Press bulletin announcing the German decision to resume unrestricted submarine warfare. First incredulous, then resolute, Wilson remarked quietly: "This means war. The break that we have tried so hard to prevent now seems inevitable." [1]

After recovering from the initial shock of Germany's action, however, Wilson vainly sought alternatives short of belligerency. Although he gave increasing attention to national preparedness, the war spirit sweeping America frightened him. War meant the submergence of the principles closest to his heart. While announcing the severance of diplomatic relations with Germany and requesting Congress to proclaim a condition of armed neutrality, the President made last, desperate efforts for peace.

Sharing the bellicose indignation of the public, Tumulty had less patience than did his chief with the still potent isolationist sentiment reflected in the Congressional filibuster against the arming of merchant vessels. Before the President accomplished this purpose by executive order, Tumulty first urged Lansing to force Wilson's hand and then made a direct plea for action. *"What I wish to impress upon you,"* he wrote to Wilson, *"is the danger of delay, no matter what course you intend to take.* The way the country has

SHADOW LAWN, 1916.

The Jackson Day Dinner, 1936.

responded on the filibuster is but a forecast of the way it will support you in case action shall be necessary." [2]

While Wilson, secluded, slowly reached the conclusion that he must lead the country into war, Tumulty recognized no other course. After the disclosure of the Zimmerman note revealed Germany's overtures to Mexico and Japan, his emotions reached fever pitch. He denounced Germany for filling the United States with spies, attacking American industry, violating neutral rights, and conspiring with Mexico and Japan. He shared the crusading zeal of his contemporaries, interpreting the war as "a struggle between democracy and feudalism," between the rights of individuals and the "hateful Kultur" which Germany threatened to extend throughout the world. "It is time for Americans to realize," he declared some months later, "that the frontiers of freedom are their frontiers. Where the battle is joined the flag must go." [3]

With Lansing and Polk, Tumulty chafed at Wilson's delay in calling Congress into session for the "great declaration." He emphasized their views in a conversation with the President a few hours before the Cabinet met to discuss the matter.[4] Before the end of March the majority of Wilson's advisers agreed that neutrality was no longer tolerable.

Long since convinced that "the right is more precious than peace," Tumulty accompanied his chief to the Capitol on April 2 to hear the war message. To preserve international law, neutral rights, and the larger rights of humanity, to liberate free peoples, to prepare for a "concert of peace" by a "partnership of democratic nations," to make the world safe for democracy, Wilson solemnly asked Congress to declare that war existed.

"It is a fearful thing," the President concluded, "to lead this great peaceful people into war, into the most terrible and disastrous of all wars, civilization itself seeming to be in the balance. But the right is more precious than peace, and we shall fight for the things which we have always carried nearest our hearts — for democracy, for the right of those who submit to authority to have a voice in their own governments, for the rights and liberties of small nations, for a universal dominion of right by such a concert of free peoples as shall bring peace and safety to all nations and make the world itself

at last free. To such a task we can dedicate our lives and our for-
tunes, everything that we are and everything that we have, with
the pride of those who know that the day has come when America
is privileged to spend her blood and her might for the principles that
gave her birth and happiness and the peace which she has treasured.
God helping her, she can do no other." [5]

It was a great speech; even Lodge was moved. The opposition
of the isolationists delayed Congressional approval only four days.
After long months of negotiations and uncertainty, the United
States was at war.

2. Wartime Routine

War brought profound changes to the government, a quickened
pace, new faces, sprawling new agencies, an aura of tension, of
makeshift solutions. At the apex of the expanding administrative
pyramid, Wilson faced a limitless task. The President had little
time for visitors, for Congress, for anything but hard work on the
complex problems of modern warfare. More than ever before he
needed his experienced Secretary.

Tumulty's routine evidenced the wartime dispensation. His hours
were longer. Washington's semi-tropical summer prostrated him.
The city, changed by the war, became, for Tumulty, particularly
lonely when Ollie James and Billy Hughes, his senatorial intimates,
died and James Kerney went abroad. There were no adequate
substitutes for Charley Swem and Warren Johnson who enlisted in
the air corps.[6] Only his family responsibilities and loyalty to his
chief kept Tumulty from following them. His job lay in the executive offices where a never-ending stream of callers with pressing demands for assistance in government business strained even Tumulty's
good nature. "I am overwhelmed here every day," he informed
Wilson, "with all kinds of requests . . . for letters of introduction
for men who are interested in promotions, contracts, etc. I am out
of excuses; and fear the use that might be made of the simplest kind

of letters. . . ." [7] To solve the problem, Wilson signed a letter drafted by Tumulty directing that all such requests be denied.

As custodian of the President's time Tumulty protected Wilson from interruptions, rarely relaxing his vigilance and often assuming larger responsibilities himself. To conserve Wilson's strength he advised that Secretary Lane or Baker should undertake to speak for the Liberty Loan.[8] When the President scheduled an interview with Congresswoman Jeannette Rankin, who had opposed the declaration of war, Tumulty protested, explaining that "this little lady . . . will use any appointment . . . for her own special purposes. . . . She can give 'cards and spades' to Joe Cannon." [9] Few visitors passed his desk. He heard their stories and sent them on their way. He politely advised George Foster Peabody and Judge John Wescott that the prosecution of the war consumed all of Wilson's business hours. Congressman Swagar Sherley's request for Administration direction on the Military Appropriations Bill was passed from Tumulty to Wilson to Newton D. Baker. Tumulty counseled the President not to comment on a draft of a speech Senator Owen had left in the outer office, warning Wilson that if he saw Owen or revised the draft he would not only waste his time but also needlessly clothe the speech with an official character. When Senator Newlands sought advice on the Priorities Bill, Tumulty informed Wilson of the situation and telephoned his chief's decision to the Senator. There were exceptions, of course. Often Congressmen had to see the President. And Tumulty requested interviews for political friends like D. W. Griffith whose motion picture companies afforded new opportunities for publicity. But the pressure of war put an end to the more casual practices of earlier years.[10]

While his duties as a buffer to the President increased, Tumulty's responsibilities as a publicity agent diminished. George Creel, appointed director of the new Committee on Public Information, considered that his was "a plain publicity proposition." [11] Mindful of Creel's prerogatives, Tumulty eliminated his official press conferences and reduced his own work in publicity to a minimum.

Tumulty's first breach of this practice in November 1917, was in response to requests from newspapermen that he enlighten them on Colonel House's activities in England. House had told the

London press that his negotiations for a single Allied war council were pursuant to Wilson's instructions, reporting the President's order in a rather inaccurate paraphrase. Word for word, Tumulty read to the Washington correspondents Wilson's comment on the Colonel's press release. Not conversant with the details of the negotiations, Tumulty failed to realize that House's paraphrase was open to question and Wilson's comment misleading. The International News Service interpreted the President's statement as a flat denial that he had communicated with House. Embarrassed by this misconstruction, House blamed Tumulty for the report. A hasty exchange of cablegrams clarified the matter, retrieving the Colonel's position in London.[12] Tumulty had unwittingly complicated American diplomacy by giving the press information he did not understand, but the fault lay equally with House and Wilson.

Tumulty forestalled the possibility of a similar mishap when he advised the President to withhold a memorandum prepared by Frank Doubleday and submitted by House for the purpose of stimulating the Allies by describing the American war effort to French and English newspapers. Dissatisfied with its phraseology and suspicious of its facts, Tumulty obtained Wilson's consent to verify and revise the statement. With the assistance of informed department heads he completely rewrote it before release.[13] With such exceptions, however, Tumulty left public relations to Creel.

The familiar preface — "Secretary Tumulty stated at the White House today" — disappeared from news items. But Tumulty's new anonymity proved to be as unwelcome as the often disagreeable publicity of former years. Although reporters no longer had occasion to mention him, rumormongers, inspired by German agents and native prejudices, kept Tumulty's name before the public. On October 9, 1917, a friend wrote from Detroit that a rumor alleging Tumulty had been imprisoned in Leavenworth as a German spy was given substance because there had been no press notices concerning him for several months. With alarming rapidity this story traversed the country, persisting in the face of specific denials. In the next few weeks official and unofficial investigators reported it in sequence from such distant points as Detroit, Pittsburgh, New York, Boston, Natchez, Toledo, Chicago, Cleveland, Atlanta, Fargo, and Birmingham. In Western Pennsylvania an itinerant Methodist minister preached it from his pulpit. Tom Watson in Georgia and his bigoted counterparts in New England spread the tale throughout their sections. In Fargo a former Republican governor told a meeting of bankers that Tumulty had been executed at Leavenworth. The *Des Moines Register* quoted a militant suffragist to the same effect, making no effort to check her account.

By early November official Washington was concerned. Wilson directed Tumulty to take steps to keep the rumor off the wires and to find some early opportunity to have himself mentioned in the newspapers. At first the President was reluctant to dignify the story by any formal reference, but on November 12 he denied it specifically. The next day Tumulty issued an official statement to the Associated Press, requesting "conspicuous publicity." On the basis of reports he had received from the federal bureau of investigation, Tumulty explained that the rumors about him were "fanciful tales . . . passed by innocent persons who are the victims of a systematic and insidious propaganda to weaken confidence in the officials of the federal government." Even this widely circulated statement failed to scotch the rumor which appeared off and on in Vermont, California, Indiana, and Pennsylvania for another six months.[14]

Although Tumulty had little official contact with the newspapermen during the war, he continued to be their informal guide and champion. He reminded Wilson to acknowledge especially favorable comments, and he sought interviews for helpful reporters. He cleared up a misunderstanding between Wilson and Louis Seibold, the friendly correspondent of the New York *World*. His tactful intercession persuaded E. B. McLean of the Washington *Post* to stop publication of a series of articles embarrassing to the government.[15] And Tumulty's table at the Shoreham remained a rendezvous for the journalists who covered Washington.

The newspapermen were constantly unhappy because of war-born conditions. Creel rarely interfered with the freedom of the press, but the reporters disliked his stereotyped, occasionally misleading bulletins. They protested vigorously against Burleson's arbitrary exclusion from the mail of mildly leftist publications. Wilson aggravated the situation by refusing to discuss their problems even at the behest of such friends as Lawrence and Cobb who felt that the relations between the newspapers and the Administration were "intolerably tangled." [16]

From the first Tumulty was on guard in behalf of the Fourth Estate and its traditional privileges. He disliked censorship in any form, preferring to rely on the personal approach. Although he regarded Hearst and Medill McCormick as vicious and irresponsible, he found the average publisher reasonable. Wilson, however, insisted on censorship. Tumulty considered the Administration's Espionage Bill so harsh that he prompted his chief in April 1917, to assure the newspaper world through Arthur Brisbane that the bill was not intended to curb legitimate criticism. "You might say," Tumulty wrote the President, ". . . 'I can imagine no greater disservice than to establish any system of censorship that would deny to the people of a free republic like our own their right to criticize their public officials. I would regret to lose the benefits of just criticism . . . while exercising the functions of the high office to which I have been elected. In these times I can be sure only of the motives which actuate me. I shall try to purge them of selfishness of every kind' . . . ." Wilson said almost exactly that.[17] A few days later Tumulty warned Wilson that the impression had gained root that the measure was "really a gigantic machine, erected for the despotic control of the press . . . by a host of small bureaucrats," [18] but the President would not temper the provisions.

The Espionage Act, the Trading With the Enemy Act, and the Sedition Act gave the Post Office Department vast powers. Before Burleson's assistants, Dockery and Lamar, had been active six months, Tumulty was uneasy about the narrowness of their interpretations. "We are bound to get into very deep water in the matter," he informed Wilson.[19] Similarly advised by other friends, the President cautioned Burleson to be more liberal, saving several periodicals from the ravages of the Post Office Department. Among these was *The Third of May*, a newspaper Paderewski wished to publish for twelve weeks. After Lamar refused to license that journal, Tumulty, reviewing the case at Wilson's request, recommended that "the President . . . insist upon a license being granted." This was typical of his attitude toward the whole censorship problem.[20]

Tumulty's experience in gauging political sentiment made him sensitive to fluctuations in wartime morale. Frequently he felt that the national spirit was unsatisfactory. He never reached the extreme of objecting to the playing of German music, nor did he fail to understand the value of such diversions as the theater and athletics,[21] but he appreciated the need to marshal mass emotions and to sustain public confidence. Tumulty realized that conditions in the South and the record of the Democratic Party there gave the American Negro cause for doubt about a war publicized as a crusade for liberty. When the President was requested to address a Negro meeting and guarantee a policy of no discrimination, Tumulty prepared Wilson's cautious reply. He declined the invitation, expressed confidence that the Negroes would give their enthusiastic support to the war, but avoided the discrimination issue. The race riots in East St. Louis in July 1917, however, forced Tumulty and Wilson to take a less evasive position. Wilson immediately declared that the Department of Justice would investigate the situation to prevent a repetition. Seeking more definite action, a delegation of Negroes requested an audience with the President. Tumulty feared this would intensify race feeling. Assuming that the tension would subside if the Administration gave the affair no further attention, Tumulty advised Wilson to decline the request, using the excuse of pressing international business. But the agitation did not decrease. Early in August, therefore, Tumulty urged Wilson to express his "deep disapproval" of the "terrible things" that had been happening in East St. Louis. Wilson agreed, directing Tumulty to phrase an appropriate statement. "America cannot countenance these things," Tumulty suggested, "without advertising to the world the fact that she is not a sincere believer in the principles of democracy." [22]

Tumulty's concern for morale induced him to propose policies which he knew Wilson would not welcome. Sharing the public's apprehension over the diplomatic situation in the Orient, Tumulty in May 1917, recommended that Elihu Root, Theodore Roosevelt's able Secretary of State, whom Wilson did not particularly like, be designated "Ambassador-at-large to the Far East." Root had already been assigned a mission to Russia. Were he also sent to Japan, Tumulty declared, "we will be indicating to Japan the importance of good relations between Japan and the United States and at the same time assuring the people of our country that we are leaving no stone unturned to win the war." [23] The President, however, preferred not to entrust Root with such large authority. He sent a relatively inexperienced man to Tokyo.

In domestic as well as foreign affairs Wilson seemed often to act without regard to public opinion. In January of 1918 he sustained an order of the Fuel Administration, issued without preliminary explanation, which shut down all factories throughout the nation for five days. Distressed by the abruptness of the order, Tumulty felt that confidence in the government would be shaken severely. He was appalled by the lack of "groundwork . . . for this radical step" and upset because the order had not distinguished between essential and nonessential industries. Wilson admitted his own concern but offered no solution except passive acceptance of the storm of criticism.[24]

When Tumulty's suggestions did not impinge on settled policies, the President was more willing to accept them. In May of 1917 Tumulty described the "general mass of people" as indifferent toward the war. To arouse "their righteous wrath," he recommended that "the character of the beasts we are fighting" be revealed in a series of speeches by Brand Whitlock, United States Ambassador to Belgium. Although unwilling to recall Whitlock for this purpose, Wilson solicited suggestions from Tumulty for his forthcoming Flag Day address, using many of his Secretary's flaming phrases. A year later, following Tumulty's advice, Wilson timed the announcement of the arrival of the first million American troops in France to coincide with the patriotic celebrations of Independence Day.[25]

3. Waging War

Tumulty followed every step in the prosecution of the war with an avid interest derived not only from his patriotism and his idealistic conception of American war aims, but also from his partisan desire that the Democratic Administration and Congress perform with skill and honor. All his loyalties, national, political, and personal were involved. And although he had no official duties in connection with military strategy and logistics, his proximity to the Commander-in-Chief brought him into contact with military men and their problems.

Even before the declaration of war Tumulty sent Wilson suggestions, based on opinions and information digested from leading Democratic newspapers, for a comprehensive military program. Believing that we should keep a free hand both in military strategy and in peacemaking, and unwilling to accept all the political objectives of England and France, Tumulty recommended American participation in the war as a co-belligerent rather than an Allied Power. But co-belligerency did not preclude full participation. "[We must] go resolutely about it," he wrote Wilson, "in dead earnest, using all the energy we can . . . swiftly to put all of our force into the struggle. . . . That is the way to compel Germany to sue for peace." The United States, Tumulty declared, would have to provide "a large number of troops, far beyond the force authorized by existing laws . . . financial aid to the Allies, probably in the form of a gift to France, [and] contributions of military and food supplies." [26] The co-belligerency plan, which the President already favored, was the one adopted.

On the troublesome submarine problem Tumulty also gave astute advice before war was declared. Like few other civilians, he saw the need for innovations in defense. In March 1917, he urged the establishment of American naval bases in the British Isles, a system of naval convoys, and the construction of a large fleet of small craft specifically outfitted for anti-submarine service in order "to maintain an uninterrupted outflow of our commodities." [27] These were the measures, already sponsored by foresighted naval officers, which ultimately conquered the submarine.

Tumulty implemented war measures where he could. To expedite the adoption of selective service, he kept "in close touch with the situation on the Hill" throughout April 1917. He informed Wilson that there was "almost panic in our ranks" over the conscription plan. Although Tumulty was sure that the Administration's Military Bill would pass in the end, he advised the President that the misconceptions of the ordinary man regarding the term "conscription" needed to be overcome.[28] The draft met opposition particularly on the grounds that it constituted an infringement of personal liberties and violated the volunteer tradition of the American people.

Theodore Roosevelt, advancing the latter proposition in a modified form, wanted special permission to raise a volunteer division, a plan which Wilson and Baker considered at variance with the program of the General Staff. Nevertheless Wilson gave Roosevelt a hearing. After receiving a "hearty slap on the back" from the ex-President, Tumulty sat in on the conference. At its conclusion, while they exchanged friendly words about children and staff work, Roosevelt good-naturedly requested Tumulty to screen his statement to the press. But Roosevelt's charm did not win Tumulty to his plan. Had the Rough Rider been permitted to raise a division, his recruiting might have popularized the war more effectively than any other scheme. Tumulty, however, defended Wilson's decision to decline the request, assuring his chief that in time of war he had to accept the guidance of professional military men.[29]

After selective service was instituted, Tumulty found certain aspects of the working of the law objectionable and discovered that the advice of professional military men was not always easy to follow. He complained to Wilson that the registration form was so phrased that young men were asked whether they "claimed" exemption. Tumulty contended that this put family men and government employees, exempt by the terms of the law, in the position of seeming to seek an excuse to evade the draft. He advised that the questionnaire be altered to avoid individual "humiliation" and misunderstandings which might be turned against future candidates for public office. Although Secretary Baker considered such a change unnecessary, he telegraphed directions for the registrars to ignore the controversial question.[30]

Wilson and Baker refused, however, to heed the protests from Tumulty, A. M. Palmer, and Vance McCormick, against the system for choosing members of the exemption boards. Foreseeing that these positions, carrying some prestige and power, could be used for political purposes, Palmer and McCormick objected to Baker's directive empowering the governor of each state to nominate the local boards. Tumulty at first refrained from criticism, commenting that since the boards should be above political consideration, he would not even attempt to influence selections in New Jersey. But in Pennsylvania, New York, and New Jersey the expectations of Palmer and McCormick materialized. Observing that Governor Edge of New Jersey had chosen only two Democrats, one of them an "out and out pro-German," Tumulty belatedly sought, without success, to persuade Wilson to intercede.[31]

Tumulty disapproved of the policy of the Secretary of War and his ranking generals in the case of General Leonard Wood. Wood had preceded his troops from Camp Funston to New York City, their port of embarkation, only to be recalled at the last moment because General Pershing, in command in Europe, had not requested his presence in France. Furthermore, since Wood was an ex-Chief of Staff of the Army, and had outranked Pershing when the latter was given command of the A.E.F., his presence in France, in a subordinate position, might well have proved embarrassing. The suddenness of the recall, however, gave substance to the claims that Wood had been denied an opportunity to go overseas because of his friendship with Roosevelt and his potential political strength in the Republican Party. But in spite of Wood's fervent pleas that he be permitted to see action, neither Baker nor Wilson would countermand the order. After an interview with the President, Wood told Tumulty that Pershing was keeping him from France because of a personal pique remaining from their difference while on duty in the Philippines. Conscious of Wood's popularity and convinced that the General was being treated unfairly, Tumulty telephoned Wilson that evening to ask that Wood be sent overseas, if not to France, at least to Italy. But the President, impatient and unsympathetic, would not reconsider his decision. The next morning Tumulty approached Baker with no better results.[32]

By influencing appointments and through unofficial conferences Tumulty attempted to minimize the jobbery and inefficiency that attended the procurement of materials of war. He warned war agencies against lobbyists who traded their influence for a percentage of profits on contracts — the "Five Percenters" of their day. He asked personal acquaintances dealing in government contracts to look elsewhere for business, explaining that otherwise they might inadvertently capitalize on his friendship. Impressed with the need for men of executive talent in the vital administrative positions, he endorsed the nomination of Bainbridge Colby, a political maverick but "a man of a constructive mind," as a member of the War Shipping Board, urging Wilson to exert his influence to hasten Colby's confirmation by the Senate.[33] With House and McAdoo he championed Bernard Baruch for chairman of the War Industries Board, the key agency for the mobilization of American business. Because many businessmen did not like Baruch, Wilson contemplated naming Edward R. Stettinius, a Morgan partner. Tumulty objected, arguing that the choice of Stettinius would permit the opponents of the war to reassert their claim that it was a capitalists' war. The appointment of a Morgan partner, he felt, would weaken the hand of Gompers, who was striving to ensure the co-operation of American labor. "One thing is certain," Tumulty contended, "we know where Baruch stands. . . . We are sure of Baruch's vision, loyalty and generous sympathies."[34] His personal inclinations strengthened by these observations, Wilson gave Baruch the job. This was a happy choice.

Tumulty was particularly interested in the railroad problem. The inability of the railroads to co-operate effectively in the essential task of moving war materials from factory to seaboard threatened the entire war effort. Early attempts at voluntary co-ordination failed. In November of 1917 Tumulty was one of several advisers to Wilson who proposed principles of management similar to those ultimately adopted. Believing that the government could manage the railroads effectively without purchasing them, he recommended the appointment of a controlling body comprised of an executive committee of general managers with a Cabinet officer as their chairman. To protect the roads he suggested that the government guarantee a reasonable income and adequate maintenance of railroad equipment.[35] Seeking the appointment of a Director General of Railroads whose views were close to his own, Tumulty urged the President to name McAdoo. Wilson feared that the joint responsibilities of the Treasury and the railroads would be too great even for his son-in-law, but Tumulty disagreed. "The essential thing," he wrote Wilson, "is that the head of the organization should be a man with vision, energy and willingness to secure able lieutenants and leave to them a wide latitude of action in the discharge of their duties." [36] After ascertaining that Louis Brandeis favored McAdoo, Tumulty persuaded Wilson to consult the Justice. Although Brandeis agreed with the President that the Treasury and railroads together would be too much, Wilson, unable to find a candidate more acceptable than McAdoo, appointed him Director when the government assumed control.[37]

Failures and delays in production occasioned by careless or inadequate administrators shocked Tumulty. Prodded by Daniel Willard, President of the Baltimore and Ohio Railroad, and Baruch's predecessor as chairman of the War Industries Board, he suggested to Wilson and to Edward N. Hurley, chairman of the Shipping Board, that a scientific follow-up system should be adopted to check the speed with which contracts were filled. He asked the same men to direct the Attorney General to investigate the disgraceful profiteering at the shipyards at Hog Island and to indict those responsible. He urged Wilson to "take some action of a radical character" to correct the deplorable sanitary conditions in Army camps. These suggestions were adopted with only minor modifications.[38]

The delay in the production of airplanes was perhaps the most publicized failure of the war effort. Pursuant to his official duties, Tumulty in January 1918, acted as an intermediary during the initial correspondence relative to the Aircraft Production Board between Wilson and Gutzon Borglum, the versatile, contentious sculptor, aeronautical enthusiast, and Progressive Republican. Although Tumulty was aware of the shortcomings of the Aircraft Board, he disapproved of the encouragement the President gave Borglum's desire to make an independent inquiry into the work of that body. Describing the sculptor as "one of Roosevelt's most intimate friends . . . [whose] intentions are not to help us if he can do otherwise," Tumulty advised Wilson to initiate remedies through official rather than private channels.[39] Tumulty's instinct was unerring. Borglum used the vague letter Wilson sent him as a mandate for an investigation of aircraft production. He announced to the public that he had discovered wilful neglect growing out of the influence of the automobile industry. Meanwhile an official committee had unearthed alarming information on the failure of the aircraft program but had found no evidence of graft or sabotage. Since Borglum's version was more severe than the situation merited and needlessly harsh on Baruch and other officials, Tumulty begged Wilson for permission to release both the President's correspondence with Borglum and the official reports, confident that these documents would clarify the issue. Wilson agreed to give out his correspondence, but he withheld the reports because of their detailed recommendations on specific policies and persons. While Borglum weakened his case by constant overstatement, Wilson restored public confidence by appointing Charles Evans Hughes to inquire into the entire aircraft program. Hughes' report, released shortly before the Armistice, contradicted most of Borglum's contentions.[40]

Reacting to Borglum's partisanship, Tumulty was tempted to forgive the Aircraft Board too much, but he fought similar conditions in other parts of the War Department. At the instance of Robert Woolley, Tumulty called on Assistant Secretary of War Cromwell to demand a reconsideration of the Roberts by-products oven, a new, more efficient process for making coke (an essential ingredient in the manufacture of steel) which the Bureau of Ordnance had rejected. Cromwell's subsequent inquiries led to the reversal of the Bureau's decision. Tumulty and Woolley also prompted Wilson and Baker to stop the waste, so extensive as to border on sabotage, of coke and toluol * by concerns specially favored by the War Department. To avoid the type of gossip that arose over the aircraft situation, Tumulty persuaded Herbert Bayard Swope, a member of Baruch's board, to apprise the President of various ineffectual policies of the Bureau of Ordnance. Tumulty and Swope were particularly concerned with the Bureau's decision to curtail production of the French "75" while experimenting with a new model. After a full year, not one improved model had been

* Toluol or toluene is a hydrocarbon obtained chiefly from coke-oven vapors and by distillation of coal tar. It is used in the manufacture of dyes, of which the United States was seriously short in 1917–18.

delivered for field use. Swope's intercession facilitated Baruch's salutary review of the whole artillery program.[41]

*   *   *   *   *   *

The waste of coke and toluol, the delays in aircraft and artillery production were evidence of growing pains. During the long period of national mobilization, a period practically co-extensive with the abbreviated belligerency of the United States, these losses seemed at times more spectacular than did American success in sending men and materials abroad. Confusion and waste were inevitable in the transition from peace. The tremendous output of vital goods, the training of a large army, the disciplining of a population unaccustomed to any regimentation were the transcendent achievements of the war effort.

But the Republicans naturally exploited the mistakes they found, insisting that only the Grand Old Party, the party of business, the party experienced in government, could manage a war successfully. Fortunately such criticism was not obstructive, but the Republicans lampooned Baker, excoriated Creel, and sponsored legislation for a bipartisan war cabinet. This agitation was a first phase in their aggressive campaign to gain control of Congress in 1918.

Tumulty's responsibilities, official and advisory, were clothed, therefore, with political as well as patriotic implications. The Democrats were as consciously partisan as the Republicans. The successful prosecution of the war involved Democratic reputation as directly as it did national survival. Tumulty's immediate antidote to Republican criticism lay in his efforts to bolster morale, in his co-operation with Congressmen for the passage of such measures as the Military Bill and the Overman Act, Wilson's alternative to a bipartisan cabinet,* and in his vigilance toward the war agencies. Even during the war, however, Tumulty's most demanding extra-official responsibilities related to domestic, political affairs with which he was thoroughly familiar. Increasingly it fell to him to oversee Democratic strategy for the political campaigns on the home front.

* The Overman Act gave Wilson increased authority over the organization of the executive departments to facilitate the prosecution of the war. The Republicans would have preferred to force upon the President a bipartisan super-cabinet.[42]

CHAPTER X

The Home Front

1. A Domestic Program

NEVER in American history has a national crisis been severe enough to overcome partisan rivalries. During the First World War party politics continued unabated. The Republicans, under the skillful direction of Will Hays, repaired the damage of the Bull Moose movement and, capitalizing on warborn issues, laid the foundations for a decade of power. The Democrats resisted stubbornly, handicapped by disagreements within the party over foreign and domestic policies, atrophy in the National Committee, and the preoccupation of the party's official leaders with nonpolitical affairs. Lacking any authority and restricted by his limited influence, Tumulty fought these conditions to the best of his ability.

The wartime redeployment of personnel left the problem of the election of 1918 largely to Tumulty and to Scott Ferris, chairman of the Democratic Congressional Campaign Committee. Administrative duties forced Vance McCormick, Robert Woolley, Burleson, and McAdoo to curtail their political activities. Colonel House devoted most of his time to diplomacy. These men never abdicated their political positions. At times their advice molded Democratic policy. But especially in the first fifteen months of Wilson's second term, Tumulty gave more consecutive attention to the interests of the Democracy than did any of the others.

Fortunately a common concern for the prosecution of the war

and the welfare of the party put an end to the personal bickering of other years. Old jealousies and animosities were forgotten. Once again Tumulty consulted the Colonel on patronage. He supported McAdoo and Woolley for important appointments.[1] In the autumn of 1918 he worked closely with McCormick and Homer Cummings. The new harmony enabled Tumulty to make political plans, not without opposition, but free from the secret intrigues that had confused Democratic tactics in other elections.

During the first months of the war Tumulty began to develop a platform for 1918. By preference always the aggressor in politics, he desired to go to the people with something more than a defense against Republican criticism. He sought to fashion an attractive program of social action by modifying and synthesizing the domestic policies of Democratic leaders in the Administration and on the Hill. Characteristically, he attempted to attract all classes and to find the most useful compromise between the ideal and the practical.

Tumulty's attitude toward labor was friendly but conservative. He felt that Wilson would hold the allegiance of the unions because of two significant acts passed during his first term: the Clayton Act, exempting unions from prosecution under the Sherman Antitrust Act, and the Adamson Law, providing an eight-hour day for railroad labor. He considered Gompers an ally and advocated the appointment of a labor man to the Council of National Defense. But the radical fringe, the violent, syndicalist International Workers of the World, and the Socialists, seemed to Tumulty to be disrupting the war effort. And he was solicitous of the approval of businessmen. "Out of the national melting pot of war," he wrote Wilson, "must come the new spirit of national co-operation between labor and employers, a new spirit of national unity and strength. . . ."[2] He proposed, therefore, while helping to consolidate labor's gains, to offer the unions nothing new and to discipline unruly elements. For legislation, pending in June 1918, to increase the hours of work of government employees he had no sympathy. Forwarding a letter of protest from Gompers, Tumulty urged Wilson to veto the measure. He asserted that since the employees would voluntarily work overtime when necessary, the bill would merely force them into unions which would interfere with the government. "I think a veto by you of this particular measure," he counseled, "would do more to hearten labor throughout the country, and would give you first call upon their services, than anything you could do." [3] But labor was not to be coddled. Protesting against a suggestion that a labor man be placed on the Federal Trade Commission, Tumulty two weeks earlier had remarked: "Our whole attitude toward labor since the beginning of this Administration has been so generous that any appointment of this kind would be misunderstood by labor and the country at large. Labor would believe that we feel we owe it something, which we do not. The country at large would think that we were making a special appeal to labor at this time. If there is any class in this country to which we have been overgenerous it has been labor. I think that this class owes us more than they have been willing to give." [4]

The caution that exemplified Tumulty's advice on labor had no part in his thinking on woman suffrage. Personally devoted to that cause, and anxious for political reasons to have the Administration credited with the reform, Tumulty tactfully combatted resistance to the suffrage amendment pending in Congress. He advised Wilson to appeal personally to Senators whose votes were in doubt. He endeavored to prevent pairing on the issue. He persuaded Wilson to request Vice-President Marshall to be prepared to break a tie. He tried to enlist the support of Republican Senator David Baird of New Jersey, his amicable political rival for many years. In August of 1918, when every doubtful vote was crucial, Tumulty's closest friend in the Senate, Ollie James, died. While in Kentucky for James' funeral, Tumulty impressed Governor A. O. Stanley with the importance of selecting a successor to James committed to woman suffrage. Later Tumulty asked Wilson to repeat this advice. Stanley's appointee gave the measure his support, but senatorial approval was delayed until after the Congressional elections, largely because of the opposition of other Southern Democrats. [5]

Tumulty stood fast against prohibition, the social reform so often associated with woman suffrage. He considered it unwise morally and inexpedient politically. Like many other "wets," he realized the influence of the "drys" too late. For political reasons in New Jersey, and by way of a delaying action, Tumulty supported local option, but the prohibition lobby was no longer content with half-way measures. In September 1918, while the Eighteenth Amendment was still unratified, the "drys" in Congress, strongest among midwestern Republicans and southern Democrats, tacked a rider onto the Agricultural Bill establishing national prohibition as of October 1, 1919. Tumulty and Burleson protested vigorously, begging the President to veto the measure. Reminding Wilson of the steps already taken as a war measure to curb the production and consumption of alcoholic beverages, Tumulty rehearsed the case against any attempt to regulate morals by legislation. He supported his views with editorials from Wilson's favorite newspapers, emphasizing the political "dangers" in further restrictions. "My principal objection to this legislation at this time," he admitted, "in view of the coming elections, I am frank to say, is political. I am afraid of its effects upon the voters of our party in the large centers of population. . . . The proponents of this measure . . . agree that it is not a conservative [sic] measure, but . . . an out-and-out attempt to declare the country dry. It is mob legislation, pure and simple." Tumulty maintained that the loss of liquor revenues would disrupt the finances of municipalities throughout the country, causing local taxes to go up at the very time federal rates were increasing. He feared the reaction of an electorate faced with the prospect of higher taxes and no beer. "So much in a great, broad humanitarian way depends upon your winning the next election," Tumulty concluded morosely, "that I look with dread . . . upon anything that stands in its way." [6] Tumulty drafted a similar protest for Burleson. Repeating the contention that the conservation of grain would not be effected, he warned that Democratic chances in New York, Ohio, Connecticut, Delaware, and Rhode Island would suffer.[7]

These letters, supplemented by fervent oral admonitions, caused Wilson to pause. The President had himself not desired further action on prohibition. Although he discounted Burleson's views as those of an incorrigible "wet," he was impressed by Tumulty's remarks on taxes. But his Secretary did not have the last word. Wilson consulted Colonel House. Speaking for McAdoo, Attorney General Gregory, and himself, House convinced Wilson that he should accept the legislation.[8]

While dealing with such current issues as labor, suffrage, and prohibition, Tumulty devised a postwar program. At first committed to a general course of radical action, he gradually retreated to a more political position. His memorandum of January 1918, entitled "The Revolt of the Underdog," declared unequivocally for a new liberalism. "The mass of the people, underfed and dissatisfied, are clamoring for a fuller recognition of their rights to life and liberty," he noted. "They are no longer interested in party shibboleths or slogans. . . . The Democratic Party will cease to live as a progressive instrumentality unless its leaders proceed to the formulation of policies which will make life more easy, more comfortable, and more prosperous for the average [man]." Not only had the regulation of railroads and the limited price-fixing of basic commodities failed to control the cost of living in wartime, Tumulty observed, but "every process of regulation [of private monopoly] has left the thing sought to be regulated stronger and more hurtful in its influence." Therefore he called on the Democracy to break new ground: "We must no longer attempt to regulate. We must control, own and operate . . . the basic needs of our life." [9] Developing this thesis, Tumulty later proclaimed the platform of the British Labor Party the "most mature and carefully formulated program ever put forth by a responsible political party." [10] These statements, appealing, as they did, for a degree of socialism still not adopted in the United States, were an uneasy, tentative attempt to find new issues. The legislation of Wilson's first administration, by bringing to fruition the reform ideas of the previous decade, had left a political void which Tumulty in 1917 and 1918 was trying to fill. Tumulty was not just fabricating a campaign platform. He could see in the frictions of the wartime economy, the retrogression in New Jersey, the continuing, even increasing power of large-scale business, that the New Freedom had not provided a final solution. Yet neither he nor most other gradualists of his generation knew exactly what to do next. He flirted, therefore, with the tempting idea of modified socialism, but, never convinced by a concept so uncharacteristic of his thought, he could not apply it to specific issues. His political training, furthermore, forbade the use of an idea repellent to most of the electorate. Tumulty wrote sincerely of government ownership of the basic needs of life, but just as sincerely he soon retreated.

Wilson, also puzzled and uneasy, temporarily used these views of Tumulty on domestic changes. His letter of March 1918, to the Democrats of New Jersey in general terms called for the provision of greater opportunity and prosperity for the average man. He warned that old party slogans were no longer significant. Tumulty, pleased, noted that the letter won the praise of the Newark *News*, the New York *World*, and the *New Republic*. In a speech immediately following the reading of Wilson's letter, Tumulty described his chief's message as the "gospel of the Democracy in this new day" and asked his fellow party members to implement it by adopting standards of social justice and common interest in dealing with state control of public utilities and state labor legislation.[11]

Tumulty had difficulty, however, in finding further concrete applications for his progressive point of view. As the election approached he instinctively dodged radical expressions. When Wilson consulted him in May about a draft of the platform for the Democrats of Indiana, Tumulty objected to an appeal for government ownership of the railroads. "It would immediately make Government ownership an issue . . ." he wrote House, "very much to the embarrassment of Mr. McAdoo. I think we ought to use the war as a laboratory . . . for the trying out of these ideas and *after* 1918 we can go to the country, standing for the permanency of those instrumentalities whose use in the War has been demonstrated to be practicable. . . ." House concurred in this view and Wilson modified his draft of the railroad plank.[12] A model for Democratic campaigners all over the nation, the Indiana platform "pointed with pride" to Democratic achievements in peace and war but contained no explicit references to a detailed domestic program for the future.

2. Preliminary Skirmishes

While helping to establish the dimensions of the Democratic appeal, Tumulty surveyed the practical application of traditional political tactics in various local salients. Until July of 1918 he exercised some direction in the Northeast, giving less attention to the rest of the country. Thereafter he was primarily concerned with the national scene, too busy with the over-all campaign to be able to concentrate on any state or section.

The New York City mayoralty contest of 1917 revived familiar problems. Machine opposition and popular disapproval of his aristocratic manner and unrestrained jingoism cost John Purroy Mitchel the Republican nomination; but supported by Theodore Roosevelt, Root, Hughes, Frank Polk, Republican Governor Whitman, Secretary of Commerce Redfield, and a group of reformers from both major parties, Mitchel ran independently on a platform of martial nationalism. The Socialists, openly opposing the war, nominated Morris Hillquit who was strong with pacifists, disaffected labor groups, and the militant Irish and German voters. Charley Murphy recognized the opportunity to regain power. To ensure party unity he gave Tammany's backing to Judge John F. Hylan, the choice of Hearst and Boss McCooey of Brooklyn. Hylan's reputation, although not white, was at least not black. Murphy strengthened the ticket by selecting Alfred E. Smith, his popular lieutenant, for President of the Board of Aldermen.[13]

Because of his penchant for regularity and his friendship with Smith and McCooey, Tumulty favored Hylan. He considered Mitchel stigmatized by the embrace of Roosevelt, and Hillquit damned by his opposition to the war. Seeking to rebuild the New York Democracy through Tammany, Tumulty had tried, with House's assistance, to persuade Wilson to show some cordiality toward the Wigwam. But Wilson refused Tumulty's repeated requests, insisting that he could not play favorites in New York City.[14]

After the mayoralty campaign began, the President's neutrality caused some trouble. A group of Democratic federal employees in New York openly opposed Hylan. Mitchel campaigned vigorously, ascribing Hearst's support of Hylan to Hohenzollern influence. The situation was compounded by the antics of Dudley Field Malone whose poor health had affected his personal and political disposition. Angry with McAdoo over a patronage squabble and distressed by Wilson's caution on woman suffrage, Malone resigned as Collector of the Port and lent his vitriolic tongue, not to his old ally Mitchel, but to Hillquit. This aberration marked Malone's demise as an important political figure, but Tumulty's immediate reaction was one of concern for the efficacy of the Collector's office in the campaign.[15]

Tumulty provided two remedies. First, with McAdoo's support, he recommended the appointment of Byron R. Newton to succeed Malone. Although an unaffiliated Democrat, Newton had no objections to Tammany. There was immediate help for Hylan in the Shipping Board in New York where Tumulty had obtained a job for N. P. Wedin, once his rival in Jersey City. Wedin now repaid his debt in dispensing patronage and furnishing data on the local political scene. Secondly, Tumulty made sure of Wilson's neutrality. Mitchel's friends, expecting help from the President, interpreted a visit to New York by Tumulty in late October as a good omen. They erred. Shortly after Tumulty's return, and probably on the basis of his report, Wilson declined a request from Redfield that he intercede in Mitchel's behalf. The President took no stand. Murphy's smoothly operating machine swept Hylan into office. After the election, Norman E. Mack, an upstate friend of Tammany, expressed Tumulty's own views in writing him that the results demonstrated the value of a disciplined organization.[16]

Still doubtful about Tammany, Wilson nevertheless deferred to the new conditions in New York. In June of 1918, he accepted the recommendation of McAdoo, Tumulty, and Mack in appointing a Collector of the Port of Buffalo. The President's response to Tumulty's enthusiasm for Al Smith, the Democratic gubernatorial candidate in 1918, was a dubious, silent smile.[17] But Wilson's personal feelings notwithstanding, his Secretary had helped re-establish Tammany as the agent of the Democracy in the Empire State, and in so doing had strengthened the party there.

Tumulty had less to work with in Massachusetts than in New York. Convinced that the Democratic Party was hopelessly weak, he was primarily interested in avoiding embarrassment for the Administration. At Burleson's request, Colonel House interceded to strengthen the Democratic ticket in 1917. After a conference with the State Chairman and Frederick W. Mansfield, the gubernatorial candidate, he asked Matthew Hale, chairman of the Progressive Party in Massachusetts, to accept the Democratic nomination for

Lieutenant Governor. Hale consented on the condition that Wilson endorse the Mansfield-Hale slate as a desirable union for the furtherance of liberal principles. Tumulty immediately objected. Although he looked forward to a merger of the "liberal forces in both . . . parties," he warned Burleson that the election in Massachusetts was "not a proper stage upon which to exploit" that idea. He argued that the efforts of "our generous Irish friends . . . to 'hog' the situation" had so disgusted Massachusetts Democrats that Mansfield, a weak candidate, won the nomination without opposition. Foreseeing Republican victory under any conditions, Tumulty hesitated to surround Mansfield "with such fine men as Hale." He counseled Burleson to keep the President out of the fight and to reserve the kind of campaign suggested for the Congressional elections in 1918.[18]

Subscribing to much of what Tumulty wrote, Wilson sent the analysis to House. The Colonel did not feel that endorsement of Hale would commit Wilson to the extent that defeat would reflect badly on the Administration. He contended that Hale had already agreed to run on assurance from Burleson that Wilson would endorse him. Obviously embarrassed by this turn of events, the President asked Tumulty to prepare a letter that would satisfy Hale without involving the Administration irrevocably. Tumulty made the most of a bad situation. The letter he drafted simply congratulated Hale for his interest in the Soldiers' Insurance Bill, a favorite project of Tumulty, and for his public spirit in accepting the nomination.[19] This equivocal approach apparently satisfied all those concerned. Even in 1918 the hyphenate complexion of the Massachusetts Democracy constrained Tumulty from recommending any more definite assistance to Bay State candidates. Tumulty was a disciple of regularity, but never to the extreme of compromising his conception of patriotism.

Tumulty's participation in New Jersey politics was more active than in New York or Massachusetts. He returned to his earliest political battleground in an effort to rescue the Democratic Party from the grasp of selfish, often inept leaders whose policies, repugnant to decent men, furnished the Republicans with superb campaign ammunition. Painfully aware of the connections between

Hague and Nugent and the saloonkeepers and brewers, Tumulty's first sally was designed to rid the party of their influence by soliciting Democratic votes for a local-option bill.[20] But the legislature of 1917 defeated the measure. Temporarily Tumulty dropped the issue.

An attempt at union of New Jersey liberals under the Democratic banner, the objective of Tumulty and Sullivan in years gone by, was the cornerstone of Tumulty's next stratagem. He proceeded cautiously. Guarding against the election of a Republican sheriff in Hudson County, he warned Otto Wittpenn against joining a fusion movement. But he struck directly at the element in the Democratic Party that made fusion popular. He appealed to the people of Jersey City to turn out Hague and his "double-dealing" political autocracy.[21] Hague, however, was all-powerful in Hudson. His victory there helped set the stage for a Republican triumph in the off-year state elections of 1917. Democratic stock had reached a new low.

Although routed, Tumulty was not permitted to withdraw. Even James Smith, Jr., realized the need for outside assistance. "We have no organization anywhere in the State that means anything," Smith lamented. ". . . Hague . . . was the best that I could get . . . but you know him. . . . Nugent means alright, but I need hardly tell you, that he lacks diplomacy. . . ." [22] Tumulty's brother echoed those sentiments. "Everyone who is truly a Democrat is disgusted with Hague and his tactics," he observed. "His method is to browbeat and to threaten. . . . No one appears at present to be able to give him a fight. . . . [You] will be needed soon." [23]

Tumulty heeded these petitions, resorting to publicity, the only weapon at his immediate disposal. In January 1918, he wrote a public letter to Alexander Simpson, a Democratic leader in the legislature, setting forth the general conception of his "Revolt of the Underdog." Beginning with a plea for reorientation in behalf of the common man, Tumulty warned the Democracy of New Jersey against the traction and brewery interests. "The influences of these two groups have been like a cancerous growth in the politics of our State," he asserted, "and they must be absolutely out if we are . . . to respond to . . . progressive impulses." He told the Democrats in the legislature that it was their duty to support local option, government ownership of all public utilities, the strengthening of the primary and corrupt-practices laws, so flagrantly violated by Hague, and a program for the construction of roads and state-owned tunnels. In the same letter he criticized the Republican schemes for accomplishing these objectives.[24] The Republicans, however, controlled the legislature where Tumulty, lacking any organization, was unable to unite even the anti-Hague Democrats.[25] For the corrupt-practices, tunnel, and local-option laws which were passed, the Republicans, with reason, claimed credit.

Tumulty's activity, especially his letter to Simpson, had one unforeseen result. It stimulated a senatorial boom for its author that reached large proportions after the death of William Hughes. Labor leaders, editors, and politicians from all over the state promised their support.[26] But Tumulty, determined not to seek public office again, in February announced that he would not run under any conditions. Wilson's need for him in Washington impelled this decision, but his deeper reasons were political and personal. He did not want to return to Hudson County where "not a corporal's guard stood ready to follow an honest man." [27] He had no personal following. He needed a larger and more certain income than politics afforded in order to give educational opportunities to his family. Finally, the barbs of the Klan and the Hyphen had struck too often. The Leavenworth rumor served as a reminder of the prejudice against Catholics, a feeling intensified by the activities of the Irish-Americans who opposed the war. In New Jersey Hague's tactics had damaged the reputation of every. Irish politician, no matter how innocent. "The idea of making the race and putting forth the things I believe in strongly appealed to me," Tumulty wrote his oldest friend, "and yet I was held back by reasons of a deep, personal nature. . . . In so far as this office is concerned — indeed as far as the governorship of the State is concerned — I have crossed the Rubicon, and I now wish to do what I can to rebuild our party in the State. Certainly no one can charge me with selfishness. It is up to the Irish in our State and elsewhere to show that they can be good privates in the ranks. I shall try to show this in every way. We must quickly gather our forces together and see what we can do to forward our cause everywhere. . . ." [28]

Tumulty did what he could to solidify Democratic ranks in New Jersey for the election in 1918 of United States Senators for the unexpired and full terms. Co-operating with Judge Hudspeth and State Chairman Charles F. McDonald, he selected Charles O'Connor Hennessy and George LaMonte, both able liberals, who won their primaries. He placated by personal and political favors disappointed Wilsonians who aspired to the offices. But the defection from the party of militant Irish-Americans and the dangerous indifference of Hague toward the national ticket assured Republican victory.[29] In New York Tumulty had bolstered the party through Tammany. In New Jersey the Democracy could prosper only on Hague's terms which Tumulty was not yet willing to accept.

3. The Election of 1918

Outside of the Northeast, Tumulty approached politics slowly and cautiously during 1917. Although he wanted to see Senator Hardwick of Georgia, an opponent of the Administration, defeated, he advised Wilson against voicing objections to Hardwick prematurely. He recommended that the incumbent Civil Service Commissioners be retained so as to avoid charges of partisanship at the beginning of the war. But in October he began to prepare for the work of the coming year. He sent Assistant Postmaster General Daniel C. Roper a list of Senators, including the "real friends" of the Administration who were "entitled to priority" in patronage and the less active supporters "entitled to secondary consideration." Classification within the former category ensured a Senator timely federal assistance in maintaining an organization.[30]

Soon the need for political planning became acute. Beginning early in 1918 the reunited Republicans took the offensive with several effective lines of attack. In the East they concentrated on the conduct of the war, relating their criticism to the bitterly partisan debates in Congress. They contrasted the failure of many Democrats to support vital war measures with the excellent record of eastern Republicans in that respect. At the same time they exploited war-weariness occasioned by food and fuel shortages, high prices, and the other inconveniences of belligerency. Eastern businessmen, long suspect of the New Freedom, looked askance at government control of the railroads and telephone and telegraph systems. They resented even more the heavy income, inheritance, and excess profits taxes which Claude Kitchin, Democratic Chairman of the House Ways and Means Committee, acknowledged to be hardest on the East. Kitchin argued that, since the East made the largest profits on the war, the East should carry the heaviest burden. This argument the Republicans interpreted as spiteful sectional discrimination. Pointing out that Kitchin could not be defeated in his own district, they called for the election of a Republican Congress to force him out of his powerful chairmanship.

In the West, where the war had always been less popular, the Republicans had an equally convincing sectional issue. Congress had empowered the President to fix the price of wheat, and in spite of requests from members of his own party, Wilson permitted no increase in the set price. But the Southern Democrats blocked regulation of the price of raw cotton which soared under the stimulus of wartime demands. The Republicans fanned the anger of wheat farmers at the Administration's apparent favoritism for the southern crop.

East and West, expression of the Republican point of view was facilitated by the attitude of the newspapers. Already bothered by censorship, the press was indignant over legislation, sponsored by Kitchin and endorsed by Burleson, to increase the postage on second-class mail.

Tumulty's channels of counterattack were limited. Neither a moderate program of social melioration nor unrelated forays in the politics of a few states were sufficient. Too little aware of the strength of the sectional argument in the West, Tumulty failed to suggest any convincing rebuttal to the Republicans as part of the Indiana platform. But he understood the feeling against Kitchin in the East and the liability imposed on the party by the opposition of Champ Clark, Kitchin, and a number of Southern Democrats to the declaration of war and essential war measures. With more determination than success he fought them at every opportunity.

Through seniority, Southern Democrats dominated the committees of the House of Representatives. Speaker Clark was their unfailing ally. Reviewing the personnel of the House in an attempt to find new leadership, one anonymous Administration adviser concluded that it was "hopeless." [31] The few able northern Democrats were no match for the experienced Southerners as floor managers or debaters. Furthermore, Wilson, House, Burleson, and Gregory, Southerners themselves, had been overgenerous to Dixie in the disposition of patronage. Long before 1917 Tumulty had protested in vain against the increasing number of major appointments given to Southerners, contrasting this development with the relatively meager contributions from the South to Democratic campaign funds.[32] By 1917 it was too late to overcome the Southern predominance in Congress and in party councils.

Tumulty considered Kitchin the most dangerous of the southern leaders. Prodded by newspaper and magazine editors, he challenged Kitchin's plan to increase postal rates. Senator Simmons, a consistent supporter of Wilson's policies, informed Tumulty, after careful inquiries, that the needed revenue could be found elsewhere. Secretary McAdoo agreed. But Kitchin and Burleson were unrelenting. Casting about for assistance, Tumulty turned to Colonel House. "It seems to me that it is both unwise and unnecessary to throttle these great engines of public opinion," he complained. "I not only think it is unwise from the business standpoint, but very unwise politically." [33] Apparently unconvinced, House did not reply. Simmons had to concede that Kitchin would prevail, and Tumulty sadly advised Wilson that executive interference would be useless.[34] Burleson's censorship and Kitchin's legislation nullified much of the good will Tumulty had assiduously cultivated among journalists.

As a reply to the Republican campaign propaganda, the Democrats emphasized their record of successful prosecution of the war. But even where loyalty and national success could be equated with membership in the Democratic Party, the effectiveness of the issue was inconclusive. And in so far as the argument was effective, it was difficult to extend credit to benefit those Democrats who had consistently opposed and obstructed the war.

Tumulty watched the first tests of public reaction to the conduct of the war carefully. In New York City the results of several Congressional elections in March 1918, promised well. In spite of a gerrymander by the Republican legislature, the Democrats won. In a detailed analysis of the New York election and its relation to national politics, Tumulty advised Wilson to encourage Hays, Hughes, and especially Roosevelt to continue their partisan attacks, explaining that the electorate reacted against their bitter criticism of the government in wartime, and predicting victory in the coming senatorial race in Wisconsin.[35] The generally agrarian, isolationist, traditionally Republican voters of Wisconsin, however, did not follow the pattern set by the urbanites of New York. They rejected an antiwar Socialist, but in spite of Wilson's strong endorsement, Vice-President Marshall's spirited stumping, and Tumulty's adroit backstage manipulations, Joseph E. Davies, the Democratic candidate, lost his race against the Republican incumbent who had opposed most of Wilson's measures.[36]

The political situation seemed ominous. About the time of Davies' defeat Tumulty failed to prevent the increase in postal rates. Worried about Democratic prospects, he persuaded Wilson to moderate the radical planks in the Indiana platform and to avoid involvement, and therefore possible embarrassment, in the primaries for United States Senator in Missouri and for Governor in Ohio. He had suggested to Wilson that a public letter would speed pending revenue legislation, reminding the President that Congressmen were eager to get home for the campaigns. But Wilson, hoping for even faster results by a direct message to Congress, pontifically announced in his address that politics were adjourned. To Tumulty's distress, Wilson appeared to give weight to this idea by neglecting to repudiate the use of his name in behalf of Republican Senators Nelson and Kenyon.[37] Clearly politics had never been adjourned, either in or out of Congress. Convinced that the time had come for more precise planning, Tumulty prepared to have the President unmask.

Early in June, after a long conversation with Wilson, Tumulty sent his chief a detailed program of action for the fall campaign. For the present he proposed a policy of continued silence, calculated to embolden Hays, Penrose, Roosevelt, and other Republican leaders to make further "rash" political statements on the tariff, prosperity, and the war. But at the propitious time he wanted Wilson to blanket Democratic candidates with a cloak of loyalty and liberalism. The President was to accomplish this by writing a public letter, such as the Underwood letter of 1914, to some Democrat "of distinction," asking the people to elect a Democratic Congress. "We ought to accept these speeches charging incompetency and inefficiency as a challenge." Tumulty declared, "and call attention to the fact that the leadership of the Republican party is still reactionary . . . that their spokesmen . . . openly sneer at everything progressive and characterize the fine things as socialistic. I think a letter along the lines of the Indiana platform . . . would carry . . . just the impression we ought to make. This letter should be issued . . . in September . . . and should be followed in October by your participation in various parts of the country in the Liberty Loan campaign." [38]

This advice was the seed from which grew Wilson's much discussed partisan appeal of October. House commended Tumulty's initial idea as "in every way admirable." [39] Scott Ferris, with whom Wilson had promised to co-operate, joined Tumulty in setting the stage. During the summer they procured Presidential letters for various Democrats throughout the country.[40] In an interview with the press in September, Ferris asked for the re-election of a Democratic Congress, attributing reform, prosperity, and the successful conduct of the war to his party.[41] Congressman Pou, inspired by Champ Clark and other old-timers, requested Wilson to issue a general endorsement.[42] Tumulty altered his views slightly, suggesting that Wilson postpone action until after the Liberty Loan drive and eliminate the speaking trip, but he reminded Wilson regularly that an appeal would be needed.[43]

Whatever Wilson's first reaction to Tumulty's plan may have been, by mid-October he had found reason to concur. His foreign policy was at stake. The war was rapidly ending and the President's thoughts were concentrated on securing a peace based on the principles of his Fourteen Points.* These had become a partisan issue.

---

* Wilson's Fourteen Points, enunciated in an address to the Senate on January 8, 1918, were the basis of his program for making peace. He intended

Simeon Fess, Chairman of the Republican Congressional Campaign Committee, Will Hays, Henry Cabot Lodge, and Theodore Roosevelt, condemning Wilson's program, urged Republican victory in 1918 as a guard against a compromise peace.[44] With the war spirit at its vindictive peak, this argument had considerable strength.

Although Tumulty subscribed to Wilson's central ideas, agreeing on the need for a "scientific and just settlement" and for a league to prevent wars, Republican tactics alarmed him. Furthermore he shared, as Wilson did not, the mass hatred of Germany. He warned the President against premature negotiations with Austria-Hungary.[45] At the same time he tried to refute Republican charges that the Democrats stood for an inconclusive peace. In an acrimonious epistolary debate with Will Hays in September, Tumulty defended Wilson's views while charging the Republicans with impeding the war effort.[46] His discussion of Wilson's war aims indicated that leaders of both parties considered the Administration's foreign policy as one issue in the election.

When the Germans made their first overtures for an armistice, Tumulty, suspicious of their purpose, feared that Wilson's desire to

that they and corollary "points" later proposed should permit a "peace without victory," a just settlement allowing continuing world peace. His Fourteen Points included both particular and general provisions. The particular provisions, over which there was in 1918 relatively little disagreement in America, called for the restoration of Russian territory conquered by the Germans and the acceptance of Russia as an equal; the evacuation of Belgium; the restoration of French territory held by the Germans, including Alsace-Lorraine, which France had ceded in 1871; the adjustment of Italy's boundary along the lines of nationality; and the construction of free states, also on the basis of nationality or "self-determination," in the area of the Austro-Hungarian Empire and the Turkish Empire in Europe. The general provisions, particularly those pertaining to trade, armaments, and an association of nations, in 1918 provoked considerable opposition in America, especially from Roosevelt, Lodge, Hays, and other Republican leaders who considered them the regrettable ingredients of a "soft peace," of a "peace without victory." These general provisions called for the end of secret diplomacy, "open covenants of peace, openly arrived at"; freedom of the seas; the removal, in so far as possible, of international economic barriers; the reduction of armaments to "the lowest point consistent with domestic safety"; an "impartial adjustment" of colonial claims recognizing equally the interests of subject peoples and ruling nations; and the formation of "a general association of nations . . . under specific covenants for the purpose of affording mutual guarantees of political independence and territorial integrity to great and small states alike."

end the war would lead to political defeat. Assuming that the American people hated the Kaiser more than they wanted peace, Tumulty wrote Wilson and House that any agreement in which the Hohenzollerns played a part would be disastrous. "It will result in the election of a Republican House and the weakening . . . of your influence throughout the world," he declared. Reminding the President that the Allies were not sympathetic with his views, Tumulty suggested that Germany sought to split the Entente by negotiating an armistice on terms distasteful to England and France. "Defeat has not chastened the Germans in the least," he told Wilson a day later.[47] And returning to this theme after a week of reflection, Tumulty insisted: "The present rulers of Germany must go. . . . They shall not gather in the fruits of peace. . . . *Guilt must be made personal in international affairs.*" "We are not directly concerned in the form of government which Germany shall have," he argued, "but we are deeply concerned in our own security and we have a right to say that we will treat with those and those alone who can give some assurance that their treaties will be observed." [48]

As negotiations proceeded, the Republicans made political capital of Wilson's demands and Germany's replies. Although the President called for far-reaching concessions as a preliminary to armistice, many Americans wanted nothing but unconditional surrender. The third German note, acceding to most of Wilson's proposals, attracted the President, but Congressional leaders considered it unsatisfactory. Burleson belligerently advised a march to Berlin, and the Cabinet agreed that the people wanted drastic terms. Homer Cummings, vice-chairman and the most vocal and active member of the Democratic National Committee, warned Wilson that any answer which did not in all respects conform to what the people wanted might lead to political ruin. He counseled that only a vigorous attitude would carry the Democracy through the election, the loss of which would imperil Wilson's whole program.[49] And Tumulty, whom Wilson and House considered an accurate sounding board of public opinion, had not changed his mind. "Germany is on her last legs . . ." he observed. "Do you not see . . . that the whole thing turns upon the question of . . . the good faith of Germany? Is this evidence sufficient? . . . The Hohenzollerns

. . . are the silent partners in every transaction. . . . If the German people wish us to accept the words of this note or any other, they must outwardly and convincingly *disassociate* themselves from the men who began and conducted this greatest of human outrages." [50]

Wilson yielded in part to the demands of his advisers. If he did not explicitly call for the overthrow of the Kaiser, the implications of his notes pushed the German people in that direction. At the time of Wilson's second note, House felt that the President became firmer almost overnight after realizing the nearly unanimous sentiment for unconditional surrender. Consulted on a draft of the President's proposals, Tumulty had approved, remarking that sober-minded Americans would view the terms without enthusiasm but with increasing appreciation of their justice.[51] Tumulty's comment suggested his own acceptance of the terms as minimal. Only public enthusiasm could have political value, and only unconditional surrender, for which Wilson would not ask, seemed capable of generating public enthusiasm.

After modifying his diplomacy to suit his political counselors, Wilson implemented their advice on the home front. Cummings had confirmed Tumulty's opinion that presidential intercession in the campaign was necessary. And Roosevelt's goading had exhausted Wilson's patience. Concentrating on the importance of the election for American foreign policy, the President prepared his celebrated appeal for a Democratic Congress. Instead of writing a letter to some distinguished Democrat, Wilson drafted a direct request to the American people. McCormick, Cummings, and Tumulty persuaded him to allay the acerbity of his message.[52] Nevertheless the call for Democratic victory, released on October 25, was unequivocal. "Many critical issues" depended on the outcome of the election, Wilson observed. The Republicans, while "unquestionably . . . pro-war," had been "anti-Administration." The United States could not afford divided leadership. Europe would interpret the return of a Republican majority as a repudiation of his policies. Therefore the President sought a vote of confidence. "If you approve of my leadership and wish me to continue to be your unembarrassed spokesman in affairs at home and abroad," he declared, "I earnestly beg that you will express yourself unmistakably to that effect by returning a Democratic majority to both the Senate and the House." [53] Wilson's emphasis was different from that suggested by Tumulty in June. Peacemaking had largely supplanted warmaking and domestic problems as the basis of the President's action. But what Tumulty had sought was accomplished. The Democratic candidates, weak and strong, pro-war and antiwar, had received an official blessing.

Wilson's appeal infuriated the Republicans. "He is a partisan leader first and President . . . second," thundered Roosevelt. Senators Lodge and Smoot, Congressmen Gillett and Fess, reminding the people that a Republican victory would frustrate such antiwar Democrats as Clark and Kitchin, explained that the Republican Party stood for a victorious peace, leaving the question of surrender to the generals in the field. Will Hays expressed the general feeling of most Republicans in describing Wilson's plea as an insult to their loyalty.[54]

As every remaining pretense of nonpartisanship was shed, Tumulty sprang to Wilson's defense. In public letters to the Cuyahoga County Republican Committee, he cited precedents for executive interference in Congressional elections. Roosevelt in 1906 and Taft in 1910 had solicited Republican victory. In 1898 Roosevelt had warned that a Democratic triumph would give heart to Spain. Tumulty quoted Hays and Penrose to show that the Republicans had never adjourned politics. But these protestations did not dignify Wilson's action. Even the apologists for the President had to admit the shortcomings of Democratic leadership in Congress. Loyal Republicans continued to feel slandered.[55]

Undeterred, Tumulty pressed Wilson to issue a second call, arguing that the Republicans were trying to equate the Fourteen Points with free trade and a soft peace.[56] Wilson would not repeat his general overture, but prodded by Tumulty and Ferris, he assisted many specific candidates, including some for whom he had little respect. In spite of his antipathy for the McGraw machine, the President even acceded to Tumulty's repeated entreaties for an endorsement of Clarence F. Watson of West Virginia.[57]

In a last-minute effort to turn the peace issue to Democratic advantage, Tumulty and William Cochran, publicity director for the

National Committee, placed a political advertisement in newspapers throughout the country calling for a vote of approval of the Fourteen Points, asking Democratic victory to prevent postponement of German capitulation, and condemning the foreign policy of Roosevelt, Lodge, and Penrose. The content and tone of the advertisement supplied further evidence that the Democrats accepted the Republican challenge to Wilson's views on the peace as a paramount factor in the campaign.[58]

Foreign policy undoubtedly affected the election returns. But the sectional question in the East and West, the superior and wealthier Republican organization, the usual mid-term reaction against the party in power, the blunders of war agencies, the hyphenate vote, prohibition, domestic reform, war-weariness and many local matters also determined the outcome. In both houses of Congress the Republicans gained control. In the Senate their one-vote margin rested on a fraudulent canvass in Michigan.[59] In spite of these complex conditions, the Republicans later claimed a mandate on foreign policy. This Wilson would never concede. Nor did Democratic analyses of the returns indicate that foreign policy was the determinant.

The call for a Democratic Congress, Tumulty's idea adjusted to Wilson's purposes, had questionable results. In several states Democratic candidates reported that it helped them, but one observer declared that it cost the party possible Republican votes in New York and Connecticut. McCormick, Burleson, and McAdoo considered the appeal a mistake.[60] Homer Cummings on the other hand, confident that Wilson's action had been justified and beneficial, concluded that it carried Democratic candidates in Kentucky, Montana, and Idaho to victory and prevented worse defeats elsewhere. The major factors in the loss of Congress, he felt, were the sectional issue, the misrepresentation of Wilson's attitude toward Germany, and the large Republican expenditures. Cochran interpreted the returns as evidencing dissatisfaction with Democrats who had not supported the President rather than indicating any lack of confidence in Wilson. And Wilson declared that he was not discouraged.[61]

Tumulty also gave no sign of discouragement, but he was clearly fighting mad. His immediate post-election plans emphasized those political conditions which were more fundamental than any statement Wilson could have made. He felt that the seclusion of the President, necessitated by the war, had made him too remote from the people. Wilson would have to stump the country before 1920. He deplored the inadequate Democratic organization. The labor, hyphenate, and farmer vote needed attention. The party needed funds. Local leadership in several states needed bolstering. But Tumulty concentrated on the sins of the South. He ascribed defeat to the resistance of southern Senators to woman's suffrage and to Kitchin's "unjust legislation" which harassed business and "antagonized" the press. The worst aspect of Southern domination was personified in Kitchin and Clark, who had consistently failed to support the war or to fix the price of cotton. *"We must fight Kitchin,"* Tumulty concluded with emphasis. *"We must fix the price of cotton."* [62]

Tumulty had some responsibility for the mistakes made. He was not the first to inject the foreign policy issue into the campaign, but in exploiting it he added to Wilson's burdens, for silence would have been safer. Both Tumulty and Wilson gambled and lost. Had they won, the President could have claimed a mandate for the League of Nations. Tumulty neglected the wheat-cotton question until too late, but on prohibition, suffrage, the conduct of the war, and the postal rate increase he did everything within his power. Kitchin simply defeated Tumulty before the Republicans defeated Kitchinism. Tumulty's shortcomings were more often the result of lack of influence than lack of insight.

In 1918 the balance of political power shifted to the Grand Old Party. In 1910 and 1912 Wilson rose to power on Republican schism, Democratic unity, and a new Democratic liberalism. In 1914 and 1916 he began to lose his advantages. Slowly the Republicans reunited. And the New Freedom trickled away into the sands of war, its mission accomplished. By 1918 the leadership of the Democratic Party seemed to have reverted in large part to Champ Clark and his southern allies.

Tumulty and Cummings understood the need to reidentify Wilson and the Democracy. The partisan appeal, Tumulty's fondest hopes notwithstanding, had not done this effectively enough. But before 1920 Tumulty hoped to remedy the situation by bolstering the Democratic organization with northern Wilsonians, by taking the President to the hustings, and by removing Clark and Kitchin from leadership in Congress. On November 11 the armistice afforded an excellent opportunity for the reassertion of Wilsonian ideals. In peacemaking, a new international program could emerge under Wilson's own hand. The President could re-establish Democratic reputation in Paris. At home, Tumulty prepared to reinvigorate the party with progressive domestic policies designed for postwar problems, and to reorient the party toward the happier political alignment of 1910 and 1912.

CHAPTER XI

Government by Cable

1. The President's Treaty

THE APOTHEOSIS of Woodrow Wilson depends on his devotion to the concept of continuous peace through world organization. His pursuit of that ideal at the council tables of Paris and in the maelstrom of American politics has provoked endless controversies. Among the earlier and most ardent champions of Wilson's course of action was Tumulty. Loyalty to his chief, consciousness of Wilson's tragedy, belief in the League of Nations, and a misplaced sense of guilt over the inefficacy of his own advice led Tumulty to defend each of Wilson's decisions on the problems and paradoxes of treaty-making and the treaty fight. Tumulty's uncritical valuation is understandable. He wrote before the prolonged, bitter partisanship had subsided. "How we did cherish and nourish our hatreds in those days," the patroness of the anti-Wilsonians has observed.[1] There was no room for tolerance in the immediate afterlook.

Yet while the battle was joined at Paris and at home Tumulty frequently questioned the wisdom of Wilson's policies. Aware always of domestic developments which would not await peace, he strove to bring the President's mind back from preoccupation with diplomacy and world order. With thousands of other Americans he resented many of the procedures and settlements of the Paris Conference. And ultimately he distrusted the methods adopted to obtain ratification of the President's treaty. His memoirs were uncritical, but his counsel was not.

Tumulty's first disagreements with Wilson arose over the selection of the American delegation. Before the armistice was signed Tumulty learned that the President planned to go abroad. Although he did not attempt to dissuade his chief, he told Lansing confidentially that he opposed the plan. And he openly objected to Wilson's choice of companions. Recognizing the desirability of placing at least one eminent Republican on the Commission, he joined Lansing in suggesting that Root be appointed.[2] Political expediency called for some gesture to appease the Republican Senators whose approval of the treaty was essential. Before Tumulty could impress Wilson with this argument, he was called to Jersey City where his father lay dying. Wilson rejected Root as too reactionary. The President conceded little to expediency. Desiring a friendly environment in the American delegation, he looked for men whose views were close to his own.*

Tumulty's protests against the choice of George Creel to handle publicity in Paris were unavailing. Tumulty considered the hostility of American journalists toward Creel reason enough to impel the selection of some other man. Colonel House, however, felt that Tumulty was merely piqued because he was to be left behind. It was true that Tumulty would have liked to accompany his chief, but he agreed with Wilson that he had better stay at home. Whereas he knew nothing of diplomacy, he was well qualified to act as the President's intermediary with Congress, the party, and the general public. Furthermore, from Washington he could estimate the effectiveness of Creel's work. "I am sure," Tumulty wrote Wilson, "that I can render better service by staying on the job . . . and keeping you in touch with affairs here, not only in reference to our own domestic situation, but to let you have, from this side, American impressions of what you are striving to do." [3]

Wilson accepted Tumulty's definition of his task. It was im-

* The American Commissioners were Wilson, House, Lansing, General Tasker H. Bliss, a member of the Supreme War Council, and Henry White, a veteran diplomatist. White, although a Republican, had no political experience, relatively little political prestige, and no influence in his party.

mense. The President today has a staff to divide the burdens of relations with the public, liaison with Congress, and the routing of department business. Tumulty had to handle them alone. The President today can make a flying trip and communicate by telephone while away. Wilson could not move back and forth between Europe and America with ease. Tumulty had to rely on slow ocean mails or clumsy cables to communicate with his chief. The stage of invention and the want of a presidential secretariat posed an extremely difficult governmental situation.

Tumulty's initial concern was with public relations. Lacking confidence in Creel, he sent Wilson and Dr. Grayson, the President's intimate as well as his physician, detailed instructions for dealing with the press. He sought to create an atmosphere of mutual trust and to induce Wilson to engage in those sentimental activities which delight American newspaper readers. The President solicited such advice, but he adopted Tumulty's ideas only at the time when they were least important.

Deep in his heart, Tumulty knew that Wilson usually inspired awe rather than affection. After Theodore Roosevelt died, Tumulty revealed the purpose underlying all his work on Wilson's public relations. "Roosevelt's death left great gap," he cabled Grayson disarmingly. "We must from now on make the people not only admire but love the President." During Wilson's triumphant tour of Europe before the peace conference convened, Tumulty had this end constantly in mind. "If the President visits hospitals have press representatives with him to get human interest story. Do not let his visits be perfunctory. Let him sit beside bed of common soldiers. Keep President in touch with Lawrence, Seibold, Swope, press associations, Hills and Gilbert. Don't forget movie men," Tumulty directed Grayson. "Can't you have President do more mixing with people . . ." he inquired. "Stories . . . only show . . . President as an official living in a palace and guarded by soldiery. . . . Try to get newspapermen Probert, Bender and Levin to inject some emotion in stories. Can't President meet poilus and American soldiers face to face . . .? President's smile is wonderful. Get this over in some way. . . ." [4]

Grayson co-operated with excellent results. Tumulty reported that the publicity in America was "very good," the President's visits to the hospitals made a "wonderful impression," and Grayson and Creel were "doing fine work." By early January 1919, Tumulty was completely satisfied. "Newspapermen without exception treating you in generous fashion," he cabled Wilson. "Your intimacy with them and their confidence in you appears in all stories. You can do nothing more serviceable to the great cause you are pushing forward than to keep close to them." [5]

But press relations, excellent while Wilson toured Europe, got off to a bad start at the Paris Conference. The President directed his fellow American Commissioners to meet daily with the correspondents. He assigned Ray Stannard Baker the task of preparing all formal news releases. Creel was to disseminate the official American point of view in Europe and the United States. These mechanical arrangements, however, were unsatisfactory to the press, for, over Wilson's protests, the Conference adopted a policy of secrecy for all the private councils at which the real negotiations were conducted. Unaware that the President had fought for publicity, American journalists blamed him for their lack of access to the news. Their irritation increased when the Paris press utilized "leaks" spread by French diplomats to publicize favorably the French objectives. Wilson took no steps to dispel the growing hostility of the Fourth Estate. Unlike the heads of the British, French, and Italian delegations, he did not meet regularly with the press, thus ignoring an effective channel for clarifying his actions and aims. Disappointed, sometimes chagrined, forced to rely on stereotyped bulletins and off-the-record "beats," American newspapermen reported the Conference without the enthusiasm or sympathy that better press relations might have produced.

In less than two weeks the tone of dispatches from Europe had changed completely. Tumulty advised Wilson that the news reports "indicated a misunderstanding" of the President's general attitude toward the problems pending at the Conference. "Situation could easily be remedied if you would occasionally call in the three press association correspondents . . . merely giving them an understanding of the developments as they occur," Tumulty suggested. Wilson agreed to do what he could, but he observed impatiently that he would not be able to check the false reports from Paris because the correspondents insisted on writing whether or not they knew the facts.[6]

The secrecy rule adopted by the Conference made knowledge of the "facts" difficult if not impossible. Negotiations may have required closed doors, but Tumulty was wedded to the concept of open diplomacy. He cabled a vigorous protest against secrecy to Grayson: "In my opinion, if the President has consented to this, it will be fatal. . . . He could have afforded to go to any length even to leaving the conference rather than to submit to this ruling. His attitude in this matter will lose a great deal of the confidence and support of the people of the world. . . . " Replying that he had won all that was possible, Wilson obscured the issue by pointing to the open plenary councils at which nothing was decided.[7]

Thereafter Wilson's relations with the press deteriorated steadily. His unwillingness to explain himself to the reporters caused misinterpretations and distortions of the causes and nature of his diplomatic compromises. Tumulty continued to remind Wilson of the necessity for better publicity. In March he warned his chief that "publicity from European end doing great damage here." To improve conditions he resorted to familiar devices. He requested the President to acknowledge favorable articles; through Grayson he sought presidential interviews for important journalists; he asked David Lawrence to show more sympathy for Wilson's point of view.[8] But on the whole Tumulty was pessimistic about the reports from Paris. He realized that the fault was not Creel's or Baker's; it lay with Wilson. Since there was no effective remedy for the President's attitude toward the press, Tumulty hoped to generate American enthusiasm by taking Wilson directly to the people when he returned, and by persuading him to champion specific measures which the people seemed to want.

Wilson, his full energy claimed by events in Paris, was not thinking about American opinion. At the secret meetings where the peace was made he daily faced determined, powerful adversaries: Clemenceau, The Tiger, stubborn spokesman of French nationalism; Lloyd George, energetic, opportunistic guardian of the British Empire; Orlando, an emotional, discerning Italian. These practical men, their arguments buttressed by secret treaties, protected their traditional national interests which frequently ran counter to Wilson's often impracticable, often vague, but altruistic aims. The President had to accept compromises, most of which were little understood in America. Nor did the American people fully understand that the President believed those compromises would be woven into a permanent and just peace by the workings of the League. They read, from the beginning, of American retreats. At the time of the armistice Wilson was forced to abandon, at Britain's insistence, any discussion of freedom of the seas; he was forced to accept in principle the French demand for reparations, a first ingredient of that nation's desire for a punitive peace. During the first phase of the Conference, from January 12 to February 14 of 1919, Wilson lost his fight for open diplomacy. He also accepted, again in principle although not in detail, a colonial settlement by which the victors, excluding the United States, divided Germany's overseas territories. Although these territories were to be governed as mandates of the League, their disposition followed the patterns of old-order diplomacy. The desires of subject peoples received no hearing. In the first period of the Conference Wilson scored one victory: he supervised the draft of the Covenant of the League and forced its acceptance before leaving France on February 15 for a short visit to the United States. He returned on March 14 to discover that his subordinates, in his absence, had yielded further to European demands. During the final phase of the Conference Wilson, compelled to reopen the subject of the League in order to satisfy American sentiment, compelled also to reach a series of detailed geographic and economic decisions within a few months, yielded more. Again he believed that Article XIX of the Covenant, empowering the Assembly of the League to consider for revision treaties the terms of which threatened to endanger peace, would save what had been lost. But to American friends of Germany, Italy, and China the territorial and economic provisions of the treaty seemed unjust. To the Irish the treaty seemed a victory for England. Not conversant with Wilson's difficulties, desiring immediate remedy, they opposed it. And the President, largely because of his poor press, failed to clarify the situation.

The Irish-Americans, both extremists and moderates, watched the peace negotiations with singular interest. Vocal and organized, their opinion was of greater political importance than that of most minority groups. Their paramount desire was that the President act in behalf of home rule for Ireland. His doctrine of self-determination seemed a sufficient mandate for this, but negotiations for self-determination were possible only in the case of conquered peoples. Wilson felt that he could not interfere in England's imperial problems, especially because interference might cause the British to oppose his primary objectives even more actively than they already were. The President held that the League would provide a sounding board for world opinion which would ultimately force England to recognize Irish aspirations. This position did not satisfy Irish-Americans. They expected something immediate and concrete, and they suspected Wilson of hostility, or at least indifference, toward their cause. The Covenant of the League, giving the British Empire six votes in the Assembly to one for the United States, seemed to confirm their suspicions. Pro-Irish and anti-League agitators, overlooking the American veto, made much of the six-to-one ratio as evidence of the President's alleged Anglophilism.

Tumulty was unhappy about the Irish situation. An advocate of home rule, he had continually requested Wilson to discuss the matter with British officials. During the war the President put him off with vague promises and assurances of sympathy.[9] Political as well as personal considerations prompted Tumulty to seek more tangible results while Wilson was abroad. He asserted that the general public as well as the Irish-Americans were "deeply interested," but Wilson seemed determined to run in the face of public opinion. When Representative Flood, a Virginia Democrat, in January 1919, introduced a resolution expressing sympathy for home rule, the President was frankly distressed. He suggested that Tumulty explain to Flood that the resolution would disrupt negotiations with the British. Tumulty replied that such a message would be misconstrued. "There is a deep sentiment here for home rule," he reminded Wilson, "and I do not wish you to be put in position of seeming to oppose it." After persuading Flood to use a concurrent instead of joint resolution, so that no Presidential veto or approval would be necessary, Tumulty informed Wilson that the passage of some kind of Irish resolution was inevitable even if the President actively opposed it.[10]

While Wilson was in the United States on his short visit in late February and early March, Tumulty hoped he could persuade him to espouse the Irish cause. With other moderate supporters of home rule, like George Creel and Sir Horace Plunkett, Tumulty foresaw that the organized effort in America in behalf of Ireland could make Wilson's attitude on the Irish question a dominant factor in the political situation in the United States. He warned Wilson that the American people wanted "to see the Irish question settled in the only way it can be settled — by the establishment of a Home Rule Parliament in Dublin." Requesting an audience for a delegation seeking to present the resolutions of a recent Irish Race Convention, Tumulty reminded Wilson that he had promised to use his influence at every opportunity to bring about a solution of the Irish problem.[11] The President, however, even though the National Democratic Executive Committee had endorsed the Irish resolutions, at first refused to see the delegates. While they waited in Washington, John Sharp Williams announced that Wilson had told him that he definitely would not discuss home rule at the peace conference. Tumulty hastily interceded to change the President's mind. He refuted Williams' statement. He assured the committee from the Irish Race Convention that he was personally sympathetic and would press Wilson on their matter.[12] On the day they visited him, he urged the President to reconsider:

> You have been so busy during the past few days that you have not been able, I think, to give sufficient thought to the importance of the request to receive a delegation to present a resolution with reference to Ireland's cause. Your attitude in this matter is fraught with a great deal of danger both to the Democratic Party and to the cause you represent. . . . Republicans are taking full advantage of this. . . . You know that I am not a professional Irishman but your refusal to see this delegation will simply strengthen the Sinn Fein movement in this country.[13]

Reluctantly, Wilson consented to meet the delegates after his speech at the Metropolitan Opera House, just before his departure to return to Europe. The President refused, however, to see their leader, Daniel F. Cohalan, whose extremism on the Irish question had been tinged with sedition. The rest of the committee resented the exclusion of Cohalan. They found Wilson's answers to their requests for assistance evasive and unsatisfactory. After the conference Eugene Kinkead, one of the Committee, wrote Wilson a polite letter clearly suggesting the displeasure of his fellow delegates.[14]

Tumulty's cables during the next months expressed his continued alarm over the situation. The President's evasiveness had done incalculable damage to the League idea. The contention of the Irish-American press that Article X * was designed to protect the British Empire would have gained less currency had Wilson been more considerate of Irish-American feelings. Sean O'Ceallaigh, delegate of the provisional Irish Republic to the Paris Conference, confidently asserted that unless the Irish question were resolved favorably, the friends of Ireland would prevent ratification of the peace treaty in America. A group of Democratic Senators repeated this warning to Wilson. Tumulty cabled Grayson that the "real intensity of feeling behind Irish question . . . not at all confined to Irishmen," could not be overestimated.[15] But these appeals were too late. Wilson replied that unofficially he had practically cleared the way for the reception of Irish representatives at the Conference when the Irish-American delegation by their indiscretions in Ireland

---

* Article X was the section of the Covenant most hotly debated in the United States. Wilson considered it the core of the Covenant, a moral commitment through which peace could be preserved. His opponents, however, argued, at times, that it underwrote the *status quo*, for example in the British Empire, and, at other times, that it violated the traditional American practice of avoiding European quarrels, the advice of Washington's Farewell Address, the *quid pro quo* for European respect for the Monroe Doctrine. The text of Article X follows:

The Members of the League undertake to respect and preserve as against external aggression the territorial integrity and existing political independence of all Members of the League. In case of any such aggression or in case of any threat or danger of such aggression the Council shall advise upon the means by which this obligation shall be fulfilled.

inflamed British opinion against their cause. He could see no way to proceed further.

Tumulty did not give up. He begged his chief not to allow the indiscretions of the delegates to influence his judgment against Ireland. "It is our own political situation here and the fate of the treaty itself that concerns me," Tumulty explained. "In this country the Irish are united. . . . Could you not ask that the Irish delegates be given a chance to present their case to the Conference." Wilson either could not or would not. Once more Tumulty tried. "Just a word for Ireland would help a great deal," he cabled briefly. But the President ended the discussion as he had begun it, on a vague, promissory note. He replied that the League as a forum of public opinion would lead to the solution of Ireland's problems.[16]

Although disappointed and apprehensive, Tumulty accepted his chief's decision. There was no use in continuing the argument. He set out faithfully, therefore, to defend the President's point of view. In a long letter to Father John F. Ryan of Jersey City, who had withdrawn his support of Wilson because of the President's attitude, Tumulty presented his case:

> . . . I am proud of my Irish blood, and . . . there has never been a time throughout my adult life in which I have not hoped for Ireland's freedom, spoken for it, and worked for it to the limit of my ability. My convictions as to the justice of Ireland's contentions are unchanged and unchangeable, for not all the mistakes of leadership nor the folly of individuals can alter the fundamental justice of the Irish cause. I am, however, an American before I am an Irishman, and not even the deep love that I bear to the land of my fathers can induce me to divide my allegiance. I do not, therefore, write to you as an Irishman, but as an American bound to Ireland by ties of blood and belief. . . .
>
> Your position . . . is taken entirely with reference to Ireland. The United States plays no part in your reasoning or emotion. . . .
>
> Is it your idea that the President should have stated to the assembled Powers that he could not discuss peace terms, or

anything else, until the rights of Ireland were recognized and allowed? You know, and I know, just as every person of intelligence knows, that this would have been an absurdity bordering on madness.

Nor was there any time throughout the entire conference when it would have been possible or proper for the President to have made demands for the recognition of the Irish Republic. Do you doubt for one single moment, or does any one of intelligence doubt, that England would have refused to give consideration to the demand, or that the other powers, concerned primarily with their own war ravaged countries, would not have joined with England in resentment? The Peace Conference would have broken up in confusion, separate peace treaties would have had to be made, and all hope of building foundations of justice for the world would have been destroyed.

What the President proceeded to do, and what he did do, was to effect the creation of a machinery that, with the coming of peace, would be able to put into force the declared ideals of America with respect to the rights of weak peoples and the high principles of self-determination. It is not alone Ireland that cried to the world for the right to determine its form of government. . . .

It was in the Covenant of the League of Nations that the President . . . kept his promise to humanity. There was no other way in which he could have kept this promise. Not only does the League of Nations grant protection to . . . weak peoples . . . but it provides opportunity for all the oppressed of the world to have their day in court. . . .

[Article XI] gives any member of the League the right to bring the case of Ireland before the League of Nations, or any case of any other people whose bitterness and revolts menace the peace of the world. . . .

Yet you, and many others like you . . . give only your hate and opposition to the one possible solution that is contained in the organization of the League of Nations. . . .

Ireland has never had a truer friend than Woodrow Wilson. . . . It has been his steadfast effort to induce the Government

of England to settle the Irish question justly and permanently.
. . . He is the most intelligent champion of the Irish cause for his
approach . . . is the only one that holds hope of success. . . .

I view this whole situation with a great deal of alarm. Meetings in which Ireland is put before America, and in which the
President of the United States is hissed, are bound to bring
reactions that may possibly restore the evil days of Know-
Nothingism and the A.P.A. We have just passed through one
painful experience with the hyphen, and the people of the
United States . . . will not stand for another manifestation of
divided allegiance.

I feel that Ireland is going to be free. . . . It can only be free
in company with the rest of the world. And the machinery for
the justice and the liberty that is to mark the new world order
is found only in the Covenant of the League of Nations.[17]

The Irish were only one of many national groups disappointed
by the negotiations at Paris. The aspirations of European peoples
were reflected by many first and second generation Americans who
condemned Wilson's part in the treaty-making. Italian-Americans
objected to the disposition of Fiume, a valuable Adriatic port which
was made part of Yugoslavia. German-Americans considered the
treaty too harsh, the reparations too large, and the war-guilt clause
unjust. Tumulty did not sympathize with them, but he feared
their growing prejudices. He implored the President to keep alive
the Division of Work with the Foreign-Born of the Committee on
Public Information, the government's only agency of counterpropaganda. But lacking sufficient funds, Wilson was forced to let
the agency disband.[18]

Native American opinions were equally worrisome to Tumulty.
The Shantung settlement, the result of prolonged efforts at compromise, seemed to many Americans to favor Japan at the expense of
China. Japan inherited the German concessions in the Shantung
Province, which violated Chinese self-determination. Japan promised, however, to restore full sovereignty in the area to China, retaining only the former German financial concessions, which she
in time did. Had Japan not received these terms, she would not

have accepted the treaty; as it was, China rejected it. The Chinese point of view captured America. Little conversant with the diplomatic difficulties confronting Wilson, Tumulty urged the President to take a stronger stand against Japan. When the compromise had been reached he reported the general hostility of the press. Wilson's careful explanation satisfied Tumulty, but Shantung remained a sore point in the American attitude toward the peace.[19]

The give and take over a redisposition of European soil, reparations, the government of backward areas, all the complexities of the peace, confused Americans. Unlearned in world politics, naïvely confident that the United States almost single-handed had won the war, distrustful of Old World diplomacy, they did not understand delay and compromise. Tumulty was as unsophisticated as most of his countrymen. He wanted Wilson in April "in some dramatic way" to "clear the air of doubts and misunderstandings and despair," but he considered the President's order that the *George Washington* return to France, presumably a threat that Wilson would leave the Conference, "an act of impatience and petulance." [20] Tumulty expected Wilson somehow to persuade the Conference to adopt each American demand, to fight for the Fourteen Points until the other diplomats gave in or departed. But not only did he fail to appreciate the difficulties in Wilson's position, he was also confused as to what the President should seek. Tumulty was anxious to dodge the problem of reparations, afraid of a soft peace, but also afraid that a harsh one would lead to Bolshevism in Germany. He was convinced that the League and a just peace were inseparable, but wary of the proposed defense treaty with France and England that gave force to the principles of the League. Wilson, harassed at the council tables, intent on rescuing what he could of his grand vision, simply ignored the well-intentioned advice of his Secretary, a reflection of American opinion. And trusting his chief to find the best way, Tumulty advised but did not interfere.

Those in Paris with Wilson could interfere as well as advise. The President treated offenders brusquely. He antagonized Lansing and young William C. Bullitt. And at Paris the long, close friendship of Wilson and House came to an end. The Colonel did not always agree with Wilson. He talked freely with the press, consulted secretly with European diplomats, and, from Wilson's point of view, endangered the League by his activities while the President was in America. Wilson felt that House had undone all that he had accomplished. Although the Colonel had agreed to various proposals that compromised the Fourteen Points, Wilson's assessment was unfair. The President himself later yielded as had House to the realities of peacemaking. But the Colonel in 1919 suffered as Tumulty had in 1916. Mrs. Wilson's jealousy of House undermined his position, and before the Conference ended Wilson had stopped speaking to his former intimate. The Colonel never fully understood why, but he realized that the President, in attempting single-handed to achieve the impossible, ruined his health and his disposition.[21] Tumulty was correct in citing petulance. Had he known of the dissatisfaction felt by House and Lansing, he would have understood better the dangers in the path his chief was taking. Wilson aimed high and strove valiantly; everything considered, he did well; possibly none could have achieved greater justice. But both friends and principles perished at Paris. And each friend lost, each principle compromised, complicated the fate of the treaty in America.

All the discouraging conditions involved in peacemaking and in domestic attitudes toward peacemaking might have been overcome had it not been for political factors. The peace treaty and the League of Nations became a partisan issue even before Wilson left for Paris. The President's failure to appoint an influential Republican to the Commission incited further partisanship. And although he knew of the prejudices which the Republicans could exploit, although he realized their strength in the Senate, Wilson made few concessions to his opponents and no serious effort to disengage the treaty or the League from American politics.

Tumulty clearly foresaw the impending battle over the treaty. Much closer than was the President to the Democratic floor leaders in the Senate, he must have had advance information on Lodge's Round Robin of March 1919. This statement, signed by thirty-three Republican Senators or Senators-elect, declared that peace should first be negotiated with Germany and only then should a League be considered — a clear warning that over a third of the

Senate — enough to defeat any treaty — opposed Wilson's policies. But while seeking to dissipate nationalistic feelings against the treaty, Tumulty almost welcomed the more dangerous partisanship, apparently confident that Wilson would emerge victorious, and, in winning, buttress the Democracy for 1920. He was sure that the settlement would be just, sure that the people and the Senate could be persuaded to accept it. "It is clear that the Republican party intends to oppose the League of Nations," Tumulty wrote William J. Cochran, the publicity director of the Democratic National Committee, in early February. ". . . In our publicity, therefore, from now on we should drive home to ordinary minds the consistency and deliberate character of the Republican opposition. Their much-vaunted cry of support to the President, put forward by them in the last campaign, is gradually being . . . shown to be a hollow mockery." He suggested that Cochran prepare a brochure of statements of Republican Senators criticizing and ridiculing the negotiations and the League. This brochure was to demonstrate that Republican arguments on specific points were merely façades for unrestrained partisanship.[22]

Tumulty relied on Wilson to popularize the treaty. He intended to make the President's visit to America between trips abroad a reception for a hero and an education for his worshipers. He advised Wilson to return through Boston and New England, the heartland of the radical Irish and the conservative Republicans, making speeches as he traveled south to Washington. Proper demonstrations would be arranged for the "effect on Capitol Hill." To mark the return to Washington, Tumulty suggested that Wilson march at the head of a parade of veterans. The President considered these plans premature since his work in Europe was far from completed, but he agreed to one impromptu speech in Boston and to the parade in Washington provided that the rest of the program was abandoned. While Wilson was in the United States Tumulty worked hard on public relations: he supervised the President's welcome in Boston; he planned a great meeting in the Metropolitan Opera House; when Wilson met the Senate Foreign Relations Committee to confer on the treaty, Tumulty made sure that the press had every comfort and facility.[23]

Brochures, speeches, headlines, and applause, however, were meager weapons against the Republicans. Will Hays, chairman of the Republican National Committee, was a public-relations expert, Lodge a masterful parliamentarian. Before returning to France Wilson saw ample evidence of the strength of the organized opposition to the League. Yet he could not believe that his opponents would reject the entire treaty. That seemed to him too sinful. Defiantly he boasted that they would have to take the League, for the League would be part of the treaty.

Tumulty made no protests against Wilson's strategy, but gradually he came to realize that the whole treaty could fail in America. The voters did not worry him; he interpreted the success of a Democratic Congressional candidate in a Pennsylvania by-election, who had made his campaign on endorsement of the League, as evidence of popular approval.[24] But even if the people were friendly, the Republicans in the Senate presented real obstacles. Lodge packed the Foreign Relations Committee with Wilson's opponents. In an effort to win the support of less adamant Republicans than Lodge, Tumulty in late March acted as intermediary for ex-President Taft, relaying Taft's suggestions for changes in the Covenant to Wilson.[25] The President agreed on the need for concessions. At the expense of his prestige and bargaining power, he reopened negotiations on the Covenant after his return to Europe and succeeded in incorporating many of Taft's modifications.

During the spring, bad publicity, the compromises at Paris, and the Republican propaganda campaign overshadowed Wilson's concessions. The Knox Resolution for a separate peace with Germany, which Wilson considered "mad," was evidence of the extremes to which isolationist and partisan sentiment would go. Tumulty warned Wilson that the Republicans were "taking full advantage" of "a decided reaction" against the League caused by the dissatisfaction of American-Irish, Jews, Poles, Italians, and Germans. He recommended strongly that Wilson, Lansing, or Henry White explain the transactions that had occasioned the most adverse comment in the United States — the failure to publish the text of the treaty, the seeming disregard of the Fourteen Points, the defense pact with England and France.[26]

Nevertheless Tumulty denied that he was discouraged. He felt that upon Wilson's return his power of persuasion would overcome opposition. Late in June, advising the President that Root and Taft would insist that ratification depend on reservations to the Covenant relative to the Monroe Doctrine, immigration, and the tariff, Tumulty opposed any further concessions. Wilson agreed, defining reservations as the equivalent of rejection. Tumulty confidently predicted to Seibold that the Republicans would make reservations "the final line of defense and they will meet failure." [27]

With Wilson on his way home, treaty in hand, Tumulty was ready for a fight. At the President's request he cabled a list of Senators, editors, and public men opposed to the treaty, a roster of the enemy.[28] Carefully he laid out the strategy by which he hoped to rout them. He had already prepared a tentative itinerary for the President, taking him over the country to address the people directly. For Wilson's immediate attention he had suggestions for a speech to be delivered to the Senate, presenting the treaty and relating that bulky document, in the precise form Wilson preferred, to the problems of world reconstruction.

Any alterations in the treaty, Tumulty argued, would cause delay beyond the margin of safety. In the United States alone, domestic conditions demanded concentrated and uninterrupted attention from an executive free from the worries of negotiation and ratification.[29] Fortunately for his peace of mind, Tumulty expected that ratification of the treaty would be quick and complete.

2. *The American Scene*

During the eight months Wilson spent in Europe, he relied on Tumulty for advice on domestic affairs. Politics and postwar adjustments could not await the making of peace. While the diplomats debated, the Democratic Party had to be strengthened. Unemployment, labor troubles, inflation, the Red scare, and prohibition came to occupy more and more the attention of the American people.

Tumulty dealt with these matters in accordance with his post-election plans of 1918. But the absence of the President was a serious handicap. The necessity for communication by cable caused delay and prevented full discussion. And without Wilson's immediate authority, Tumulty had no way of disciplining the Democratic members of the Administration and Congress.

Tumulty endeavored, with little success, to remove the political liabilities of 1918. While the lame-duck Congress still sat, he helped Senator Simmons in January 1919, renew the attack on Kitchin's increase of postage on second-class matter. Tumulty advised Wilson that Simmons could prevail only with Presidential support. Two weeks later, describing Kitchin as indifferent to party or public interests, Tumulty again sought Wilson's aid. This time Wilson complied, but he acted too late. Kitchin's views, accepted by the Senate and House conferees, were part of the badly needed revenue bill. Simmons and Tumulty agreed that it would be dangerous to revive the issue.[30]

In the matter of prohibition Tumulty was blocked by law. The war measure prohibited the manufacture and sale of alcoholic beverages until demobilization should be completed. Tumulty suggested that Wilson, by proclamation, could lift the ban on the theory that the purpose of the act had been accomplished. Once the treaty was signed, he argued, the tenure of the act would expire. The conservation of grain would no longer be necessary. And six months of beer, a boon to returning veterans and the laborers of the nation, would be possible before the Eighteenth Amendment took effect. Wilson was willing to follow this suggestion if the Attorney General would attest to the legality of such a decree, but the Justice Department ruled that it could not be done.[31] Frustrated by this ruling, Tumulty then tried to put the blame for prohibition on the Republican Congress. He persuaded Wilson to insert a passage in his message to Congress of May 1919, recommending that the wartime statute be revised to permit the manufacture and sale of light wines and beers until the Eighteenth Amendment took force.[32] But Congress did not act. As a lure to the "wet" vote, Wilson's words were a poor substitute for a glass of beer.

In the case of woman suffrage Tumulty could find satisfaction.

The excellent work done by American women during the war strengthened their claim to a vote. Tumulty continued to champion their cause. Following his advice, Wilson helped to secure the necessary votes in the Senate by personal requests and in his formal messages.[33] Not until the new Congress convened, however, was Tumulty's persistence rewarded. In June, with the support of many once hostile Democrats, the suffrage amendment passed the Senate.

Southern domination of the Democracy, in Tumulty's view the most important factor in the defeat of 1918, continued unchallenged in Congress. Neither Tumulty nor the Democratic Congressmen from the North and West could dispute the claims of the Southern Representatives to the best minority positions. Champ Clark became minority leader and Kitchin retained his influence. The southern delegation had survived the election relatively intact, whereas their northern colleagues had lost heavily to the Republicans. Recognizing that the Northerners were inferior in seniority as well as in number, Tumulty avoided a futile struggle which would only have divided the party further.[34]

Outside of Congress, however, Tumulty gave battle to the South. Changes in the Cabinet precipitated a sectional fight. Shortly after the armistice, McAdoo and Attorney General Gregory having resigned, Carter Glass and Walker D. Hines, both Southerners, divided McAdoo's jobs as Secretary of the Treasury and Director General of the Railroads respectively. But when Gregory urged Wilson to elevate Carroll Todd, Assistant Attorney General, a Virginian, to his place, Tumulty, McCormick, Cummings, Woolley, and even Burleson objected to the appointment.[35] Tumulty organized the opposition to Todd, relaying the unfavorable views of the party's leaders to Wilson. As a positive antidote, he marshaled support for A. Mitchell Palmer for the vacancy. One of the original Wilsonians, Palmer had been identified with the Administration in various capacities since its beginning. He was a friend of Tumulty, and sympathetic with his plans for reorganization of the party. Resolved to keep the patronage of the Justice Department from the South, Tumulty expounded Palmer's virtues in presenting his name to Wilson:

Frankly our party here is dispirited and needs stimulation. Todd's selection . . . without value as affecting morale. . . . Your attitude toward the future of our Party will be measured by this appointment. Palmer young, militant, progressive and fearless. . . . Stands well with country, Congress, appeals to young voter; effective on stump. McCormick, Cummings and whole Democratic Committee in favor his selection. Roper, a Southern man, one of our wisest friends, heartily endorses him; says it would be disastrous to appoint Southern man. . . . This issue is more acute than you realize. Republicans taking full advantage. . . . This office great power politically. We should not trust it to any one who is not heart and soul with us. . . . Our enemies and some of our friends have the feeling that you do not care to recognize the services of those who stood by us in the dark days. . . . The ignoring of men of high type of Palmer who have been faithful throughout will accentuate this feeling. The Democratic party, under your inspiring leadership, by slight changes can be made a great and militant organization. I know you will supply us with the tonic. . . .[36]

The President acquiesced. He informed Gregory that Palmer was the most available man. After learning of his appointment, Palmer wrote Tumulty a deserved letter of thanks.[37]

Tumulty was encouraged by changes in the National Committee. He had learned to respect Vance McCormick, and missed him when he resigned the chairmanship. This loss, however, was overbalanced by the election of Homer Cummings of Connecticut to the vacancy. Wilson preferred Cummings to anyone else. He was experienced, energetic, of liberal reputation, and decidedly pro-League. Although not intimate with Cummings, Tumulty found communication with him easier and more rewarding than with his predecessors.[38] The new chairman had agreed with Tumulty on political strategy in 1918 and on the causes of defeat, and he had never been a satellite of Colonel House. Moreover he was closely identified with the Northern wing of the Democracy.

Offsetting the strength that Palmer and Cummings commanded

were new political difficulties. McAdoo's resignation cost the Administration the services of its most forceful and ambitious statesman. With Wilson away McAdoo's executive capacity was badly needed. The rest of the Cabinet lacked proper direction. Disagreements on policy between William Wilson and Burleson, between Hines and Redfield, weakened the Democratic front, particularly in regard to controlling inflation.[39]

In Congress the Republicans exploited their position skillfully. They forced Wilson to call the new Congress into session by refusing to vote needed appropriations in the old, thus taking over control of the committees in May 1919. Their investigations of the conduct of the war embarrassed the Democrats even when no evil was discovered. Tumulty warned Wilson that Republican inquiries into court-martial procedures would cost the Democrats the veterans' vote unless the War Department democratized the military courts and reviewed wartime convictions.[40] To overcome the inertia of military institutions, however, called for more energy than the President cared to expend.

Congressional investigation of profiteering caused Tumulty personal pain. Again as in 1917, he suffered only because his office was a handy political target. The Senate Agricultural Committee, while conducting hearings on the meat-packing industry, found that an anonymous "Diamond T" had given the packers advance information on government plans. The Committee also discovered that Thomas F. Logan, a journalist and a close friend of Tumulty, was the packers' lobbyist in Washington. For several days gossip in the capitol identified Tumulty with "Diamond T." All the unpleasantness of the "leak" investigation was revived. But further hearings disclosed that Logan himself was "Diamond T." Tumulty had no connection with the packers' lobby.[41]

The aggressiveness of the Republicans, the memory of Democratic defeat in the mid-term elections, the lack of executive leadership, and the intra-party friction that developed with long rule demoralized many Democrats. Tumulty and Cummings recognized and combated inertia and defeatism. But they needed Wilson who still personified the success of bygone days. Consequently, when the question of a third term was broached by the Springfield

Republican, Tumulty was cautious. In his own mind, he firmly opposed the idea. He had heard Wilson tell the National Committee that he would return to private life in 1921,[42] but Tumulty feared that a public announcement to that effect would further dispirit those Democrats who felt lost while the President was away. Furthermore, until the disposition of the treaty was settled, Cummings could threaten another Wilson campaign if the League were not ratified. On his Secretary's advice the President refused comment on the *Republican's* editorial.[43]

To overcome Democratic weakness in Washington, Tumulty turned to effective organization on state levels. In 1912 Wilson's strength had rested as much on friendly machines as on friendly liberals. For 1920 Tammany had already been won, but Tumulty, McAdoo, and House gave the Wigwam further assurance of amity by seeking a major federal appointment for the New Yorker Martin Glynn.[44] Turning to a newer but even more powerful machine, Tumulty in 1919 made peace with Hague.

Early in January, at Tumulty's instigation, the Democratic leaders of New Jersey gathered to attempt to resolve their differences and unite on a gubernatorial candidate. But Hague and Nugent distrusted each other and the liberals distrusted them both. After the conference the anti-Hague Democrats of Jersey City proposed to Tumulty that he enter the primary as a candidate for governor. They suggested that even if he could not win the support of all the factions, his prestige and Wilson's would carry the day. But Tumulty rejected the plan. He had learned from Hague that the Hudson organization was committed to E. I. Edwards. To defeat Edwards would have been prohibitively expensive if not politically impossible. Realizing that Tumulty's refusal was a recognition of Hague's power, the liberals abandoned their plans to contest the election. Campaigning almost exclusively on the liquor issue, obviously supported by the "beer barrel," Edwards routed Jim Nugent in the primary. Hague had gained control of the state.[45] Tumulty's silence, in contrast to his letter to Simpson in 1918, indicated once more Tumulty's realistic knowledge of when to surrender. Wilson's program and Democratic unity for 1920 had made opposition to the power in Jersey City unwise.

In contrast to the concert with Tammany and Hague, was Tumulty's plan for postwar reconstruction at home — the counterpart of the New Freedom of 1912. The treaty and the League were to be only one part of the Democratic achievement. Of more direct concern to the voters were the domestic problems arising from readjustment to peace. In his consideration of these issues, Tumulty proposed an amalgam of laissez-faire and paternalism, a program designed to remedy specific economic conditions, to conform with current political attitudes, and to combat the spread of Bolshevism.

The Russian Revolution disturbed Tumulty profoundly. His political and religious convictions precluded sympathy for its methods or purposes. This instinctive repulsion for Bolshevism was impeccable, but with many of his fellow countrymen Tumulty overestimated communist strength in 1919. Like them, he interpreted a few instances of radical violence as portents of revolution. While self-appointed vigilantes, confused state and local governments, and circulation-minded editors manufactured a Red scare, no responsible Administration official interceded to define the situation properly or to protect the civil and personal liberties of individual victims of hysteria. Attorney General Palmer, at once a victim of hysteria and, to generate his presidential boom, a sponsor of it, ordered midnight raids and arbitrary imprisonments. His agents rounded up and deported many aliens whose activities did not clearly endanger this or any other nation. Against Palmer's deplorable policies Tumulty failed even to protest, but he did with courageous conviction forward to Wilson, with a favorable endorsement, a request for the pardon of Eugene Debs, the Socialist leader.[46] The pardon was refused.

Releasing their leftover wartime emotions in red-baiting, Americans transferred this antipathy to milder forms of socialism. Tired of all restrictions, they opposed a continuation of existing controls. Tumulty bowed to public opinion. Forsaking the principles of his "Revolt of the Underdog," he abandoned all hope of government ownership of the systems of transportation and communication. The Republicans were skillfully exploiting public sentiment, promising to return the railroads, telephones, and telegraph to private management by acts of Congress. Tumulty, less than a month after the armistice, urged Wilson to pre-empt that issue: "I hope you do not intend to advocate government ownership or even hint at the permanent control either of the railroads, the telegraph, telephone or cable lines," he advised his chief. "The result would be to divide the country on an economic issue when . . . you may be called upon to ask the backing of the country in favor of . . . the League of Nations." [47]

Although Wilson, in his message to Congress of December 1918, left the fate of the railroads up to Congress and refrained from discussion of the other nationally managed industries, his party continued to be identified with government control. Burleson opposed the return of the telegraph and telephone systems until provision could be made for adequate compensation to the owners and more extensive government regulation of rates and services in the future, the very questions delaying the return of the railroads. [48]

Tumulty considered Burleson's recommendations "fraught with grave peril." He saw no chance of their passing Congress. And Burleson aggravated matters by his administration. Clarence Mackay, the president of the Postal Telegraph Company, complained to Tumulty that the Postmaster General discriminated against his firm. Both Postal and Western Union maintained that even a financial loss was preferable to continued government control. Laborers employed by the telephone and telegraph companies found Burleson unreasonable and oppressive. [49] Politically, Burleson's most dangerous act was an increase in rates, ordered in May 1919. Tumulty tried to get Wilson to stop the Postmaster General, but the President would do no more than ask Burleson whether he was sure the new rates were necessary. Palmer, Scott Ferris, and Tumulty were distressed by the unfavorable public reaction. Thirty-seven states protested against the increase. [50] Discovering labor, management, and the public for once in complete agreement, Tumulty implored the President to announce that the telephone and telegraph systems would be returned at an early date, leaving the problem of compensation to Congress:

. . . There is no present source of irritation and popular discontent . . . comparable with that growing out of the continuance of control. . . . Public opinion is not ready for Government control of railroads, telegraph, or telephone lines or cable. . . . The wise, constructive thing to do is to announce . . . that you have definitely determined to return all of these instrumentalities to private control, but that you will insist upon the immediate enactment by the Congress of appropriate legislation to protect the rights of security holders. . . . This is the practical politics of the situation. Frankly, the people are sick of all kinds of control and war restriction. . . . [They] are going through a period of reaction . . . and they are irritable and impatient of every interference, however laudable its purpose.[51]

. . . The Government's control of these systems has produced nothing but criticism and discontent. The sooner we can get rid of them the better. . . . Mr. Mackay of the Postal, is begging for the return of his systems, claiming that no legislation is necessary to protect his property. You can have no idea of the intensity of feeling of the people in these matters. . . .[52]

But Wilson, while physically and intellectually removed from the situation, would not make a final decision on the problem of government management.

Although opposed to a continuation of wartime control, Tumulty did not wish the government to abdicate its rôle in the national economy. Interpreting Bolshevism as a symptom of unrest, he wisely sought an antidote in constructive economic policies. In part he relied on such earlier legislation as the Federal Reserve Act and the Rural Credits Act to help the country through the difficult period of reconversion. He also advocated new measures. To assist business he recommended that burdensome taxes be repealed. He advised Wilson to consult with Professor Taussig, the leading American tariff authority, about readjusting the tariff to protect those industries which had grown up during the war. Tumulty also suggested that the President remove the ban against the construction of foreign-owned vessels in American shipyards in order to revive production and permit re-employment of the workers who had been laid off.[53]

Tumulty did not trust industry to do the job alone. By direct government action he proposed to stimulate the economy through public works projects. He felt that only aggressive, remedial action would insure prosperity. Drawing on the plans of the departments of Agriculture, Labor, and Interior, Tumulty prepared a broad program for Wilson's consideration during his few days in America between trips abroad. With some of the projects the President was already familiar, but none had previously progressed beyond the blueprint stage. Tumulty called attention to Secretary Lane's plans for land reclamation which would provide employment for thousands of soldiers and civilians, and new farms for veterans. He suggested that Logan Page of the Good Roads Bureau, by conferring with chiefs of the road departments of the various states, could stimulate highway construction throughout the country. He recommended that Wilson call a conference of governors to encourage an exchange of ideas and information on other public works projects. Washington was too relaxed, Tumulty declared. The great need was to renew the energy of tired officials, replacing them where necessary by fresher men, not unqualified lame-ducks, but young men with vision and a capacity for work. The wartime spirit had vanished in the executive departments. "The President," Tumulty concluded, "ought to get on the job. . . . with both feet." [54]

Wilson, however, was not ready in February and March to face domestic problems. He was willing to review such legislation as Houston or Lane might draft, to sponsor Logan Page's conference, even to summon the governors, but anxious to hurry back to Europe, and preoccupied with the treaty while in America, he was unwilling to sit down with the governors or to attempt a reorganization of personnel.[55] He accomplished little, postponing serious consideration of unemployment and public works as he had postponed consideration of government control of the telephone and telegraph.

During the spring of 1919, while the President was again in France, high prices and labor troubles disturbed Washington. Unemployment decreased as a postwar boom began, but government officials were unable to agree on any antidote for the high cost of living, a condition that harassed the employed as well as the jobless.

Redfield proposed that voluntary price reductions be sought through action of a special committee to be appointed by the Department of Commerce. But Senators of both parties from the wheat belt, whose votes were needed in the treaty fight, protested that Redfield's plan would cut the price of agricultural products.[56] The farm bloc was powerful at both ends of Pennsylvania Avenue. The purchases of the Wheat Administration sustained the price of foodstuffs, the major source of public discontent. Tumulty informed Wilson of the unpopularity of that agency among consumers. "Issue of high cost of living most acute," he cabled. ". . . Wheat is keystone in arch of high prices. . . . You cannot understand how acute situation is brought about by rising prices of every necessity of life." [57] But again the President was lost in diplomacy. Lacking guidance, department heads pursued independent, conflicting courses, some advancing, others retarding inflation.

The rising cost of living contributed to the labor problem. Voluntarily restrained during the war, American unions sought a larger share of the postwar income and a fuller recognition of their bargaining rights. Tumulty supported these objectives. At first he spoke vaguely for industrial democratization, but after clashing with Burleson during a strike of telephone workers in New England, he formulated a program of specific measures in behalf of organized labor.

When the Postmaster General refused to advance wages after he had increased rates, the employees of the New England Telephone and Telegraph Company prepared to walk out. Felix Frankfurter, then Secretary of the War Labor Policies Board, reported that Burleson had consistently refused to recognize the principle of collective bargaining, discriminated against union men, and ignored the grievances of telephone workers whose pay was inadequate. Tumulty agreed with this analysis. He warned Wilson that unless he acted to modify Burleson's attitude, the movement in New England would spread. Telegraphers all over the country had taken a strike vote. But the Postmaster General insisted that wages and bargaining facilities were adequate, ascribing discontent to the agita-

tion of a small number of radicals.[58] Wilson issued no orders from
Paris. On April 16 the strike in New England began.

Acting on his own responsibility, Tumulty attempted to mediate
between the union officials and the representatives of the Post
Office Department. As a last resort he promised to appeal to
Wilson. Meanwhile New England Republican Governors Coolidge,
Bartlett, and Beeckman requested the President to intervene. But
Wilson declined, holding that he was too far away to exercise judg-
ment. His declination, disrupting Tumulty's private negotiations,
left the issue with Burleson.[59]

With Mayor Peters and ex-Mayor Curley of Boston supporting
his arguments, Tumulty went to work to persuade Burleson to
adopt a more conciliatory attitude. The Postmaster General agreed
to promise the strikers fair treatment. With Tumulty he proposed
that they submit their demands to the General Manager of the New
England Telephone Company. Tumulty appealed to their leader,
Miss Julia O'Connor, to accept this plan, but she wanted something
more substantial than Burleson's promise. Only after six days of negotiations was the strike settled. The strikers received an increase in
wages, but rates were to be raised to cover the increment.[60]

The long period of suspended telephone service had hurt the
Democrats. Calvin Coolidge, Republican Governor of Massachusetts, had suggested that his state take over the telephone lines "for
the duration of the disability of the United States Government to
furnish telephone service." The president of the Democratic Club
of Massachusetts had cabled Wilson that Burleson was "wrecking
the party." This opinion, shared by many leading Democrats, fortified Tumulty's growing conviction that the Postmaster General
had become a political liability and should be dismissed from office.[61]

The political implications of the telephone strike forced Tumulty
to crystallize his thinking on labor. To prevent disturbances in
private as well as government-controlled industries some definite
program was needed. In his recommendations for Wilson's message to Congress in May, Tumulty began to spell out a plan. He
suggested that a system of shop committees to bargain with employ-

ers could be useful. To co-ordinate and direct those conciliation agencies already existing, he proposed that a national labor conference committee be established. And he advocated new child-labor legislation to circumvent judicial nullification of earlier statutes.[62] In the next few weeks Tumulty's ideas matured. The day after A. Mitchell Palmer's home was bombed, he presented them to Wilson. Demanding something "vitally reconstructive" to save the country from Bolshevism, Tumulty suggested that the President summon a national industrial conference of employers and employees "to recommend a national plan for the improvement of relations between capital and labor." This conference would be directed to consider many large questions affecting business: government ownership of the railroads; the stock-piling of oil, steel, and coal; the affairs of bankrupt public utilities companies; a definition of reasonable return on investments. But primarily the conference was to concern itself with the labor problem.[63]

Tumulty, however, had already made up his mind on a minimal labor program. Overcoming his normal middle-class sympathies, breaking through the economic naïvete that he shared with most Wilsonians, transcending the prejudices engendered by the Red scare, he demonstrated the wisdom of mature statesmanship. With his letter on the industrial conference, he sent an outline of legislation intended to remove the causes of strikes and to strengthen the position of labor. In this, perhaps the most penetrating memorandum of his career, Tumulty foreshadowed the Democracy of the nineteen thirties. He recommended government assistance in the development of consumer co-operatives to reduce labor's cost of living, and the establishment of federal home loan banks to extend credit on easy terms for the construction of workmen's homes. He called for federal vocational training for those injured in industrial pursuits, and for a permanent federal employment agency. He advocated federal health insurance and old age pensions, and he sought federal laws fixing minimum wages, establishing an eight-hour day, and recognizing the right of collective bargaining. For these matters he asked the President's immediate attention. Only by volunteering real concessions to industrial unrest, Tumulty declared, could America resist the radicalism sweeping Europe.[64] This was an enlightened answer to bomb-throwing. Its usefulness rested initially on the approval of Wilson, who promised to study Tumulty's program on his way home.[65]

* * * * *

Tumulty awaited his chief's return impatiently. The fate of the peace treaty, the solution of domestic problems, the future of the Democratic Party depended on a resumption of leadership in the White House. In Wilson's absence, while the Republicans exploited the opposition to his foreign policy and the crises in the economy, the Democrats had been disunited and enervated. Tumulty lacked the prestige and the power to whip the party into action. But he had formulated definite plans for the treaty fight and for domestic reconstruction. Confident that these would save the situation as soon as Wilson could implement them, he took pains to reassure his chief:

> You are in possession, I know, of . . . many evidences of a depressing character. . . . There is a great depression in our ranks here, but with a definite thing presented by you to the people in the League of Nations and your explanation to the people [of the treaty] . . . our enemies will be left in a most pitiable plight. . . . Your absence has been a tremendous handicap to us, but we have weathered the storm better than I had expected. . . . Your return, presence and leadership will be of great psychological value. We must have a definite program with aggressiveness written all over it. . . . There have been many dangerous symptoms of economic unrest, but we have succeeded, at least, in lessening them and keeping them in check.
>
> I hope, when you return, that you will get in touch with the members of the House and Senate who show strong desire to support you in every way. I hope you will initiate a new program of meeting members of the House and Senate and newspapermen a certain hour of each day, so that we may . . . push our program forward. . . . We must take the offensive and never cease until our foe is driven back. I am the most op-

timistic Democrat in America and see strong evidences of
the turning of the tide in our favor.[66]

On July 8 Wilson's ship reached the United States. He shared
the headlines the next morning with Irish agitators and with the
high cost of living. But Tumulty was happy. He was working on
the itinerary for Wilson's tour; he could discuss politics and legislation with his chief, and he was again in charge of public relations.
Government by cable had come to an end.

CHAPTER XII

Regency and Defeat

1. Problems of Peace

THE PRIMARY OBJECTIVE of Wilson and Tumulty upon the President's return was ratification of the Treaty of Versailles. Wilson considered the treaty with its League his great achievement. On them he pinned his hopes for permanent peace. Sharing those feelings, Tumulty sought ratification as an end in itself, but for Tumulty it was also a means to other ends. He believed no proper solution of domestic problems was possible until the United States completed making peace. He also considered the treaty the crux of the record on which the Democracy could campaign in 1920.

Ratification, however, depended on the will of the Senate. The necessary two-thirds vote was out of the question unless the President would accept some changes. In the ensuing battle, the real issue was between Wilson's interpretive reservations to the League of Nations and Lodge's harsher reservations which Wilson considered crippling. But even Lodge's version was not ruinous, and except for the League, the treaty was not in danger of alteration.

Political prejudice mixed with honest conviction to confound the fight. For too long the President, his spokesmen in the Senate, and, to a lesser degree, his Secretary, made the unamended treaty their alternative to rejection. For too long they proposed no practicable compromise to the "mild reservationists," Republican Senators whose views were similar to Wilson's. Lodge and his party, equally politically minded, were intent on Republicanizing the League. The "irreconcilables," those opposed to any league, were largely Republicans. Both sides played on prejudice, both stretched the truth.[1]

Wilson set his own course. Frequently he acted without reference to his party in the Senate or his colleagues in the executive departments. He was not impervious to advice, for he realized that he needed help; but he was so intent on his League, so sure that he was right, that he was less receptive to counsel and less co-operative with his legislature than in any other struggle of his political career.

The Democratic team of other years had broken up. House, like Bryan and Malone before him, had fallen out of favor with Wilson. McAdoo, in private life a candidate for the presidential nomination, preferred to observe rather than participate in what he apparently thought was a losing cause. Lansing and the President had drifted apart at Paris. Their separation was increased when Lansing, testifying before the Senate Foreign Relations Committee, gave only lukewarm support to the treaty. Burleson had lost face. Furthermore, although he worked faithfully for Wilson's ends, the Postmaster General was in favor of some compromise with Lodge.[2] Gilbert Hitchcock, ranking Democrat on the Foreign Relations Committee and acting floor leader in the Senate, did not have Wilson's confidence. The President could not forget that Hitchcock had not been sympathetic with his neutrality policies.

Tumulty, by contrast, had demonstrated his unswerving loyalty. He had been close to Wilson longer than had any other political figure. His work while his chief was abroad had restored much of the prestige he had lost in 1915 and 1916. Above all, Tumulty sought to refine Wilson's tactics but never to challenge his objectives. Wilson, emotionally involved in the treaty fight, wanted just such sympathetic counsel.

Tumulty worked hard to hide Wilson's impatience with the Senate. The President's conferences with individual Senators who might be won to his point of view on the treaty were in keeping with Tumulty's recommendation for personal contact. But Tumulty was dissatisfied with his chief's attempts at liaison. He tried to bolster Hitchcock's prestige by denying that any disagreement existed between Wilson and the Senator. He urged Wilson to consult Key Pittman with regard to conditions in the Senate.[3] Considerate of the feelings of friend and foe alike, Tumulty warned the President against rudeness toward Lodge. Referring to Wilson's draft of a public letter, he declared: "I do not think you ought to address Lodge as 'My dear sir.' I know how you feel toward him, but . . . I think you ought to use the words, 'My dear Mr. Chairman.' " [4]

While awaiting the time to begin Wilson's tour of the country, Tumulty gave careful attention to public relations. He solicited complimentary letters from the President for friendly editors and for Cardinal Gibbons, who had spoken favorably for the League.[5] Unduly optimistic about the Cardinal's influence with the Senate, Tumulty expected his support to counterbalance the antagonism of Cardinal O'Connell and Archbishop Hayes. Senators who were cultivating the Irish vote, however, realized that Cardinal Gibbons spoke only for himself.

Although the Irish could not be won, other Americans were still undecided. With an eye to the friendly and the neutral, Tumulty interceded to prevent Wilson from making a dangerous mistake. When the Senate requested a copy of a letter written by General Tasker Bliss on behalf of himself, Lansing, and White, protesting against tentative provisions in regard to Shantung, Wilson's first inclination was to supply the document. After reading Bliss' letter Tumulty objected. "To put it mildly," he cautioned his chief, "his [Bliss'] reply is astounding." The General, referring to the first plan proposed for Shantung, had declared it abandoned the democracy of China "to the domination of the Prussianized militarism of Japan." He had concluded that this price was too great to pay even for peace. Tumulty observed that publication of these statements would insult Japan and make a "profound impression" on the Senate and the American people. He urged Wilson to withhold the letter and to explain that the ultimate settlement of Shantung met many of the objections set down by Bliss.[6] Wilson followed this advice.

Meanwhile Tumulty had concluded that some reservations had to be made to the Covenant. The Democrats could command the

votes to defeat Lodge's proposals, but to get enough votes for ratification, they would have to agree to some changes. Only Wilson,
Tumulty observed, could draw the line between destructive amendments and harmless additions. Late in July he advised the President
to declare that he was not opposed to interpretive resolutions. This
policy, Tumulty argued, by indicating flexibility in Wilson's views,
would strengthen his stand against Lodge's amendments.[7]

In order to gain the support of the mild reservationists, Tumulty
considered it important that Wilson adopt his plan quickly. But
the President delayed. On the floor of the Senate, pleading Wilson's
case, Pittman contended that any reservation would have to be submitted to the signatories of the treaty for their approval. The Solicitor of the State Department, however, contradicted the Senator.
In a private letter to Wilson, the Solicitor held that interpretive
reservations could be deposited at Paris without further action by
the other governments, although these interpretations would not
then be binding on the other governments.[8] But by the middle of
August Wilson had still not acted. He was preparing an address to
the Senate Foreign Relations Committee in which he planned to
ask for ratification without reservations.

Both Pittman and Tumulty urged the President to reconsider.
Tumulty declared that unless Wilson announced that he would not
oppose reasonable interpretations before he met with the Foreign
Relations Committee, he might have to defer to suggestions advanced by the Republicans. Wilson would be wiser to take the
initiative.[9] The President accepted this advice only in part. He
told the Committee that he would accept interpretations, but even
then he did not clearly define the difference between interpretation
and amendment.

Before Wilson made this concession to political reality, Republican strategy in the Senate had crushed Tumulty's hopes for prompt
ratification. Lodge and his colleagues, sure that time was on their
side, were prolonging consideration of the treaty. Their manipulation of the hearings and their propaganda aired and intensified
prejudices against Wilson's work. Delay not only threatened ratification except on Lodge's terms but also kept the Senate from its
other business. While popular interest in the treaty flagged, labor

unrest and the high cost of living bore directly on the lives of the people. The solution of these problems, in Tumulty's view, depended on the resolution of the treaty problem. Yet the issues complicated each other. As the Administration lost ground in the treaty fight, it incurred blame for economic disorder. The disorder, on the other hand, demanded Wilson's attention, forcing him to delay his tour in behalf of the treaty, Tumulty's favored propaganda device.

Throughout August Tumulty tried to break the log jam. Hoping to create public demand for speedy ratification, he advised Wilson to point out the relation between the domestic economy and world settlement. In his suggestions for a message on the high cost of living, Tumulty wrote:

> There can be no approach to normal conditions in this country until the treaty of peace is out of the way and the work of liquidating the war has become the chief concern of Government as well as of the victims of the existing situation. Business of all kinds is largely speculative because of indefinitiveness and uncertainty, and gambling has to be paid for by somebody. In this case it is paid for by the consumer. . . . It is futile to expect that peace prices can be approximated under a Government and under a financial and economic system that are still legally on a war basis. . . .
>
> The high cost of living is but a phase of the whole question of social and industrial unrest. It is but a reflex and reaction of what is happening throughout the world. . . . None of the problems of peace, from the high cost of living to the control of the railroads, can be dealt with by the Government of the United States until this treaty is disposed of.
>
> We must have world peace and tranquillity at the earliest possible moment. Here at home we should be made ready for peace by wise legislation dealing with . . . reconstruction and readjustment. Congress alone can quicken this process.
>
> Europe will not really get busy again until she knows exactly where she stands on this peace proposition. While there is any possibility that the peace terms may be changed or may be held

in abeyance or may not be enforced . . . the conditions under which European industry and commerce can resume are so uncertain that only the necessary activities will be revived.[10]

Tumulty urged the President to re-emphasize this theme by telling the Senate Foreign Relations Committee that their delays were disrupting domestic reconstruction. The disposition of the railroads, the re-establishment of an American merchant marine, the stabilization of prices, Tumulty held, called for legislative action that was impossible while the treaty debate continued. "Further inaction in this vital matter [the treaty]," Tumulty wrote, ". . . can only delay the return of normal conditions throughout this country and the world. Failure to act produces uncertainty and aggravates those conditions which from day to day grow more acute and make definite action absolutely necessary." Inaction permitted the spread of Bolshevism, "more terrible than the war itself," in Europe. In the United States, it could result in the enlargement of difficulties "to a point where they will be almost insoluble." [11]

Tumulty's reasoning, which Wilson adopted, did not hasten the progress of the treaty. While neither Lodge nor Wilson displayed any inclination to compromise, most of the energy of the government was dissipated in debate. Where executive action was possible without reference to Congress, however, Tumulty urged Wilson to take steps to overcome the atrophy. It was partly Tumulty's prodding that caused Wilson to give special attention to the high cost of living. The President implemented his message on that subject by ordering Attorney General Palmer to prosecute retail profiteers.[12]

The labor situation, closely related to the high cost of living, also called for some definite policy from the White House. Fearful that wage increases would be passed on to the consumer, Tumulty opposed the growing demands of unions for higher pay. The first requisite, he felt, was increased production, which was impossible in the face of a wave of strikes. In his suggestions for Wilson's cost of living speech, Tumulty remarked: "Labor can't expect any campaign to reduce the cost of living to win if strikes are to predominate. One way labor can help is to increase production." [13]

Other circumstances modified Tumulty's friendliness toward labor, whose troubles embarrassed the Administration. When efforts for settlement were rejected by union leaders, Tumulty blamed them for Democratic discomfort. Furthermore, although he did not subscribe to newspaper analyses which equated all labor difficulty with Communist agitation, he considered labor radicals to be American Bolsheviks. Referring to outbreaks of violence in Seattle, Tumulty wrote Wilson: "Everything I hear from the most reliable sources . . . impresses upon me the importance of your giving expression to some vigorous declaration with reference to the attitude of the Government toward peremptory demands made . . . by . . . various labor organizations. . . . It is clear to me that it is the first appearance of the soviet in this country. . . ." [14]

A strike vote by the railroad shopmen brought the problem into sharp focus. Since the government still controlled the roads, Wilson had to settle on a policy quickly. Tumulty opposed the shopmen's demands for higher wages and their decision to resort to a strike. He urged Lansing to advise the President to resist them. He also spoke for himself. "Gently but firmly," Tumulty wrote Wilson, "you must let the leaders of the railroad brotherhoods understand that any attempt to enforce their demands by 'direct action' is an unfriendly act against the United States of America. . . ." Since the people depended on the railroads for their food, Tumulty argued, no curtailment of service could be tolerated. Wilson's cost of living speech had been well received, he continued, but now the request for an increase in railroad wages involved a possible increase in the prices of all commodities carried by the roads. The brotherhoods were "the aristocracy of labor," seeking special privilege, upsetting "the hopeful efforts to curb the cost of living." The interests of the rest of labor as well as those of the public needed protection. "In any eventuality," Tumulty contended, Wilson should be prepared "to make good this position." A law compelling the men to stay on their jobs should be drafted. The army and navy should be readied to man the roads in an emergency. It should be made clear, Tumulty concluded, with the treaty fight in mind, that the government was not refusing the demands outright. Some alterations in the wage scale might be justified and necessary, but the future of the railroads was still uncertain. "All the Government is asking for," Tumulty held, "is time to permit a discussion of these things with the idea of providing a permanent remedy." [15]

Wilson used Tumulty's ideas on the relation of wages and the cost of living. He persuaded the shopmen to abandon their strike. With the approval of Tumulty, Walker D. Hines, and McAdoo, he took firm measures to stamp out wildcat strikes on the roads.[16] The end of the railroad strike was followed by the collapse of a steel strike. In the latter case, Tumulty and Baruch advanced the claim of Judge Gary, the head of U.S. Steel, that the strikers' organization deserved no government support.[17] Management won without the government's assistance. Labor tension began to subside. In his Labor Day address, adopting the recommendations of Tumulty and Hines, Wilson generalized his theme on wages and the cost of living, and appealed for increased production to combat inflation.[18]

By early September 1919, the pressure of domestic affairs had relaxed temporarily. The major strikes were over. Palmer was attacking profiteering. Congress was considering various plans for the disposition of the railroads. The final solutions of these problems were not in sight, but Wilson and Tumulty considered the situation stable enough to permit the President to leave Washington. "If things quiet down," Tumulty had written Wilson in mid-August, "I hope you will follow up the conference with the Senators by an appeal to the country. . . ." [19] In September the time had come to take the treaty to the people.

2. Across the Continent

Wilson's decision to stump the country for his League was open to question. His critics have argued that he should have stayed in the White House, directed Democratic strategy in the Senate, attempted to reach a rapport with the mild reservationists, and concentrated on domestic reconstruction as well as the treaty. They have also contended that he had nothing to gain by going to the country, for public opinion, even if he could arouse it, would not affect the Senators. Finally, Wilson was tired. While in Paris he had suffered a severe intestinal ailment that may have involved a minor stroke. He had aged. In his weakened condition, an extended speaking tour, as Dr. Grayson realized at the time, was a serious threat to his health if not to his life.[20]

Wilson and Tumulty were aware of these arguments. Tumulty had pointed out the need for careful executive leadership on the treaty and on domestic issues. He had constantly sought a closer rapport with the Senate. He did not expect such Senators as Lodge or Borah or their allies to be influenced by public sentiment. And he was cognizant of Wilson's physical condition.

Tumulty had various reasons, however, to which the President apparently agreed, for urging the tour. The first, in point of time, was political. Before the election of 1918 Tumulty had advised Wilson to show himself to the country. After the election he had reiterated this advice. Tumulty, from the time of his experiences in New Jersey, considered Wilson the most effective spokesman of his own cause. He intended the tour for the League to strengthen the party and to reidentify it with the President. Tumulty considered this of great importance for 1920 even though he never contemplated a third term for his chief.

Tumulty's second reason related to his confidence in Wilson's persuasiveness. He expected the President to create such overwhelming sentiment for the League that the mild reservationists would adopt the Democratic view. Wilson had consented to interpretive resolutions. Before leaving Washington, he drafted four reservations for Hitchcock's use. Although the President would not permit the Senator to reveal their authorship, they were the basis for ratification to which Tumulty hoped the mild reservationists, moved by the weight of public opinion, would agree.[21]

Finally, Tumulty believed that the tour had to precede any permanent settlement of domestic problems, since he felt that reconstruction awaited ratification and that ratification depended on the tour. For these ends, he was willing to gamble on the President's health. Wilson, thinking of himself as one of the army who had gone forth for "the right," welcomed the gamble.

Tumulty planned the tour carefully. He drew on the experience of the League to Enforce Peace which had arranged shorter trips for Taft. In preparing the itinerary, he considered whether it covered the best possible news-distributing centers, what correlation there should be between states visited and the party and views of the Senators of those states, and how to reach unvisited states through stops in cities near their borders. He concentrated on the Midwest and Far West, avoiding the Democratic South and Republican East. The itinerary he proposed called for ten thousand miles of travel in twenty-seven days, with twenty-six major stops. He also allowed for twelve short, rear-platform speeches daily. In spite of Wilson's fatigue few changes were made in this schedule.[22]

Tumulty suggested a larger party to accompany the President than it proved possible to accommodate. He wanted at least one labor leader, suffrage leader, and Irish-American politician in the entourage, as well as representatives of all the important press associations. Lack of space on the President's train reduced this list to only the newspapermen. Wilson's personal retinue included Mrs. Wilson, Dr. Grayson, Tumulty, and a corps of clerks, stenographers, messengers, and secret service men.[23]

Tumulty made the arrangements for Wilson's receptions. He relied on advance agents and groups of pro-League citizens in each locality to prepare detailed schedules for his review. These "maneuver sheets" of accommodations, intra-urban transportation, and appointments covered every minute from the President's arrival to his departure, allowing little time for privacy or relaxation. To assure good publicity, Tumulty gave copies of the "maneuver sheets" to the traveling newspapermen twenty-four hours before each stop, and an advance agent supplied the local press with promotional information.[24]

Tumulty cultivated the appearance of nonpartisanship, taking care that some Republicans were on all the local committees and in evidence at all the large meetings. Nonpartisanship in fact, however, was far from his mind. McAdoo sent him a list of Democratic politicians in Columbus, Portland, San Francisco, and Los Angeles for whom a presidential handshake was mandatory. Much of Tumulty's time en route was given over to Democratic committees. Even Wilson did his best to be a "good mixer." [25]

The presidential party left Washington on September 3. For almost a month they were to live on wheels, a small, closely confined group, plagued by dust and cinders, finding little relief in the commercial hotels and amidst the noisy crowds at their places of call. Tumulty took it upon himself to enliven his fellow travelers. He started the trip on a jocular note by substituting a colored messenger from the executive offices, whom Wilson knew, for the railroad's porter. On the train, every evening after dinner, with Grayson as his "end man," Tumulty amused the President and Mrs. Wilson with his unfailing Irish wit.[26]

Wilson needed these diversions. To add to the discomfort of travel, he received, through Tumulty, discouraging reports from Washington. Billy Cochran informed Tumulty that the West was confused and upset about the British Empire's six votes to the United States' one. Rudolph Forster, after talking to Senator Simmons, telegraphed that the Democrats needed definite proposals endorsed by the President for interpretive reservations. Democratic Senator Pomerene of Ohio, reporting that Lodge was negotiating with the mild reservationists, feared that the Democrats would have to choose between rejection and hurtful amendments unless they reached an agreement with the mild reservationists at once. Vance McCormick warned Tumulty that the treaty could not be ratified without reservations. Although still confident that the President could arouse "the folks back home," McCormick felt that Wilson's initial speeches had had no effect except to stiffen the opposition. He was particularly unhappy about Wilson's attacks on the Senate.[27]

Disturbed by these reports and by the restrained attitude of Midwestern audiences, Tumulty began to make written suggestions for Wilson's speeches. The day before the President's Tacoma address, Tumulty submitted his first memorandum. Seeking to guide Wilson away from further attacks on the Senate, Tumulty proposed three specific arguments: he maintained that the League fulfilled the purposes of the United States in entering the war, as expressed in

Wilson's speech of April 2, 1917; he presented the League as a non-partisan instrument, observing that former Attorney General Wickersham, a Taft Republican, after seeing the destruction in Europe, had changed his views and endorsed the League; and he described the League as the device which in the future would eliminate the cost of war in money and dead and wounded, underlining this point with statistics on the cost of the war just ended.[28]

Wilson used these arguments in Tacoma. As the tour continued he relied more and more on Tumulty's suggestions. Tumulty excerpted a speech made by Lodge in 1916 and an interview given by Theodore Roosevelt in 1914 to show their early adherence to the idea of a League. The President read these excerpts at San Diego. At Los Angeles Tumulty advised him that "the issues that are most acute in this part of the country are . . . Shantung, Great Britain, isolation. . . . I am sending . . . for a copy of Mr. McKinley's speech . . . in which he . . . said the age of isolation was past." Quoting McKinley, Wilson concentrated on the issues Tumulty had mentioned. In the same city the President adopted Tumulty's idea for a reply to California Senator Hiram Johnson, an "irreconcilable" Republican, who had charged that the League meant partnership with bankrupt nations. "No matter what may be said about our associates," Tumulty wrote, "for three years they fought to serve civilization. If they are bankrupt in money, it is because they expended it and their precious blood to save the world." [29]

The West Coast showed great enthusiasm for Wilson. Although this did not necessarily mean enthusiasm for the League, and although the cheering failed to alter the situation in the Senate, Tumulty was encouraged. The tour was beginning to resemble the mass tribute he had long sought for his chief. If the exuberant response could be sustained while Wilson headed back East, the Senate might feel pressure from "the folks back home." The mild reservationists might then come into the Democratic camp.

There were, however, discouraging signs. In San Francisco the rudeness of an Irish-American committee toward the President evidenced the continuing hostility of the Irish toward the League. Wilson's speeches had not altered their thinking. The effect of the tour on the uncompromising opponents of the treaty, the Irish, the isolationists, the irreconcilables, was to provoke increasing and more caustic counterpropaganda. Most disconcerting of all, the President was perilously tired.

Wilson's speech in the hot, crowded auditorium at Salt Lake City on September 23 revealed his fatigue. "Frankly," Tumulty advised the President, "your 'punch' did not land last night in Salt Lake. As a newspaperman put it this morning, you simply pushed the ball; there was no snap in your stroke." Tumulty warned Wilson that he would have to spell out in detail why Lodge's reservations would constitute a rejection of the treaty. The press and the audience had not "really caught the point in its full significance." [30]

Agreeing with Wilson's interpretation of Article X as the moral commitment which formed the heart of the League, Tumulty asserted that Lodge's changes weakened the obligations of the Covenant. This "would be a base betrayal of our American boys," "would inevitably force a separate peace with Germany." Tumulty felt that those who had cheered Wilson agreed on this point. To supply the "punch," missed at Salt Lake, Tumulty drafted a passage for the President's next speeches:

> My experience during the last three weeks has convinced me that the heart of America is in this great enterprise. . . . With this conviction in mind . . . I shall resist with all my heart and soul any attempt to dishonor or besmirch the integrity of the United States. The men at Château-Thierry and Belleau Woods went into this great enterprise without reservation; they did not come out until they had provided us with a way to accomplish the ultimate and greatest result for which they fought — the establishment of a permanent peace. This is the most solemn hour in the life of America. A mistake now would be irreparable. . . . It is your duty as much as it is my duty to impress upon the Senate of the United States the danger of repudiating the principles of permanent peace and failing to ratify this treaty as it was written at Paris. . . . The honor, good faith, and integrity of this nation in this great matter must not be betrayed.[31]

Wilson utilized the ideas and the emotions in Tumulty's draft because he also believed and felt them. At Denver and Pueblo the President's fervor struck the hearts of his audiences. The crowd at Pueblo was moved to tears. Tumulty always recalled that address as the finest of the tour.[32] His reverence arose in part from the context and reception of the speech; in part he venerated it because it was the last of Wilson's public career.

The night after leaving Pueblo Wilson experienced nausea, insomnia, and a racking headache. Near Baxter the train was stopped and the President took a short walk. He felt no better for the exercise. His symptoms were those of nervous and physical exhaustion. Grayson demanded that the rest of the tour be canceled. Reluctantly Wilson consented. Before the scheduled stop at Wichita, Tumulty issued an explanatory bulletin:

> The President has exerted himself so constantly and has been under such a strain during the last year and has spent himself without reserve on this trip, that it has brought on a nervous reaction. . . . Dr. Grayson, therefore, insists upon the cancellation of his remaining appointments and his immediate return to Washington, notwithstanding the President's earnest desire to complete the engagements.[33]

Wilson had agreed to return only after Tumulty assured him that the trip had been successful. But Tumulty must have felt despair in his heart. The ovations of the last two weeks had been gratifying but insufficient. Conditions in the Senate were unchanged. Wilson could make no further attempt to arouse public opinion for his League. The gamble was lost, the President exhausted, the Democrats in the Senate in an increasingly uncomfortable situation. Worse was to come.

3. Regency

On October 2, a few days after arriving at Washington, Wilson collapsed. A victim of arteriosclerosis, he had suffered a thrombosis which resulted in paralysis of his left side. Probably the collapse had been preceded by minor thromboses which were not diagnosed. Ultimately arteriosclerosis caused Wilson's death.[34]

From October 1919, until his death Wilson was a sick man. His thrombosis was accompanied by intestinal disorders which, on October 17, developed into an obstruction of the urethra. For days he was in a coma. It was a wonder and a tragedy that he lived. After a month of complete inactivity he began to resume some of the duties of his office. For another month he was a secluded convalescent. Thereafter he was again accessible, partially recovered, but still paralyzed. Never again was he able to dictate for more than a few moments at a time. Fortunately his mind was unimpaired, but besides physical pain, arteriosclerosis brought its companion affliction of emotional instability.[35]

There is no question but that for at least a month Wilson was incapacitated within the meaning of the Constitution. He considered no legislation, made no appointments to office, issued no proclamations. For at least another month his capacity was doubtful. There is no provision, however, for the determination of presidential disability. No one forced an investigation of Wilson's condition. The Democrats would not discredit their elected leader, the Republicans found they could profit by his weakness. Even the malicious Fall Committee, the snooping creature of the most partisan Republicans, visited Wilson after the crisis in his illness had passed. For a month the United States had no President; for many months the country had only a shell of a President.[36]

Tumulty came to realize the implications of Wilson's collapse only slowly. He was not permitted to see his chief, but he received periodic reports from Mrs. Wilson. On October 7, he had "a most interesting and encouraging talk" with her. She was hopeful that "positive evidence" of recovery would "soon manifest itself." "No more devoted wife lives," Tumulty declared. On the fourteenth he wrote one of the President's oldest friends that Wilson was "on the mend" but far from a complete recovery. Just before the crisis of the seventeenth he finally admitted, confidentially, the severity of the President's condition.[37]

Congress and the public, however, were not told the truth about Wilson. Nor did the Cabinet receive any direct word.

Tumulty, for the only time in his career, did not release even off-the-record information. His daily bulletins from the White House, written with Grayson, were intentionally vague and optimistic. The people knew only that the President was too ill to transact business. The lack of information permitted the proliferation of rumors, invented by political opponents, that the President was the victim of a venereal disease, that he was insane, or that he had had a "cerebral lesion." [38]

The secrecy, imposed in part to avoid alarm, was necessary primarily because Mrs. Wilson decided that the President was not to resign; he was too ill himself to make any decision. She, putting her duties as a wife above her duties as a citizen, refused to endanger her husband by upsetting him emotionally; Wilson's physicians were bound to secrecy by their professional oaths; Tumulty had no first-hand information. In any event, his loyalty to his chief probably would have caused him to approve of Mrs. Wilson's decision.

Another important reason for Wilson's retention of office was the reputation of Thomas R. Marshall. No one high in the councils of the Administration had great respect for the Vice-President. That affable politician, typifying the mediocrity of most of the holders of his office, stood for little but a good five-cent cigar. Neither as a Governor of Indiana or as presiding officer of the Senate had he demonstrated the vision or capacity for leadership in such critical times. He had attended a few Cabinet meetings while Wilson was abroad but contributed nothing to discussions. Fearful that he would accept Lodge's changes to the League, Mrs. Wilson would not trust him with her husband's precious treaty. Lansing considered him vain and incompetent; Tumulty found him rude and uninformed.[39]

Marshall first learned of Wilson's serious condition from J. Fred Essary, a newspaperman chosen as informant by Tumulty. The Vice-President was stunned by the news. Some of Wilson's opponents suggested that Marshall take steps to assume office, but he would not. He did not want to challenge Wilson or disrupt the party, and he was reluctant to face the responsibilities of the Presidency. During Wilson's illness and convalescence, Marshall assumed certain social obligations of the White House, but otherwise he was ignored by the President's guardians.[40]

Throughout October and most of November the Presidency was held by a regency. Mrs. Wilson then and later had great power, for she alone decided what business could be brought before her husband. He was given very little. Lansing wrote the Thanksgiving Day proclamation. Tumulty, correlating the suggestions of the Cabinet, prepared the President's December message to Congress.[41] Each department head made his own decisions, but many matters had to be postponed. By the middle of December there were eight major diplomatic vacancies and over a dozen important unfilled offices in the executive branch.[42] While these vacancies existed, incalculable damage was done to the efficiency of the government. When Wilson was again able to transact some business, the situation improved, but for two crucial months his wife, his Secretary, and his Cabinet attended as best they could to the duties of the President's office.

Tumulty assumed tremendous responsibilities. His work while Wilson had been abroad prepared him for his task. He was the executive clearing house, the liaison officer between the departments and the sick room, the moderator of intra-Administration disputes. He did not presume to set policies alone. Immediately after the President's collapse, while the nature of his illness was a closely guarded secret, Tumulty indicated to Lansing, by pointing significantly to his left side, that Wilson was paralyzed. The Secretary of State met the emergency resolutely. To co-ordinate executive policy and to sustain public confidence in the government, he called periodic meetings of the Cabinet members and the heads of wartime agencies. Tumulty publicized the meetings. He helped Lansing summon the officials and prepare agenda for their consideration.[43]

However essential, the meetings had no legal status, for only the President had the authority to convene the Cabinet. Although Mrs. Wilson disliked Tumulty and distrusted Lansing, she did not protest against their action. Houston and Newton D. Baker, presumably the President's favorites, approved of the procedure. Wilson himself learned of the sessions late in October, if not before, but took no steps to prevent them.[44]

Much of the President's work fell directly on Tumulty. Pressed for time and unable to obtain Wilson's attention on patronage, he abandoned his efforts to rebuild the party. But the enforcement of prohibition presented a clearly political problem. In analyzing the election of 1919, Tumulty ascribed Democratic losses largely to hyphenism and the liquor issue. Just before the election, he had attempted to divorce the national Democracy from the southern "drys," to appeal to Irish and German "wets," and to please the urban Democratic machines by drafting a veto of the Volstead Act, a measure calling for strict interpretation of the Eighteenth Amendment. Houston put the veto in final form, but Congress, to Tumulty's dismay, overrode it.[45]

With the exception of the Volstead Act, however, Tumulty was too acutely aware of his responsibilities to play politics. In dealing with larger issues, his conception of national interest governed his thought, although he inevitably saw national problems through Democratic eyes. Loyally he attempted to act as he felt Wilson would have him act. But he had good reason to resent imputations that partisan motives lay behind his work. Even in the case of the Volstead Act his objections were moral as well as political. Tumulty explained his position to Arthur Sinnott:

> In all the suggestions I am called upon to make . . . in these critical days, I strive not to tarnish them by selfish interests of any kind. . . . I seek . . . in all my judgements to comprehend the general interests of the country and to try to bring to bear on my interpretations . . . the needs of the country and that which is just and for the lasting interests of all classes. . . .[46]

The class question was a constant irritant. Lasting industrial peace seemed remote as the Red scare and labor violence persisted. Tumulty consulted with Lansing to determine how to combat the dissemination of Bolshevik propaganda in the United States. He declared that the Democratic gubernatorial candidate in Massachusetts endangered the state and the party by criticizing Calvin Coolidge for his celebrated action in ending the Boston police strike. When Coolidge was re-elected, Tumulty drafted a congratulatory telegram for Wilson, describing the outcome as "a clear-cut victory for law and order." [47]

Tumulty continued to hope for a solution to the general problem of labor relations. With Bernard Baruch and Secretaries Lane and Wilson he communicated the Administration's program to the first Industrial Conference, which Wilson had called partly on Tumulty's advice.[48] The disagreements between labor and management, however, could not be resolved by discussion. While the Conference was meeting, a major coal strike intensified their differences. With the strike in progress the representatives of management refused to assent even to a compromise formula proposed by the representatives of labor and the public. Shortly thereafter the labor representatives walked out and the Conference adjourned.

4. The Coal Strike

The coal strike, a typical example of the postwar labor problem, created a difficult situation for the national government. To save the nation's fuel supply the government had to act during the period of the President's disability. The nature of the intervention was characteristic of the divided authority and confusion of the regency.

In September 1919, at the biennial convention of the United Mine Workers, the union's Scale Committee, referring to the increased cost of living, submitted a report of the changes desirable in the union's contract with the operators of bituminous coal mines. The committee recommended a sixty per cent increase in wages for all day laborers, a six-hour workday, and a five-day week. It advised a strike if these demands were not met. John L. Lewis, who had just become acting president of the U.M.W., endorsed this report in a fiery speech. He took pains to deny that radicals or Reds inspired his position. The convention thereupon adopted the report and voted to strike if the operators would not comply by November 1.[49]

The contract between the U.M.W. and the operators in the central competitive bituminous fields had been made in 1917 with the approval of the Fuel Administration. The parties agreed that the contract should extend for the duration of the war but not beyond April 1, 1920. The officials of the U.M.W. contended that the war was over after the armistice and the negotiation of the peace treaty. The operators, backed up by the government, denied that the war was over and maintained that the old contract was still in force. At a series of conferences they refused the miners' demands. Consequently Lewis called a strike for midnight, October 31.

Railroad Director Walker D. Hines, Secretary of Labor William Wilson, and Tumulty attempted to avert the strike. Realizing early in October that the miners and operators would not agree, Hines and Tumulty resolved that the Administration must control the situation. Their plan was first to arouse public opinion against a strike by releasing full information on the matters at issue, and then to make an official appeal against the strike so authoritative that the miners would respect it.[50] At the same time Secretary Wilson undertook to settle the disagreements by holding special conferences with both sides.

After the Secretary of Labor failed and the Industrial Conference adjourned, Hines, his assistant, and Tumulty drafted the official appeal against the strike. It is not clear whether this statement, later issued over Wilson's name, ever received his approval, but the Cabinet was in accord with its context. Tumulty wrote most of it, incorporating suggestions by Hines in almost every paragraph. The statement asserted that as the war was not over, the war contract still obtained. Although the union's demands were a threat to the government's efforts to control the cost of living, the government would appoint a tribunal to investigate and help to settle the questions at issue if both parties so requested. But whatever the justice of the miners' demands, no strike would be tolerated. A strike would disrupt vital functions of national and local government and interfere with the transportation of troops and the supply of food to the Allies. "A strike under these circumstances," Tumulty inserted on one draft, "is not only unjustifiable; it is unlawful." [51]

While awaiting the union's reaction to this statement, Hines and Tumulty prepared to deal with a strike. Hines drew up plans, which Tumulty endorsed, for the rationing of coal to ensure adequate supplies for railroads and public utilities. At the request of the Cabinet, Harry Garfield returned to his position as Fuel Administrator, ready to supervise the rationing. Hines and Tumulty also obtained Attorney General Palmer's approval of their contention that the wartime Lever Act, which forbade strikes at least until the membership of a union had been polled, was still in force.[52]

Shortly before the U.M.W. rejected the government's plea to call off the strike, Tumulty and Secretary Wilson were planning a last move to avert it. Tumulty felt that both sides would submit to arbitration if a commission of investigation were appointed at once by the Administration.[53] But it was too late. Before Tumulty's plan could be considered, Lewis announced that the miners would walk out.

The Administration then moved to force the U.M.W. to stay at work. Federal troops were sent to West Virginia and state militia to other bituminous areas. Attorney General Palmer visited the sick President to obtain his assent to the use of an injunction under the terms of the Lever Act. Tumulty sent Palmer a long memorandum justifying resort to injunction. The coal miners, like a city's police force, had no right to strike, Tumulty declared, because in both cases a strike threatened the "general welfare" of the people which the government was founded to protect. He wrote Palmer in part:

> This is a critical hour in the life of America which will . . . test the right of the Government . . . to vindicate its own authority and sovereignty. The offer of a peaceful settlement of the miners' strike through the instrumentality of an impartial tribunal has been rejected and the alternative of submission to the demands of a group . . . is upon us for decision and action. . . . There can be but one answer to that challenge, and that is . . . [the] assertion by the Government itself of the right to protect the very life, property and fortunes of the whole people of the country. . . .
>
> While the right to strike, in all ordinary industries and under

ordinary circumstances, cannot be denied, yet there are some industries which concern the public so closely and whose uninterrupted continuance is so vital to the well-being or even the life of the public, that the right to strike in such cases must be subordinated to the superior right of the public. . . . Fair wages and just conditions of labor must be granted to the soft coal miners as to the workers in every other industry . . . but the great public interest must not be held in contempt while adjustments are being sought. . . .[54]

With Wilson's approval, using Tumulty's argument and many of his words, Palmer instigated injunction proceedings. Lewis, supported by Samuel Gompers, protested loudly. Informed of Gompers' denunciation of the injunction, Tumulty remarked: "The situation is in the hands of the courts. This is no time to get cold feet." [55] His attitude revealed that political pressure would not move the Administration. On November 14, Lewis obeyed the court's order and called off the strike.

Lewis' action did not send the miners back to work. In return for Lewis' agreement not to fight the injunction in the higher courts, the Cabinet had promised that Secretary Wilson would hold conferences to settle the miners' grievances. The miners would not enter the pits until some increase in pay was granted. The operators offered 20 per cent. The union asked 31 per cent which Secretary Wilson described as fair. While they were parleying over the difference, Fuel Administrator Garfield announced that the government would permit an increase of only 14 per cent, all of which the operators were to absorb. His declaration produced a deadlock, for the miners refused 14 per cent when they had been offered 20 per cent.[56] Meanwhile Palmer spoke of further injunctions, the presence of troops in mining towns threatened to lead to violence, and the nation's coal supply dwindled.

Tumulty, Secretary Wilson, and McAdoo felt that Garfield was unreasonable. Breaking his silence, McAdoo wrote Wilson that Garfield and Palmer were aiding the "implacable enemies" of the Democratic Party. The President could not afford, McAdoo warned, "to make the triumph of reaction, toryism and privilege certain in 1920." [57] Tumulty and the Secretary of Labor set out to win the Cabinet to this view. While Hines, Garfield, and Secretary Wilson were preparing possible statements for the President's use, the Cabinet had instructed Carter Glass, then Secretary of the Treasury, Palmer, and Secretary of Agriculture Houston to formulate its policy. Tumulty prevailed on Palmer to reconsider his position, persuading the Attorney General to hear the union's cause. Gradually Garfield was isolated.

On December 6, Palmer called a conference at his home to discuss the strike. Garfield attended under the impression that the President had agreed to issue the statement he had prepared restricting an increase to 14 per cent and refusing to consider any increase in coal prices. He and Glass maintained at the conference that any adjustment in wages in excess of 14 per cent would result in higher prices. But Palmer and Tumulty had seen Lewis and William Green earlier in the day. The Attorney General reported that the miners considered 31 per cent the authorized government offer. After the conference, Tumulty and Palmer, on their own responsibility, withheld Garfield's statement.[58]

On December 6 and 7, Palmer and Tumulty talked again with Lewis and Green. They showed the labor leaders a statement they had written as an alternative to Garfield's. This proposal, which was ultimately used, granted an initial increase in wages of 14 per cent, to be absorbed by the operators, and left further adjustments as to wages and prices to a board of investigation to be appointed by the President. The board was to consist of one representative each of the miners, the operators, and the public. Lewis and Green accepted this plan and agreed that John P. White should represent the miners and Rembrandt Peale the operators. On the completion of these negotiations, Lewis and Green left Washington.[59]

On December 8, Palmer informed Garfield of what had occurred. Garfield, unwilling to consent to any change in prices, wrote Wilson protesting against the plan. The President at first agreed with Garfield that prices should not be subject to consideration or increase. Tumulty, however, warned Mrs. Wilson that such a limitation "would be disastrous to any possible settlement." Lansing, speaking for the Cabinet, endorsed the statement prepared by Tumulty and Palmer, and informed Wilson that the Cabinet disapproved of Garfield's limitation. The President then changed his mind, and Tumulty immediately telegraphed to Palmer, who had gone to Indianapolis to meet with the U.M.W. officials. The Attorney General presented the plan to the miners' convention. It was accepted by the miners and later by the operators. Late in December work in the mines was resumed. Garfield, defeated but unconvinced, resigned his office.[60]

Tumulty's course in the coal strike offended both labor and management. His efforts to avert the strike ran counter to Lewis' plans; his advocacy of the injunction antagonized Lewis and Gompers; his proposals for the final settlement permitted a potential increase in wages and decrease in hours greater than the operators wished to consider. "The general interests of the country," not those of a class, had been Tumulty's concern. In pursuing those interests, as he interpreted them, Tumulty had not thought of himself as labor's enemy. The question of the legitimacy of injunction in time of labor crisis, especially when the crisis is precipitated by John L. Lewis, remains unsettled to this day. The overruling of Garfield, on the other hand, earned the gratitude of Lewis and Green.

The President had little to do with the coal strike. Hines and Tumulty prepared one of his statements, Palmer and Tumulty the other. In approving the injunction and the ultimate basis of settlement, Wilson merely followed the advice of his Cabinet. His subordinates were running the government, but they could not exercise the forceful direction for which Tumulty had yearned in June. Delay, friction, and conspiracy encumbered the regency. These conditions, troublesome during the coal strike, were in the same period fatal to the President's treaty.

5. Defeat of the Treaty

Just before Wilson's collapse, Tumulty tried to hearten his chief by reporting that there was no need to worry any longer about amendments to the treaty.[61] This advice, good medicine for the sick man's nerves, was palpably false. Senator Hitchcock, a few days later, was coldly realistic. "We are face to face with a serious crisis," he informed Bryan, writing about Wilson's collapse. ". . . The situation is unusually bad." [62] During the President's illness and convalescence the situation steadily deteriorated.

Wilson dominated Democratic strategy in the treaty fight although he rarely issued any specific directions. In October he was completely inaccessible; in November he was ill informed, uncompromising, and emotional. But his dictates, as he had expressed them earlier and as he reiterated them from his sickbed, guided Tumulty and Hitchcock. The Senator, well informed, personally willing to compromise, and not emotionally involved, dutifully abided by the wishes of the leader of his party, while Tumulty loyally repeated Wilson's views as he understood them. Even Lansing, an unco-operative dissenter, was not openly rebellious.

The plan on which Wilson and Hitchcock agreed has been aptly described as the "strategy of deadlock." [63] Clearly Lodge was going to succeed in having his reservations passed. Wilson and Hitchcock planned to have the Democrats vote down the treaty with the Lodge reservations, to permit the unamended treaty also to be voted down, and then to present the interpretive resolutions the President had drafted as a basis for compromise and ratification. The difficulty with this scheme was that Lodge could control enough votes to prevent the Administration's resolutions from reaching a vote. Twice Hitchcock was permitted to interview Wilson. On both occasions he was frankly pessimistic. But the ailing Wilson would not hear of giving ground to Lodge.

Unwilling to cross the President, Tumulty was deaf to argument. Bernard Baruch, Herbert Hoover, House, and Lansing, all able advisers, were willing to concede to Lodge. Lansing, who consulted with Tumulty regularly during October and November, had good reasons for concession. The Solicitor of the State Department had assured the Administration that Lodge's reservations would not necessitate renegotiation of the treaty. Lord Grey, with whom Lansing discussed the treaty, revealed England's willingness to have the United States enter the League on Lodge's terms; the French were also agreeable. But Tumulty would not bend. He and Lansing could not agree on methods to assist the Democrats in the Senate. Lansing wanted Colonel House to testify before the Foreign Relations Committee. Tumulty, voicing Wilson's attitude, objected. The Colonel remained in New York, his letters to Wilson appealing for compromise unanswered. Tumulty asked the Secretary of State to confer with the Senators, but Lansing, reluctant to sponsor Wilson's views, refused.[64]

Although Tumulty could not work with Lansing, he had powerful allies in the Senate. Hitchcock buried his personal doubts and co-operated with the White House. Democrats Pittman, Phelan, and T. J. Walsh, long Tumulty's trusted friends, could be counted on to subordinate their preferences to his directions. Oscar Underwood, who was preparing to challenge Hitchcock for the Democratic leadership in the Senate, subscribed to the President's general strategy. With proper assistance from Wilson, these leaders could discipline all the Democrats except the few irreconcilables.

As the day for a vote on the treaty approached, Tumulty, Underwood, and Hitchcock agreed that some word from Wilson was necessary to keep wavering Democrats from voting in favor of the treaty with the Lodge reservations. They wanted the President to throw all the blame for the rejection of Lodge's version on the Republicans by again defining Lodge's terms as tantamount to nullification, and by accusing the Republicans of blind partisanship in their opposition to Wilson's League. On the anniversary of the armistice Tumulty asked Wilson to write Hitchcock a public letter telling the country "what the real purpose of the Republican opposition is." The draft Tumulty proposed held that adoption of the "vital changes advocated by Senator Lodge" would force reconsideration of the treaty by all signatories. Like Wilson, Tumulty, ignoring the opinion of the Solicitor of the State Department, perpetuated this falsehood. Lodge's amendments, Tumulty emphasized, delayed peace beyond the margin of safety. Economic reconstruction in America and Europe should not be postponed any longer.[65]

A few days later Hitchcock wrote Mrs. Wilson that he needed definite word from the President to ensure the defeat of the treaty with the Lodge reservations. Before the Senator was given an appointment with the President, Mrs. Wilson informed him that in no case would her husband accept the Lodge reservations. If the

treaty passed on Lodge's terms, Wilson would pocket it. Nevertheless, even after the President himself repeated this threat, Hitchcock asked permission to show the reservations drafted by Wilson
to Lodge in order to get the Massachusetts Senator's consent to a
vote on them. The implication in his letter was that some last-minute compromise with Lodge could and should be arranged.[66]

Underwood, however, opposed negotiation with Lodge as
strongly as did Wilson. He told Tumulty "that the President ought
to insist on his friends in the Senate voting to defeat the Lodge resolution of ratification, and that he should insist upon Senator
Hitchcock's favoring a vote on unconditional ratification. . . ."
Underwood declared that "this will put the President in a position
to dictate the terms of settlement between the different forces in the
Senate." [67] This advice, though unrealistic, by contrast to Hitchcock's was calculated to please Wilson. Underwood reasserted
the "strategy of deadlock." He spoke of ratification through
Democratic dictation. Whatever his convictions, his counsel was
certain to increase his chance of getting White House support in
his coming contest with Hitchcock for the Democratic leadership.
If he became leader, he might arrange ratification after Lodge's version and the unamended treaty had been beaten. Such an achievement would further his presidential ambitions. Underwood was
a calculating friend.

Tumulty, whether or not he suspected Underwood's purpose,
agreed with his advice. He transmitted Underwood's message to
Mrs. Wilson for the President's attention. On the same day he sent
Wilson a draft for a letter to Hitchcock calling on the Democrats
to defeat the treaty with the Lodge reservations, and proposing ratification on Wilson's basis. Tumulty's letter to Wilson, with the
suggested letter to Hitchcock, was his final appraisal of the situation
before the treaty was put to vote:

> As we approach a climax in the Senate, the Republicans are
> beginning to give the impression that by failing to vote for the
> Lodge Resolution, the Democrats will be assuming the responsi-
> bility for killing the treaty. All of us know, of course, that this
> is not true, but the country generally is confused about parlia-

mentary procedure and tactics, and we must see to it that they have a clear understanding of the meaning of the vote on the Lodge Resolution.

We can hold our ranks all right, I think, when it comes to the necessary one-third to block the Lodge Resolution, but it would hearten our supporters and at the same time make it easier for certain of the mild reservationists to come over to our programme later on if they had as a basis for their action a definite statement from you analyzing the Lodge Resolution and stating clearly to the country that if it is adopted by two-thirds vote of the Senate, you will be obliged to notify other governments that the Senate of the United States has rejected the treaty.

My idea of a letter to Senator Hitchcock, to be issued not after the vote is taken but just before the Lodge Resolution is acted upon, would be this:

"My dear Senator Hitchcock:

The Senate is about to vote on a resolution containing a number of reservations to our acceptance of the Peace Treaty. I deem it my duty to tell you, in order that you may advise both Republican and Democratic supporters of the Treaty, that if the pending resolution receives a two-thirds vote, it will be necessary for me to notify our associates in the war that the Senate of the United States has rejected the Peace Treaty adopted at Versailles, and that it is necessary for me to reopen negotiations with them with a view to making a new treaty. I feel confident from my knowledge of the attitude of the foreign governments associated with us that they cannot accept some of the reservations which are at present a part of the ratifying resolution, and that they would be embarrassed by a request from us that they recede from positions which they are bound in honor, by treaty entered into before we came into the war, to support.

I feel confident, also, that there are enough friends of the treaty and League of Nations in the Senate who can together draft a compromise set of reservations which would be acceptable to foreign governments, but if the pending resolution is passed, such a process cannot be undertaken, for I will be obliged at once to proclaim that the Senate has rejected the treaty.

I therefore am in hopes that the pending resolution of ratification will fail to get a two-thirds vote and that another ratifying resolution acceptable to two-thirds of the Senate may be drafted and speedily adopted." [68]

This letter expressed Wilson's views. It was, however, poor policy. Tumulty, as his counsel in the earlier stages of the treaty fight indicated, understood the need for concessions. At this first crisis in the fight, however, he sustained Wilson instead of challenging him. This was a loyal act performed at the wrong time. Tumulty had deliberately falsified the issue: the Lodge reservations did not necessitate renegotiation. In counseling Wilson to say that they did, Tumulty, like Underwood, sponsored a dangerous strategy that threatened the whole treaty for the sake of Wilson's pride and Democratic prestige. The President of course welcomed Tumulty's draft. After conferring with Hitchcock, he rephrased it for the Senator's use. He wrote Hitchcock that the friends of the treaty should vote against Lodge's resolution. The Democrats obeyed. On November 19, 1919, the treaty with the Lodge reservations was voted down. Immediately thereafter the unamended treaty was voted down. The Republicans, following Lodge, prevented any further vote. The Senate then adjourned *sine die*. Wilson, Tumulty, Underwood, Hitchcock, and the other friends of the treaty, Democratic and Republican, were shocked. At least until the Senate reconvened, the United States was still at war.

The Senate's rejection of the treaty was the worst defeat Wilson or Tumulty had suffered. All of Tumulty's hopes of the previous July were shattered. His domestic program and Wilson's League were further from realization than they had ever been. The appeal to the people had failed. The Democracy had lost ground in the elections of 1919 and lost face in the treaty fight. The President was physically broken.

Wilson's illness in large part accounted for the disaster. Had he retained his health, Democratic tactics would have been more forceful and might have been more flexible. Without him the Democrats lacked dynamic, undivided leadership. Because of his illness, he received insufficient information and was unable to appreciate what he received. As late as August he had agreed to interpretations. After September he would listen to no suggestions for concessions.

The Wilson of 1911 or 1913 was better able to deal with reasonable Republicans than was the Wilson of 1919. The President's subordinates missed his direction. Only Wilson could have induced Tumulty to change his views on the treaty. Bound by his loyalty, lacking guidance, Tumulty adhered to and even fortified the President's position. Even if he had changed his views, he, like Hitchcock, would have found Mrs. Wilson a difficult intermediary in communication with the President. The basis for Hitchcock's unrealistic action and for Tumulty's unrealistic thinking was their obedience, a political asset turned liability.

From July to December, 1919, Tumulty experienced setback after setback. By December he no longer had a domestic program. The defeat of the treaty made its reconsideration his paramount, almost single problem for 1920. He had persistently maintained that the solution of domestic problems had to await peace. He had persistently expected that peace, in the form of Wilson's treaty, would provide Democratic capital for the election of 1920.

There was still a chance that, by skillful politics, the treaty, in some form acceptable to both parties, could be saved. This would spark the Democratic campaign, perhaps to victory, and then permit the start of reconstruction. By December, moreover, the regency was over. Wilson was well enough to be President in fact. He was not able to give adequate time to his job, but he was able to make top-level decisions, particularly in regard to the treaty fight. For Tumulty this was a promising sign. Unfortunately, however, Wilson's querulous disposition and emotional fixations, by-products of his little-understood disease, were to prove even more troublesome than his earlier incapacity.

CHAPTER XIII

Götterdämmerung

1. *Death of the Treaty*

FOR TUMULTY, the year after the first rejection of the Treaty of Versailles was a succession of catastrophes. Long before the election of Warren G. Harding, the last glimmer of hope had faded. While other Democrats sulked or retired, however, Tumulty, with continuing courage, almost alone of the Wilsonians, fought each losing battle to the limit of his abilities.

The defeat of the treaty in November convinced almost all the Democratic leaders except Wilson that a compromise with the Republicans had to be arranged. Lansing, long committed to compromise, found Senators Hitchcock, Underwood, Owen, and Pomerene prepared to concede to their political rivals. Hitchcock was hopeful that even on Article X a satisfactory adjustment could be devised. Underwood was willing to sever the League from the treaty in order to get at least partial ratification. Owen and Pomerene wanted to bolt Wilson's leadership and force a settlement. Others actively seeking some basis for agreement included peace negotiators House and Bliss, Assistant Secretary of the Treasury Norman H. Davis, Ambassador to England John W. Davis, Baruch, Hoover, and William Jennings Bryan.[1]

The force of these opinions and the desire of the mild reservationists to salvage the treaty strengthened Tumulty's personal belief in the necessity for compromise. Profoundly aware of the implications of the first defeat of the treaty, he was prepared to resist, loyally and tactfully but none the less firmly, Wilson's uncompromising attitude. The United States, for the sake of international order, Tumulty felt, must join the League, if necessary in a limited partnership. The Democratic Party could not afford to go to the country without first making peace. The party had struggled for Wilson's terms and lost. World peace and political expediency now dictated concession.

Tumulty, however, faced an impossible situation. Wilson, his strength returning, began in December to resume the functions of his office. He asserted himself with increasing vigor as the weeks passed. But Wilson still felt the effects of his disease. He was petulant, irascible, unreceptive to advice. Furthermore, Mrs. Wilson, fearful that pessimistic communications might cause a setback in the President's health, maintained her close surveillance over his correspondence and routine. To many of those who had pressing affairs of state to review with the chief executive she seemed also to be jealous of the power she had inadvertently acquired. Even to Tumulty and Hitchcock, Wilson was for the most part inaccessible, and they found dealing with Mrs. Wilson increasingly difficult.

Tumulty could never communicate directly with his chief. Desirous of compromise on the treaty, he had to clothe his messages in words that would not offend the President or Mrs. Wilson. Had he been able to speak his mind, he would probably have tempered his feelings out of concern for Wilson's health, but he was forced to be overcautious because of Mrs. Wilson's attitude. Characteristically, he deferred to the President's decisions when Wilson rejected his advice. Less careful and less loyal advisers either failed to get a hearing, or were dismissed, or deserted.

Tumulty delayed his offensive for compromise for over a month. On December 15, when Wilson announced that he had no compromise or concession in mind, Tumulty lauded the statement. He had, however, already begun to lay plans with Lansing and Hitchcock. On the eighteenth, after consulting Hitchcock, he asked Mrs. Wilson to ascertain "whether the President would look with favor upon any effort on his [Hitchcock's] part to make an adjustment with the mild reservationists by which to soften the Lodge reservations and thus avoid splitting the Democratic party." Hitchcock felt, Tumulty reported, that Lodge's preamble, calling for specific endorsement of the reservations by the signatories, a scheme offensive to Wilson, could be "knocked out." Mrs. Wilson informed Hitchcock that the President wanted the Democrats to propose nothing. He had no objections to purely interpretive resolutions, but he insisted that the initiative come from the Republicans.[2]

About this time, while pro-Wilson newspapers were demanding concession, while many Democratic Senators were ready to vote with the Republicans on the treaty, the President concocted a fantastic scheme. He planned to suggest that all Senators opposing his treaty resign so that an election with the treaty as the issue could be held for their seats. If the opposition won, Wilson would resign and turn the government over to the Republicans. The President was serious enough to consult Attorney General Palmer on the legal procedures by which senatorial seats could be vacated.[3] Impossible of execution, out of keeping with the philosophy of American government, this plan revealed the deterioration of a once effective talent.

Tumulty must have learned of Wilson's scheme either from the President or from Palmer, for he later used the phraseology of Wilson's proposed statement of the plan when he drafted the President's Jackson Day letter. This letter, composed at Wilson's direction, advanced an idea only less fantastic than the earlier one. Insulting the mild reservationists, playing into the hands of Lodge, Wilson asked the Democrats to refuse compromise. If the treaty failed again, it would be taken to the people for a "solemn referendum" in the election of 1920.[4] The President was throwing the already battered treaty into the maelstrom of politics.

Opposed to the "solemn referendum," Tumulty nevertheless dutifully drafted Wilson's Jackson Day letter. Sometimes borrowing the President's words, sometimes expressing the President's intention in his own words, he worked and reworked the document. Houston and Newton D. Baker helped him, eliminating errors in fact and polishing the style. Edith Wilson, recording the President's wishes, made final revisions.[5] Homer Cummings read the letter at the Jackson Day Dinner on January 8. Most of the audience cheered. Bryan and many others protested. To the Democrats attempting to arrange a compromise, the letter was a tremendous obstacle.

While Tumulty was preparing the Jackson Day letter, he and

Hitchcock, after a conference on December 31, tried again to persuade Wilson to take the initiative for compromise. Tumulty struck first in a letter of January second. Taking care not to antagonize the President, he talked of concession as an adjunct to Wilson's conviction that the treaty, in some way, be made an election issue. Combining lip service to Wilson's idea with advice that rendered it nugatory, Tumulty suggested a compromise which, had it been achieved, could have resulted in ratification before an election could have been held:

> I know you will believe me sincere when I tell you that in my opinion we cannot longer adhere to the position we have taken in the matter of the Treaty. The people of the country have the impression that you will not consent to the dotting of an "i" or the crossing of a "t." In fact, these words have appeared in nearly every report of the interview Senator Hitchcock had with you at the White House. The result is that the country is slowly coming to the belief that we will accept no offer of compromise, even as to interpretative resolutions.
>
> The plan I would propose will not in its final result be at all inconsistent with the larger plan you already have in mind. Briefly, it is this: That you take the proposed substitute reservations offered by Mr. Hitchcock in the Senate on November fifteenth and make them your own, with the necessary modifications — adding whatever you think necessary to complete them. For instance, you might add a clause with reference to mandates — that no mandate shall be accepted by the United States without the consent of Congress. Senator Hitchcock informs me that before he introduced these reservations he consulted you and that they met with your approval. I have looked them over and attach hereto a copy of them.
>
> Frankly, the only objection to a plan like this is that we have yielded to the reservation idea and that you have given up the position which you took in the statement issued by you on Sunday [December 15], three weeks ago. But therein lies the very virtue of the thing I propose. It would force the mild reservationists to come to your side and would put upon Lodge the

whole responsibility of defeating the Treaty, and thus you would be in a position to go to the country in the way that you have in mind. In proposing these reservations, you could make a public statement outlining your reasons for doing so, and the country will applaud your effort by a reasonable compromise to reach a settlement. If you will look over the Hitchcock reservations, you will find that they follow the terms of your Denver speech and the other speeches you made in the West.[6]

This was a far cry from the dangerous strategy Tumulty had sponsored before the first defeat of the treaty. His caution was shared by Hitchcock, who on January 5 supplemented Tumulty's letter. Public opinion, he wrote Mrs. Wilson, was strong for compromise. Lodge, he declared, was primarily interested in Republican harmony and would accept compromise if he saw that enough Republicans were going to. But to persuade enough Republicans, concessions were needed, and as yet Hitchcock had had no encouragement from Wilson to make them.[7]

Mrs. Wilson quickly indicated that Tumulty was *non grata* and that Hitchcock had made no progress. In a sharp letter, she directed Hitchcock to send directly to her the original copy of the suggestions Wilson had given him the previous June. No one (by implication Tumulty) was to see them. Three days later the Jackson Day letter contained no suggestion of compromise. To Hitchcock's request for assistance from Wilson in his contest for the leadership with Underwood, Mrs. Wilson sent a polite refusal.[8] Hitchcock retained his position, but his victory owed nothing to the White House.

Less resolute men, or men with a smaller problem than the Versailles Treaty, might have given up. Tumulty and Hitchcock redoubled their efforts. Hitchcock, with Democratic Senators McKellar, Owen, Simmons, and T. J. Walsh, began, on January 18, a series of conferences with Republicans Kellogg, Lenroot, Lodge, and New to try to find a bipartisan basis for ratification. Tumulty attempted to smooth Hitchcock's path. With the assistance of Lansing, Lane, Baker, and later Houston, he composed a letter which he wanted the President to send to Hitchcock. This document, conciliatory in tone, considered, modified, and endorsed each important part of the Lodge resolution of ratification. The modifications were calculated to win the support of the mild reservationists. Even Lodge could have had little objection to them, for although they gave the Executive a larger part in determining the nature of American action within the League than he had contemplated, they accepted the core of his proposals. A masterful effort at compromise, Tumulty's suggested letter offered circumspect solutions even for Article X.[9] Lansing declared that if Wilson used the letter, the treaty would be ratified quickly. Later Houston repeated this view.[10] Certainly the letter would have given the bipartisan conference important material for discussion and high hopes for success.

Tumulty sent his proposal to Mrs. Wilson, urging that it be used:

It now appears that without any initiative on the part of the President, efforts are being made in the Senate to reach a compromise on the Peace Treaty. Those negotiations will soon approach a point at which both sides will reach their irreducible minimum. It is at this psychological moment that action must be taken — if it is to be taken at all — in making clear that the President is not insisting upon an unqualified adoption of the Treaty. . . . If we say nothing, and a compromise is reached, it will be too late to revise or change the agreement. . . .

Therefore, it would seem to me to be wise to inject at the proper moment, if negotiations have seemed to reach a compromise — our own interpretation of the Treaty.

In the accompanying letter, I have sketched what the President might use as the basis of a communication to Senator Hitchcock. The letter was framed after carefully eliminating the obnoxious parts of all the resolutions proposed by the majority and minority in the Senate Foreign Relations Committee, and by including, of course, the main thread running through the President's western speeches and the proposals made from time to time by Senator Hitchcock. . . .

Action along the lines suggested in this letter would make the issue clear and clean-cut and remove from the President's shoulders the burden of the responsibility which would be his for a seeming unyielding attitude.

If the President wishes to place full responsibility squarely upon Lodge and the Republicans, this, in my opinion, is the way. It has in it, the great opportunity of obtaining speedily the ratification of the Treaty.[11]

Mrs. Wilson did not reply to Tumulty's letter. Possibly she did not transmit his suggestion to the President. The next day Tumulty sent her Houston's endorsement of his plan. Still she did not reply. On the same day Hitchcock informed Tumulty that much progress had been made at the conferences. Only Article X remained at issue.[12] Referring to this progress, Tumulty repeated his appeal to Mrs. Wilson: "The psychological moment is approaching when the President could strike with great force along the lines suggested in the letter to Senator Hitchcock. . . ."[13] In another note he requested Mrs. Wilson to read the President a friendly editorial from the Oregon *Journal*. She answered abruptly that she would not.[14] Either at Wilson's wish or on her own, she had closed the door to communication as well as to compromise. For several weeks Tumulty sent no messages to the President or Mrs. Wilson.

The bipartisan conferences stalled on Article X. Wilson's aloofness hampered Hitchcock and the Democrats. Borah's opposition to any compromise inhibited Lodge and the Republicans. On January 22 Hitchcock again asked the President for help. Too late, on the twenty-sixth, after the conferences had failed, Wilson complied. His letter to Hitchcock contained several of the ideas that Tumulty had suggested almost two weeks earlier but offered no solution for the deadlock on Article X.[15]

At the end of January the Republican position was reinforced from abroad. Writing as a private citizen, Lord Grey published a letter in the London *Times* accepting all but one of the Lodge reservations. Perhaps suspecting Grey's feelings, Wilson, to Tumulty's dismay, had refused to see him the previous December.[16] Lloyd George, with Grey's letter in mind, declared that the United States could define any restrictions as long as the other powers did not have to express agreement with the American definition. But these statements failed to clear the air. They served only to anger Wilson.

The President's disposition became a matter of public comment in the first part of February. Tumulty and Lansing had been distressed by Wilson's recent diplomatic appointments, which Tumulty described as "terrible." Lansing protested to Mrs. Wilson against the man selected for Switzerland. This protest precipitated a crisis. Long dissatisfied with his Secretary of State, Wilson sent him a letter criticizing him for convening the Cabinet without authority. In another letter the President dismissed Lansing's objections to the Switzerland appointment. Lansing, exercising restraint, wrote the President explaining his reasons for calling the Cabinet meetings and notified the Cabinet that there would be no further meetings except at Wilson's direction. The Secretary of State withheld a letter of resignation only because Frank Polk appealed to his sense of duty. Wilson, however, again citing the unauthorized Cabinet meetings, requested Lansing's resignation, which the Secretary immediately submitted.[17]

The incident shocked the country. Tumulty, surprised by Wilson's first letter to Lansing, broke his silence to protest against the forced resignation. Grayson also tried to restrain the President. Polk, Lane, Redfield, and Baker expressed sympathy for Lansing. Even Mrs. Wilson admitted her husband's argument was weak. The dismissal could have been justified on the ground that Lansing's views on the treaty were hopelessly different from Wilson's, but Lansing should not have been chastised for convening the Cabinet. When the Lansing-Wilson correspondence was published, even the pro-Wilson press was appalled.[18]

Lansing's resignation further weakened Tumulty's influence. The President and Mrs. Wilson resented his intrusion. Lansing's departure cost him a friend in the Cabinet. When Tumulty suggested to Mrs. Wilson that Polk or Cummings be made Secretary of State, his letter was unanswered.[19] Wilson chose Bainbridge Colby, a capable phrase-maker but a man of no diplomatic experience. Although Tumulty eventually became friendly with Colby, during the first months of his tenure they constantly took opposite sides on important issues.

The failure of the bipartisan conference, Grey's letter, Lansing's resignation, and a growing public demand for compromise destroyed the morale of many Democratic Senators. Hitchcock reported a "strong disposition" among Democrats to "abandon the fight against the Lodge reservations." Only another command from the White House, he warned, would hold the party in line.[20] Concurring in these views, Tumulty begged the President to surrender. Let Wilson express his dissatisfaction with the Lodge reservation on Article X; make that a campaign issue, he advised, but only after the treaty had been accepted and peace had been made:

> I had a long talk with Senators Robinson and Glass the other day regarding the Treaty situation and there is no doubt that it is critical; that our forces are rapidly disintegrating. Both Glass and Robinson say that nothing but a statement from you will prevent a complete collapse. Robinson, who has been a devoted supporter of yours throughout the whole Treaty fight, says that Senators are influenced by an overwhelming sentiment from "back home" demanding immediate action on the Treaty, even with the Lodge reservations. Whether you should make a statement now or await the action of the Senate in ratifying the Treaty with the Lodge reservations, is a problem. There is great danger in taking action now irrevocable in character. There is no doubt that the country is tired of the endless Senate debate. The ordinary man on the street is for ratification even with the Lodge reservations. He yearns for peace and an early settlement of the whole situation. If the Treaty is ratified with the Lodge reservations, brought about with the aid of a majority of the Democrats, the Democratic party might as well not hold a convention this year. It wouldn't be possible under those circumstances to make the Treaty an issue in the next campaign and thus all the advantage would be with the Republicans.

> *My judgment is that we should accept the ratification of the Treaty with the Lodge reservations* with an address by the President to the American people, showing wherein these reservations weaken the whole Treaty and make it a useless instrument; showing what the real essence of Article X is — a checking of imperialism; that the purpose of the President in standing for unqualified ratification was to keep America's influence in the affairs of the League undiminished; that the imperialists of

the world were the real opponents of Article X; that the President's ambition was to have America enter the League with a great moral influence behind her so as to be in a position to check and prevent those things that in the past have been the breeders of war. Now that the Senate has acted, the question is whether the President by his action is going to postpone peace and thus aggravate a world situation which is now very serious.

If we pocket the Treaty, will we not be responsible for all the consequences and all the perils that may come because of the failure to bring about peace? [21]

Once again Wilson's failure to reply showed Tumulty that his counsel was unwelcome. There was no point in repeating his arguments. As he had so often done before, therefore, he adopted his chief's attitude as his own. For the rest of his life he expressed only Wilson's view on the treaty.

In March Tumulty helped draft Wilson's last statements against the Lodge reservations. The President's public letters to Hitchcock and to Simmons were deathblows to compromise. Slapping at Grey for his interference, antagonizing Britain and France by references to Article X as a means to check their imperialisms, the letters left Democrats loyal to the President with no choice.[22] The last votes on reservations were clearly political. The reservations adopted were gentler than those of November. In the last roll call on the treaty with reservations a majority of the Senate voted "aye." But enough Democrats, mostly Southerners, observing the dictum of party responsibility, heeded Wilson's wishes and joined the irreconcilables against the "Republicanized" treaty, preventing a two-thirds vote. The treaty was dead.

2. The Party's Choice

Tumulty's greatest concern, during the first half of 1920, other than the treaty itself, was the forthcoming Democratic convention. Although he felt that Wilson had made tactical errors, he hoped that the Republican failures to keep their campaign promises of 1918 and possible dissension in Republican ranks would permit Democratic victory. He realized, however, that, on their part, the Democrats needed solidarity and an appealing platform. He gave continual attention, therefore, to the contest for the Democratic nomination and to healing intra-party differences on domestic and foreign policies.

Tumulty's ideas for the platform were substantially those he had long held. He hoped to commit the party to them by persuading Wilson to make them White House policies before the convention met. With the urban Democrats of the East and Middle West he favored revision of the Volstead Act to permit the manufacture and sale of light wines and beer. Wilson, unwilling to request Congress to make that change, adopted Tumulty's plan in a plank dictated for the consideration of the convention, but the President abandoned the plank before June because he considered it politically inexpedient.[23]

Tumulty also failed to have his way on the issue of civil rights. Out of personal conviction and with an eye to the political left, he urged Wilson to grant an amnesty to those Americans, including Eugene Debs, who had been imprisoned because of their attitude toward the war. The President, however, refused even to permit Tumulty to receive a petition for the pardon of Debs.[24]

On the railroads and labor Tumulty and Wilson were in agreement. Tumulty approved of the President's decision to delay the return of the roads to private management until March 1920. He sympathized with his chief's objections to the Esch-Cummins Act which governed the return. Late in June he applauded the firm stand Hines took against a railroad strike. Increasingly cool to union labor, he abandoned the position he had taken while Wilson was in Paris. Making no reference to wages, hours, or compulsory collective bargaining, he suggested a labor plank which simply endorsed the ineffectual recommendations of the business-controlled Second Industrial Conference.[25]

Tumulty hoped to please labor as well as the middle class by a general economic program. To increase real income, he suggested that Wilson ask Congress for authority to control prices. He recommended tariff adjustments to protect young industries, and he advocated the reduction of taxes, especially the excess profits tax. On these matters Wilson agreed. He declined to use a long message Tumulty prepared on them, but in June he signed a public letter, written completely by Tumulty, castigating Congress for its delay in dealing with the railroads and its failure to act on the cost of living, tax revision, and other "similar urgent" matters. Congress, Tumulty declared, had been motivated only by political expediency.[26]

The outstanding issue for the Democrats was the treaty and the League. Tumulty agreed with Wilson that unqualified approval of the Administration's stand on the treaty was the first requisite for an acceptable platform. Tumulty and Burleson whipped the Democrats in Congress into active opposition to the Knox Resolution for a separate peace with Germany. Tumulty, praising Wilson's strong veto message, maintained that the failure of the Knox Resolution would disclose the inability of the Republicans to legislate peace.[27] The veto, following Wilson's Jackson Day letter, his final messages on the treaty, and its defeat, left the Democrats with no retreat. The time for repudiating the President had long since passed. At the convention, Tumulty felt, the Democracy had to stand on Wilson's record.

Tumulty was resolved to discipline the party on the treaty issue. He prompted Wilson's letter to G. E. Hamaker of Oregon, defining support of the treaty without the Lodge reservations as the criterion for White House endorsement of candidates in Democratic primaries. This letter, in spite of Tumulty's denials, was a specific challenge to Democratic Senator Chamberlain of Oregon. Tumulty also intended it to be a "smashing rejoinder to Lodge and Knox" and a general warning that in Wilson's "solemn judgment" it was "the duty of the Democratic party to endorse the Versailles Treaty without the Lodge reservations." [28] Shortly after the Hamaker letter Tumulty called Wilson's attention to a plank on the League which Carter Glass had written for the Virginia platform.[29] This was to be the Administration's proposal for the delegates at San Francisco.

Disagreement on home rule for Ireland complicated Tumulty's work with Wilson on the treaty plank. Hoping to make the Demo-

cratic point of view on the treaty and the League more attractive
to Irish-Americans, Tumulty co-operated with Attorney General
Palmer and Senators Gerry, Glass, and T. J. Walsh in framing a
plank endorsing Ireland's aspirations. The President, however, ignored Tumulty's request for assistance.[30]

A greater complication was Wilson's attitude toward a third term.
It was ridiculous for a man in Wilson's health to contemplate a
presidential campaign; even before his illness he had renounced the
idea. But after his partial recovery, possibly confused as a result
of his sickness, he conducted himself like a candidate. His Jackson
Day and Hamaker letters caused widespread speculation on his intentions. Instead of denying any desire for renomination, he kept
silent, refusing to support any candidate or to eliminate himself.
His silence increased the difficulties of those striving for a Wilsonian
plank on the League, for Democrats and Republicans, alike opposed
to a third term, identified the President's position on the treaty with
his apparent personal ambition.

A receptive although not an active candidate, Wilson would not
take Tumulty's advice that he declare against renomination. Late
in March, while the Knox Resolution was before Congress, Tumulty
urged Wilson to speak out. His letter to Mrs. Wilson, which the
President may never have seen, set forth the arguments for an
immediate statement:

> I do not know how the President feels about making an an-
> nouncement with reference to his attitude toward a third term
> and I am wondering if, in view of the Treaty situation and the
> proximity of the convention, this is not the time to consider
> making a final statement with reference to his attitude toward
> this important matter. *In my opinion this is the time to act*, so
> that we may garner whatever advantage would flow to the
> President and the Administration from such a course.
> It is clear that the Republicans industriously circulate the
> story that the President was attempting to create out of the
> League of Nations an issue upon which he would soon base
> a reason for demanding a third term. . . . I think that a dignified
> statement of withdrawal.made now would greatly help all

along the line and will strengthen every move the President wishes to make during the remainder of his term. . . .

I think the statement of withdrawal could, in its preparation, be made a ten-strike for the League of Nations. It should be most intimate and generous in character and should embody the President's real feelings with reference to the League. . . . No purpose of self-exploitation was in the Treaty; the only desire of the President was to accomplish a great purpose and thus prevent another and what might turn out to be a final war.

Then the President should, in a striking way, say that he wishes his name not to be considered in connection with a third term; that were he nominated by a convention he would decline, but that his withdrawal must not be considered as a withdrawal of his interest in this great project; that he intends to fight with all of his energy for the fulfillment of the great purpose that lay behind the League, whether in office or out of office.[31]

This letter elicited no response. To eliminate the President and further the treaty plank, therefore, Tumulty and Louis Seibold of the New York *World* evolved a complicated stratagem. Seibold, anxious to be the first reporter to interview Wilson since his collapse, suggested to Tumulty that such an interview would result in a better understanding of Wilson's attitude toward the League. Tumulty, recognizing the publicity value of Seibold's idea, helped make the arrangements. Their scheme, developed in April, was not broached until June when both men felt that the proceedings of the Republican convention set the stage for comment by Wilson. Together they prepared a letter asking Mrs. Wilson's permission for the interview. She and the President consented, and the interview was set for June fifteenth and sixteenth. Meanwhile, Tumulty and Seibold developed their plans in detail.[32]

Tumulty was determined to use the interview for his ideas on the Democratic platform. Seibold could demonstrate that Wilson was sound of mind and competent to pass judgment on current questions. These questions, with loaded answers, Tumulty and Seibold drew up together. Gathering pertinent material for replies from the *Congressional Record*, newspaper reports of the Republican convention, and current periodicals, Tumulty composed questions on every phase of American foreign policy, including the treaty, the League, and the Mexican issue. He also prepared questions and answers on the tariff, labor, taxes, prices, and the Volstead Act, in each case emphasizing his own views. Finally, and perhaps most important, Seibold and Tumulty planned to interrogate Wilson on the third term tradition and his post-presidential plans. They expected to obtain a renunciation of any desire for renomination.[33]

Wilson, however, had his own plans for the interview. Before Seibold arrived, the President indicated his intention to turn the scheme to his own ends. Tumulty discovered, after submitting a tentative list of questions, that his chief would answer few. In reference to the suggested questions on the Presidency, Mrs. Wilson told Tumulty that nothing but exaltation of Wilson would be permitted. Tumulty's private comment on these instructions registered his disgust: in pencil, alongside of her order, he wrote a note for his private files inviting her to go to hell.[34]

Seibold, who eventually won a Pulitzer prize for his article, had to confine it to the topics Wilson approved. As published throughout the country, the article told of the President's amazing recovery, "splendid intellect," vigor, and "saving sense of humor." It pictured him as fully able to discharge his duties. The article presented Wilson's request that the Democratic platform contain no "ambiguity or evasion" on the League. The Prussian-like Republican leaders, Wilson told Seibold, had beclouded the issue. The Democrats, he trusted, would give the people the chance for a solemn referendum by declaring in "positive and definite" language for the treaty without the Lodge reservations. Beyond this point Wilson had nothing to say. He would not discuss politics, suffrage, prohibition, prices or candidates. To such questions he simply replied that he was sure the Democratic platform would be "progressive." [35]

Wilson effectively frustrated Tumulty's intentions. The public interpreted the interview as a bid for a third term. The President received offers of support and financial assistance. McAdoo, sure that Wilson was definitely receptive, declared himself out of the running. And Wall Street made Wilson the favorite in the betting on the Democratic choice.[36]

While Wilson was receptive, Tumulty could not effectively check the President's boom. Loyalty to his chief prevented him from building up any other candidate. Consequently his maneuvers were largely negative. Differing from Bryan on the League and on prohibition, he had diverted patronage from the Commoner's friends. He had ignored Vice-President Marshall and New Jersey's Governor E. I. Edwards whose managers were Walter Vick and Hague. On the positive side he had kept on good terms with McAdoo, Palmer, and Governor Cox of Ohio. While McAdoo conducted a campaign by the questionable device of denying interest in the nomination, Tumulty helped him try to get some top-level patronage for his supporters and warned him to terminate his legal connections with Harry Doheny. Palmer was an old friend whose attributes Tumulty well knew, and whom he probably preferred to any other candidate. But recognizing the Attorney General's unpopularity with labor, Tumulty made no effort to give him a disproportionate share of political favors. Governor James M. Cox a moderate "wet," sponsored by Taggart, McGraw, McCombs, Murphy, and Brennan, was the central figure in the "stop McAdoo" movement of anti-Administration Democrats. Yet Tumulty maintained cordial relations with Cox, whose record marked him as something better than a stalking horse. He was ready to give his full support to McAdoo, Palmer, or Cox after the convention but unwilling to be an active partisan for any of them before the nomination.[37] If Tumulty had wished to be less neutral, the obligations of his office and Wilson's refusal to withdraw would have constrained him.

The Democrats who met at San Francisco late in June 1920 were sharply divided on policies and personalities. Administration leaders were intent on retaining their control. Their opponents were resolved to regain the suzerainty lost at Baltimore in 1912. State bosses, nursing old grievances over patronage, had little sympathy with Wilson's treaty which their immigrant and first generation constituents for the most part disliked. Their interest, besides power, was in beer. United behind the treaty, the Wilsonians were at odds on the nomination. Bainbridge Colby and Burleson had cultivated the President's third term ambitions. Colby, Wilson's political manager at the convention, communicated with the White

House by secret code. Glass, who carried Wilson's platform to the convention, and Cummings, whose keynote speech lauded the President, were for Wilson's policies but against a third term. Both were receptive "dark horses." A majority of federal officeholders, led by Roper and Woolley, worked for McAdoo. Burleson, in spite of his relations with Wilson, co-operated with them. Others supported Palmer. The Wilsonians proved strong enough to control the convention on the platform but, divided on the nomination, they lost out to the leaders of the opposition.

Tumulty followed the proceedings at San Francisco closely. Ray T. Baker of California, Louis Seibold, and Joseph E. Davies sent him up-to-the-minute bulletins. After a plank on the League was adopted with few changes from what Wilson had endorsed, Tumulty persuaded his chief to express his approval in a public telegram to Cummings.[38] But he could not persuade the President to discuss the nomination even in private.

Wilson's continued silence, an indication of his ambitions, complicated the balloting. Had he spoken out for McAdoo or Palmer, the long deadlock that developed could probably have been prevented. But Palmer, McAdoo, and Cox, the strongest possibilities, held each other off. On the twelfth ballot Cox, for the first time, took the lead. Bryan had denounced him as a "wet" and Glass had declared that he was unacceptable to Wilson. Cox, with victory in sight, telephoned Tumulty, requesting a denial of Glass' statement. The President, however, would issue no denial. On his own initiative, Tumulty then told the press that he was authorized to say that Wilson was impartial.[39]

The President was, in fact, decidedly partial, but only to himself. The day Cox telephoned, Ray Baker also called Tumulty to convey the astonishing news that Colby was planning to take the floor and move Wilson's nomination by acclamation. Baker did not know it, but Wilson had approved this plan subject to the consent of his friends at San Francisco. Their unanimous dissent dissuaded Colby, but before that development Tumulty begged Mrs. Wilson to prevent Colby's proposed action. Guarding his words so as not to offend her, but reminding her of his objections to a third term, Tumulty pointed out that if Wilson was intent on renomination, he should at least employ a tactic more feasible than that suggested by Colby. He advised Mrs. Wilson to delay any move until a complete deadlock had wearied the delegates.[40] Doubtless he anticipated that before such a deadlock the convention would select someone other than the President.

As usual, Mrs. Wilson did not reply. Nevertheless, another report from Ray Baker prompted Tumulty to write her again. Warning her that the approaching deadlock was helping John W. Davis, whom he knew Wilson opposed, Tumulty urged her to have the President act at once. He suggested that McAdoo, Cox, Colby, or Cummings could be "put across" with Wilson's endorsement. In a second note on the same day, Tumulty simply informed Mrs. Wilson that unless the President spoke out, Bryan might be able to force the nomination of an undesirable candidate.[41] Neither note was answered. Wilson made no comment.

Two days later, on July 7, after more than forty ballots, Cox was nominated. The long battle had produced hard feelings. Bryan, still unreconciled to any "wet," announced that his heart was "in the grave." McAdoo devoted the next decade to a bitter quest for the nomination. Palmer and Cummings were openly unenthusiastic. Wilson's telegram of congratulations to Cox was perfunctory. Toward those who had discouraged Colby, the President was unmistakably cold.[42]

Of all the Wilsonians, only Tumulty displayed unreserved satisfaction with the party's choice. His habit of regularity committed him to wholehearted support for Cox, who needed help from the White House. Tumulty stood ready to render it, prepared to fight to the last minute in spite of the vanishing chances of victory.

3. The People's Choice

The campaign of 1920, from its beginning, was a losing battle for the Democrats. The Republican Party was united, better organized, and wealthier. The electorate, relatively uninterested in politics, was, as in 1918, tired of Democratic rule. The idealism, the fervor for reform, that had characterized Wilson's campaigns was spent. The average voter, it seemed, wanted most of all to be left alone. Warren G. Harding invented the word "normalcy," a relaxing panacea connoting a golden age of other years, and made it his most effective issue. On the issue of the League, which Wilson had hoped would decide the contest, Republican leaders stood squarely on both sides while Harding straddled. Disunited, badly organized, the Democrats offered no convincing answer to their opponents who promised all things to all men.

Few Democrats put up a good fight. Bryan, sulking, for the first time since 1896 had nothing to say. House conceded victory to the Republicans. Wilson, curiously optimistic, did little to help. The burden fell on Cox and his running mate, Franklin D. Roosevelt, who campaigned vigorously, on Pat Harrison and Key Pittman, who were of great assistance at party headquarters, and on Tumulty, who devoted himself completely to the contest.

For Tumulty the campaign presented several distinct but related problems. He tried to repair the disintegrating Democratic organization and improve the clumsy tactics of the National Committee. He helped Cox define the party's stand on domestic issues, defend Wilson's record, and explain Wilson's position on the League. Finally, he attempted to get Wilson to participate actively in the campaign.

Immediately after the Democratic Convention, Cox's supporters took over the National Committee. George White, a dapper, affable mediocrity replaced Homer Cummings as chairman. Ed Moore of Ohio, Cox's prenomination manager, was the power behind White. Cummings, distrustful of both men, refused to have anything to do with them. Unfortunately for the party, they proved to be incompetent on the very level of politics for which they were presumably well trained.

Tumulty liked White and Moore personally, but after observing their work for two months, he begged Cox to force a reorganization. "The campaign, so far as the National organization is concerned," he wrote the candidate, "is an utter and tragic failure. There is no executive or campaign committee; no plan of campaign;

no contact between the National organization and the various state organizations." The National Committee had raised little money. Inactivity discouraged possible contributors. "No bureau . . . is functioning," Tumulty lamented. "They have not merely ceased to function, they have never functioned at all." Only "heroic methods" could counteract the "demoralization and chaos." Tumulty urged Cox to call a meeting of the Committee at once. If White, whose health was poor, was unable to continue in his post, "a man of the type of Roper" should be put in his place. Cox telegraphed Tumulty to "get hold of Ed Moore" and "agree upon . . . action to be taken." [43] But this suggestion was useless. Moore, even more than White, was responsible for the conditions Tumulty had described.

Tumulty failed in his efforts to vitalize the party through the use of federal patronage. Hoping to interest disaffected leaders in the campaign by rewarding them for past services, he recommended Homer Cummings and Martin Glynn for Cabinet posts. Wilson rejected the suggestions. Left to his own devices, Tumulty persuaded Cummings and Palmer to take the stump late in the campaign. Using memoranda Tumulty prepared, they made a few speeches, but their efforts were spiritless.[44]

Tumulty supplemented and improved the work of the Democratic publicity agencies. He called Cox's attention to the editorial counsel of the Springfield *Republican*, New York *Times*, New York *Post*, and Newark *News*, papers which, he felt, best understood the desires of the independent voters. By-passing the National Committee, he supplied Frank Cobb of the New York *World*, and Albert Dear, publisher of the Jersey City *Journal*, with editorial materials. With McKee Barclay and George Creel he prepared memoranda for the Democratic Publicity Bureau.[45]

Two incidents connected with the public relations, however, revealed the collapse of Democratic morale. The usually cautious and normally pro-Democratic New York *Times* embarrassed Tumulty by accusing him of collaboration in a motion picture publicity stunt. After Tumulty's denial, the *Times* retracted the story, but the damage had been done.[46] Later in the campaign Colonel House failed Tumulty, who with Woolley had almost convinced the publisher of the Republican Philadelphia *Public Ledger* to announce that journal's support for Cox. Woolley advised House that only his assistance was needed to complete arrangements. The Colonel, however, declaring that no newspaper could change the vote in Pennsylvania, told Woolley and Tumulty to abandon the project.[47] Unimportant in themselves, the *Times'* mistake and House's disinclination to co-operate were symptomatic of the difference in the Democratic attitude between 1912 and 1920.

Poor morale, desperation, or sheer malice led some Democrats to circulate a false report that Harding was partly Negro. Tumulty has been blamed unjustly for that unpleasant episode. Actually he did his best to prevent the spread of the story. Dr. William E. Chancellor of Ohio gave Tumulty affidavits from several Ohioans certifying that various of Harding's ancestors were colored. Chancellor and Virginia Williams, an employee at Republican headquarters in Chicago, wanted the Democrats to distribute the affidavits. Tumulty, however, told Chancellor "that under no consideration would the White House lend its influence" to the scheme. He refused to acknowledge Chancellor's letters and he consistently informed inquiring newspapermen that responsible Democratic officials knew nothing about Chancellor's story and were not interested in it.[48]

Tumulty hoped to win votes by emphasizing what he considered the genuine issues. Even before the convention he declared that "the whole case of the Democratic party in this campaign is built around its sympathy in behalf of welfare legislation." [49] In October, appealing to progressives in both parties, he directed an attack on Harding for his criticisms, in 1912, of Theodore Roosevelt. Assisted by Secretary of Agriculture Meredith, he supplied Cox with data on the Democratic legislation which had benefited farmers. Tumulty and Governor W. P. G. Harding of the Federal Reserve Board also sent Cox information on the salutary effects of the Federal Reserve Act.[50]

In spite of his contentions about "welfare legislation," however, Tumulty made no explicit gesture toward the labor vote. Contrary to newspaper reports, he took no part in the government's efforts to ration fuel and to settle the coal strike during the summer of 1920. He did not suggest to Cox the comprehensive labor program he had previously recommended to Wilson. Probably as a result of his experience in the coal strike of 1919, he had the middle class rather than labor in mind when he urged the President, during the campaign, to reassert the need for federal authority in all cases of labor trouble in vital industries.[51]

Frequently Tumulty helped Cox defend Wilson's record. He drafted replies to Republican criticisms of the canal tolls legislation, the conduct of the war, and the President's tariff policy and tariff commission. When Penrose blamed the Democrats for keeping the excess profits tax in effect after the war, Tumulty pointed out that the Republicans in Congress, ignoring Wilson's recommendations, had failed to repeal it.[52]

Tumulty encouraged Cox to attack prohibition and Republican campaign expenditures. Cox had favored legalizing light wines and beer, but personnel at the Democratic headquarters in New York City and James Kerney in New Jersey urged the candidate to declare himself on the "dry side of the liquor issue." Such a reversal, they argued, would bring Bryan into the campaign and win approval from women voters. Tumulty disagreed. "You would not only lose the liberal support," he wired Cox, "but you would not gain the dry support." Even honest drys, Tumulty maintained, preferred "frankness" to "wobbling." [53] Cox took Tumulty's advice. He also agreed with Tumulty on "slush." After John W. Weeks asked businessmen to raise fifteen million dollars "to get rid of the Administration now in Washington," Tumulty suggested Cox pillory the Republican use of money. He was within his rights, for the Republicans raised and spent almost four times as much as the Democrats, but Cox was severely criticized for discussing "slush" by those who felt he should have confined himself to more elevated topics.[54]

From the beginning of the campaign Tumulty made the Treaty of Versailles, as Wilson had presented it, his primary concern. It was the subject of most of his communications to Cox. Unlike most Wilsonians, Tumulty was confident that Cox would adopt the President's point of view. Nevertheless he undertook to persuade the candidate to increase the emphasis and the frequency of his statements on the treaty and the League. Tumulty made the arrangements for Cox's visit to Wilson; he represented the Administration at the acceptance ceremony at Dayton; finally he helped Cox draft his acceptance speech, writing an unequivocal passage on the League:

> I am in favor of going in. This is the supreme test. . . . This question must be met and answered honestly. . . . We must say in language which our own people can understand, whether we shall unite with our former Allies to make effective the only plan of peace and reconstruction which has been formulated or whether we propose to play a lone hand in the world and guard our isolation with a huge army and an ever increasing navy. . . . I repeat: I am in favor of going in.[55]

In September Tumulty advised Cox to stress the League in every speech. "Your friends hope you will stick to the League issue," he wrote, "driving home every day Harding's inconsistencies and forcing him to say for what substitute for peace he now stands." [56] To assist in this effort Tumulty drew up a series of memoranda for Democratic speakers. He sent Cox his file on the German-American Alliance, contending that the Alliance was supporting Harding and isolation in order to recoup Germany's position in Europe. He prepared a memorandum demonstrating that religious leaders of all faiths in America had endorsed the League as an application of Christian ethics in international affairs. After the League settled a Polish-Lithuanian dispute, Tumulty advised Cox to point out the effectiveness of the new institution as a means to avert war. He supplied Cox with quotations from wartime speeches of Lodge, Taft, and Root in favor of the League principle, and at the candidate's request, he replied to Corinne Roosevelt Robinson, who had asserted that her brother, Theodore Roosevelt, in December 1918, helped frame the Lodge reservations. This proved, Tumulty declared, that for purely partisan reasons the Republicans had always been prepared to condemn any plan proposed by Wilson.[57]

Cox was co-operative and grateful. As he concentrated more and more on the League, Democratic analysts felt that he was gaining ground. But Cox, Moore, and Tumulty realized that they lacked time and prestige to overcome Harding's obvious lead. Aware of the odds against them, they felt that only Wilson's continual, overt assistance could make victory possible. The President's silence was being interpreted as disapproval. If he spoke out, his many admirers, both disgruntled Democrats and indifferent independents, might give Cox their essential support.[58]

Tumulty endeavored to persuade Wilson to enter the campaign. He knew that the President's health permitted no speeches, but after conferring with Moore, he tried to get Wilson to issue a series of statements. "The idea," Tumulty wrote his chief, "is to have you, beginning in October, issue a weekly address to the American people." Harrison and White repeated this request.[59] Wilson, however, unwilling to engage in any direct exchange with Harding, at first refused.

Hoping to alter the President's decision, Tumulty and George Creel prepared a statement for his use. Intended to counteract the "poison spread by Lodge" to the effect that Wilson had failed to "consult anyone about possible changes in the treaty," the statement quoted the cables exchanged beween Wilson and Taft on the League. Wilson wrote Tumulty that he was pleased that he and Creel were at work. He hoped Tumulty would send the material to the Speakers' Bureau, but the President would not answer Lodge or Harding himself.[60] Recognizing the finality in Wilson's tone, Tumulty sent the Taft material to Cox for his release to the press. A memorandum of Tumulty to Wilson on the churches of America and his suggested reply to various speeches of Elihu Root met the same fate.[61]

However, continuing pleas from Tumulty and Cox had some effect on Wilson. During October he made three contributions to the campaign. Republican Senator Spencer of Missouri provoked him to one effort. Spencer claimed that Wilson had promised to send American troops to defend the boundaries of Rumania in case of invasion. Tumulty issued an unqualified denial for Wilson. Spencer then declared that Tumulty spoke without authority. At Tumulty's suggestion, Wilson repeated the denial, maintaining that the voters of Missouri would determine whether he or Spencer told the truth.[62] Late in October the President, speaking from his wheel chair, asked the American people to vote for pro-League candidates.[63] Before this address he had issued his only other important statement.

On October 3, in a message to the voters, Wilson declared that the election was a "genuine national referendum." [64] Believing that, he was confident that the people also believed it and would elect Cox. Tumulty, however, was distressed. After going over a draft of the statement with Creel, he begged the President to delete the paragraph on the election as a referendum:

> However much we want this to be the truth, the fact remains that it is not true in any degree. There is not a single national magazine . . . presenting our side of the case, not ten per cent of the daily press is presenting the case of the League, and there is the added fact that the lack of money and lack of proper organization has deprived us entirely of any machinery that might enable us to make a proper presentation of our own. Because of this . . . it is not a genuine referendum. For you to make such a statement at this time would stop us, in the event of defeat, from pointing out the utter unfairness of this imperfect referendum.[65]

Wilson, unconvinced, replied briefly that he was sorry, he could not agree.[66]

By the end of October the battle was clearly lost. Tumulty was momentarily encouraged when Colonel Harvey, Wilson's old backer who was now a leading sponsor of Harding, published a cartoon distasteful to the Catholic Church,[67] but Tumulty's enthusiasm was merely a façade. Before the campaign ended, his one speech, at Bethesda, Maryland, on October 28, suggested his real feelings. With deep emotion he praised Wilson as a man and a public figure. On the eve of defeat, this was a powerful elegy on a statesmen whose era was about to close.[68]

In a letter to Mrs. Wilson, Tumulty tacitly admitted defeat. "We are associated with the greatest force for good in the world," he wrote. "We know this in our very souls and no mere results of tomorrow can alter . . . this in the least." To Cox's telegram of thanks for his "helpfulness and confidence," Tumulty replied: "I was . . .

proud to serve." He knew what mistakes had been made, but he felt that the cause had been just. The next day Harding was elected. Tumulty remarked that the result was not a landslide but an "earthquake." [69] Harding chose to accept Wilson's view that it was a solemn referendum.

4. Last Days

Between the election and the inauguration, the White House was clothed in gloom. Tumulty agreed with Stockton Axson, Wilson's brother-in-law, that "the people didn't vote to seat Harding . . . [the] vote was . . . for nothing except 'a change.' " [70] That change was a departure from all the things with which Tumulty identified his chief. Defeat brought idealization and sentimentalization. The last days were "melancholy," but there were a few things left to do.

Mindful of the financial needs of his family and unwilling to assume a sinecure, Tumulty decided to leave public life and return to the practice of law. He was concerned, however, about loyal Democrats who lost their offices in the Republican deluge. Although declining Wilson's offers to nominate him to the Customs Court of Appeal or the Canadian-American Joint Commission,[71] Tumulty recommended Cordell Hull and Champ Clark for these positions. "Clark," Tumulty wrote Wilson, "has been defeated and . . . is brokenhearted. . . . It would be a most generous thing if you could appoint [him]." [72]

In defeat, the enemies of other years were forgiven. "Will you tell the President," Tumulty asked Mrs. Wilson, "that William F. McCombs just died? Would he care to send a telegram of condolence . . . ?" "You and I have not always agreed . . . " Tumulty reminded Frank Hague, "but . . . when you did agree to give your friendly support to anything . . . you never deserted or forgot your obligations." To Dr. Cary Grayson Tumulty wrote: "This is not a plea of confession . . . but a word of tribute from one whom you probably misunderstood to one whom I unfortunately misunderstood. . . . I have witnessed so wonderful a demonstration of . . . a true heart interest in the President, that your fine character and generous nature stand self-revealed." [73]

At the very end, Tumulty bade farewell to his friends. To the members of the Cabinet he expressed his faith in the ultimate triumph of Wilson's principles. He thanked his intimates among the newspapermen for their co-operation. For James Kerney he had a special message: ". . .You have the small credit . . . of having discovered me and whether or not you are proud of the discovery . . . I am very proud of the discoverer. . . . [You] have kept the faith." [74]

Tumulty's last letter from the White House was to his brother, Philip:

> Eight years ago tomorrow . . . I arrived at the White House offices and telephoned my first message to Pop. . . . I want the last official letter I shall write to be . . . to you. . . . I want you to feel that I have tried to hold our banner high and do while I was here just the things my dear father and mother would have me do. Her generosity, her fine emotions, and his common sense, have been my greatest assets. I have lived in the presence of a great man and I tried hard to serve him. . . . The happy feeling that I have now is that the many people who have come in contact with me do, in truth, feel sorry that my work has come to its close. How God must laugh at the petty men who think that election returns settle everything. . . .[75]

The next day Warren G. Harding became President of the United States. Charles Evans Hughes, his Secretary of State, refused to reply to communications from the League of Nations. Wilson, a broken man, retired to his new Washington home on S Street.

* * * * *

The failure was complete — the grand vision gone; the treaty dead; the election lost; the party disabled; the leader fallen, and with him his associates. Most of them never recovered from the shock. Yet in the distant perspective the mechanics of failure appear less shocking. Wilson came to power with the support of an uneasy alliance of organization Democrats and crusading liberals, joined, after his nomination, by Southerners who distrusted both. He conquered in 1912 a divided opposition. Defeat reunited his opponents while the fruits of victory gradually destroyed his coalition. The liberals, after accomplishing their purpose — the purpose of their generation — had left neither the energy nor the imagination to cope with the problems of America which, intensified during war, came into focus by 1920. By 1916 they had lost their program, by 1918 their organization. Meanwhile the organization Democrats of the North and South, never compatible, drifted further and further apart. Openly hostile by 1918, they were by 1920 dueling venomously over the sorry issues of patronage, prejudice, and prohibition. Not until 1932, and then only in time of crisis, could a new generation of liberals with a new leader restore the still uneasy triple alliance.

There was no one who could have prevented the disruption of Wilson's Democracy. The President, like his fellow liberals, after 1916 had no policy except a foreign policy. Of what he had done at home, conservatives had had enough. To labor, to farmers, to consumers, he had nothing more to offer. In spite of the continuing efforts of his political counsellors, he had too often spurned the professional politicians of the North. The South, well rewarded, was willing to follow its benefactor, particularly on foreign policy, but the South alone was insufficient. Southern Congressmen and Cabinet officers in 1917 and 1918 managed primarily to antagonize Northern reformers and organization men alike. After 1918 these Southerners, unchanged, essentially unchangeable, had more power within the party than they had had in a decade. And even in the South Wilson had no personal organization which he could turn over, had he desired, to a successor. This, as well as his disinclination, prevented his having a successor. The aspirants for that rôle, mostly undiscerning and clumsy men, in large part lacked inspiration, organization, and ability. The best of them, McAdoo, a victim of his own ambition, while alienating many who might have helped him, had curdled his own disposition and integrity. The worst of them, Palmer, fouled the Democratic tradition as well as his personal reputation by his irresponsible red-baiting. Where these men failed, Tumulty could not succeed in saving the party. But he tried. He had no personal following. He had largely lost, by 1916, access to the stuff of political power. Yet, conscious of the party's disintegration, he attempted to restore the coalition that had in 1912 produced victory and, as a means to that end, he attempted to redefine political issues. Just as he could not, without power, restore the lost sectional balance, he could not, even with vision, find new political directions. Where he almost succeeded in this latter task, his memorandum on labor proved so disturbing, so unprecedented in politics as well as in Wilsonian liberalism, that he quickly abandoned its conclusions. Above all, however, his loyalty, the compulsive product of temperament and training, bound him to his chief and therefore to Wilson's limitations.

The Democracy was disabled, but to it Wilson entrusted his treaty. As a party leader he perhaps had no choice. The Democrats after 1918 desperately needed an issue on which they could unite and win. This, Tumulty and Cummings among others, felt, foreign policy could provide. The Republicans, aggressively confident after 1918, were bound to attack anything Wilson produced. His product, it developed, was vulnerable. Whatever the merits of the decisions of the Paris Conference, they were frequently, as Tumulty's reactions demonstrated, liabilities in domestic politics. The treaty simply lacked the winning potential for which the Democrats had hoped. In the Senate, moreover, the Republicans controlled the votes and the parliamentary processes which could have encumbered a much more popular proposal. If, at this point, concessions were in order, they were nonetheless out of the question. Democratic strategists still hoped to win without them. The Republicans still asked for more than Wilson was willing to give. After the treaty, in this difficult environment, had for the first time been rejected, responsible men on both sides tried to save it from the ravages of partisanship. It was, regrettably, too late. Tumulty, like too many others, fully understood the need for compromise only after Wilson's physical and emotional condition made compromise impossible for him and consequently for the many Democrats still loyal to him. The Republicans, of course, would not surrender. While they considered compromise, the Democrats could not present a proposal for which they had their leader's support. The treaty died. Already the election of 1920 had ceased to be a doubt, but the ineptitude of the divided, disabled Democrats turned their defeat, in any case probable, into rout.

The failure was complete, and shocking, but the process of failure is clear in retrospect. The defeat of the League no longer shocks, for it is now also clear that an international organization in itself cannot guarantee peace. Yet the shock persists because the grand vision of continuing peace through international organization, a vision inexorably associated with Wilson's treaty, is precious still to men who would believe, as Wilson and Tumulty and so many of their generation believed, that in a good world reasonable human beings can solve amicably and finally the problems of living together. Tumulty should have known that this was doubtful. The microcosm of experience with which he was so familiar, the processes of politics, of party structure and partisan propaganda, suggested that men were wicked and unreasonable, political solutions painful and ephemeral. Neither he nor Wilson should have expected any League, or tariff, or antitrust law to end rivalries for power or to overcome the strong attachments of men to other men and institutions. Yet because they did expect these things, the premises of Wilsonian liberalism suffered when his treaty fell. Men were shocked, for they had founded their hopes on a dream. Wilson, crushed, blamed his enemies. Tumulty in part agreed, but also, perhaps for the wrong reasons, he blamed himself. He probably could not have rescued the treaty. It perhaps would have made very little difference, in the long run, if he had. But it seems likely that he blamed himself, not for some technical political error, made or imagined, but, as his generation and other generations have blamed themselves, for the wickedness of men. This pains especially those who, like Tumulty, believe that the grand vision, even if only a dream, is a precious one.

CHAPTER XIV

Epilogue

ALTHOUGH he missed the excitement of office, Tumulty returned to private life and the practice of law with enthusiasm. Still young, accustomed to hard work, he devoted himself to his profession with rewarding energy. Long hours at the office and social, charitable, and family obligations filled his days. But time was never lacking for political discussion and planning. Residing in the nation's political center, Tumulty kept in touch with party affairs and party leaders. More often an interesting observer than a participant, he abided by two political loyalties — to the Democracy and the Wilson tradition as he interpreted it.

In the first weeks after leaving the executive offices, while establishing himself as a member of the Washington bar, Tumulty recorded his view of Wilson in his widely read memoir. For some time he had contemplated such a book. In part it was a labor of love, for he wanted to give extended expression to the sentiments in his Bethesda speech and to answer the critics of Wilson's policies. The book, however, was not easy to write. Aware of his lack of training, Tumulty made no pretense of scholarship, and the criticisms of scholars bothered him less than did the wounded feelings of his erstwhile associates. House took issue with several of Tumulty's interpretations. Other Wilsonians felt, in varying degrees, that they had been praised too little or blamed too much. Furthermore, Wilson himself did not like the book.[1] Anticipating misunderstandings and resentment, Tumulty would not have attempted his *Woodrow Wilson* had he not needed the royalties to underwrite his legal career.[2]

Tumulty's memoir strained old friendships less than did his political activity. He expended his political energy largely within the party where defeat and rivalry had created a difficult atmosphere. The supporters of McAdoo, led by Roper, Glass, Woolley, Baruch, and Chadbourne, began in 1921 to attack George White and others of the Cox faction then in control of the National Committee. Tumulty, personally friendly with Cox and cool to McAdoo, agreed that White ought to resign but objected to the tactics of the McAdoo men. Putting the party above any faction, he particularly resented their refusal to contribute to campaign funds while White continued in office. As a result of Tumulty's attitude, Baruch concluded erroneously that he would resist any change on the National Committee. Notwithstanding Tumulty's co-operation with Cordell Hull, who replaced White, Baruch's misconception persisted, reached Wilson, and made the ex-President suspicious of Tumulty's political purposes.[3]

Wilson, a secluded invalid, drew further and further away from his former secretary. Tumulty's book and his friendship with Cox intensified the discord which had begun to develop in 1916. Mrs. Wilson, long Tumulty's bitter critic, had kept him from her husband since the President's collapse. At S Street her brothers helped her guard Wilson's door, and the ex-President, seeing Tumulty infrequently, never took him into his confidence. Unable to realize that he was being rejected by his idol, ignorant of Wilson's plans and ambitions, Tumulty groped toward what was to be the most severe blow of his life.

Wilson was no longer a completely competent man. His illness produced a petulance and egocentricity out of keeping with his former character. Occasionally he showed flashes of his old intellectual abilities, but increasingly he entertained ideas and prejudices he would once have rejected or at least resisted. He even contemplated running for the Presidency again. This impossible dream made him hostile to other candidates. Even McAdoo, although a son-in-law, was not wanted at S Street; Cox was a favorite whipping boy; Tumulty and others who had opposed Wilson at San Francisco and would have opposed him again were only less in disfavor.[4]

Partly as an adjunct to his candidacy, Wilson worked intermittently on a platform. At the very least he envisioned himself as the party's leader and the platform as his program for 1924. He consulted his close political friends, Colby, Newton D. Baker, Baruch, Brandeis, Cobb, Norman Davis, and Houston on his statement of Democratic aims, which they all knew as the "Document." The work of tired liberals, the "Document," as it evolved and in its final form, was an unimpressive repetition of old ideas. Its first objective was the League, followed by demands for a lower tariff, the creation of a Federal Department of Transportation, the extension of federal conservation projects, and the rigid enforcement of the Volstead Act. In the United States of the early twenties it had little political appeal, but Wilson expected great results. Fearing that premature exposure would spoil the effect, he consistently refused to discuss publicly the issues defined in his precious manuscript.[5]

Silent, even secretive, Wilson nevertheless distrusted those who disagreed with his hidden views. Tumulty's forthright objections to the Volstead Act were no longer tolerable to the ex-President. Furthermore, with his collaborators, Wilson tended to classify all "wets" with Tammany ward heelers. There was an intellectual and social snobbery at S Street that allowed no room for Tumulty.

Tumulty should have sensed Wilson's aloofness. His advice was clearly unwelcome. Mindful of Wilson's public relations, Tumulty, with Bainbridge Colby and J. Fred Essary, suggested, when Cardinal Gibbons died, that Wilson praise the Cardinal's career, but their letter was ignored. Later, when Tumulty asked Wilson to wish General Smuts godspeed in his attempt to settle the Irish question, Wilson again did not reply.[6] In January 1922, Tumulty recommended that Wilson send "a telegram of greetings" to Governor Cox who was to preside at the Jackson Day Dinner at Dayton, where "all the speeches" were to "center around" Wilson's work.[7] Adverse to public statements, hostile to Cox, Wilson did not answer Tumulty's wire. On his own initiative Tumulty told the Dayton audience that the "expressions of devotion and affection . . . evidenced tonight are comforting to Woodrow Wilson." [8] This statement, innocuous but unauthorized, caused no comment. A second, similarly harmless statement, however, precipitated the final break between Tumulty and his old chief.

On April 8, 1922, the Democrats of New York City held their Jefferson Day Dinner. Tumulty was a guest of honor. After receiving his invitation to the dinner, he asked Wilson for a message to read. Still unwilling to break his silence, Wilson would not so much as express regret at his inability to attend.[9] Before leaving Washington, however, Tumulty visited Wilson, discussed the political situation in general terms, and went away under the impression that "the Governor" was not adverse to honoring the dinner with a platitudinous greeting. Although he had no official, authorized message from his former chief, at the dinner Tumulty gave the chairman a statement over Wilson's name. It read: "Say to the Democrats of New York that I am ready to support any man who stands for the salvation of America, and the salvation of America is justice to all classes."[10] The audience cheered these words, then turned its attention to other messages of greeting, speeches, and the major address by Cox.

The enthusiastic response to Cox and to his forceful attack on Harding led the press to interpret the dinner as a Cox boom. These reports upset Wilson who felt that he had been made to seem to give support to Cox. He immediately wrote Tumulty, demanding an explanation of the message that had been read. Before replying, Tumulty told the press that the statement was not a telegram, as it had been reported to be in some places, but merely a casual remark Wilson had made to him. Tumulty then wrote Wilson, accepting "full responsibility for the message of greeting." "It is only fair to you to say that there was no express direction on your part that I should convey any message," Tumulty explained, "but I think I was justified by every fair implication, from what you said to me, in conveying a word of greeting. . . . Of course your remarks were casual. . . . Unfortunately, the newspapers 'played it up' and placed . . . an unwarranted interpretation upon it."[11]

The next day Tumulty wrote Wilson again. Repeating the substance of his earlier letter, he added that no "sane" person could have misconstrued the message "as an endorsement of anybody."

"I will never engage in a controversy with you," Tumulty concluded. "No . . . public rebuke from you can in any way lessen my devotion to and respect for you. . . . If you decide that this message of greeting . . . has embarrassed you in any way and that I must be rebuked, I shall not complain. . . ." [12]

Wilson had already reached that decision. The *Times* of April 14 printed his letter stating that he did not send any message or authorize anyone to convey any message. The *Times* also carried Tumulty's statement: "If Mr. Wilson says the message was unauthorized then I can only say I deeply regret the misunderstanding which has arisen between us. I certainly would not have given the message if I had not believed it to be authorized." [13] On the fourteenth Tumulty received a cordial letter from Mrs. Wilson, answering his letters to her husband. "When one finds himself out in the cold of No Man's land," he replied, "a kind word from a real, devoted friend, like you, goes a long way to help." [14]

There the trivial, unfortunate episode should have closed. But it did not. Tumulty never saw Wilson again. He was never explicitly forgiven. Years later, Mrs. Wilson, in her memoirs, condemned him unsparingly. When Wilson died she did not invite him to the funeral — he was invited by McAdoo who noticed that his name had been omitted. In the funeral procession he rode in the last coach.

These were crushing blows for one whose feeling for Wilson approached infatuation, terrible punishment for a small error that resulted, at one stroke, in ostracism after a decade of service. Tumulty was not blameless. By his own admission he had acted without authority. In his letters of explanation perhaps he argued too much. The break, however, was not his fault; it was the culmination of a series of personal and political frictions, some many years old, which would not have produced so unhappy an end had not Wilson been ill.

Only personal reasons can account for Edith Wilson's scathing criticism of her husband's Secretary. Before and after her obloquy, however, Tumulty found solace in the sympathy he received from Stockton Axson, Helen Bones, and other old friends of his and Wilson's. [15] Furthermore, before he died, Wilson in part healed the wound he had made. Recommending Tumulty for the United States

Senate, Wilson indicated to James Kerney that he had not forgotten his Secretary's abilities. Edith Wilson attempted to prevent the publication of the letter but she failed. Even had she succeeded, the knowledge of that letter assured Tumulty the happiness she tried to deny him.[16]

After the break with Wilson and particularly after Wilson's death, Tumulty gave decreasing thought to politics. His law practice grew, absorbing his time and attention. Besides routine business, he handled several difficult receiverships and won the gratitude of Manuel Quezon for his legal work in behalf of Philippine independence. He gave many hours to Community Chest drives and other charitable activities. His leisure was also filled. His luncheon table at the Shoreham, still a celebrated Washington rendezvous, attracted his political, journalistic, and theatrical friends. In the late afternoon at his office, where the Volstead Act was always suspended, an informal caucus of Congressmen gathered daily to gossip about affairs on the "Hill." At home his children were a source of delight and pride. One son achieved distinction as a doctor, one as a lawyer, becoming, in time, his father's partner. Profession, friends, and family provided a pleasant pattern of private life enriched by memories of the political years.

Tumulty did not abandon politics completely. The office caucus kept him up to date. Presidential campaigns captured his attention and brought him out of retirement. In the middle twenties he initiated a movement to establish a Democratic newspaper modeled after that of Tom Pence.[17] The project failed for lack of funds, but later Charles Michelson, devastating Hoover, made a similar journal the effective organ of a successful Democracy. In 1924 and 1928 Tumulty assisted the preconvention campaign of Al Smith. He preferred Smith or Garner to Franklin D. Roosevelt in 1932, but after Roosevelt's nomination, and again in 1936, he campaigned extensively in New York, New Jersey, and New England.[18]

Through Coolidge prosperity, Hoover depression, and Roosevelt New Deal, Tumulty's political thinking was conditioned by his interpretation of the significance of Wilson's career. The New Freedom was no longer "new," but its purpose and accomplishments remained, for Tumulty, the standards of political comparison. Republican policies in the twenties lent substance to his bias that that party was a "brutal thing . . . which has preyed upon our people." [19] Answering the contention that it was the only party fit to rule, he recalled, privately and publicly, the reform legislation of Wilson's first term. He spoke for a lower tariff in the twenties and praised Hull's reciprocity program in the thirties.

Like most of his former colleagues in office, Tumulty was concerned largely with the freedom of the individual and the protection of individuals and minorities. He had intellectual as well as personal reasons for objecting to Coolidge's silence on the Ku Klux Klan and Hoover's attitude toward prohibition. The same frame of reference, allowing sympathy for Roosevelt's social reforms, excluded sympathy for the methods the new President employed. To most Wilsonians the New Deal seemed too paternalistic; the aggrandizement of the federal government, dangerous. Tumulty praised the early New Deal, maintaining that, where Hoover had thought only of the well born, Roosevelt assisted the re-establishment of self-respect among all the people. He objected strongly, however, to the later New Deal. Nevertheless, spurning the Liberty League, he remained a loyal Democrat. Roosevelt, although never friendly to Tumulty, recognized his campaign assistance and party regularity with an appointment to the Jefferson Memorial Commission.

Wilson's associates, like Wilson's domestic policies, were close to Tumulty's heart. Within a decade after their chief's death, recollections of service together restored the friendship of Tumulty with House and McAdoo. He sustained lesser participants in times of adversity, helping many of his former political associates who were "down in their luck" during the great depression. Later he was one of the few who had a kind word to say for Samuel Insull. While a legal adviser to Insull, Tumulty had warned him to submit to the laws he was so profitably circumventing. When Insull's utilities empire collapsed and his name became anathema, Tumulty, not in the least condoning his business practices, reminded Insull's critics that during the war he had served his country well.[20]

For Tumulty, even before the shadows of age engulfed him, as for most men, one memory of Wilson transcended all others. World peace through international organization was the enduring, overwhelming basis of the Wilson tradition. To this ideal Tumulty gave his supreme devotion. In his mind Wilson and the League merged, forming together an image of unselfish purpose and world salvation. On anniversaries of Wilson's birthday and death, a letter from Tumulty reminded newspaper readers of Wilson's ideal. In other public letters, Tumulty took Viereck and Ludwig to task for their unsympathetic characterizations of his chief. Lodge's *Senate and the League of Nations* he dismissed as a "hymn of hate." He criticized public men as well as publicists, attacking Franklin Roosevelt and Newton D. Baker for their evasions on the League in 1932. To the press, on the podium, over the radio Tumulty pointed to Wilson as the creator of the instrument by which peace could be assured.[21]

Tumulty's vision of Wilson, the peacemaker, dimmed his other memories. The political skirmishes in New Jersey and Washington, the frustrations of his last months in office, the heartbreak of 1922 faded. In Tumulty's own career, his rise from the Horseshoe to the White House, was the stuff of American promise, a chapter from Horatio Alger, in which any man could take pride. But Tumulty's abiding pride was in his chief, his fondest hope in Wilson's mission. He expressed this fervently:

Yes, Woodrow Wilson is dead.
But I catch a vision of his indomitable courage. I see him on his memorable tour, struggling for national and international life. I hear the sound of preparation for his welcome in city, town, hamlet, and crossroads. I hear . . . drums. I hear . . . bugles . . . I see thousands of assemblages. And then I hear him at Pueblo. . . . Again I see Woodrow Wilson, stricken down in the zenith of his power. . . . Now he lies dead. . . . But his spirit still lives — the spirit that tried to wipe away the tears of the world, the spirit of justice, humanity, and holy peace. . . .[22]

NOTES AND
BIBLIOGRAPHY

INDEX

NOTES AND BIBLIOGRAPHY

Introduction

THE NOTES and bibliography for this book are arranged by chapter on the following pages. The annotation, reduced to a minimum, includes only references of immediate pertinence. The bibliographical paragraphs discuss only the most relevant and useful sources. For the whole book and for each chapter the comparative volume of citations of manuscripts, newspapers, memoirs, or secondary works reveals the nature of the materials relied upon. Full citations are given the first time only; thereafter the short form. An essay on method, fuller annotation, documentary appendices, and a complete list of all works consulted, including those which proved barren for this subject, may be examined at the Archives, Harvard University Library, in my dissertation, "Tumulty and the Wilson Era," on which this book is based.

Chapter I

A POLITICAL APPRENTICESHIP

For Tumulty's life before 1910 there are no adequate published sources. My discussion of his boyhood and youth is based largely on interviews with his brother, Felix Tumulty, on interviews Tumulty himself gave to reporters, and on the brief account in Joseph P. Tumulty, *Woodrow Wilson as I Know Him* (Garden City, 1921). Intermittent accounts of Tumulty's political work and legislative career are in the Jersey City *Evening Journal* and the excellent daily discussions of Jersey politics in the New York *Tribune*. The *Minutes of the Votes and Proceedings* of the *General Assembly of the State of New Jersey* and the *Journal of the Senate of the State of New Jersey* contain the data on all bills introduced in the legislature. They do not, however, contain debates. Because of the absence of good manuscript materials, the history of the progressive movement in New Jersey from 1900 to 1910 cannot be fully narrated. I profited greatly, however, from the one excellent scholarly book on the subject, Ransom E. Noble, Jr., *New Jersey Progressivism Before Wilson* (Princeton, 1946). Other helpful analyses of conditions in New Jersey, focused on a later period, are in Dayton D. McKean, *The Boss, The Hague Machine in Action* (Boston, 1940), and McKean, *Pressures on the Legislature of New Jersey* (New York, 1938). There are two useful but not entirely reliable "annals" of New Jersey's political history in the first decade of the century: William E. Sackett, *Modern Battles of Trenton* (New York, 1914), and Hester E. Hosford, *The Forerunners of Woodrow Wilson* (East Orange, 1914).

My prefatory account of Inauguration Day is based on reports in the New York *Tribune*, March 5, 1913, and the account in Ray Stannard Baker, *Woodrow Wilson, Life and Letters*, 8 vols. (Garden City, 1927–39), IV, 8-11. I share the continuing debt of all students of the Wilson period to Baker's multivolume works on Wilson.

1. Baker, *Wilson*, IV, 10.
2. New York *Tribune*, March 5, 1913.
3. *Ibid.*
4. *Ibid.*
5. McKean, *The Boss*, pp. 16–17.
6. Tumulty, *Wilson*, p. 2.
7. Boston *Post*, March 10, 1913.
8. *Ibid.*
9. New York *Tribune*, January 10, 1911; Tumulty, *op. cit.*, p. 10; Noble, *New Jersey Progressivism*, pp. 10, 13; James Kerney, *The Political Education of Woodrow Wilson* (New York, 1926), p. 38. Atwood C. Wolf, sometime clerk in Tumulty's law office, to the author.
10. McKean, *op. cit.*, p. 19.
11. Tumulty, *op. cit.*, p. 5.
12. Joseph M. Sharkey to Tumulty, March 3, 1913, *Joseph P. Tumulty Manuscripts*, Washington, D. C. (privately owned).

13. Tumulty, *op. cit.*, pp. 7, 8.
14. Noble, *op. cit.*, pp. 12, 13; Sackett, *Modern Battles of Trenton*, pp. 179 ff.; J. Lincoln Steffens, *Upbuilders* (New York, 1909), chap. I; Felix Tumulty to the author.
15. "Catalogue of St. Peter's College" (Jersey City, 1907).
16. Noble, *op. cit.*, chaps. I, II; Steffens, *op. cit.*, chap. I.
17. Boston *Post*, March 10, 1913.
18. New York *Tribune*, October 15, 1906.
19. *Ibid.*, October 31, November 7, 8, 9, 10, December 11, 1906; Noble, *op. cit.*, pp. 80–82.
20. J. Lincoln Steffens, *The Struggle for Self-Government* (New York, 1906), p. 246.
21. Noble, *op. cit.*, pp. 56, 70, 71, 78, 79.
22. New York *Tribune*, December 11, 12, 15, 18, 19, 1906; January 9, 1907.

23. *Ibid.*, January 14, 23, February 6, 1907; Sackett, *op. cit.*, pp. 246–48; Tumulty, *op. cit.*, pp. 10–13. The fullest accounts of the attempt to secure the Democratic endorsement for Wilson are in Baker, *op. cit.*, III, 18–30, and Arthur S. Link, *Wilson: The Road to the White House* (Princeton, 1947), pp. 93–107.

24. New York *Tribune*, March 20, 1907.

25. *Ibid.*, February 23, 28, April 15, 17, 1907; Noble, *op. cit.*, pp. 136, 137, 143.

26. *Minutes of the Assembly of New Jersey, 1907*, especially pp. 168, 228, 757, 1375; New York *Tribune*, March 27, April 10, 1907; Noble, *op. cit.*, pp. 102–4.

27. Hosford, *Forerunners*, pp. 68–75; Noble, *op. cit.*, pp. 35–37; Sackett, *op. cit.*, p. 137; Steffens, *Upbuilders*, pp. 62 ff.; New York *Tribune*, March 14, 1907.

28. Josephus Daniels to Tumulty, February 6, 1913, *Woodrow Wilson Manuscripts* (Library of Congress, Washingtin, D.C.).

29. New York *Tribune*, February 8, 15, April 29, July 9, August 6, 8, 1908.

30. These measures are indexed in the *Minutes of the Assembly* for 1907, 1908, 1909, and 1910. See also the Jersey City *Evening Journal*, March 10, 21, 1910.

31. Jersey City *Evening Journal*, April 13, 1910.

32. New York *Tribune*, March 12, April 11, 1908; April 15, 16, 17, 1909; Noble, *op. cit.*, p. 144.

33. Jersey City *Evening Journal*, March 25, 1908; New York *Tribune*, January 19, 20, March 8, 11, 15, 24, 25, 30, April 1, 2, 1909; Noble, *op. cit.*, pp. 110–11.

34. Jersey City *Evening Journal*, March 10, 16, 1910; New York *Tribune*, January 19, March 17, 25, 1910.

35. Jersey City *Evening Journal*, March 17, 1910.

36. New York *Tribune*, November 25, 1907.

37. Jersey City *Evening Journal*, April 12, 1910.

38. Sharkey to Tumulty, March 3, 1913, *loc. cit.*

Chapter II

ENTER WOODROW WILSON

Of the many authors who have written on the topics covered in this chapter, I replied particularly on three: Ray Stannard Baker, Arthur S. Link, and James Kerney. Baker's third volume contains a comprehensive and sympathetic treatment of Wilson's governorship. Link, *Wilson, The Road to the White House* (Princeton, 1947), is the best analysis of that period. Less sympathetic than Baker, Link has produced a more careful and better-documented account. He is complete and incisive on Wilson's nomination and campaign, on the Smith-Martine contest, and on the legislative session of 1911. James Kerney, *The Political Education of Woodrow Wilson* (New York, 1926), is based in large part on the recollections of the author, a participant in the events he describes, and on information he received from Tumulty, his intimate friend. Its strongest section is that on the governorship. These books provided material on Tumulty as well as on Wilson which I constantly used.

Tumulty's own memoir is helpful but brief. Charles R. Bacon, *A People Awakened* (New York, 1912), contains the author's contemporary newspaper stories on the campaign of 1910. Hester E. Hosford, *Woodrow Wilson and New Jersey Made Over* (New York, 1912), is uncritical but detailed. For background material and data on Tumulty's work the Jersey City *Evening Journal*, New York *Evening Post*, and New York *Tribune* are all good. I found few but valuable documents in the manuscript collections of Tumulty, Wilson, and Ray Stannard Baker.

1. Tumulty, *Wilson*, p. 15.
2. Sharkey to Tumulty, March 3, 1913, *loc. cit.*
3. The Wilson Mss. contain endorsements from New Jersey progressives of whom many, including the following, mentioned his speech as an impelling factor in their support: W. F. Cox, Sept. 15, 1910; C. E. Hendrickson, Sept. 16; G. S. Silzer, Sept. 16; J. M. Wescott, Sept. 16; G. R. Tennant, Sept. 17; J. H. Christie, Sept. 19; D. F. Platt, Sept. 19; W. Hughes, Sept. 20. See also Tumulty, *op. cit.*, p. 22; Link, *Wilson*, pp. 169–72.
4. Platt to Wilson, September 19, 1910, *Wilson Mss.*
5. Tumulty to Dolan, April 17, 1915, *Tumulty Mss.*
6. Tumulty, *op. cit.*, pp. 26–30; Link, *op. cit.*, pp. 175–85. The following letters to Wilson, all in *Wilson Mss.*, urged him to concentrate on specific issues: J. L. O'Connell, October 3, 1910; J. W. Wescott, October 3; H. W. Lewis, October 6; H. Marshall, October 13; H. E. Alexander, undated.

7. *Literary Digest*, LXIV, pp. 71 ff.
8. J. G. Warner to Wilson, October 15, 1910, *Wilson Mss.*
9. Warner to Wilson, October 25, 1910, *Wilson Mss.*; Bacon, *A People Awakened*, pp. 111, 145, 149, 189; New York *Evening Post*, September 30, October 22, 1910.
10. The best accounts of this celebrated exchange between Record and Wilson are in Baker, *Wilson*, III, 69–102, and Link, *op. cit.*, pp. 189–97. That Record himself considered Wilson's reply a master stroke is obvious in Record to Baker, June 5, 1926, *Ray Stannard Baker Manuscripts* (Library of Congress, Washington, D.C.). See also Tumulty, *op. cit.*, pp. 38–43; Tumulty and M. A. Sullivan to Wilson, October 26, 1910, *Wilson Mss.*
11. New York *Tribune*, October 24, November 7, 1910. The year-by-year returns from the suburban counties suggest that Link, in his otherwise excellent analysis of the election of 1910, paid too little attention to the commuter vote; ref. *Manual of the Legislature of*

New Jersey: 1908, pp. 506–7; 1909: pp. 553–54; 1910: p. 531; 1911: pp. 531–32; 1912: p. 570. Howard Marshall, President of the Commuters League of New Jersey, emphasized the importance of normally Republican votes to Wilson's victory; ref. Marshall to Wilson, October 13, December 22, 1910, *Wilson Mss.*

12. New York *Evening Post*, November 9, 1910; New York *Tribune*, November 9, 1910; *The Commercial and Financial Chronicle*, XCI, 1287; *Harper's Weekly*, LIV, 2–8; *The Outlook*, XCVI, 607–8.

13. Kerney, *Wilson*, pp. 84–86.

14. Tumulty, *op. cit.*, pp. 53–55. Tumulty quotes this from memory, but the general tone, at least, is confirmed in Tumulty to Wilson, January 17, 1916, *Tumulty Mss.*

15. Tumulty to Wilson, November 30, 1910, *Wilson Mss.*

16. Tumulty to Wilson, December 7, 1910, *Wilson Mss.*; Link, *op. cit.*, p. 217.

17. Kerney, *op. cit.*, pp. 83–84; Jersey City *Evening Journal*, January 13, 1911; Wilson to O. G. Villard, January 2, 1911, *Wilson Mss.*

18. Tumulty to Wilson, December 15, 1910, *Wilson Mss.*

19. Baker, *op. cit.*, III, 122.

20. New York *Evening Post*, December 20, 27, 1910; Tumulty, *op. cit.*, pp. 60, 63; Link, *op. cit.*, p. 225.

21. New York *Tribune*, January 6, 1911.

22. Tumulty, *op. cit.*, p. 66.

23. R. S. Baker Memo of Interview with Hudspeth, November 3, 1927, *Baker Mss.* Tumulty, *op. cit.*, p. 65 lists the leaders who supported Martine.

24. Tumulty, *op. cit.*, p. 70.

25. Kerney, *op. cit.*, pp. 115–21; Baker, *op. cit.*, III, 152–54; C. O. Hennessy to Baker, July 1, 1926; Hudspeth to Baker, November 11, 1927, *Baker Mss.*

26. New York *Tribune*, February 7, April 4, 1911; Kerney, *op. cit.*, p. 120; Link, *op. cit.*, p. 270.

Chapter III

JOE TUMULTY'S MASTER PLAN

On Tumulty's personal relations with Wilson and Ellen Wilson my best sources were interviews with Joseph P. Tumulty, Jr., Mary Tumulty Cahill, Felix Tumulty, Warren F. Johnson, Charles L. Swem, Robert Norton, and Eugene Buck. Also helpful were Eleanor Wilson McAdoo, *The Woodrow Wilsons* (New York, 1937), and a memorandum by Ray Stannard Baker of his interview with Judge Hudspeth, November 30, 1927, *Baker Mss.*

There are three valuable studies of the details of New Jersey politics in 1911–12 in Link, *Wilson*; Kerney, *Wilson*; and McKean, *The Boss*. On these, particularly Link's, I drew heavily. Sackett is also informative.

The New York *Tribune* and Jersey City *Evening Journal*, as the annotation indicates, were indispensable for this topic. Manuscript sources were only rarely of use.

1. Kerney, *Wilson*, pp. 115–19.
2. C. O. Hennessey to Baker, July 1, 1926, *Baker Mss.*
3. Alexander to Wilson, August 27, 1911, *Wilson Mss.*
4. New York *Tribune*, July 28, 29, August 12, 25, 1911; Kerney, *op. cit.*, pp. 148–49; Link, *Wilson*, pp. 280–82; Tumulty, *Wilson*, p. 65; William F. McCombs, *Making Woodrow Wilson President* (New York, 1921), p. 43.
5. New York *Tribune*, May 22, June 26, November 6, 1911; Link, *op. cit.*, pp. 282–83.
6. To follow every eddy in Hudson politics would be confusing and unrewarding. Kinkead and the "Big Five," for example, did not always co-operate, but by the middle of June 1911, their policies were usually the same. For a time the "Big Five" was the "Big Six." Hague switched from camp to camp as the situation changed. The Jersey City *Evening Journal* from June through September, 1911, contains long accounts of every local alignment and issue; see also McKean, *The Boss*, pp. 34–36.
7. Hudspeth to W. C. Liller, in New York *Tribune*, August 7, 1911.
8. Jersey City *Evening Journal*, June 17, July 9, August 15, 18, 1911; New York *Tribune*, July 10, 1911.
9. New York *Tribune*, June 19, 1911.
10. *Ibid.*, November 16, 1911.
11. *Ibid.*, September 7, 1911; Jersey City *Evening Journal*, September 6, 9, 12, 13, 1911.
12. Jersey City *Evening Journal*, September 5, 18, 22, 26, 1911.
13. *Ibid.*, July 19, 29, August 9, 10, September 27, 28, 1911; New York *Tribune*, August 4, 1911.
14. Jersey City *Evening Journal*, September 28, October 4, 1911; New York *Tribune*, October 14, 19, 23, 1911.
15. New York *Tribune*, November 8, 9, 22, 1911.
16. Kerney, *op. cit.*, p. 203.
17. New York *Tribune*, February 22, March 6, 8, 14, 1912.
18. *Ibid.*, January 23, February 28, March 25, 28, April 11, 1912; Kerney, *op. cit.*, pp. 197–99; Link, *op. cit.*, pp. 301–2.
19. Tumulty, *op. cit.*, pp. 78–80; Link, *op. cit.*, pp. 302–3.
20. Kerney, *op. cit.*, pp. 194–96. Evidence for the Tumulty-Walker alliance is in section VI of the *Wilson Mss.* It continued through the period of agitation for jury reform in 1913, discussed below in chap. VI.
21. New York *Tribune*, March 12, 1912; Sackett, *Modern Battles of Trenton*, pp. 338, 344.
22. Link, *op. cit.*, pp. 299–300.
23. New York *Tribune*, March 21, 1912; New York *Evening Post*, February 3, 1913.
24. New York *Tribune*, April 3, 1912; Kerney, *op. cit.*, pp. 187–90; Sackett, *op. cit.*, p. 345.
25. Jersey City *Evening Journal*, April 2, 13, 1912; New York *Tribune*, April 5, 15, May 20, 30, 1912; New York *Evening Post*, May 22, 1912.
26. Jersey City *Evening Journal*, April 15, 16, 19, 22, May 11, 1912;

New York *Tribune*, December 18, 1911; April 3, 1912; Sackett, *op. cit.*, pp. 338–39.

27. Jersey City *Evening Journal*, April 2, 12, 13, 15, 17, 18, 24, 25, 26, May 18, 27, 1912.

28. *Ibid.*, April 13, 1912. A copy of the list of Catholic appointments is enclosed in Kerney to Drummond, August 13, 1912, *Wilson Mss.* There are several copies in the *Tumulty Mss.* which he used at various times between 1912 and 1927.

29. Jersey City *Evening Journal*, May 15, 1912; see also *Ibid.*, May 16, 17, 1912.

30. *Ibid.*, May 22, 23, 27, 1912.

31. *Ibid.*, May 29, 1912.

Chapter IV

BROADER HORIZONS

By far the best accounts of the national Wilson movement are in Baker, *Wilson*, III, and Link, *Wilson*. They supplied the essential background data for my narrative and, often, relevant material on Tumulty. Link is more discerning than Baker, particularly on the conservative reaction against Wilson. Both authors, from different points of view, deal ably with the Baltimore Convention. They tend to balance each other, for Link's fuller analysis, it seems to me, undervalues Bryan's importance, while Baker, as Link demonstrates, underrates McCombs' contribution. Of various memoirs and biographies covering these topics, the most helpful were William J. and Mary B. Bryan, *The Memoirs of William Jennings Bryan* (Philadelphia, 1925); Willis F. Johnson, *George Harvey* (Cambridge, 1939); Kerney, *Wilson*; Maurice F. Lyons, *William F. McCombs, the President Maker* (Cincinnati, 1922); William F. McCombs, *Making Woodrow Wilson President* (New York, 1921); Charles Seymour, *The Intimate Papers of Colonel House*, 4 vols. (Cambridge, 1926–28), I; and Tumulty, *Wilson*. For the reception in Sea Girt of the news from Baltimore, Eleanor W. McAdoo, *The Wilsons*, is excellent.

Most of the rest of this chapter is based on materials from newspapers, the *Wilson Mss.*, *Tumulty Mss.*, and the *Edward M. House Manuscripts* (Yale University Library, New Haven).

1. Baker, *Wilson*, III, 230; Kerney, *Wilson*, pp. 146, 171.

2. Tumulty, *Wilson*, chap. XII.

3. R. F. Pettigrew, *Imperial Washington* (Chicago, 1922), pp. 240–42.

4. E. W. McAdoo, *The Wilsons*, p. 123.

5. Tumulty, *op. cit.*, pp. 95–97; Link, *Wilson*, pp. 355–57; Baker, *op. cit.*, III, 256–67.

6. Tumulty, *op. cit.*, pp. 108–16;

Link, *op. cit.*, pp. 432–33; Baker, *op. cit.*, III, 334–37.

7. Link, *op. cit.*, chap. XIII.

8. Tumulty, *op. cit.*, pp. 110, 113, 114, 117, 120–22; Link, *op. cit.*, pp. 450–51; E. W. McAdoo, *op. cit.*, pp. 156–63; William Gibbs McAdoo, *Crowded Years* (Cambridge, 1931), p. 154. Tumulty's account is substantiated in W. G. McAdoo to Tumulty, September 24, 1930, and Tumulty to McAdoo, October 10, 1930, *Tumulty Mss.*

9. E. W. McAdoo, *op. cit.*, p. 164; see also Link, *op. cit.*, pp. 452–58; W. J. and M. B. Bryan, *Memoirs*, pp. 161 ff., p. 185.

10. E. W. McAdoo, *op. cit.*, pp. 164–65; see also Link, *op. cit.*, pp. 458–62.

11. Form Letters in *Wilson Mss.*, section II.

12. Tumulty to Wilson, August 26, 1912, *Wilson Mss.*

13. Stanchfield to Wilson, July 22, 1912, *Wilson Mss.*

14. The first use of "Joe Tumulty" I found was in the New York *Evening Post*, July 2, 1912. Soon thereafter it became common, whereas earlier it had not been used even by the Jersey City press.

15. Tumulty, *op. cit.*, pp. 112, 114; Kerney, *op. cit.*, p. 264; Robert Norton to the author.

16. New York *Tribune*, June 17, July 1, 8, August 18, 20, 21, 31, September 4, 22, 25, 1912.

17. *Ibid.*, September 19, 1912; Link, *op. cit.*, pp. 497–98.

18. Tumulty to Wilson, September 16 (?), 1912, *Wilson Mss.*

19. New York *Tribune*, September 25, 26, 1912; New York *Evening Post*, September 26, 1912.

20. New York *Tribune*, October 7, November 6, 7, 1912.

21. Davies to Tumulty, November 20, 1912, *Wilson Mss.*

22. New York *Tribune*, November 6, 1912.

23. Wilson to Tumulty, November 30, December 3, 11, 1912; Tumulty to Wilson, December 6, 1912, *Tumulty Mss.*; Newark *Evening News*, December 3, 6, 1912.

24. New York *Tribune*, January 2, 13, 15, 1913; Kerney, *op. cit.*, pp. 253–56.

25. New York *Tribune*, February 12, 1913; Baker, *op. cit.*, III, 434–35; Sackett, *Modern Battles of Trenton*, pp. 349–55, 367–84.

26. Kerney, *op. cit.*, p. 252. For the later relations of McCombs, Vick and Tumulty, see chap. VIII.

27. Alexander to Wilson, August 27, 1911; W. W. All to Wilson, November 26, 1912; "A Patriotic American" to Miss Jessie Wilson, undated, *Wilson Mss.*; C. Vann Woodward, *Tom Watson, Agrarian Rebel* (New York, 1938), pp. 426, 452.

28. Diary of E. M. House, December 15, 1912, *House Mss.*; Baker, *op. cit.*, III, 458.

29. New York *Evening Post*, January 31, February 3, 1913; see also New York *Tribune*, February 4, 1913; Newark *Evening News*, February 3, 1913; New York *Times*, February 9, 1913.

30. Diary of E. M. House, December 15, 18, 19, 1912, *House Mss.* Tumulty considered House's influence the most important factor in his appointment, ref. Tumulty to House, March 18, 1921; December 5, 1935, *Ibid.*

31. Baker, *op. cit.*, III, 458–59; E. W. McAdoo, *op. cit.*, pp. 196–97.

32. Charles W. Thompson, *Presidents I've Known and Two Near Presidents* (Indianapolis, 1929), pp. 277–78.

33. Hilles to Tumulty, February 4, 1913, *Wilson Mss.*

34. Barclay to Tumulty, February 5, 1913, *Wilson Mss.*

35. Tumulty, *op. cit.*, p. 137; Baker, *op. cit.*, III, 439–43.

36. Tumulty, *op. cit.*, p. 138; Baker, *op. cit.*, III, 454–55; Kerney, *op. cit.*, pp. 293–99.

Chapter V

DAILY ROUTINE

The material in this chapter is drawn from a variety of sources, cited below, of which no single one is particularly informative. David Lawrence, *The True Story of Woodrow Wilson* (New York, 1924), and James E. Pollard, *The Presidents and the Press* (New York, 1947), deserve special mention, however. The latter book is the only study of its kind; Lawrence's biography, often the product of his personal observations, is illuminating on Tumulty. Like Kerney a personal friend of Tumulty, Lawrence was often more critical and usually more conscious of the area of Tumulty's influence. The "portrait" of Tumulty at the end of the chapter is based on information contributed to me in letters and interviews by Joseph P. Tumulty, Jr., Felix Tumulty, Warren F. Johnson, Charles L. Swem, Eugene F. Buck, James A. Farley, Joseph F. Guffey, Helen W. Bones, and the late Robert Norton.

1. Boston *Herald*, February 15, 1914; A. G. Baker, "The Ladies of the Cabinet," *Independent*, LXXIV, 1029; Notebook of Invitations, Acceptances, and Declinations, in *Tumulty Mss.* Tumulty's salary was $7500 a year.

2. New York *Times*, October 5, 1913; January 9, 16, 1915.

3. Boston *Herald*, February 15, 1914; New York *Times*, May 8, 1914.

4. Notebook of Invitations, *Tumulty Mss.*; New York *Times*, May 8, 1914, April 15, May 6, November 27, 1915; December 13, 1916.

5. J. D. Bedle to Tumulty, December 2, 1913; J. A. Hamill to Tumulty, December 3, 1913; M.

A. Sullivan to Tumulty, December 3, 1913; *Tumulty Mss.*

6. Interviews with Robert Norton, Eugene Buck, Warren F. Johnson, and J. P. Tumulty, Jr.

7. Joseph E. Davies to Tumulty, November 24 (?), 1913, *Tumulty Mss.* See also George F. Milton, *The Use of Presidential Power* (Boston, 1944), p. 208.

8. Tumulty to Cutley, March 31, 1913, January 5, 1914; Tumulty to F. W. Gnitchel, February 25, 1916, *Tumulty Mss.*

9. New York *Tribune*, March 6, 1913.

10. Edward G. Lowry, *Washington Close-ups* (Cambridge, 1921), p. 120.

11. R. S. Baker Memo of Interview with Swem, July 16, 1925, *Baker Mss.*; Interview with Warren F. Johnson.

12. Simon Wolf, *The Presidents I Have Known* (Washington, 1918), pp. 404, 416.

13. D. Wilhelm, "When You Drop in on Mr. Wilson," *Independent*, XCVIII, 442.

14. Baker Memo of Interview with Swem, *loc. cit.*

15. O. G. Villard, "Ways of Tumulty," *Nation*, C, 490; D. Wilhelm, "When You Drop in on Mr. Wilson," *loc. cit.*; *Literary Digest*, LXIV, 71; New York *Times*, January 16, 1915.

16. O. G. Villard, *Fighting Years, Memoirs of a Liberal Editor* (New York, 1939), p. 237; J. L. Steffens, *The Letters of Lincoln Steffens*, E. Winters and G. Hicks, eds. (New York, 1938), 2 vols., I, 334; Samuel Gompers, *Seventy Years of Life and Labor* (New York, 1925), 2 vols., II, 60, 355.

17. Tumulty to Wilson and Wilson to Tumulty, December 20, 1916, *Wilson Mss.*; Lawrence, *Wilson*, p. 89; New York *Tribune*, June 8, 1913.

18. Mrs. J. Borden Harriman, *From Pinafores to Politics* (New York, 1923), pp. 132–35; New York *Times*, July 6–15, 1913.

19. John L. Heaton, ed., *Cobb of "The World"* (New York, 1924), p. 214.

20. I. M. Tarbell, "A Talk with the President of the United States," *Collier's Weekly*, LVIII, 6.

21. Interviews with Warren F. Johnson and Charles L. Swem. There are hundreds of sheets of the "Yellow Journal" in the *Tumulty Mss.*

22. Ray Stannard Baker, *American Chronicle* (New York, 1945), p. 285.

23. W. F. Sapp to Tumulty, February 3, 1916; C. M. Selph to Tumulty, February 4, 1916; Sullivan to Tumulty, July 19, 1913, *Wilson Mss.*; Lawrence to Tumulty, June 5, 6, 1916, *Tumulty Mss.*; Villard, *Fighting Years*, p. 237.

24. Johann H. A. von Bernstorff, *My Three Years in America* (New York, 1920), p. 34.

25. Edward N. Hurley, *The Bridge to France* (Philadelphia, 1927), p. 317.

26. Pollard, *Presidents and the Press*, p. 632.

27. New York *Times*, January 29, 1914; Lawrence, *op. cit.*, p. 89; Interviews with Eugene Buck and Robert Norton.

28. Pollard, *op. cit.*, pp. 630–36; Lawrence, *op. cit.*, pp. 64, 65, 350; J. Fred Essary, *Covering Washington* (Cambridge, 1927), p. 99; Villard, *Fighting Years*, p. 257.

29. Essary, *op. cit.*, p. 89; Milton, *op. cit.*, p. 211; New York *Tribune*, March 16, 1913.

30. Boston *Herald*, February 5, 1913; Kerney, *Wilson*, p. 270.

31. J. J. Hopkins to Tumulty, April 5, 1913, *Tumulty Mss.*

32. J. P. Tumulty, "In the White House Looking Glass," New York *Times*, December 31, 1921.

33. Essary, *op. cit.*, p. 47; Pollard, *op. cit.*, p. 659; New York *Tribune*, March 6, 1913; *Literary Digest*, LXIV, 71; *Public*, XXI, 1283.

34. Diary of E. M. House, January 5, 1913, *House Mss.*

35. Tumulty to Kerney, April 25, 1913, *Tumulty Mss.*

36. Bryan to Wilson, February 18, 1915; Wilson to Tumulty, February 20, 1915; Tumulty to Wilson, February 20, 1915; Lawrence to Wilson, March 24, 1915; Villard to Wilson, June 7, 1915, *Wilson Mss.*

37. New York *Herald*, August 30,

1915; Wilson to Randolph Marshall, September 2, 1915; Marshall to Wilson, September 6, September 10, 1915; Donald Craig to Wilson, September 13, 1915; Craig to Tumulty, September 14, 1915; Marshall to Tumulty, September 16, 1915; A. J. Sinnott to Tumulty, September 9, 1915; Lane to Wilson, September 9, 1915; Wilson to Lane, September 10, 1915; Tumulty to Wilson, September 15, 1915; T. Pence to Wilson, September 15, 1915, *Wilson Mss.*; Tumulty to House, August 31, 1915, *House Mss.*; George M. Stephenson, *John Lind of Minnesota* (Minneapolis, 1935), pp. 298–99; Villard, *Fighting Years*, pp. 491–92.

38. Tumulty to Wilson, June 23, 1914; April 20, 1916; Wilson to Watterson, September 21, 1914; Wilson to Ely, April 6, 1914; Wilson to Essary, June 24, 1914, *Wilson Mss.*; Tumulty to Swope, January 21, 1915; Tumulty to Krock, August 14, 1915; Tumulty to Lawrence, April 22, 1916, *Tumulty Mss.*

39. Arthur W. Dunn, *Gridiron Nights* (New York, 1915), pp. 280, 281, 288, 370.

40. Cary T. Grayson to Tumulty, July 4 and 29, 1915, *Wilson Mss.*

41. Interview with C. L. Swem; Villard, *Fighting Years*, p. 257; Lawrence, *op. cit.*, p. 89; Essary, *op. cit.*, p. 89.

42. Baker Memo of Interview with Swem, *loc. cit.*

Chapter VI

POLITICAL MANAGER

The most complete account of the domestic policies of Wilson's first two years in office is in Baker, *Wilson*, IV. The best analysis of Wilson's intentions is in William Diamond, *The Economic Thought of Woodrow Wilson* (Baltimore, 1943), a superb, scholarly study. For background material I relied constantly on these books. Arthur Link's forthcoming volumes will surely add valuable factual and interpretive data to that now available. On the much-debated question of who deserved credit for the Federal Reserve Act there is provocative, often contradictory material in Baker, *Wilson*, IV; Bryan, *Memoirs;* Carter Glass, *An Adventure in Constructive Finance* (Garden City, 1927); McAdoo, *Crowded Years*; Robert L. Owen, *The Federal Reserve Act* (New York, 1919); Seymour, *House*, I; Tumulty, *Wilson*; and Samuel Untermyer, *Who is Entitled to Credit for the Federal Reserve Act?* (New York, 1927).

On the central issue of this chapter, national and local politics, there is a little data in Baker, *Wilson*, IV; Kerney, *Wilson;* and Tumulty, Wilson. The newspapers are more helpful. From 1913 on, however, beginning with this topic, my most fruitful sources, as the annotation indicates, were manuscript collections. Those of Bryan, Burleson, House,

Tumulty and Wilson were useful on this chapter. Of these the Tumulty Manuscripts, to which I was the first to have access, are alone privately owned. Since here and later they were my most valuable source, they merit some description: Although some of the documents in the Tumulty Manuscripts are also in the Wilson Manuscripts, most of them are to be found nowhere else. The collection consists of fourteen large looseleaf notebooks containing, for the most part, Tumulty's letters and memoranda to Wilson; fifteen letter-press books of Tumulty's general correspondence; several packing boxes of incoming and outgoing correspondence and clippings and a room of files of Tumulty's correspondence after 1921. The looseleaf notebooks are most important; the letter-press books are excellent on patronage for which the best source is the "Black Book," now kept apart from the rest of the collection.

1. Joseph P. Tumulty, "Democratic Solidarity," a campaign document dated October 10, 1914, *Tumulty Mss.*

2. This devolution was natural. The Postmaster General by virtue of his office handled the patronage allotted to members of the House; the Secretary of the Treasury bore a similar relationship to the Senators. Bryan had many offices at his personal disposal and tremendous influence elsewhere by virtue of his many years' party leadership. Tumulty's part is explained in the text. See also Baker, *Wilson*, IV, chap. I; W. G. McAdoo, *Crowded Years*, pp. 180, 189–92; Burleson to Houston, February 6, 1926, *Baker Mss.*

3. Burleson to Daniels, February 19, 1926, *Baker Mss.*; Bryson to Wilson, *ca.* May 7, 1913, *Wilson Mss.*

4. Tumulty, *Wilson*, pp. 175–81; Josephus Daniels, *The Wilson Era: Years of Peace* (Chapel Hill, 1944), p. 277; W. J. and M. B. Bryan, *Memoirs*, pp. 371–73.

5. Tumulty, "Democratic Solidarity," *loc. cit.*; Baker, *op. cit.*, IV, 394–421; New York *Times*, March 23, 30, April 1, June 12, 1914, January 7, 1915; T. R. Marshall to Tumulty, April 9, 1914, *Wilson Mss.*; R. S. Baker Memo of Interviews with A. S. Burleson, March 17, 18, 19, 1927, *Baker Mss.*; M. C. Adamson to Burleson, April 7, 1914, *Albert Sidney Burleson Manuscripts* (Library of Congress, Washington, D.C.); Tumulty, *Wilson*, pp. 165–67.

6. Tumulty to Matthew Ely, April 3, 1914; Tumulty to Alexander Hamill, April 3, 1914; Tumulty to Wittpenn, September 4, 1915; Tumulty to Burleson, September 11, 1914, *Tumulty Mss.*; J. A. Hamill to Wilson, March 5, 1914, *Wilson Mss.*

7. New York *Tribune*, April 19, 1913.

8. Watterson to Tumulty, July 8, 1914, *Wilson Mss.*; Wilson to Watterson, September 21, 1914; Watterson to Wilson, September 24, 1914; Wilson to Watterson, September 28, 1914, *Tumulty Mss.*

9. Tumulty to Wilson, September 27, 1914, *Wilson Mss.*; Johnson, *Harvey*, pp. 234–39; Tumulty to Harvey, October 9, 1914, *Tumulty Mss.*; Tumulty, *Wilson*, pp. 91–93.

10. McCombs' rôle in the post-convention campaign of 1912 has been

much discussed. The consensus is that he was of little assistance, and probably a nuisance. His own memoirs indicate the emotional tensions which must have torn him to pieces. The memoirs of McCombs, McAdoo, Lyons and Tumulty, and the works of Baker and Link cited in chapter IV, cover this question thoroughly.

11. Trenton *Times*, November 9, 1913; Washington *Times*, March 22, 1913; Mark Sullivan to McCombs, April 2, 1913; McCombs to Tumulty, April 3, 1913; *Tumulty Mss.*; Tumulty, *Wilson*, pp. 128–37.

12. McCombs, *Wilson*, p. 225.

13. Pence to Burleson, June 12, 1913; September 21, 1914, *Burleson Mss.*

14. Joseph P. Tumulty, "In the White House Looking Glass," New York *Times*, December 29, 1921.

15. This little volume, hereafter designated the "Black Book," is in the Tumulty Papers. The memoranda therein are the source of much of the information in this chapter.

16. In the *Wilson Mss.*, section VI, as those papers are presently arranged, filed by subject are the sets of correspondence on appointments with which the President was concerned. The documents within each file are too numerous to cite. For evidence of Tumulty's influence, see especially the data on James J. Walsh and Thomas J. Spellacy.

17. In *Wilson Mss.*, section VI, see files on P. J. O'Connor, John T. Essary, Maurice F. Lyons; see also R. S. Baker Memo of Interview with Tumulty, November 6, 1927, *Baker Mss.*

18. Tumulty, "Democratic Solidarity," *loc. cit.*; Baker, *op. cit.*, IV, chap. I.

19. Baker, *op. cit.*, V, 92; Tumulty, *Wilson*, p. 101; Baker Memo of

Interviews with A. S. Burleson, March 17–19, 1927, *loc. cit.*

20. Newark *Evening News*, March–May, 1913; Tumulty to Treacy, March 17, 1913; Tumulty to Grosscup, April 19, May 9, 1913; Tumulty to LaMonte, May 14, 1913; Tumulty to Gannon, May 7, 1913; Tumulty to Taylor, May 8, 1913; Tumulty to Collins, May 8, 1913; Tumulty to Kinmouth, May 8, 1913; Tumulty to Daly, May 9, 1913; McGovern to Tumulty, April 2, May 3, 1913, *Tumulty Mss.*

21. New York *Tribune*, April 21, 1913; Tumulty to Honnecker, April 5, 1913, *Tumulty Mss.*

22. Kernan to Tumulty, June 14, 1913, *Wilson Mss.*; Newark *Evening News*, June 26, July 9, 1913.

23. Tumulty to Ely, June 17, 1913; Tumulty to Binder, June 24, 1913; Tumulty to Thomas, June 30, 1913, Tumulty to Lippincott, July 3, 1913, *Tumulty Mss.*; McTague to Tumulty, June 27, 1913; Thomas to Tumulty, July 2, 1913; Stevens to Wilson, July 3, 1913; Russell to Tumulty, July 19, 1913; Fallon to Tumulty, July 29, 1913; Bacon to Tumulty, July 29, 1913, *Wilson Mss.*

24. Ref. Kernan-Tumulty correspondence now filed in *Wilson Mss.*, section VI; Newark *Evening News*, June 26, July 17, 23, 26, 1913.

25. R. F. Kernan to Tumulty, July 17, 31, August 1, 1913; R. F. Kernan to Fielder, August 1, 1913, *Wilson Mss.*

26. Tumulty to Fielder, October 2, 9, 21, 1913, *Tumulty Mss.*; Kernan to Tumulty, August 1, 1913; Dwyer to Tumulty, October 16, 1913, *Wilson Mss.*

27. Tumulty to Kerney, February 26, 1914, *Tumulty Mss.*; Tumulty, "Democratic Solidarity," *loc. cit.*;

Kerney, *Wilson*, p. 258; Davis to Tumulty, November 13, 1913; J. A. Hamill to Tumulty, November 17, 1913; McBride to Tumulty, January 24, 1914; Thomas to Tumulty, January 26, 1914; Record to Tumulty, February 10, 1914, *Wilson Mss*.

28. Tumulty to Fielder, November 7, 1913, March 27, 1914, *Tumulty Mss*.

29. Tumulty to Fielder, October 4, 1913, *Tumulty Mss*.; Kerney, *op. cit.*, p. 258; New York *Times*, October 4, 1913. McGovern to Tumulty, November 3, 1914, *Tumulty Mss*.

30. In section VI of the *Wilson Mss*. and in the letter press books in the *Tumulty Mss*., there is a falling off of Tumulty's correspondence relative to New Jersey shortly after the beginning of 1914. The volume of such correspondence declines steadily, except for two or three short periods, for the rest of Tumulty's tenure in office, one evidence of the change in his interests.

31. New York *Times*, April 5, 8, 1914; Tumulty to Hughes, March 31, 1914; Tumulty to Wittpenn, September 4, 1914; Tumulty to Philip Tumulty, Jr., September 11, 1914; Tumulty to Devlin, September 19, 1914, *Tumulty Mss*.; Wilson to T. J. Scully, October 16, 1914, *Wilson Mss*.

32. New York *Tribune*, April 25, 26, 30, 1913; House to Wilson, May 4, 1913; Wilson to O'Gorman, May 5, 1913; Kerney to Wilson, May 6, 1913, *Wilson Mss*.; Kerney, *op. cit.*, pp. 320–22.

33. Kerney, *op. cit.*, pp. 323–24; Baker, *op. cit.*, IV, 186, 191. New York *Times*, November 6, 11, 1914; Diary of E. M. House, August 31, September 13, 1913, *House Mss*.

34. J. M. Power to Tumulty, March 7, 1913; T. D. McCarthy to Tumulty, August 28, 1913, *Tumulty Mss*.

35. Malone to Wilson, August 1, 1914; *Wilson Mss*.

36. Diary of E. M. House, July 8, 1914, *House Mss*.; Kerney, *op. cit.*, pp. 323, 325.

37. H. H. Childers to Tumulty, February 16, 1914, *Wilson Mss*.; New York *Times*, February 10, March 3, July 23, August 16, September 16, 1914.

38. Wilson to Bryan, July 10, 1914; Glynn to Tumulty, July 16, 1914, *Wilson Mss*.

39. Diary of E. M. House, September 12, November 30, December 18, 19, 20, 1913; January 22, July 30, 1914; House to McAdoo, March 4, 1914; McAdoo to House, June 28, 1914, *House Mss*.

40. Malone to Wilson, January 26, August 1, 1914, *Wilson Mss*.

41. Malone to Wilson, June 22, 1914; Rush to Tumulty, August 15, 1914; Rush to McAdoo, undated, *ca*. October 29, 1914, *Wilson Mss*.; New York *Times*, September 16, 1914.

42. McReynolds to Wilson, November 14, 1913; McAdoo to Wilson, November 24, 1913; Wilson to McReynolds, November 13, 1913; McCombs to Tumulty, April 9, 1914; Elkins to Tumulty, June 12, 1914; McCarthy to Tumulty, August 14, 1914; Schneider to Tumulty, August 24, 1914; Seitz to Tumulty, September 4, 1914, *Wilson Mss*.

43. Malone to Wilson, March 6, 1914; F. D. Roosevelt to Wilson, October 10, 1914; Mitchel to House, October 14, 1914; Felix Tumulty to Tumulty, January 16, 1914, *Wilson Mss*.

44. Malone to Wilson, March 31,

September 8, 1914; Wilson to Malone, September 8, 1914, *Wilson Mss.*

45. New York *Times*, October 31, 1914.

46. House to McAdoo, October 7, 1914, *House Mss.*; House to Wilson, October 9, 14, 15, 1914; Wilson to Glynn, October 15, 1914; Kerney to Wilson, October 1, 1914; Wilson to Kerney, October 3, 1914; Wilson to McAdoo, October 3, 1914; McAdoo to Wilson, October 29, 1914; Rush to Tumulty, October 27, 1914, *Wilson Mss.*; Tumulty to Malone, October 5, 1914, *Tumulty Mss.*; New York *Times*, October 5, 6, 7, 20, 23, 24, 27, 1914.

47. New York *Times*, October 8, 14, 31, 1914; Tumulty to Garrison, October 29, 1914; Tumulty to George Harvey, October 29, 1914; Tumulty to McAdoo, October 30, 1914; *Tumulty Mss.* These documents show that Tumulty drafted the message for the President. Originally Garrison was going to read the telegram which conveyed the message, but because McAdoo was a New Yorker, Wilson decided to have McAdoo read it. The telegram was read at a meeting at Cooper Union on October 30 and published in full in the New York *Times* the next day.

48. House to McAdoo, July 29, 1913, *House Mss.*; Quincy to Tumulty, July 21, 25, 1913, *Wilson Mss.*; Tumulty to McReynolds, March 17, 1913, *Tumulty Mss.*

49. "Black Book," *loc. cit.*

50. Thayer to McAdoo, September 10, 1913; Taylor to Tumulty, September 10, 1913; McAdoo to Wilson, September 10, 22, 1913; House to Wilson, September 11, 1913; Fitzgerald to McAdoo, September 8, 1913; Higginson to Wilson,

September 11, 1913; H. O. Sullivan to Tumulty, September 11, 1913; Nutter to Wilson, September 11, 1913; R. Olney to Wilson, September 12, 1913; Hoar to Wilson, October 3, 1913, *Wilson Mss.*; New York *Times*, October 8, 1913.

51. House to McAdoo, August 2, 1913; Tumulty to House, August 18, 1913, *House Mss.*; Tumulty to Wilson, Memorandum attached to Hoar to Wilson, October 3, 1913, *Wilson Mss.*; New York *Times*, November 5, 1913; Boston *Evening Transcript*, November 4, 1913.

52. Vrooman to Bryan, June 14, 1914; Dunne to Bryan, May 25, June 15, 1914; Harrison to Bryan, June 15, 1914, *William Jennings Bryan Manuscripts* (Library of Congress, Washington, D.C.); R. L. Owen to Wilson, June 5, 1914, *Wilson Mss.*

53. "Black Book"; Tumulty to Roger Sullivan, October 22, 1913, *Tumulty Mss.*

54. Ladd to Wilson, May 2, 1914; R. L. Owen to Wilson, June 5, 1914; J. M. Page to Rainey, September 26, 1914, *Wilson Mss.*; Stringer to Wilson, January 30, 1914; Page to Tumulty, July 20, 1914; Snively to Tumulty, July 28, 1914, *Tumulty Mss.*; Dunne to Bryan, May 25, June 23, 1914; Vrooman to Bryan, June 14, 1914; Harrison to Bryan, June 15, 1914; Thompson to Bryan, June 21, 1914; Vrooman to Bryan, July 6, 1914, *Bryan Mss.*

55. Charles to Tumulty, October 22, 1914; Wheeler to Tumulty, October 27, 1914; Page to Tumulty, October 28, 1914; Shannon to Tumulty, November 3, 1914, *Tumulty Mss.*

56. Williams to Tumulty, September

21, October 14, 1914; Glenn to Tumulty, October 2, 1914; Rainey to Tumulty, October 23, 25, 1914; Rosenthal to Tumulty, October 27, 1914, *Tumulty Mss.*; Tumulty, *Wilson,* pp. 101–4.

57. Vanee to Williams, October 30, 1914; Pindell to Wilson, October 30, 1914, *Tumulty Mss.*

Three drafts of the letter from Wilson which was intended for Henry T. Rainey but was not sent are in the Tumulty Mss. A flimsy of one of these is in section II of the Wilson Mss. An analysis of the handwriting of the interlineations and of the typewriting establishes the sequence of the drafts.

Rainey and Tumulty prepared the original, which Warren Johnson, Tumulty's secretary, typed. Tumulty revised this copy and had a clean revision typed by Charles L. Swem, Wilson's stenographer. This second draft Wilson signed. He also made extensive changes in phraseology on the copy. Swem then typed a third draft, incorporating Wilson's revisions. The President never signed it or mailed it. In his memoirs Tumulty quoted the final draft. Baker quoted the second draft, the carbon of which is the only one in the Wilson Mss., in his biography of Wilson.

Tumulty's loyal attempt to clear his chief of charges of ingratitude to Sullivan has beclouded the whole incident. Tumulty explained that one of Sullivan's managers telephoned him, advising that Wilson should keep out of the campaign so as not to arouse the antagonism of Theodore Roosevelt who was about to begin a tour in behalf of the Bull Moose's senatorial candidate. Since neither Tumulty nor Wilson ever balked at giving battle to Roosevelt, this story is not convincing.

Rainey identified John P. Hopkins, a wealthy and influential Illinois Democrat and personal friend of Sullivan, as the caller to whom Tumulty referred, but Rainey wrote Ray Stannard Baker that Hopkins either wrote or telephoned to Wilson directly. Hopkins told the President that he realized that an endorsement of Sullivan would embarrass Wilson and that no such endorsement was necessary (Rainey to Baker, August 5, 1932, *Baker Mss.*).

This message, for which Hopkins had no authorization, must have reached Wilson after he had signed the second draft of his letter to Rainey and while the final draft was in preparation. It gave him an excuse to yield to the pressure of Illinois progressives to withhold support for Sullivan. Rainey believed that Wilson's change of heart cost Sullivan the election. Tumulty was obviously embarrassed by his chief's reversal. He tried to avoid seeing Rainey. His correspondence with Burleson and Rainey indicates that he considered Wilson's course a mistake (Rainey to Tumulty, October 25, 1914; Burleson to Tumulty, October 22, 1914, *Tumulty Mss.*). And in his memoirs he attempted to exonerate Wilson from blame for Sullivan's defeat.

58. Burleson to Tumulty, October 22, 1914; Shannon to Wilson, November 3, 1914; King to Wilson, November 2, 1914, *Tumulty Mss.*
59. Baker, *op. cit.,* IV, 367–69.
60. *Ibid.,* pp. 319–72.
61. "Programme for the Fall Campaign," *Tumulty Mss.*
62. Compare Tumulty's memoran-

dum with Wilson to Doremus, September 4, 1914 and Wilson to Underwood, October 17, 1914, as quoted in R. S. Baker and W. E. Dodd, eds., *The Public Papers of Woodrow Wilson, The New Democracy*, 2 vols. (New York, 1926), I, 164–67, 187–94.

63. Tumulty to Wilson, undated memorandum, *Tumulty Mss.* Beginning, "I have examined the Underwood letter and . . . my feeling is that it is too argumentative . . ." this memorandum sets forth ideas similar to those in the "Programme for the Fall Campaign." Comparison to the final draft of the Underwood letter indicates that Tumulty's advice was followed.

64. "Democratic Solidarity," dated for release October 10, 1914, *Tumulty Mss.*

65. On October 26, 1914, Tumulty sent the following telegram to the Congressmen listed below: "Please wire me name and address of man to whom the President should address a telegram in your interest." To: Augustine Lonergan (Conn.); H. R. Fowler (Ill.); L. FitzHenry (Ill.); E. W. Townsend (N.J.); L. Brown (N.Y.); C. B. Smith (N.Y.); J. A. McGuire (Neb.); W. A.

Ashbrook (Ohio); H. D. Flood (Va.); C. C. Carlin (Va.), *Tumulty Mss.;* see also Tumulty to Kerney, November 4, 1914, *Tumulty Mss.;* Tumulty to Wilson, January 20, 1914, *Wilson Mss.*

66. New York *Times*, November 4, 5, 6, 7, 9, 1914.

67. Tumulty to Wilson, *ca.* December 1, 1914, *Wilson Mss.*

68. Tumulty to McCrea, November 6, 1914; Tumulty to T. J. Burns, November 6, 1914; Tumulty to Philip Tumulty, Jr., November 6, 1914, *Tumulty Mss.*

69. Tumulty to Kerney, November 6, 1914, *Tumulty Mss.*

70. "Message of the President," Tumulty to Wilson, undated, *ca.* November 4–12, 1914, *Tumulty Mss.*

71. Compare Tumulty's memorandum with Wilson to McAdoo, November 17, 1914, as quoted in Baker and Dodd, eds., *New Democracy*, I, 210–14.

72. Tumulty to Wilson, December 4, 1914, *Tumulty Mss.*

73. Compare Tumulty's letter to Wilson's second annual message of December 8, 1914, as quoted in Baker and Dodd, eds., *New Democracy*, I, 215–28, especially 215.

Chapter VII

THE KLAN AND THE HYPHEN

For background material on American-Mexican relations, American neutrality policies, and the preparedness campaign, I depended largely on the comprehensive accounts in Baker, *Wilson*, V and VI, supplementing these particularly with data from Seymour, *House*; Bryan, *Memoirs*; and Tumulty, *Wilson*. The last, useful on Tumulty's rôle, quotes letters which are in places slightly altered or condensed. Although this has not affected their meaning, in all cases I relied on original documents from the manuscript sources. Manuscripts, as the annotation indicates, furnished most of the detailed information in this chapter. Without them Tumulty's part could not have been followed. On Mexican-American relations there is a good brief narrative and analysis, generally, like Baker's, favorable to Wilson, in Samuel Flagg Bemis, *A Diplomatic History of the United States* (New York, 1936). A critique of the vast bibliography on American neutrality policies and intervention, a considerable part of which I consulted, would be out of place in a biography of Tumulty, for his influence, while not insignificant, was but an infinitesimal part of the complicated general problem. Without a critique a list would have little meaning. For a discussion of the changing historical attitudes on neutrality and intervention, see the excellent essay of Richard W. Leopold, "The Problem of American Intervention, 1917: An Historical Retrospect," *World Politics*, II (April, 1950), 405–25.

For public opinion on all topics discussed in this chapter, I relied upon the New York *Times;* the *Literary Digest; America, A Catholic Review of the Week*; and *The Irish World and American Industrial Liberator. The Irish World* was excellent for extreme Irish-American opinion; *America,* usually a more moderate periodical, was equally good on Catholic opinion.

1. Tumulty to Reverend W. T. Russell (undated), 1913, *Tumulty Mss.*; New York *Times,* November 28, 1913; August 15, 16, November 7, 1916.

2. Wade to Tumulty, February 14, March 18, 1915; Tumulty to Wilson, February 22, 1915, *Wilson Mss.*

3. Arthur Sinnott to Tumulty, December 2, 1915; Burleson to Tumulty, December 3, 1915; Kernan to Tumulty, January 12, 1916; Kerney to Wilson, January 15, 1916; Nugent to Burleson, January 19, 1916; Wilson to Tumulty (January ?), 1916, *Wilson Mss.*; Newark *Evening News,* January 22, 24, 27, February 16, 1916.

4. Williams to Watson, June 30, 1914, *Tumulty Mss.*

5. Williams to Wilson, January 31, 1914; Williams to Tumulty, February 14, 1914, quoted in George C. Osborn, *John Sharp Williams* (Baton Rouge, 1943), p. 439.

6. A. D. Bulman to Wilson, May 20, 1914; L. E. Carter to Wilson, November 24, 1914; Wilson to Carter, November 26, 1914, *Wilson Mss.*; New York *Times,* February 18, 1914.

7. "Tumulty and Rome," *Life, LXVI* (August 5, 1915), 230–31.

8. Wilson to Tumulty, August 6, 1915, *Tumulty Mss.*; see also Tumulty, *Wilson,* p. 187.

9. Tumulty, *op. cit.,* pp. 151–53.

10. New York *Times,* December 6, 1914.

11. *America, A Catholic Review of the Week,* XI (June 20, September 19, 26, October 3, 10, 1914),

especially 220, 227–28, 544, 568, 597.

12. Rev. R. Tierney, *et al.*, to Wilson, September 29, 1914; Wilson to Cardinal Gibbons, August 21, 1914; Malone to Wilson, December 7, 1914; January 8, April 22, 1915; McAdoo to Wilson, April 12, 1915, *Wilson Mss.*; Bryan to Wilson, March 11, 1915; Wilson to Bryan, March 17, 1915; Bryan to Father F. C. Kelley, March 20, 1915, *Bryan Mss.*

13. *America*, XIV (October 23, 1915), 38.

14. Tumulty to McGuire, November 27, 1915, *Tumulty Mss.*

15. New York *Times*, November 29, 30, December 3, 9, 1915; Boston *Herald*, December 11, 1915.

16. Rev. R. H. Tierney, "Mr. Tumulty and Mexico," *America*, XIV (December 4, 1915), 173–74.

17. *North Western Christian Advocate*, January 5, 1916, clipping in *Wilson Mss.*

18. Wilson to Tumulty (January ?), 1916, *Wilson Mss.*

19. Tumulty to Wilson, March 15, 1916, *Tumulty Mss.*

20. Tumulty to Wilson, June 24, 1916; Tumulty to Lansing, June 24, 1916, *Tumulty Mss.*

21. Lansing's Desk Book, June 24, 1916, *Robert Lansing Manuscripts* (Library of Congress, Washington, D.C.)

22. New York *Times*, November 23, 1916.

23. Tumulty, *op. cit.*, pp. 229–30.

24. *Ibid.*, p. 237; Baker, *Wilson*, V, 333–34, 340.

25. Baker, *op. cit.*, V, 338–40.

26. Henry Cabot Lodge, *The Senate and the League of Nations* (New York, 1925), pp. 44–54. Lodge's version of the "postscript" affair was wrong only in its minor details. He asserted that the qualifying statement had been in-tended as part of the note and that it was withdrawn only when certain Cabinet members threatened to resign. Wilson immediately denied these allegations. Inferentially this denial invalidated any claims that the President had intended to temper the note to Germany, so that whereas Wilson told the exact truth, his statement carried false connotations. Lodge withdrew his charges, as he felt he was bound to do. See also Baker, *op. cit.*, V, 341.

27. Garrison to Tumulty, November 18, 1928, *Tumulty Mss.*; Baker Memo of Interview with Garrison, November 30, 1928, *Baker Mss.* Garrison wrote his letter after first reading Tumulty's book. Of the book he said: ". . . It is certainly a testimonial to your magnanimity. . . . No reference whatever was made to your achievement in preventing the sending of the so-called 'postscript'. . . ." He then recounted the same story he told Baker a few days later. Two years earlier, after the publication of Seymour's *House*, Thomas B. Love had written Tumulty reviewing his memory of the "postscript" incident as Tumulty had once told it to him. Love's letter conforms to Garrison's testimony; see Love to Tumulty, March 4, 1926, *Tumulty Mss.* Tumulty apparently gave a similar version to David Lawrence, who accepted it as true; see Lawrence, *Wilson*, pp. 145–46. A New Jersey man supplied Lodge with some of the details he used in his charges in 1916. Lodge asserted the account came by way of Tumulty. His version also largely conformed to Garrison's; see Lodge, *op. cit.*,

pp. 44–54. Ray Stannard Baker refers only briefly to the rôles of Garrison, Lansing and Tumulty, leaving it unsettled as to whether their "remonstrances" or his own "reconsideration" influenced Wilson to change his mind; see Baker, *op. cit.*, V, 340.

28. Baker, *op. cit.*, V, 342–58.
29. Tumulty to Bryan, June 9, 1915, *Tumulty Mss.;* New York *Times*, June 9, 1915.
30. Robert J. Bender, "*W.W.*" (New York, 1924), p. 9; Villard, *Fighting Years*, p. 277.
31. Tumulty to Wilson, July 21, 1915, *Tumulty Mss.*
32. Tumulty to Wilson, July 14, September 7, 10, 1915, *Wilson Mss.*, Lansing's Desk Book, February 23, 1916, *Lansing Mss.;* Tumulty to Lansing, May 18, 1916, *Tumulty Mss.*
33. *The Irish World and American Industrial Liberator*, June 19, 1915. See also May 22, June 12, 1915; April 29, 1916.
34. Tumulty to Wilson, February 24, 1916, *Tumulty Mss.*
35. Tumulty to the Editor, the Jersey City *Evening Journal*, March 8, 1916, *Tumulty Mss.*
36. Baker, *Wilson*, VI, 4.
37. Tumulty to Wilson, August 9, 1915, *Tumulty Mss.*
38. Tumulty to Wilson, undated Memorandum on Manhattan Club speech, *Tumulty Mss.* Compare to text of speech in Baker and Dodd, eds., *The New Democracy*, I, 384 ff.
39. Tumulty to Wilson, November 19, 1915, *Tumulty Mss.* Compare to Wilson's address as published in Baker and Dodd, eds., *op. cit.*, I, 406 ff., especially 423 ff.
40. Tumulty to Wilson, November 29, 1915, *Tumulty Mss.*, cf. as above.

41. Tumulty to Wilson, January 17, 1916, *Tumulty Mss.*
42. W. F. Sapp to Tumulty, February 3, 1916; A. W. Kopke to Tumulty, February 4, 1916; C. M. Selph to Tumulty, February 4, 1916, *Wilson Mss.;* Edith B. Wilson, *My Memoir* (New York, 1938), p. 94.
43. Tumulty to Wilson, January 15, 1916, *Tumulty Mss.*
44. Baker, *op. cit.*, VI, 33–34; Tumulty, *op cit.*, pp. 243–44.
45. Tumulty, *op. cit.*, p. 247.
46. Tumulty to Wilson, June 13, 1916, *Tumulty Mss.*
47. Husting to Tumulty, June 12, 1916, *Tumulty Mss.*
48. Tumulty to Wilson, June 13, 1916, *loc. cit.*
49. Lane to Wilson, undated, *ca.* June 13, 1916, *Tumulty Mss.*
50. Cox to Tumulty, June 21, 1916, *Wilson Mss.* The letter Cox forwarded was from F. W. Durbin to Cox, June 19, 1916.
51. Philip Zoercher to Tumulty, June 26, 1916; Paul Boyton to Tumulty, June 28, 1916, *Wilson Mss.*
52. Flannery to Tumulty, August 10, 1916, *Wilson Mss.*
53. Press release, August 15, 1916; Kinkead to Tumulty, September 4, 1916; Roper to Tumulty, September 15, 1916, *Wilson Mss.*
54. Flannery to Tumulty, August 24, 1916, *Wilson Mss.*
55. N. W. Mullen to Tumulty, October 4, 1916, and clipping therein from *The Catholic News Bulletin*, October 1916, *Wilson Mss.; The Irish World*, June 24, September 23, October 7, 14, 1916.
56. Tumulty, *op. cit.*, pp. 214–15.
57. C. M. Selph to Tumulty, August 28, 1916, *Wilson Mss.* Selph wrote that Father Collins had spoken to 5000 priests all over the

United States. He reported that 3500 favored Wilson because he had maintained peace.

58. *The Irish World*, April through August, 1916, especially May 6, 20, June 17, July 8, 29, August 3, 12.

59. Doyle to Tumulty, April 29, July 6, 1916; Lansing to Tumulty, *ca.* April 30, 1916; Polk to Tumulty, June 2, 1916; Page to Lansing, July 1, 1916, *Wilson Mss.*

60. Congressmen London, Carey, Burke, *et al.*, to Wilson, June 30, 1916; Tumulty to London, Carey, *et al.*, June 30, 1916, *Wilson Mss.*

61. Krebs to Tumulty, July 7, 1916, *Wilson Mss.*

62. Doyle to Tumulty, July 6, 1916; Tumulty to Wilson, July 20, 1916; Wilson to Tumulty, July 20, 1916, *Wilson Mss.*

63. R. P. Troy, R. C. O'Connor, and J. Mulhern to Wilson, July 20, 1916, *Wilson Mss.*

64. Polk to Tumulty, August 2, 7, 1916; Lansing to Tumulty, September 2, 1916, *Wilson Mss.*; *The Irish World*, July 29, August 13, 1916.

65. Phelan to Tumulty, August 4, 1916; McGuire to Tumulty, August 5, 1916; Doyle to Tumulty, August 28, 1916; Polk to Tumulty, August 2, 7, October 5, 1916; Lansing to Tumulty, September 2, 1916, *Wilson Mss.*; Polk to House, August 18, 1916, *House Mss.*

66. Tumulty to Lansing, September 7, 1916, *Wilson Mss.*

67. Polk to Tumulty, October 5, 6, 1916, *Wilson Mss.*

68. Tumulty to Polk, October 11, 1916; Polk to Tumulty, October 12, 1916, *Wilson Mss.*

69. Tumulty to Doyle, October 14, 1916, *Wilson Mss.*

70. Doyle to Tumulty, October 18, 1916, *Wilson Mss.*

Chapter VIII

STRATAGEMS AND SPOILS

Most of this chapter is based on the manuscript and newspaper sources cited below. There are, however, a few useful background works, none of which contain much on Tumulty. On the San Domingo episode, see Baker, *Wilson*, IV, 441–51; Melvin M. Knight, *The Americans in Santo Domingo* (New York, 1928), chap. VI. Baker wrote with beauty and understanding of the life and death of Ellen Axson Wilson, see especially his *Wilson*, IV, 461–81. His sixth volume treats Wilson's second marriage and the campaign of 1916 in detail. Seymour, *House*, II, is excellent on the campaign. On Tumulty's relations with Edith Wilson in 1915–17 and his difficulties with the President, the best account is in Lawrence, *Wilson*. Edith Wilson's unfriendly attitude toward Tumulty is evident throughout Edith B. Wilson, *My Memoir* (New York, 1938).

The last section of this chapter rests almost entirely on my note, "The

'Leak' Investigation of 1917," *American Historical Review*, LIV (April, 1949), 548–52 (see note 49, *infra.*). That article, in turn, was largely based on the reports of the investigation in the New York *Times*, December 1916–February 1917. Further details on the "leak" may be found in the *Times* or in "Alleged Divulgence of the President's Note to Belligerent Powers," *Hearings Before the Committee on Rules, House of Representatives, Sixty-Fourth Congress, Second Session* (Washington, 1917). Of these two sources I prefer the *Times*, for it contains not only testimony but also a good indication of public feeling toward the investigation in each of its stages.

1. Cummings to Tumulty, May 20, 1913; Hamill to Tumulty, June 22, 1913; Hamill to Tumulty, Memorandum, August 1, 1913; Whitman to O'Gorman, April 23, 1913, *Wilson Mss.*

2. Bryan to Wilson, June 9, 1913; May 19, 1915; McAdoo to Wilson, July 30, 1913, *Wilson Mss.*

3. Platt to Wilson, March 17, 1913; McCombs to Wilson, April 17, 1913; Vick to Tumulty, April 21, 1913; Cummings to Wilson, April 22, 1913; Davies to Wilson, April 22, 1913; House to Tumulty, May 14, 1913; Garrison to Wilson, June 16, 1913, *Wilson Mss.*; New York *Times*, January 20, 1915.

4. Pence to Bryan, September 4, 1913; Vick to Tumulty, August 19, September 5, 1913, *Wilson Mss.*; New York *Times*, August 29, 1913.

5. Bryan to Vick, August 20, 1913, published in New York *Times*, January 15, 1915.

6. Tumulty to Vick, July 31, August 5, September 25, October 15, 1913; Vick to Tumulty, August 2, 19, October 7, 27, 1913, *Wilson Mss.*; Tumulty to Hamill, November 3, 1913, *Tumulty Mss.*

7. Bryan to Wilson, March 24, 1914; Vick to Tumulty, February 20, May 5, June 8, 1914; Vick to Bryan, April 14, 1914; Vick to Wilson, December 1, 1914, *Wilson Mss.*; New York *Times*, January 17, July 27, 1915.

8. Vick to Tumulty, February 20, 1914; J. M. Sullivan to Bryan, December 10, 1913, *Wilson Mss.*; New York *Times*, January 14, February 10, 1914.

9. Lyons to Tumulty, October (?), December 11, 1914, January 21, 1915, *Wilson Mss.*

10. Vick to Wilson, June 9, 1914, *Wilson Mss.*

11. See Note 7, *supra*; also Vick to House, May 17, 1914; Vick to Wilson, June 9, 1914; Wilson to Vick, June 22, July 20, December 7, 1914; House to Wilson, December 5, 1914; Wilson to Garrison, December 8, 1914; Wilson to Bryan, December 10, 1914, *Wilson Mss.*; New York *Times*, January 19, 22, 1915.

12. New York *Times*, January 13, 14, 15, 19, 20, 26, 29, 1915.

13. See Note 9, *supra*; also John J. Rooney to George W. Loft, January 23, 1915, and enclosures; Affidavit of Edo. Pellerano, June 5, 1914, *Wilson Mss.*

14. New York *Times*, January 16, 22, February 10, 1915; Tumulty to Charles H. Strong, February 8, 1915, *Tumulty Mss.*

15. Knight, *Santo Domingo*, p. 65.

16. New York *Times*, January 23, 1915.

17. Tumulty to Hennessy, August 27, 1915, *Tumulty Mss.*

18. Bryan to Wilson, March 24, 1914; Wilson to Bryan, March 26, 1914, *Wilson Mss.*

19. House to Wilson, December 4, 1915; November 14, 1916, *Wilson Mss.*

20. Diary of E. M. House, September 12, November 30, December 13, 18, 19, 20, 23, 1913; January 22, May 7, July 30, November 6, 17, 1914; May 2, 1915, *House Mss.*

21. Tumulty to Wilson, March 24, 1916, *Tumulty Mss.*; Diary of E. M. House, April 15, 1914, *House Mss.*

22. Baker Memo of Interview with N. D. Baker, April 6, 1921, *Baker Mss.*

23. Diary of E. M. House, May 7, 11, 1914, *House Mss.*

24. Grayson to House, September 10, 1915, *House Mss.*; Baker Memo of Interview with L. M. Garrison, November 30, 1928, *Baker Mss.*; Lawrence, *Wilson*, pp. 177–79; Interview with Charles L. Swem.

25. Bender, "*W. W.*", p. 14; Lawrence, *op. cit.*, p. 179; New York *Times*, October 7, 1915.

26. New York *Times*, October 8, 9, December 19, 1915; Notebook of Invitations, *Tumulty Mss.*

27. McAdoo to Wilson, December 9, 10, 1915; Tumulty to Wilson, December 17, 1915, March 3, 1916; N. E. Mack to Tumulty, April 18, 1916, *Wilson Mss.*

28. Tumulty to Kinkead, November 16, 1915, *Tumulty Mss.*

29. Woolley to House, March 2, April 1, 3, 6, 1916, *House Mss.*

30. Diary of E. M. House, April 6, 1916, *House Mss.*

31. Tumulty to Wilson, January 25, February 15, March 17, 1916, *Tumulty Mss.* Tumulty's ideas were much the same as those he had advanced for the campaign of 1914.

32. Fielder to Wilson, May 19, 1916; Fielder to Tumulty, May 19, 1916, *Wilson Mss.*; Statement by Tumulty, *ca.* May 19, 1916, *Tumulty Mss.*

33. House to Wilson, May 19, 30, 31, June 2, 9, 10, 1916, *Wilson Mss.*

34. Tumulty to McAdoo, July 3, 1916; Tumulty to McCormick, July 7, 1916; Steckman to Tumulty, July 8, 1916, *Tumulty Mss.*; Woolley to House, July 8, 1916; Polk to House, July 16, 17, 1916, *House Mss.*

35. Tumulty to Woolley, July 27, 1916; Tumulty to Wilson, August 18, 1916, *Tumulty Mss.*; Palmer to Tumulty, October 17, 1916, and enclosures, *Wilson Mss.*

36. Tumulty to Wilson, August 10, 1916, *ca.* September 30, October 26, 1916, *Tumulty Mss.*; Tumulty's suggestions were used as the basis for a perfunctory telegram to local Democratic chairmen but not in any public speech by the President.

37. Woolley to House, August 5, 1916, *House Mss.*

38. Tumulty to R. T. Baker, August 4, 1916, *Tumulty Mss.*; New York *Times*, August 16, September 15, October 8, 18, November 6, 7, 1916.

39. New York *Times*, November 7, 8, 9, 10, 1916.

40. *Ibid.*, November 11, 12, 1916.

41. *Ibid.*, November 14, 1916; Tumulty to John McCormick, December 11, 1916, *Tumulty Mss.*

42. New York *Times*, November 14, 1916.

43. Baker Memo of Interviews with Vance McCormick, July 15, 1928; Burleson, March 17–19, 1927, *Baker Mss.*; Diary of E. M.

House, November 15, 1916, *House Mss.*

44. Baker Interview with Burleson, *loc. cit.*

45. Diary of E. M. House, November 15, 1916, *House Mss.*

46. Tumulty to Wilson, November 18, 1916, *Wilson Mss.*

47. Lawrence, *op. cit.*, pp. 333–34; Interview with Charles L. Swem.

48. Diary of E. M. House, January 13, 1917, *House Mss.*

49. The remainder of this chapter, except where references to manuscript sources indicate otherwise, is based on Blum, "The 'Leak' Investigation," *loc. cit.*

50. J. H. James to Lansing, January 6, 1917; Lansing to J. H. Hammond, January 18, 1917, *Lansing Mss.*

51. Lansing to E. N. Smith, January 21, 1917, *Lansing Mss.*; Wilson to Lansing, December 21, 1916, *Wilson Mss.*

52. Desk Book of Robert Lansing, January 2, 6, 7, 8, 15, 16, 18, 1917, *Lansing Mss.*

53. Memorandum by Tumulty, January 9, 1917; Affidavits of J. A. Rodier and E. W. Smithers, January 9, 1917, *Tumulty Mss.*

54. Reports by Detectives of the William J. Burns Agency, January 19–February 3, 1917, *Tumulty Mss.*

55. Tumulty to F. B. Kent, February 9, 1917, *Tumulty Mss.*

56. See the following letters to Tumulty, all 1917, in *Wilson Mss.*: Smith, January 9; Hearst, January 26; House, January 6; see also J. H. Lewis, January 8; J. Daniels, January 9; J. F. Fort, January 16; R. W. Woolley, January 22; see also Tumulty to Philip Tumulty, Jr., February 15, 1917, *Tumulty Mss.*

57. Tumulty to Mrs. T. F. Logan, February 9, 1917, *Tumulty Mss.*

Chapter IX

THE GREAT WAR

For the first section of this chapter I relied largely on Baker, *Wilson,* VI, chaps. XI, XII. In these chapters Baker gives an excellent, detailed description of Wilson's feelings, diplomacy, and executive actions, and of Congressional and public opinion in the trying days of February, March and April, 1917. Also useful were the New York *Times* and relevant sections of the following books: Josephus Daniels, *The Wilson Era: Years of War and After* (Chapel Hill, 1946); Heaton, *Cobb;* David F. Houston, *Eight Years With Wilson's Cabinet,* 2 vols. (Garden City, 1926); A. W. Lane and L. H. Wall, eds., *The Letters of Franklin K. Lane* (Cambridge, 1922); Robert Lansing, *War Memoirs of Robert Lansing* (Indianapolis, 1935); G. W. McAdoo, *Crowded Years*; Thomas R. Marshall, *Recollections of Thomas R. Marshall* (Indianapolis, 1925); Seymour, *House,* II; Tumulty, *Wilson*; and Villard, *Fighting Years.*

For the sections of this chapter pertaining to the war, the most detailed published source is Baker, *Wilson*, VII, VIII. These volumes contain Baker's notes on the war period chronologically arranged. Regrettably, he was too ill to synthesize his material, but the volumes are nevertheless useful for a day-by-day account of the war, of Wilson's activities, and, to a lesser extent, of Tumulty's work. The New York *Times* is also good on a day-by-day basis. For more generalized descriptions of the war effort as it formed a background for this chapter, two useful volumes were Bernard M. Baruch, *American Industry in the War* (New York, 1941), and Frederic L. Paxson, *America at War, 1917–1918* (Boston, 1939). My detailed information, however, came almost exclusively from manuscript sources.

1. Tumulty, *Wilson*, pp. 254–55.
2. Tumulty to Wilson, March 8, 1917, *Tumulty Mss.*; ref. also Desk Book of Robert Lansing, March 6, 8, 9, 1917, *Lansing Mss.* Lansing, McAdoo, and Polk, and, to a lesser degree, the other Cabinet officers except for Wilson and Burleson, were as ardent and sometimes more ardent than Tumulty in urging stringent measures toward Germany and, later, the declaration of war.
3. Tumulty to Wilson, undated memorandum, *ca.* June 10, 1917, *Tumulty Mss.*
4. Desk Book of Robert Lansing, March 19, 20, 1917, *Lansing Mss.*
5. New York *Times*, April 3, 1917; Baker, *Wilson*, VI, 509 ff.
6. Tumulty to Johnson, August 3, 1918; Tumulty to Alexander Simpson, August 7, 1917; Tumulty to McAdoo, August 8, 1917; Tumulty to House, August 20, 1917, *Tumulty Mss.*
7. Tumulty to Wilson, May 11, 1918, and Wilson to Tumulty, undated, attached, *Wilson Mss.*
8. Tumulty to Wilson, October 15, 1917, *Tumulty Mss.*
9. Tumulty to Wilson, undated memorandum, *ca.* June 20, 1917, *Tumulty Mss.*
10. Tumulty to Wilson, May 31, June

2, October 7, October 19, 1917, *Tumulty Mss.*; Baker, *op. cit.*, VII, 112–13.
11. Baker, *op. cit.*, VII, 20–21.
12. Tumulty to House, November 22, 1917, *House Mss.*; Tumulty to Wilson, November 19, 1917, *Wilson Mss.*; Seymour, *House*, III, 219–25; Baker, *op. cit.*, VII, 361 ff., especially 364–66, 369–70.
13. House to Wilson, August 9, 1918; Tumulty to Wilson, August 14, 1918; House to Wilson, August 24, 1918; Wilson to Tumulty, August 26, 1918; Tumulty to Wilson, September 4, 1918, *Wilson Mss.*
14. John M. Blum, "Tumulty and Leavenworth: A Case Study of Rumor," *The Journal of Abnormal and Social Psychology*, XLIV (July, 1949), 411–13.
15. Tumulty to Wilson, June 26, July 11, July 12, 1917; October 3, 1918; October 9, 1918; Tumulty to E. B. Wilson, October 16, 1918, *Tumulty Mss.*; Tumulty to Wilson, October 17, 1918; Wilson to Creel, January 2, 1918, Wilson to Glynn, January 30, 1918, *Wilson Mss.*
16. Cobb to House, undated, enclosed in House to Wilson, July 13, 1917; Lawrence to Wilson, May 24, 1917; Wilson to Lawrence, May 25, 1917; Lansing to Wilson, September 1, 1917; Wilson to Lan-

sing, September 4, 1917; House to Wilson, October 17, 1917, *Wilson Mss.*

17. Cf. Tumulty to Wilson, April 20, 1917, and Wilson to Brisbane, April 25, 1917, *Tumulty Mss.*

18. Tumulty to Wilson, May 8, 1917, *Tumulty Mss.*

19. Tumulty to Wilson, October 10, 1917, *Tumulty Mss.*

20. Tumulty to Wilson, April 4, 1918, *Tumulty Mss.* See also Wilson to Burleson, October 11, 1917, *Tumulty Mss.*; Wilson to Burleson, October 18, 1917, *Wilson Mss.*

21. Tumulty to Wilson, May 19, 1917, *Tumulty Mss.*; Baker, *op. cit.*, VII, 4, 364.

22. J. M. Waldron to Wilson, April 12, 1917; Tumulty's draft of Wilson's letter to Waldron, April 19, 1917; Tumulty to Wilson, July 10, 1917; Wilson to France, July 11, 1917; Tumulty to Wilson, August 1, August 3, 1917, *Tumulty Mss.*

23. Tumulty to Wilson, undated, *ca.* May 10, 1917, *Tumulty Mss.*

24. Tumulty to Wilson, January 17, 1918, *Tumulty Mss.*; Tumulty, *op. cit.*, pp. 362–64.

25. Tumulty to Wilson, May 31, 1917, June 4, 1918, *Tumulty Mss.* Cf. Tumulty's suggestions for the speech in undated memorandum to Wilson in *Tumulty Mss.* and Wilson's address as published in R. S. Baker and W. E. Dodd, eds., *The Public Papers of Woodrow Wilson: War and Peace,* 2 vols. (New York, 1927), I, 60–67.

26. Tumulty to Wilson, March 24, 1917, *Tumulty Mss.*

27. *Ibid.*

28. Tumulty to Wilson, April 12, 1917, *Tumulty Mss.*

29. Tumulty to Wilson, April 20, 1917, *Tumulty Mss.*; New York *Times,* April 11, 1917, Tumulty, *op. cit.*, pp. 285–89.

30. Tumulty to Wilson, May 24, 1917; Baker to Wilson, June 1, 1917, *Tumulty Mss.*; F. Palmer, *Newton D. Baker, America at War,* 2 vols. (New York, 1931), I, 325–26.

31. Palmer to Wilson, June 20, 1917; Wilson to Palmer, June 22, 1917; Palmer to Wilson, July 2, July 5, 1917, *Wilson Mss.*; Tumulty to J. D. Moriarty, June 15, 1917; Tumulty to Wilson, undated, *ca.* October 1, 1917, *Tumulty Mss.*

32. Tumulty, *op. cit.*, pp. 289–93; Palmer, *op. cit.*, II, 244–45.

33. Tumulty to E. N. Hurley, January 21, 1918; Tumulty to Rev. J. F. Kelihan, December 7, 1918; Tumulty to J. B. Regan, July 24, 1918; Tumulty to G. E. Cutley, August 9, 1918; Tumulty to Wilson, July 30, 1917, *Tumulty Mss.*

34. Tumulty to Wilson, September 17, 1917, February 7, 1918, *Tumulty Mss.*; House to Wilson, February 6, 1918, *Wilson Mss.*

35. Tumulty to Wilson, November 21, December 10, 1917, *Tumulty Mss.*

36. Tumulty to Wilson, December 7, 1917, *Tumulty Mss.*

37. Baker, *op. cit.*, VII, 401–2, 435; A. T. Mason, *Brandeis, A Free Man's Life* (New York, 1946), pp. 521–22.

38. Tumulty to Wilson, September 12, December 29, 1917, February 11, 1918; Tumulty to Hurley, September 18, 1917, *Tumulty Mss.*

39. Tumulty to Wilson, January 24, 1918, *Tumulty Mss.*

40. Tumulty to Wilson, May 3, May 8, 1918; Wilson to Tumulty, *ca.* May 8, 1918; Tumulty to House, May 6, 1918, *Tumulty Mss.*; Swope to Tumulty, March 18, 1918, *Wilson Mss.*; Baker, *op. cit.*, VII, 372, 407, 412, 430, 446, 495, 507, 517; VIII, 36, 62–63, 92, 140, 193, 522, 536, 562–63.

41. Woolley to House, May 22, 28,

29, June 15, 1918, and enclosure, *House Mss.*; Swope to Wilson, April 16, 1918, *Baker Mss.*

42. For information on the Overman Act, see Baker, *op. cit.*, VII and VIII. Index references lead to the legislation itself and the Congres-sional background. Tumulty and Burleson shared the responsibility for liaison to Congress on behalf of the measure; refer Tumulty to Wilson, April 26, 1918, *Tumulty Mss.*

Chapter X

THE HOME FRONT

Certain aspects of the central topic of this chapter, the elections of 1918, have received excellent, detailed treatment. There is a good account of the campaign in the East and of the "Kitchinism" issue in Alex M. Arnett, *Claude Kitchin and the Wilson War Policies* (Boston, 1937). The best account of the significant sectionalism issue in the West is in Seward W. Livermore, "The Sectional Issue in the 1918 Congressional Elections," *Mississippi Valley Historical Review*, XXXV (June, 1948), 29–60. Livermore gives a restrained, balanced, and scholarly picture of the whole campaign. Thomas A. Bailey, *Woodrow Wilson and the Lost Peace* (New York, 1944), contains, in chaps. I–IV, a concise, cogent discussion of the relation between foreign policy and the election. Mowry, *Roosevelt and the Progressive Movement*, describes Roosevelt's part. To these authors I am indebted. Particularly on the subjects they did not cover, the chapter is based on newspaper and manuscript sources. Of these the *Baker Mss.* contain the best general material, for Baker interrogated the participants in the campaign. His most significant findings, in letters and memoranda, are filed in his manuscripts under N. D. Baker, Burleson, Cummings, Daniels, Gregory, Lawrence, McCormick, Rainey, and Woolley. The most useful contemporary documents are in the *Wilson Mss.* and *Tumulty Mss.*

1. Tumulty to House, August 20, 1917; May 27, 1918, *House Mss.*

2. Tumulty to Wilson, March 18, 1917; May 21, 1917; June 6, 1917; undated memorandum, *ca.* July, 1917, on business and the war, *Tumulty Mss.*

3. Tumulty to Wilson, June 27, 1918, *Tumulty Mss.*

4. Tumulty to Wilson, June 15, 1918, *Tumulty Mss.*

5. Tumulty to Wilson, March 10 (?); March 12, March 14, May 8, May 23, June 20, June 24, July 31, November 9, 1918; Tumulty to Kerney, September 10, 1918, *Tumulty Mss.*; Tumulty to Wilson, August 29, 1918; Wilson to

Stanley, August 30, 1918; Stanley to Wilson, September 7, 1918; Arthur Krock to Wilson, September 7, 1918, *Wilson Mss.*

6. Tumulty to Wilson, September 7, 1918, *Tumulty Mss.*

7. Burleson to Wilson, September 12, 1918, *Tumulty Mss.* In pencil at the end of this letter the following note appears: "This was prepared by Mr. Tumulty for the Postmaster General."

8. Tumulty to Wilson, September 7, November 9, 1918, *Tumulty Mss.*; Diary of E. M. House, September 24, 1918, *House Mss.*

9. Memorandum, January 1918, "The Revolt of the Underdog," *Tumulty Mss.*

10. Tumulty to Wilson, February 21, 1918, *Tumulty Mss.*

11. New York *Times*, March 21, 1918; Tumulty to Wilson, April 4, 1918, *Tumulty Mss.*

12. Tumulty to House, May 23, 1918, and enclosure; House to Tumulty, May 25, 1918; Tumulty to Wilson, June 18, 1918, and enclosure, *House Mss.*

13. New York *Times*, June 18, 19, August 11, 12, 14, 15, 16, 19, 22, 23, 24, 26, September 1, 13, 19, 21, 28, 30, October 2, 3, 5, 7, 9, 12, 13, 15, 18, 23, November 7, 1918.

14. Tumulty to House, June 8, 9, 19, 1917, with Wilson's notes to Tumulty appended, *House Mss.*

15. New York *Times*, September 8, 1917; House to Wilson, July 26, August 10, 1917; Malone to Wilson, September 7, 15, 1917; Wilson to Malone, September 12, 1917, *Wilson Mss.*; Diary of E. M. House, July 26, 1917, *House Mss.*; Tumulty to E. B. Wilson, September 30, 1918; Tumulty to Wilson, October 7, 1918, *Tumulty Mss.*

16. Tumulty to McAdoo, September 12, 1917, *Tumulty Mss.*; Wedin to Tumulty, July 3, 21, 30, 1917; Mack to Tumulty, March 11, 1918; Redfield to Wilson, October 27, 1917, *Wilson Mss.*; New York *Times*, October 27, 1917.

17. Mack to Tumulty, June 20, 1918; Tumulty to Wilson, July 26, 1918, *Wilson Mss.*

18. House to Burleson, September 13, 1917; Olney to Burleson, September 13, 1917; Tumulty to Burleson, September 15, 1917; Tumulty to Wilson, September 15, 1917, *Tumulty Mss.*

19. Wilson to House, September 17, 1917; House to Wilson, September 19, 1917; Wilson to Tumulty, September 21, 1917; Tumulty to Wilson, September 24, 27, 28, 1917; *Tumulty Mss.* The letter of September 28 suggested the draft which Wilson adopted, cf. Wilson to Hale, October 1, 1918, *Wilson Mss.*

20. Newark *Evening News*, March 19, 20, 21, 22, 23, 27, 29, 1917.

21. Tumulty to Norton, July 23, 1917; Tumulty to Wittpenn, July 28, 1917, *Tumulty Mss.* Also Statement to the Press on Hudson County Special Election, September 1917, *ibid.*

22. Smith to Tumulty, October 23, 1917, *Wilson Mss.*

23. Thomas Tumulty to J. P. Tumulty, October 20, 1917, *Tumulty Mss.*

24. Tumulty to Simpson, January 18, 1918; Tumulty to Townsend, January 29, 1918, *Tumulty Mss.*; see also New York *Times*, January 20, 1918; Newark *Evening News*, January 19, 21, February 6, 1918.

25. Newark *Evening News*, February 6, 8, 12, 27, March 1, 1918; Tumulty to Simpson, February 21, 1918; Tumulty to Ely, February 22, 1918; Tumulty to Dwyer, March 11, 1918, *Tumulty Mss.*

26. The following is a sampling from

the letters in the *Tumulty Mss.* from men offering him their support. The citations give the name of the writer, a brief description where necessary, the date of the letter, and, in a few instances, an excerpt. W. J. Morgan, of Newark, January 30, 1918; W. D. Johnson, Managing Editor, the New York City *Gazette,* January 31, 1918: ". . . I promise you . . . to assist in your election. I would readily go to your state. . . ."; Carmelo Amoruso, of Jersey City, February 2, 1918; John E. Dunn, Secretary, the Supreme Council of the Catholic Benevolent Society, former Jerseyman, February 2, 1918; D. Robinson, Executive Manager of the "Downtown League," February 3, 1918: Speaking for the commuters, offers "whatever service I can render"; L. B. Plumer, Presbyterian Minister of Branchville, February 4, 1918; Thos. B. Delker, publisher, the *South Jersey Star,* February 6, 1918; Simon P. Northrup, Fidelity Trust Co., February 6, 1918; J. R. Riggs, Maryland Democrat, February 6, 1918, promising to provide labor speakers; J. A. Matthews, U.S. Labor Commissioner for New Jersey, February 7, 1918; G. B. Jackson, president, National Civic Improvement Association, Department of Negro Economics, February 11, 1918. Various outsiders offered good wishes and support if they could be effective: Colin R. Selph, January 31; Rev. R. B. Robinson, president, National Cooperative Association, February 4; Frank H. Polk, February 4; Abram I. Elkus, February 6; W. J. Burns, February 7.

27. Interview with Joseph P. Tumulty, Jr.

28. Tumulty to Mark A. Sullivan, February 9, 1918, *Tumulty Mss.*

See also Tumulty to Wade, February 8, and Tumulty to Dolan, February 8, 1918, *Tumulty Mss.*

29. Tumulty to Hudspeth, March 12, June 24, 1918; Tumulty to McDonald, June 17, 1918; Tumulty to Wilson, June 28, July 16, and enclosures, August 7, 14, 1918; Tumulty to Waldron, August 16, 1918; Tumulty to Wittpenn, October 24, 1918, *Tumulty Mss.;* Newark *Evening News,* June 10, 1918; Tumulty to Wilson, October 9, 1918; LaMonte to Wilson, October 19, 1918; Wilson to LaMonte, October 22, 1918, *Wilson Mss.;* New York *Times,* March 21, September 21, 22, November 6, 1918.

30. Tumulty to Wilson, July 10, August 8, 1917; Tumulty to Roper, *ca.* October 15, 1917, *Tumulty Mss.* Foreknowledge of the events of the coming year would have caused Tumulty to change these lists. On the priority list were Senators Chamberlain (Ore.), Culberson (Tex.), Fletcher (Fla.), Hughes (N.J.), Husting (Wisc.), James (Ky.), Johnson (S.D.), Jones (N. Mex.), Kendrick (Wyo.), King (Utah), Lewis (Ill.), Martin (Va.), Meyers (Mount.), Overman (N. C.), Owen (Okla.), Phelan (Cal.), Pittman (Nev.), Pomerene (O.), Ramsdell (La.), Robinson (Ark.), Saulsbury (Del.), Shafroth (Colo.), Sheppard (Tex.), Simmons (N.C.), Smith (Md.), Smith (Ariz.), Swanson (Va.), Tillman (N.C.), Walsh (Mont.), Williams (Miss.). On the secondary list were: Ashurst (Ariz.), Bankhead (Ala.), Beckham (Ky.), Hitchcock (Neb.), Hollis (N.H.), McKellar (Tenn.), Smith (S.C.), Thomas (Colo.), Trammell (Fla.), Underwood (Ala.), Wolcott (Del.). Of the former group,

Chamberlain especially proved unfriendly, and Sheppard led the prohibition forces.

31. Unsigned memorandum, "Analysis of Democrats in the 65th Congress," *Wilson Mss.*

32. Tumulty to Wilson, *ca.* December 1, 1914, *Wilson Mss.*; Tumulty to Wilson, August 8, 1917, *Tumulty Mss.*

33. Tumulty to House, May 7, 1918, *House Mss.*

34. Tumulty to Wilson, June 7, 1918, *Tumulty Mss.*

35. Tumulty to Wilson, March 4, 1918, *Tumulty Mss.*

36. A complete analysis of this celebrated Wisconsin election is beyond the scope of this biography, for Tumulty's rôle was confined to enlisting newspaper and organization support for Davies, see Tumulty to Wilson, February 27, March 7, 1918; Tumulty to Cobb, March 17, 1918; Tumulty to McAneny, March 17, 1918; *Tumulty Mss.*

37. Tumulty to Wilson, May 23, 29, June 7, 18, 1918, *Tumulty Mss.*

38. Tumulty to Wilson, June 18, 1918, *Tumulty Mss.*

39. House to Tumulty, July 29, 1918, *Wilson Mss.* House did not approve, however, of the final form of the partisan appeal.

40. Wilson to Ferris, March 16, July 13, 1918; Wilson to Lewis, July 13, 1918; Wilson to Gregory, July 26, 1918; Folk to Tumulty, August 7; Folk to Wilson, August 7; Wilson to Folk, August 8, 1918; Tumulty to Wilson, July 26, 1918; Tumulty to Wilson, August 7; Heney to Creel, July 17; Wilson to Heney, August 8, 1918; Krock to Wilson, September 7; Wilson to Beckham, September 19, 1918; Tumulty to Wilson, September 19; Wilson to Morrison, September 20, 1918; Decker to Wilson, August 28; Wilson to Decker, August 31, 1918, and attached notes, *Wilson Mss.* These letters show Tumulty's work for Folk, Heney, Stanley, Sherley, and Decker. They are cited in groups by man assisted. Inconsistently Tumulty was cold toward the use of these specific endorsements, especially to the many Ferris requested Wilson to make, preferring a blanket appeal as a more effective method, ref. Tumulty to Wilson, September 18, 1918, *Tumulty Mss.* But not only did the specific letters probably help the candidates, they also prepared the way for broader presidential intercession.

41. Press release in *Wilson Mss.*, dated September 9, 1918; New York *Times*, September 23, 1918. Apparently written by September 9, the statement was withheld until an attack on the Administration by Republican Simeon Fess provided a good excuse for issuing it.

42. Pou to Wilson, October 11, 1918, *Wilson Mss.* Describing a possible Republican victory as a "calamity," Pou suggested Wilson prevent it by direct action. Henry T. Rainey wrote R. S. Baker that the idea for a partisan appeal originated with Champ Clark and other veterans in Congress, ref. Rainey to Baker, August 20, 1932. *Baker Mss.*

43. Tumulty to Wilson, September 18, October 16, 1918, *Tumulty Mss.* Tumulty to Wilson, September 4, 1918, *Wilson Mss.*

44. New York *Times*, March 29, May 30, August 12, 28, 29, September 4, 11, 12, 13, 14, 15, October 26, 1918.

45. Tumulty to Wilson, September 16, 1918, *Tumulty Mss.*
46. New York *Times*, September 12, 13, 14, 1918.
47. Tumulty to Wilson, October 7, 8, 1918; Tumulty to House, October 7, 1918, *Tumulty Mss.*
48. Tumulty to Wilson, October 14, 1918, *Tumulty Mss.*
49. Cummings to Wilson, October 22, 1918, *Wilson Mss.*; Baker, *Wilson*, VIII, 495, 500, 501.
50. Tumulty to Wilson, October 21, 1918, *Tumulty Mss.*
51. Diary of E. M. House, October 9, 1918, *House Mss.*
52. Memorandum by Cummings, November 21, 1928, *Baker Mss.*
53. New York *Times*, October 26, 1918.
54. *Ibid.*, October 26, 28, 1918.
55. *Ibid.*, October 26–30, 1918; Tumulty to Cuyahoga County Republican Committee, October 26, 28, 1918, *Tumulty Mss.*
56. Tumulty to Wilson, October 25, 1918, *Tumulty Mss.* This was written after the evening newspapers showed the reaction of Republicans to Wilson's message.
57. Tumulty's requests and Wilson's responses are in the *Wilson Mss.* The following citations are to some typical examples, arranged in groups by man assisted: Tumulty to Wilson, October 9, Wilson to LaMonte, October 26; Shaine to Wilson, October 21, Tumulty's note attached, Wilson to Shaine, October 24; Mullen to Tumulty, October 24, Wilson to Tumulty, October 25, Tumulty to Wilson, October 25, Wilson to Smith, October 28; Tumulty to Wilson, October 31, Wilson to Higgins, November 1, Wilson to Murchie, November 1, Wilson to Frazier, November 1. On Watson, see McGraw to Wilson, October 16, 1918, and Tumulty's note attached; Tumulty to Wilson, October 31, 1918; McGraw to Tumulty, October 31, 1918; Wilson to McGraw, November 1, 1918, *Wilson Mss.*; Tumulty to Wilson, October 24, 1918, *Tumulty Mss.*
58. Tumulty to Wilson, November 3, 1918, and enclosure, *Wilson Mss.*
59. Spencer Ervin, *Henry Ford vs. Truman H. Newberry, The Famous Senate Election Contest* (New York, 1935). Tumulty had no part in Ford's nomination or campaign.
60. In analyzing the election, most of those who wrote the President or Tumulty declared that the appeal had helped. They advanced reasons discussed in this chapter for the defeat. A few felt the appeal hurt. The following citations are all from the *Wilson Mss.* Among the letters which took the position that Wilson's message had helped were: McGraw to Tumulty, October 31; Pittman to Wilson, November 6; A. J. Peters to Wilson, November 7; D. V. Stephens to Tumulty, November 9; J. T. Heflin to Wilson, November 12; J. H. Lewis to Wilson, November 16. Of a contrary opinion were the following: S. H. Armstrong to Wilson, November 2; Jouett Shouse to Wilson, November 7. See also Baker Interview with Burleson, March 17–19, 1927; Baker Interview with Woolley, February 2, 1929; Baker Interview with McCormick, July 15, 1928, *Baker Mss.*; Baker, *op. cit.*, VIII, 513–14.
61. Cummings to Wilson, November 7, 1918; Cochran to Wilson, November 8, 1918; Wilson to Shouse,

November 12, 1918; Wilson to Ferris, November 7, 1918, *Wilson Mss.*

62. Memorandum, "Things to be

Attended to at once: Program for 1920," November 9, 1918, *Tumulty Mss.*

Chapter XI

GOVERNMENT BY CABLE

In this and the following chapters, my main sources on the transactions at Paris were: Thomas A. Bailey, *Woodrow Wilson and the Lost Peace* (New York, 1944); Ray Stannard Baker, *Woodrow Wilson and World Settlement,* 3 vols. (Garden City, 1923), and Paul Birdsall, *Versailles Twenty Years After* (New York, 1941). For background on American opinion and on the treaty fight, in this and following chapters, I have relied constantly on Bailey's *Lost Peace* and his *Woodrow Wilson and the Great Betrayal* (New York, 1945). Familiarity with Bailey's manuscript sources increased my admiration of his analyses. On these problems Tumulty's memoir is misleading, for he wrote to defend Wilson. But his *Wilson*, indispensable to a biographer, contains, usually in complete form, most of the letters and cables Tumulty and Wilson exchanged. These documents reveal Tumulty's views fully. On public opinion the New York *Times* and *Tribune* were helpful; for extreme Irish-American opinion the *Irish World* was excellent.

Although the peace negotiations and the treaty fight have constantly been the concern of American historians, there is no good, comprehensive study of the domestic situation in America in 1919–20 apart from the politics of the treaty fight. In the parts of this chapter and later chapters on domestic affairs, therefore, manuscripts and newspaper sources proved even more valuable than in those sections on the treaty. Of the available secondary works, the most useful for background on economic problems were Selig Perlman, *A History of Trade Unionism in the United States* (New York, 1922), and George Soule, *Prosperity Decade, From War to Depression: 1917–1929* (New York, 1947). There is a graphic account of the Red scare in Frederick Lewis Allen, *Only Yesterday* (New York, 1931). My own detailed interpretation of that episode, "Nativism, Anti-Radicalism, and the Foreign Scare, 1917–1920," is scheduled for publication in either the winter or the spring issue of the *Midwest Journal* for 1951. Frederic L. Paxson, *Postwar Years, Nor-*

malcy, 1918–1923 (Berkeley, 1948), contains a rather full but disappointing general account of the period.

1. Alice Roosevelt Longworth, quoted in Bailey, *Great Betrayal,* p. 40.
2. Desk Book of Robert Lansing, November 12 through November 20, 1918, *Lansing Mss.*; Tumulty, *Wilson,* pp. 337–38.
3. Desk Book of Robert Lansing, November 25, 29, 1918, *Lansing Mss.*; Diary of E. M. House, December 14, 1918, *House Mss.*; Tumulty to Wilson, November 21, 1918, *Tumulty Mss.*
4. Tumulty to Grayson, December 16, 17, 1918, January 16, 1919, *Wilson Mss.*
5. Tumulty to Grayson, December 22, 1918; Tumulty to Wilson, December 23, 1918, January 3, 1919, *Wilson Mss.*
6. Tumulty to Wilson, January 13, 1919; Wilson to Tumulty, January 16, 1919, *Tumulty Mss.*
7. Tumulty to Wilson, January 16, 1919; Wilson to Tumulty, January 21, 1919, *Tumulty Mss.*
8. Tumulty to Wilson, March 14, 1919; Tumulty to Grayson, January 8, January 16, 1919; Tumulty to Gilbert Close, February 26, 1919 (Close was Wilson's private secretary in Paris); Tumulty to Wilson, March 24, 1919; Tumulty to Grayson, March 26, 1919; April 8, 1919, *Wilson Mss.*
9. See Tumulty, *op. cit.,* pp. 397–400. The correspondence there published is also in the *Tumulty Mss.*
10. Tumulty to Wilson, December 29, 1918; Wilson to Tumulty, January 26, 1919; Tumulty to Wilson, January 28, February 5, 1919, *Wilson Mss.*
11. Tumulty to Wilson, February 25, 1919, *Tumulty Mss.* See also Creel to Wilson, March 1, 1919; Plunkett to Wilson, March 2, 1919, *Wilson Mss.*
12. New York *Times,* March 1, 2, 1919.
13. Tumulty to Wilson, March 1, 1919, *Tumulty Mss.*
14. New York *Times,* March 4, 5, 8, 10, 1919; Kinkead to Wilson, March 8, 1919, *Wilson Mss.*
15. New York *Times,* March 8, 1919; Senators Gerry, D. I. Walsh, *et al.,* to Wilson, *Wilson Mss.*; Tumulty to Grayson, June 7, 1919, *Tumulty Mss.*; see also Tumulty, *op. cit.,* pp. 401 ff. for the final exchange of messages on Ireland between Tumulty and Wilson.
16. Tumulty to Wilson, June 9, 18, 1919; Wilson to Tumulty, June 27, 1919, *Tumulty Mss.*
17. Tumulty to Rev. John F. Ryan, *ca.* July 12, 1919, *Tumulty Mss.*
18. Tumulty to Wilson, April 25, 1919, Wilson to Tumulty, May 1, 1919, *Wilson Mss.*; Tumulty to Wilson, May 26, 1919, *Tumulty Mss.*
19. Tumulty, *op. cit.,* Appendix C; see also Bailey, *Lost Peace,* chap. 18.
20. Tumulty to Grayson, April 5, 9, 1919, *Tumulty Mss.*
21. For antithetical views on the causes of Wilson's break with House, compare G. S. Viereck, *The Strangest Friendship in History* (New York, 1932), chap. XII, and E. B. Wilson, *My Memoir,* pp. 227 ff. Mrs. Wilson's rôle in the affair is clear from her own account. Bailey in *Lost Peace* shows the differences be-

tween Wilson and House on things diplomatic, as does Birdsall, in a concise form. See also R. Lansing, *The Peace Negotiations: A Personal Narrative* (Boston, 1921). On January 9, 1938, House wrote Tumulty that there were many around Wilson trying to cause a rupture between them, that they finally succeeded, but only after they were dealing with a sick man. House declared that he believed there would have been no trouble had Wilson kept his health; see House to Tumulty, Jan. 9, 1938, *House Mss...*

22. Tumulty to Cochran, February 4, 1919, *Tumulty Mss.*

23. Tumulty to Wilson, January 7, February 8, 15, 18, 19, 28, 1919; Wilson to Tumulty, February 19, 20, 1919; Tumulty to Grayson, February 20, 1919; Tumulty to Wilson, February 22, 1919, *Wilson Mss.*; Lawrence, *Wilson*, p. 272.

24. Tumulty to Wilson, March 6, 1919, *Wilson Mss.*

25. See Appendix B in Tumulty, *op. cit.*, for the messages from Taft to Wilson.

26. Tumulty to Wilson, May 26, 1919, *Tumulty Mss.*

27. Tumulty to Wilson, June 21, 23, 1919; Wilson to Tumulty, June 23, 25, 1919; Tumulty to Seibold, June 30, 1919, *Tumulty Mss.*

28. Tumulty to Grayson, July 2, 1919, *Tumulty Mss.* As unreservedly opposed to the treaty Tumulty listed the following Senators: Borah, Brandegee, Reed, Johnson, Knox, La Follette. As opposed unless reservations were adopted: Cummins, Curtis, Fall, France, Frelinghuysen, Hale, Harding, Kellogg, M. McCormick, Lodge, Moses, Nelson, New,

Penrose, Poindexter, Phipps, Sherman, Newbery, Smoot, Spencer, Sterling, Capper, Townsend, Wadsworth, Warren, Watson. The leading public men opposing the treaty listed by Tumulty were: G. W. Pepper, J. N. Beck, H. A. Wisewood, Beveridge, Root. Editors and periodicals listed as virulently "anti" were W. R. Hearst, George Harvey, the N.Y. *Tribune*, N.Y. *Sun*, Chicago *Tribune*, Kansas City *Star*, Indianapolis *News*, Detroit *Free Press*, *New Republic*, Philadelphia *North American*, *Nation*, *Ohio State Journal*, San Francisco *Chronicle*, Detroit *Journal*, N.Y. *Herald*, Providence *Journal*.

29. Tumulty to Wilson, June 4, 1919, *Tumulty Mss.* See also Note 63, *infra.*

30. Tumulty to Wilson, January 10, 23, 31, 1919, *Wilson Mss.*

31. Tumulty to Wilson, May 9, 12, 1919; Wilson to Tumulty, May 12, 1919, *Tumulty Mss.*

32. Wilson to Tumulty, May 9, 1919; Tumulty to Wilson, May 9, 1919 (two letters of same date from Tumulty to Wilson), *Tumulty Mss.* Grayson to Tumulty, May 19, 1919, *Wilson Mss.*

33. Tumulty to Wilson, January 23, February 6, February 7, April 30, May 2, 3, 9, June 4, 1919; Wilson to Tumulty, May 6, June 6, 1919, *Wilson Mss.*

34. In an undated memorandum *ca.* May 1919, *Tumulty Mss.*, Congressman McClintock requested Tumulty to help him and Congressmen Mays, Lever, Rainey, Whaley, Ayers, and Lesher prevent the election of Clark as minority leader. McClintock's request was ignored.

35. Tumulty to Wilson, January 12,

30, February 4, 1919; McCormick to Wilson, February 18, 1919, *Wilson Mss.*; Woolley to House, January 23, 1919, *House Mss.*

36. Tumulty to Wilson, February 1, 1919, *Wilson Mss.*

37. Wilson to Gregory, February 26, 1919, *Wilson Mss.;* Tumulty to Palmer, March 3, 1919, *Tumulty Mss.*

38. Tumulty to Wilson, December 26, 1918; Wilson to Tumulty, January 14, 1919, *Wilson Mss.* Tumulty's letter press books from 1919 to 1921 contain many letters to Cummings. Cummings and Palmer were among his most frequent correspondents in that period. See also Woolley to House, February 1, 1919, *House Mss.* The House coterie did not like Cummings, partly because they felt him too friendly with Tumulty.

39. Tumulty to Wilson, March 18, 1919; McAdoo to Tumulty, March 15, 1919, *Wilson Mss.*

40. Tumulty to Wilson, March 22, May 9, 1919, *Wilson Mss.*

41. New York *Times,* January 23, 26, February 1, 12, 1919; Woolley to House, February 1, 1919, *House Mss.*

42. On February 28, 1919, the President addressed the Democratic National Committee at the White House. His extemporaneous remarks were recorded and transcribed by a government stenographer. A copy of this transcription is in the *Tumulty Mss.* In his *Wilson,* Tumulty quoted this speech in full in two sections: pp. 332–34, 367–79. On p. 378 in Tumulty's book, in the second paragraph on that page, appears the correctly quoted sentence in which Wilson announced his intention to return to private life at the expiration of his term. Although the White House at that time denied that this was the President's final decision, it was clearly at least his firm preference.

43. Wilson to Tumulty, June 2, 1919; Tumulty to Wilson, June 3, 1919, *Wilson Mss.*

44. Cobb to Tumulty, April 2, 1919; McAdoo to Tumulty, July 14, 1919; Phillips to Tumulty, September 9, 1919, *Wilson Mss.* Glynn's friends wanted him appointed Secretary of Commerce to succeed Redfield in the autumn of 1919, but Wilson refused that request. The President, however, selected Glynn as chairman of the Industrial Conference.

45. Tumulty to C. F. McDonald, December 31, 1918; Tumulty to Kerney, January 30, 1919, *Tumulty Mss.*; New York *Times,* January 18, 1919; New York *Tribune,* September 23, 25, 1919.

46. Tumulty to Wilson, March 24, April 4, 1919; Wilson to Tumulty, March 26, 1919, *Tumulty Mss.*

47. Tumulty to Wilson, December 1, 1918, *Tumulty Mss.*

48. Tumulty to Wilson, May 5, 1919, transmitting message from Burleson, *Tumulty Mss.*

49. Tumulty to Wilson, May 8, 1919; Mackay to Tumulty, May 7, 1919, *Tumulty Mss.*; Frank Morrison, Secretary of the A. F. of L., to Wilson, March 1, 1919, *Wilson Mss.*

50. Wilson to Tumulty, May 7, 1919, message for Burleson; Tumulty to Wilson, May 5, 1919, *Wilson Mss.*

51. Tumulty to Wilson, April 25, 1919, *Tumulty Mss.*

52. Tumulty to Wilson, May 8, 1919, *Tumulty Mss.* See also Tumulty to Wilson, May 9, 1919, suggestions for message to Congress, *Tumulty Mss.*

53. Tumulty to Wilson, November 14, 1918; May 9, 13, 1919, *Tumulty Mss.*; Tumulty to Wilson, May 5, 7, 1919, *Wilson Mss.*

54. Tumulty to Wilson, January 30, 1919, *Tumulty Mss.*

55. Wilson to Tumulty, undated reply to Tumulty's letter of January 30, 1919, *Tumulty Mss.*

56. Tumulty to Wilson, February 6, 1919, message from Redfield; Senators Sheppard, Curtis, Gore, Grona, *et al.* to Wilson, February 14, 1919, *Wilson Mss.*

57. Tumulty to Wilson, May 12, 1919, *Tumulty Mss.* See also Tumulty to Wilson, May 10, 1919, in *ibid.*

58. Frankfurter to W. B. Wilson, February 4, 1919; J. P. Noonan, Acting President, International Brotherhood of Electrical Workers, to Tumulty, March 26, 1919; Tumulty to Wilson, March 27, 1919; Burleson to W. B. Wilson, March 15, 1919; Burleson to Wilson, March 28, 1919, *Wilson Mss.*

59. Wilson to Tumulty, April 17, 1919, Tumulty to Grayson, April 19, 1919, *Wilson Mss.*

60. New York *Times*, April 16 through 22, 1919; Tumulty to Wilson, April 19, 20, 1919, *Wilson Mss.*

61. New York *Times*, April 18, 19, 1919; Woolley to House, June 17, 1919, *House Mss.*

62. Tumulty to Wilson, May 9, 1919, *Tumulty Mss.*

63. Tumulty to Wilson, June 4, 1919, *Tumulty Mss.*; the letter and enclosed memo, with no significant omissions, follow:

I hope you will have a chance to read the suggestions I have sent you by pouch with reference to your speeches on the League of Nations and the suggestion of a special address on reconstruction. It is clear to me, as it must be to you after witnessing the aftermath of war in Europe and the reaction in this country, that something vitally reconstructive must be done to save the world from something more terrible than European War. What happened in Washington last night in the attempt upon the Attorney General's life is but a symptom of the terrible unrest that is stalking about the country. Very few people, and especially the gentlemen on the Hill, realize the absolute seriousness of the whole situation. As a democrat I would be disappointed to see the republican party regain power. That is not what depresses me so much as to see growing steadily from day to day, under our very eyes, a movement that, if it is not checked, is bound to express itself, in an attack upon everything that we hold dear. In this era of industrial and social unrest both parties are in disrepute with the average man. The country realizes that everything of a constructive character which you succeeded in obtaining was given to it most reluctantly by Congress and that Congress has ceased to be a constructive instrument. It is, therefore, your duty as the leader of the liberal forces of the world to speak the truth about the whole situation and to propose the remedy.

If you will read the outline of the suggestions I have made you will find that I propose a definite thing in the idea of a *national industrial conference composed of employers who represent big and little business and of employees, to recommend a national plan for the improvement of relations between capital and labor.* The republican leadership of the Senate and House will scoff at this and refuse to make you an appropriation. Whereupon you will be in a position to call a national conference upon your own initiative and draw from the pockets of patriotic individuals enough to meet the needs of this conference.

This conference could outline certain steps to be taken in order to bring about a happier relationship between capital and labor. Out of it might come a programme similar to the Whitley programme.

This might adopt a profit sharing plan. You might also adopt a plan to give labor representation in the management of business. Whatever plan would be put forth by the conference would be the subject of sharp discussion throughout the country.

My suggestion is that in the same address to Congress on these matters of reconstruction, you ask Congress to avow its faith in the principles found in the Peace Treaty with reference to the fundamental rights of labor. I think this plan will do more than anything else to save the situation which now threatens us.

Suggestions of Mr. Tumulty

When the President returns he should immediately address the Senate and House and put before the Senate the Peace Treaty, and after submitting it to the Senate he should make a tour of the country, especially touching the middle west, the coast and New England.

Message by the President to Congress, covering the League of Nations.

In outlining the League of Nations to Congress the President should lay stress upon the burdens of war, as found by him in Europe, calling attention to the attendant effects of war, the burdensome taxation . . . citing the cost . . . social unrest, Bolshevism. In other words the President should make the issue before the Senate and the country one of War or Peace. It is either the League of Nations or another final war. Either the League of Nations should be accepted in its entirety or rejected, for those who clamor for its amendment are really urging its defeat. Show why this is so. Because of the impossibility of bringing all the nations together in another international conference. The message of the President to Congress and his subsequent messages should *not* have a defensive or apologetic note in them. He must take an offensive position and never digress from it for a moment. The President in his addresses should inject more punch and should use language that will bring home to the ordinary man just what he is trying to accomplish by establishing a League of Nations, and emphasize where the interest of the ordinary man is involved in this whole business. In other words, the speeches which he makes through the country should be of such a character as to satisfy every kind of opinion in this country. . . . A particular note should be struck in those speeches to the mothers and fathers of the country.

1. The speeches of the President on the League of Nations should contain arguments of a practical character; arguments that will strike home . . . that will stick. . . . Peace . . . disarmament of Ger-

many. Reduction of armaments. . . . Justice for France. . . . Protection of American interests. . . . Labor given its due. . . .

2. The President should discuss the causes of war. The wars of the past caused by attempt of great nations to exploit smaller nations and peoples; balance of power used to oppress. . . .

It is either the League of Nations or a final war; Europe paralyzed; Bolshevism spreading through all the European countries. The cause of Bolshevism is unrest. . . .

Cost to the allies, showing cost to the allies in money and in dead and wounded.

The President is the one man in the world, in my opinion, whose leadership can unite the liberal forces of the world in favor of a great program of international and domestic reconstruction. In my opinion, the real antidote for Bolshevism is social reconstruction throughout the world. We took the leadership in the matter of the League of Nations; we must follow it up by suggesting America's remedy for this ugly thing, Bolshevism. . . .

Now is the time for the President to strike and thus make the democratic party the great liberal party of the country. A new dispensation must come, either quietly or abruptly, a new adjustment between capital and labor. In the past capital got the apple and labor got the core. . . .

The President should describe economic and social conditions in Europe. . . .

Mr. Vanderlip makes a very thorough diagnosis and says that the economic and social conditions in England, France and Spain threaten revolution. In other words, that the English statesmen have allowed this cancerous growth to extend itself until now the very heart of Europe is threatened. Let us beware, therefore, and put our own house in order lest the fires that are now burning in Europe shall spread and destroy our own country. . . .

The President shortly after he delivers his address to Congress on the League of Nations ought to be ready to submit to Congress a plan of reconstruction, embodying in this plan the things that he believes necessary to bring about a better understanding between capital and labor. . . . We must treat Bolshevism as a fact and diagnose its causes and suggest a remedy. American political thought on this subject represents a great lake full of eddies but with no current moving forward.

The President could diplomatically call attention of the Congress to . . . "Labor's Bill of Rights," in the Treaty of Peace. . . .

In addition to these I believe the President should recommend to Congress the following:

Passage by Congress of an act fixing minimum wages and establishing Federal eight hour day, affecting all business and industry; Old age pensions; Health Insurance; Democratization of Industry; Federal Housing; Control of fundamental raw materials like oil, steel . . .; An act recognizing the right of collective bargaining; Appointment of a War Labor Board for the settlement of labor disputes between capital and labor; Extension of Federal vocational training to those injured in industrial pursuits . . . the appointment by the President of a committee to be known as the National Industrial Conference, composed of employers who represent big and little business and of employees, to recommend a national plan for the improvement of relations between capital and labor . . .; Establishment of cooperative organizations throughout the different towns, cities and states for the purchase of necessities of life; Establishment of Federal employment agencies on a permanent basis; The recognition of labor's right to a voice in determining the laws within industry and commerce which affect them; A reavowal of all the principles accepted in the labor declarations of the Peace Conference; Declaration by the President to protect in full the La Follette Act and the high standards of life and wages now given our seamen; The establishment of what is known as Home Loan or Neighborhood Banks, on which loans are made to workmen on easy terms of credit. . . . The Administration should encourage small farm owners and also home owners in industrial communities. Industrial unrest has vanished in the labor communities where a large percentage of the workers own their own homes. The good sense of this idea is already recognized by some of the large corporations; the Standard Oil Company, for one, is spending $500,000 on a scheme to facilitate home purchase by workers.

The President should urge the establishment of some governmental bureau under the Department of Labor to facilitate the development of the co-operative system in the United States whenever the workers or farmers or members of any other class desire to set it up. . . . In the reconstruction programme of American labor, strong endorsement is given to this movement. As in many other factors in the industrial situation, it is impossible for the Government to do anything, save provide the necessary aid and guidance for development where the workers themselves desire it.

Much good has developed from the work of the Capital Issues Committee in restraining the issuance of spurious stocks. . . . It might be unwise . . . to retain the authority permanently to *prevent* stock issues, but the Government certainly should maintain the function of investigation upon request of the investor with freedom to publish its opinions respecting the soundness of new stock issues. It probably would be better to remove this function from the Treasury Department and rest it in the Federal Reserve Board.

While developments at this time point to a constructive attitude generally on all matters to be taken up by the next Congress, it is important to anticipate a larger echo of European agitation and to volunteer real concessions to industrial unrest. American opinion is undoubtedly less radical than that of Europe, but these tendencies may change, and the only way to prevent change is to look far ahead in removing possible causes of unrest. It is possible to do radical things that will please both elements of American opinion.

64. See Note 63, *supra*.
65. Wilson to Tumulty, June 17, 1919, *Tumulty Mss.*
66. Tumulty to Wilson, June 16, 1919, *Wilson Mss.*

Chapter XII

REGENCY AND DEFEAT

In this, as in the preceding chapter, I drew heavily from the excellent study of the treaty fight in Bailey, *The Great Betrayal*. For a general discussion of the labor situation and railroad, steel, and coal strikes, Perlman, *Trade Unionism* and Soule, *Prosperity Decade* were helpful. Cecil Carnes, *John L. Lewis, Leader of Labor* (New York, 1936), contains a particularly good account of the coal strike. Tumulty, *Wilson*, is misleading on Wilson's tour and illness. On the President's illness, however, there are good discussions in Bailey, *op. cit.*, and Charles M. Thomas, *Thomas Riley Marshall* (Oxford, Ohio, 1939). Important first-hand accounts are in Irving H. Hoover, *Forty-Two Years in the White House* (Cambridge, 1934); Houston, *Eight Years with Wilson's Cabinet*, II; Lane and Wall, eds., *The Letters of Franklin K. Lane*, and E. B. Wilson, *My Memoir*. Lansing's rôle during Wilson's incapacity is well handled in Lawrence, *Wilson*. See also Note 35, below. That Wilson relied on Tumulty's suggestions, and to a lesser degree the suggestions of his other advisers, from the time of his return from Europe and particularly after his illness, is obvious by comparison of the drafts in the *Tumulty Mss.*, cited below in this and the following chapter, with the President's public papers as published in Baker and Dodd, eds., *The Public Papers of Woodrow Wilson: War and Peace*, 2 vols. (New York, 1927). After his illness the President used these drafts almost verbatim.

On all topics covered in this chapter, as the annotation indicates, manuscripts supplied the best material. The collections of Hitchcock, Lansing, and Tumulty were particularly important.

1. For the situation in the Senate in July 1919, see W. H. Taft to Hitchcock, July 21, 1919, *Gilbert M. Hitchcock Manuscripts* (Library of Congress, Washington, D.C.).

2. Baker Memo of Interview with Burleson, April 28, 1927, *Baker Mss.*

3. Press Release, dated July 12, 1919; Tumulty to Wilson, July 25, 1919, *Tumulty Mss.*

4. Tumulty to Wilson, August 14, 1919, *Tumulty Mss.* The letter in question was not used.

5. Tumulty to Wilson, July 17, 25, 1919, *Tumulty Mss.*

6. Tumulty to Wilson, August 4, 1919, *Tumulty Mss.* Tumulty's letter to Wilson contained the quotations from Bliss' letter.

7. Tumulty to Wilson, July 25, 1919, *Tumulty Mss.*

8. Solicitor of the State Department

to Wilson, July 29, 1919, *Wilson Mss.* The Lodge Resolution of November called on foreign governments to acknowledge the American reservations. In March this was eliminated. Clearly the Solicitor felt that even the November version was not binding on the foreign governments.

9. Tumulty to Wilson, August 14, 1919, *Tumulty Mss.*; Tumulty to Wilson, August 15, 1919; Pittman to Wilson, August 15, 1919, *Wilson Mss.*

10. Tumulty to Wilson, August 6, 1919. *Tumulty Mss.* See also Tumulty to Wilson, August 7, 1919, in *ibid.*

11. Tumulty to Wilson, August 14, 1919, *Tumulty Mss.*

12. New York *Times*, August 5, 7, 9, 11, 1919. Homer Cummings joined Tumulty in advising Wilson to address himself to the high cost of living.

13. Tumulty to Wilson, August 7, 1919, *Tumulty Mss.*

14. Tumulty to Wilson, August 7, 1919, *Tumulty Mss.* This was a separate memorandum from that cited immediately above.

15. Desk Book of Robert Lansing, August 21, 1919, *Lansing Mss.*; Tumulty to Wilson, August 22, 1919, *Tumulty Mss.*

16. Tumulty to Hines, August 27, 1919; Tumulty to Wilson, August 28, 1919, *Wilson Mss.*; McAdoo to Tumulty, August 29, 1919, *Tumulty Mss.*

17. Tumulty to Wilson, August 30, 1919, *Tumulty Mss.*

18. Tumulty to Hines, August 27, 1919; Tumulty to Wilson, August 28, 1919, *Wilson Mss.*

19. Tumulty to Wilson, August 15, 1919, *Tumulty Mss.*

20. Bailey, *Great Betrayal*, chapters VI, VII.

21. Hitchcock added a fifth reservation to Wilson's list. For many years it was not revealed that the President had given Hitchcock the reservations. Tumulty's memoranda, however, indicate that he knew what had transpired (see especially his appraisal of the situation in the Senate in November, quoted below in this chapter). The same memoranda indicate that the support of the mild reservationists was his objective. The other points in his argument have been documented elsewhere.

22. "Agenda for the Consideration of the Proposed Tour," undated memorandum, ca. July 1, 1919, *Tumulty Mss.* See also Tumulty to Wilson, June 9, 1919, *Tumulty Mss.*, and Tumulty to Wilson, June 5, 11, 17, 20, 1919, *Wilson Mss.*

23. "Agenda for . . . the Proposed Tour," *loc. cit.*; New York *Tribune*, September 4, 1919.

24. "Agenda for . . . the Proposed Tour," *loc. cit.*

25. *Ibid.*; McAdoo to Tumulty, August 29, September 2, 1919, *Tumulty Mss.*; New York *Tribune*, September 22, 1919.

26. E. B. Wilson, *My Memoir*, pp. 275 ff. Mrs. Wilson's descriptions of the tour, the arrangement of the train, the personnel, the crowds, etc., are interesting and useful.

27. Forster to Tumulty, message from Cochran, September 9, 1919; Forster to Tumulty, September 8, 1919; N. D. Baker to Tumulty, confidential message for Wilson from Pomerene, September 15, 1919; McCormick to Forster, message for Tumulty, September 11, 1919, *Wilson Mss.*

28. Tumulty to Wilson, September 12, 1919, *Tumulty Mss.*

29. Tumulty to Wilson, September 19, 20, 20, 1919, *Tumulty Mss.*

30. Tumulty to Wilson, September 24, 1919, *Tumulty Mss.*

31. Tumulty to Wilson, September 24, 1919, *Tumulty Mss.*, a memorandum to supplement that cited immediately above.

32. Tumulty, *Wilson*, p. 449; Interview with Warren F. Johnson.

33. New York *Tribune*, September 27, 1919.

34. Grayson to Baker, January 22, 1936, *Baker Mss.*

35. Charles L. Swem, in an interview, told me that after his collapse, Wilson never dictated more than five minutes at a time. He said that the President, even after his partial recovery, passed most of his time sitting in silence. Mrs. Wilson had to help with the dictation. Swem, who took Wilson's dictation for a decade, was in a good position to evaluate the effects of the disease. In his opinion, Wilson was never again competent to hold office.

Edith Wilson in her *Memoir* describes the President's collapse, illness, and partial recovery in detail, pp. 288 ff. Her account is the source for my information on her activities during the period. A conflicting and less reliable account of the collapse and illness is in Hoover, *Forty-Two Years in the White House*, pp. 95 · ff. Hoover was chief usher in the White House at that time.

Dr. Walter C. Alvarez has written an article discussing Wilson's symptoms in a general analysis of arteriosclerosis, W. C. Alvarez, "Cerebral Arteriosclerosis, With Small Commonly Unrecognized Apoplexies," *Geriatrics*, I, 189–216. His analysis is extremely helpful for any layman interested in the problem. He presents a series of case studies to show that the debilitating strokes of old age or middle life are frequently preceded by thromboses which are not so diagnosed at the time. These often, but not always, produce changes in the personality. The fatal stroke is the last stage of a progressive disease which, in its earlier periods, involves gradual deterioration of ability, personality, and, not infrequently, morals. Alvarez, summary reads in part: "One of the commonest ways of dying is to take ten or twenty years to peter out with cerebral arteriosclerosis and occasional episodes of thrombosis of a small intracranial artery. . . . The first episodes can come on in the forties, or even in the thirties. . . . Some become somewhat psychopathic. . . . Some fall unconscious. Some are overly emotional. Acute episodes are often thought to be attacks of 'acute indigestion'. . . ."

It is likely that the indigestion Wilson suffered in Paris was the first episode of his crippling illness; that the second major episode was at Baxter; the third his collapse. The reminiscenses of his contemporaries suggest that he was "overly emotional" after his partial recovery. His breaks with Lansing and Tumulty confirm that idea. There is no evidence, however, that he was irrational. Indeed, some of his post-presidential prose was extremely lucid and well organized. Finally, it should be noted that even in a period of coma, the heart patient is capable of sporadic, lucid moments.

36. Evidence of Wilson's disability lies in the fact that for over three weeks he signed no pardons,

issued no proclamations, and permitted many bills to become law without his signature.

37. Tumulty to Louis Seibold, October 7, 1919; Tumulty to Helen Bones, October 14, 1919; Tumulty to Joseph R. Wilson, October 16, 1919, *Tumulty Mss.* Joseph Wilson was the younger brother of the President.

38. New York *Times,* October 3 through 27, 1919, especially October 3, 4, 5, 7, 13, 14, 18.

39. Desk Book of Robert Lansing, October 3, November 4, 1919; Marshall to Lansing, October 6, 9, 1919; Lansing to Marshall, October 7, 1919, *Lansing Mss.* Lansing discussed the advisability of Marshall assuming the position of Acting President with Tumulty and Grayson on October 3. He apparently made no effort to force that condition. Tumulty to Miss Benham, October 28, 1919, *Tumulty Mss.*

40. Thomas, *Marshall,* pp. 206–8, 215; T. R. Marshall, *Recollections,* pp. 364–65; New York *Times,* October 3, 7, 19, 1919.

41. Desk Book of Robert Lansing, November 3, 1919, *Lansing Mss.* Tumulty to E. B. Wilson, letter and memorandum, November 24, 1919, *Tumulty Mss.*

42. Tumulty to E. B. Wilson, December 18, 1919, *Tumulty Mss.*

43. Desk Book of Robert Lansing, October 3, 4, 6, 7, 9, 14, 21, 22, 25, 28, 30, November 18, 25, December 1, 9, 12, 19, 23, 30, 1919, *Lansing Mss.;* New York *Times,* October 7, 1919; Tumulty to Lansing, October 28, 1919, *Tumulty Mss.*

44. Desk Book of Robert Lansing, October 3, 9, 1919, *Lansing Mss.* Houston attended without complaint, but objected to meetings called at irregular intervals. See

also R. S. Baker Memo of Interview with N. D. Baker, April 6, 1928; R. S. Baker Memo of Interview with W. B. Wilson, January 12–13, 1928, *Baker Mss.*

45. Memorandum by Tumulty, undated, *ca.* November 10, 1919; Louis Seibold to Tumulty, November 21, 1919; Draft of Veto by Tumulty, undated, *ca.* October 24, 1919, pencil changes in Houston's hand, *Tumulty Mss.*

46. Tumulty to Sinnott, October 31, 1919, *Tumulty Mss.* Sinnott, an old friend, was with the Newark *News.*

47. Tumulty to Lansing, October 28, 1919; Tumulty to E. B. Wilson, November 5, 7, 1919, *Tumulty Mss.*

48. Tumulty to Wilson, October 2, November 4, 1919; Tumulty to Baruch, November 1, 1919, *Tumulty Mss.;* New York *Times,* October 5, 6, 7, 22, 1919.

49. Wilson to H. M. Robinson, December 19, 1919, *Tumulty Mss.*

50. Hines to Tumulty, October 10, 1919, *Tumulty Mss.*

51. Tumulty to Hines, October 24, 1919, with enclosure; Hines to Tumulty, October 24, 1919, *Tumulty Mss.* In these letters, Hines and Tumulty exchanged and correlated the ideas and phraseology that formed the statement, which was then taken to the Cabinet for approval.

52. Hines to Tumulty, October 21, 28, 1919, *Tumulty Mss.;* Garfield to Lansing, January 13, 1920, *Lansing Mss.* This long letter, written at Lansing's request, was a resumé of all the events leading up to Garfield's resignation in December. The letter included copies of the correspondence between Garfield and Wilson, dated December 5, 7, 9, 11, and 13, 1919; Garfield's statements of his

negotiations with William Green; and Garfield's recollection of his negotiations with the Cabinet. It is an invaluable document for an account of the government's part in the coal strike. Hereafter I shall cite it as "Garfield's Resumé."

53. Tumulty to W. B. Wilson, October 29, 1919, *Tumulty Mss.*

54. Statement of October 31, 1919, prepared by Tumulty and sent to Palmer, *Tumulty Mss.*

55. New York *Times,* November 11, 1919.

56. Garfield's Resumé *loc. cit.*.

57. McAdoo to Wilson, December 2, 1919, *Tumulty Mss.*

58. Garfield's Resumé, *loc. cit.*

59. *Ibid.*

60. Tumulty to E. B. Wilson, December 9, 1919; the Cabinet to Wilson, December 9, 1919; Palmer to Tumulty, December 8, 1919, *Tumulty Mss.*; Lansing to Wilson, December 9, 1919, *Wilson Mss.* The Commission appointed was White, Peale, and Henry M. Robinson. They failed to agree on an adjustment, White dissenting. In March 1920, their disagreement resulted in a recurrence of the friction of November 1919, but not in a major strike, for Lewis stamped out the wildcat strikes of

March led by Frank Farrington, a radical labor organizer from Illinois; ref. Carnes, *Lewis,* pp. 60–61; Hines to Tumulty, March 17, 1920, Reynolds to Tumulty, March 13, 1920, *Tumulty Mss.*

61. Tumulty to Wilson, September 30, 1919, *Tumulty Mss.*

62. Hitchcock to Bryan, October 4, 1919, *Bryan Mss.*

63. Bailey, *op. cit.,* chapter XI.

64. Desk Book of Robert Lansing, October 12, 20, November 4, 5, 6, 7, 8, 17, 1919, *Lansing Mss.* The French and British positions were made public after the first defeat of the treaty. That Lansing was informed of them by Grey in November seems to me to be clear, judging from Lansing's point of view after seeing Grey.

65. Tumulty to Wilson, November 11, 1919, *Tumulty Mss.*

66. Hitchcock to E. B. Wilson, November 13, 15, 18, 1919, *Wilson Mss.* Desk Book of Robert Lansing, November 17, 1919, *Lansing Mss.*

67. Tumulty to E. B. Wilson, November 17, 1919, *Tumulty Mss.* Tumulty quoted Underwood.

68. Tumulty to Wilson, November 17, 1919, *Tumulty Mss.*

Chapter XIII

GOETTERDAEMMERUNG

The outstanding secondary work on the topics covered in this chapter, particularly on public opinion and on Republican tactics in the treaty fight and the election of 1920, is Bailey's *Great Betrayal.* I am again indebted to him. There is, regrettably, no adequate study of the Democratic preconvention campaigns and the convention of 1920. A few published accounts are helpful: Josephus Daniels, *The Wilson Era: Years of War and After* (Chapel Hill, 1946), pp. 551–55 (the reminiscences of an observer); McCombs, *Wilson,* pp. 295–99 (the report of an anti-Wilson leader); R. Smith and N. Beasley, *Carter Glass* (New York, 1939), pp. 205–13 (excerpts from Glass' revealing diary). C. W. Stein, *The Third-Term Tradition* (New York, 1943), contains a detailed study of Democratic politics in 1920, based on the best available sources. It suffers, however, because of the author's weak thesis that Wilson began to seek a third term before going to Paris. In all sections of the chapter, as the annotation indicates, my most fruitful source was the *Tumulty Mss.* On the nomination and convention, the *Baker Mss.* and *Burleson Mss.* were also excellent.

1. Desk Book of Robert Lansing, November 20, 22, 29, December 1, 2, 3, 1919; C. D. Warner to Lansing, November 29, 1919; J. W. Davis to Lansing, December 23, 1919; *Lansing Mss.*; Hitchcock to Bryan, November 30, 1919, *Bryan Mss.*; N. H. Davis to Tumulty, December 1, 1919, *Wilson Mss.*

2. Tumulty to E. B. Wilson, December 16, 18, 1919, *Tumulty Mss.*; E. B. Wilson to Hitchcock, December 19, 1919, *Hitchcock Mss.*

3. Draft of Proposed Statement, tentatively dated January 26, 1920; Palmer to Wilson, December 22, 1919, *Wilson Mss.* The January date, affixed by the custodians of the Wilson Papers, is, I believe, wrong. Palmer's letter indicates that the plan was proposed to him in some form in December. Tumulty's draft of the Jackson Day letter, composed early in January, contains sections identical with the senatorial resignation statement. I believe, therefore, that the correct date for the statement should be about December 20, 1919. The January date was affixed, I think, because in late January Wilson consulted Burleson about the plan. It is possible, but I think unlikely, that in December Wilson outlined the plan

and late in January wrote the statement, drawing on Tumulty's draft of the Jackson Day letter. In either case, however, before December 22, 1919, the President had the senatorial resignation scheme in mind.

4. There are three drafts of the Jackson Day letter in the *Tumulty Mss.* The final draft is the same as that published in the New York *Times*, January 9, 1920.

5. Drafts of the Jackson Day letter, *Tumulty Mss.* See also Houston, *Eight Years with Wilson's Cabinet*, II, 47–48.

6. Tumulty to Wilson, January 2, 1920, *Tumulty Mss.*

7. Hitchcock to E. B. Wilson, January 5, 1920, *Hitchcock Mss.*

8. Hitchcock to E. B. Wilson, January 13, 1920; E. B. Wilson to Hitchcock, *sa.* January 6, January 15, 1920, *Hitchcock Mss.*

9. The following letter from the *Tumulty Mss.* was drafted by Tumulty for Wilson to send to Hitchcock. The draft was completed on January 14, 1920:

You have asked me to tell you frankly what interpretations I had in mind when I wrote the letter of January eighth, saying: "I have endeavored to make it plain that if the Senate wishes to say what the undoubted meaning of the League is, I shall have no objection. There can be no reasonable objection to interpretations accompanying the act of ratification itself."

I am very glad indeed to tell you, so that you may inform your Democratic and Republican colleagues who desire an early ratification of the Peace Treaty, what I would construe as reasonable interpretations. I fully agree with you that delay is most unfortunate and that if there is an opportunity to obtain an agreement on the part of those who sincerely desire to see the Treaty ratified, we should make every effort, in a spirit of accommodation, to accomplish that result as quickly as possible. Each day's delay brings an unsettlement of conditions throughout the world which not only invites disaster to our sorely-tried associates, but brings the contagion of world unrest nearer our own shores.

I have had from the first no doubt about the good faith of our associates in the war; nor have I had any reason to suppose that any nation would seek to enlarge our obligations under the Covenant of the League of Nations, or would seek to commit us to lines of action which under our Constitution only the Congress of the United States can in the last analysis decide, but if any doubts remain in the minds of Senators that in future generations ambiguous constructions may be placed upon various clauses in the Treaty, I am glad to summarize what seem to me reasonable interpretations on the points which have been the subject of controversy in the Senate for many months.

1. It is evident that when ratifications have been exchanged,

the interpretations set forth by the United States therein will become a part of the Treaty of Peace.

2. The United States is of course able to withdraw from the League of Nations, under Article I of the Covenant, and being a sovereign state is naturally the sole judge of whether all its international obligations have been fulfilled at the time of withdrawal. But, in my judgment, it would seem to be wiser to give to the President of the United States in the future the right to act upon any such resolution as may be adopted by Congress giving notice of withdrawal, and it would seem, therefore, advisable to make it necessary that any resolution giving notice of withdrawal shall be a joint instead of a concurrent resolution. This would permit the President of the United States, who is charged by the Constitution with the conduct of foreign policy, to have a voice in saying whether so important a step as withdrawal from the League of Nations shall be accomplished by a simple majority vote or by a two-thirds vote, which would be the case if he vetoed the resolution. Our fathers provided that whenever the legislative body was to be consulted in treaty-making, a two-thirds vote was required, and it seems to me that there should be no departure from the wise course which they outlined at the beginning of the Republic.

3. With respect to the much-discussed Article X, it seems to me to be clearly a question of whether the moral influence which the Executive branch of the Government of the United States, under this or future ad-

ministrations, can always exert for the preservation of peace shall not be diminished, but that, on the other hand, it should be clearly understood by our associates at all times that whenever the employment of military or naval forces is recommended by the League of Nations, the power of the Congress of the United States to accept or reject such a recommendation is inviolate. And there must be no misunderstanding at any time on the part of our associates in the League if any President of the United States in the exercise of his constitutional functions submits the matter for decision by Congress before casting the vote of the United States. Disregard of the right of Congress in this respect was never contemplated by the members of the American Peace Commission in Paris, nor was it misunderstood by our colleagues, who were as jealous as we were to guard their own sovereignty and preserve the right of their own legislative parliaments to participate in momentous decisions involving the use of military or naval forces. . . .

5. As to the sovereign right of the United States to determine what questions are within its domestic jurisdiction, the Covenant expressly excludes interference with domestic questions relating wholly or in part to international affairs. Therefore, I see no objection to stating that immigration, the tariff, the suppression of the traffic in opium, or any other questions which the United States may by its sovereign rights determine are domestic in character, shall not be submitted in any way either to arbitration, inquiry or decision without our consent.

6. With respect to the Monroe Doctrine, the Covenant expressly states that "nothing shall impair the validity of such regional understandings as the Monroe Doctrine." I see no objection to an even more specific declaration, if it is desired by the Senate, to the effect that any question which in the judgment of the United States depends upon or relates to our long-established policy, commonly known as the Monroe Doctrine, shall be interpreted by the United States alone and declared entirely unaffected by any provision contained in the Treaty of Peace with Germany. . . .

7. Clearly, the desire of those who do not approve of the so-called Shantung Settlement must be, not merely to condemn, but to do something salutary which will assist in the future settlement of this troublesome question. Therefore, I should see no objection to a declaration reserving to us full liberty of action with respect to any controversy that may arise between the Republic of China and the Empire of Japan, if the pledges made by the Japanese delegation, and which are contained in the minutes of the Conference at Paris, are not fulfilled.

8. There is no necessity, in my judgment, to insert in the Treaty of Peace provisions that relate entirely to the method by which the United States will provide for the appointment of the representatives of the United States in the Assembly and Council of the League, since each nation must retain its sovereign right of selecting those representatives in whatever way it shall choose. The appointment of individuals to

conduct the foreign policy of the United States is fully covered in the Constitution of the United States, and Congress is authorized to pass laws appropriating or refusing to appropriate money for the maintenance of such representation. Congress can always pass laws forbidding participation by citizens of the United States on commissions of the League of Nations if those citizens have not already been duly appointed as representatives of the United States in accordance with the laws of the United States.

9. With respect to the Reparation Commission and the functions of the American commissioner, it is obvious that the commerce of the United States can be regulated under the Constitution only by the Congress, but that this in no way impairs the power of the Executive branch of the Government to negotiate commercial agreements with foreign powers, subject, of course, to the approval of our legislative body. (See Lansing on this.)

10. Those questions which relate to whether or not the United States shall be obliged to contribute to any expenses of the League of Nations unless and until an appropriation of funds for such expenses shall have been made by the Congress of the United States are, of course, in line with what has been recognized would be our practice, and is the practice of parliamentary governments in all parts of the world who control foreign policy by means of the budget. So, there can be no objection to notifying foreign govenments that appropriations for the maintenance of American representa-

tions in the Secretariat or on commissions organized under the League of Nations can be made only by the Congress of the United States.

11. No programme for disarmament has as yet been adopted by any of the powers. Provision alone has been made for inquiry into this subject. It is to be expected that when any definite programme is finally presented to the United States for approval or disapproval by the League, this country, of course, reserves the right to say under what conditions, such as when threatened with invasion or when engaged in war, the United States would feel justified in increasing those armaments.

12. The right of the United States to permit in its discretion the nationals of a covenant-breaking state to continue their commercial, financial and personal relations with the nationals of the United States is entirely covered in the right of the Executive branch of the Government to sever diplomatic relations with foreign countries and to withdraw consular protection to commercial transactions.

13. See Lodge reservation 13.

14. It was the unanimous opinion of the men who framed the League of Nations Covenant that under no circumstances should one nation have greater voting power than any other. So, I have no objection to stating specifically, as it has been stated in the Senate, that in case of a dispute between members of the League, if one of them have self-governing colonies, dominions or parts which have representation in the Assembly each are to be considered parties to the dispute,

the same shall be the rule if one of the parties to the dispute is a self-governing colony, dominion or part, in which case all other parts, as well as the nation as a whole, shall be disqualified.

I sincerely hope, my dear Senator, that the interpretations which I have set forth will be of use in bringing about an early ratification of the Peace Treaty, so that we may take our place alongside the great nations who helped to fight the war to a successful conclusion and who bound themselves together by the terms of the Armistice to establish a concert of power that would preserve the peace of the world. The only stabilizing influence left to bring order out of this chaos of distress is the League of Nations, whose power and effectiveness would be more or less nullified by the refusal of America manfully to accept her full measure of responsibility with her associates. If there have been any mistakes in the making of the Peace Treaty, the League of Nations furnishes the means for revision in the future. America covets the opportunity to serve humanity and to help save the world. She ought not to be denied of this opportunity.

10. Desk Book of Robert Lansing, January 9, 13, 14, 21, 1920, *Lansing Mss.*; Lansing to Tumulty, January 15, 1920; Tumulty to E. B. Wilson, including message from Houston, January 16, 1920, *Tumulty Mss.*

11. Tumulty to E. B. Wilson, January 15, 1920, *Tumulty Mss.*

12. Tumulty to E. B. Wilson, January 16, 1920, *Tumulty Mss.*; Hitchcock to Tumulty, January 17, 1920, *Wilson Mss.*

13. Tumulty to E. B. Wilson, January 17, 1920, *Tumulty Mss.*

14. Tumulty to E. B. Wilson, January 17, 1920, with pencil comment by E. B. Wilson in return, *Wilson Mss.*

15. Hitchcock to Wilson, January 22, 1920; Wilson to Hitchcock, January 26, 1920, *Wilson Mss.*

16. Desk Book of Robert Lansing, December 29, 1919, *Lansing Mss.*

17. New York *Times*, February 14, 1920; Desk Book of Robert Lansing, January 19, February 7, 8, 9, 10, 11, 12, 13, 1920, *Lansing Mss.*; Lansing to Burleson, February 10, 1920, *Burleson Mss.*

18. New York *Times*, February 14, 16, 17, 1920; Desk Book of Robert Lansing, February 14, 15, 18, 22, 24, 25, 27, December 24, 1920, *Lansing Mss.*; Interview with Charles L. Swem (Swem said that Tumulty was surprised and shocked by Wilson's action); David Lawrence in the Washington *Star*, February 17, 18, 19, 1920; K. E. Brand Interview with Josephus Daniels, August 8, 1936, *Baker Mss.*; R. S. Baker, *American Chronicle*, p. 480 (Baker's diary, here published, described Wilson's action as petulant and irritable, a harsh criticism from a good friend); Bailey, *Great Betrayal*, pp. 245–50; Houston, *op. cit.*, II, 67; E. B. Wilson, *My Memoir*, pp. 300–301.

19. Tumulty to E. B. Wilson, February 13, 1920, *Tumulty Mss.*

20. Hitchcock to Wilson, February 24, 1920, *Tumulty Mss.*

21. Tumulty to Wilson, February 27, 1920, *Tumulty Mss.* The emphasis is mine.

22. Tumulty to E. B. Wilson, March 1, 1920, *Tumulty Mss.*, enclosed a draft of Wilson's letter of March 8 to Hitchcock. "You will notice," Tumulty observed,

". . . a gentle slap at Sir Edward Grey's unwarranted interference in our politics." Tumulty to E. B. Wilson, March 7, 1920, *Tumulty Mss.*, enclosed a revision of the March 1 draft. Tumulty to E. B. Wilson, March 11, 1920, *Tumulty Mss.*, enclosed a draft of Wilson's letter to Simmons of that date, which simply referred Simmons to the March 8 letter to Hitchcock. These letters were the last call for an uncompromising attitude on the treaty.

23. Tumulty to E. B. Wilson, March 26, June 24, 1920; C. L. Swem to Tumulty, May 10, June 3, 1930, and enclosures, *Tumulty Mss.* Swem's letters contain his shorthand notes, transcribed, of the plank Wilson dictated.

24. Tumulty to Wilson, March 23, May 12, 1920, *Tumulty Mss.* Wilson returned the letter of May 12 after writing in pencil at the bottom that Tumulty was not to receive the petition.

25. Tumulty to E. B. Wilson, December 23, 1919, February 10, 14, 1920; Tumulty to Wilson, February 24, March 4, April 1, 8, 1920, *Tumulty Mss.*

26. Tumulty to E. B. Wilson, March 26, 1920; Tumulty to Wilson, June 4, 1920, *Tumulty Mss.*

27. Tumulty to E. B. Wilson, March 24, 1920, *Tumulty Mss.*

28. Tumulty to Wilson, May 7, 1920, *Tumulty Mss.*; New York *Times*, May 10, 11, 12, 1920.

29. Tumulty to Wilson, May 17, 1920, *Tumulty Mss.*

30. Tumulty to Wilson, April 20, 1920; Tumulty to Walsh, Gerry, Glass and Palmer, June 15, 1920, *Tumulty Mss.*

31. Tumulty to E. B. Wilson, March 23, 1920, *Tumulty Mss.*

32. Seibold to Tumulty, April 1, 4,

May 13, 27, June 11, 13, 1920; Seibold to E. B. Wilson, May 12, June 12, 1920, *Tumulty Mss.*

33. The questions, answers, and excerpted materials were attached to the incoming Seibold correspondence, cited above. The various memoranda are undated. They are in Tumulty's longhand or shorthand as well as in typed form.

34. *Ibid.*

35. New York *World*, June 18, 1920. The *World* was Seibold's paper. The article was also distributed by the Associated Press.

36. New York *Times*, June 18, 19, 20, 21, 22, 23, 24, 1920; A. I. Elkins to Wilson, June 24, 1920; K. Guild to Wilson, June 26, 1920; Mingo County Democratic Committee to Wilson, June 26, 1920; J. J. Schuyleman to Wilson, July 2, 1920, *Wilson Mss.*

37. Tumulty to Krock, December 2, 1919; Tumulty to E. B. Wilson, March 16, 1920; Tumulty to McAdoo, November 20, December 5, 1919; Tumulty to Wilson, March 17; Tumulty to Palmer, J. E. Davies, T. T. Ansberry, March 10, 1920; Tumulty to Cox, January 14, 1920, *Tumulty Mss.*; J. M. Cox, *Journey Through My Years* (New York, 1946), p. 244; McAdoo to Tumulty, May 14, 1920, *Wilson Mss.*

38. Tumulty to Wilson, July 2, 1920, *Tumulty Mss.*

39. Tumulty to Glass, July 4, 1920; Tumulty to Wilson, July 4, 1920; Press Release, July 4, 1920, *Tumulty Mss.*; Glass to Baker, February 4, 1929, *Baker Mss.*

40. Tumulty to E. B. Wilson, July 4, 1920, *Tumulty Mss.*; see also Colby to Wilson, July 2, 1920, *Wilson Mss.*

41. Tumulty to E. B. Wilson, July 5,

5, 1920, *Tumulty Mss.* (two letters of the same date).

42. New York *Times,* July 7, 1920; Hoover, *Forty-Two Years in the White House,* pp. 106–7.

43. Tumulty to Cox, September 23, 1920; Cox to Tumulty, September 24, 1920, *Tumulty Mss.*

44. Tumulty to Wilson, August 4, *ca.* August 10, 1920; Tumulty to Palmer, September 30, October 10, 13, 1920; Tumulty to Cummings, August 4, September 16, 1920, *Tumulty Mss.*

45. Tumulty to Cox, July 9, September 24, 1920; Tumulty to Cobb, August 2, October 11, 1920; Tumulty to Dear, September 21, 1920; Tumulty to Barclay, undated, *ca.* September 1, 1920, *Tumulty Mss.*

46. New York *Times,* July 30, 31, 1920; Tumulty to the Editor of the *Times,* July 30, 1920; Tumulty to Swann, July 31, 1920; Tumulty to Measday, August 2, 1920; Swann to Tumulty, July 30, 1920; Reichenbach to Tumulty, July 30, 1920; Measday to Tumulty, July 31, 1920, *Tumulty Mss.*

47. Woolley to House, October 23, 1920; House to Woolley, October 25, 1920, *House Mss.*

48. Memorandum, October 19, 1920, signed by Tumulty; Chancellor to Tumulty, October 24, 1920, *Tumulty Mss.*; Tumulty, *Wilson,* pp. 278–80; M. Sullivan, *Our Times: the Twenties* (New York, 1935), pp. 131–37. Mrs. Wilson accused Tumulty of wanting to use the affidavits in the campaign. Her caustic account is in E. B. Wilson, *My Memoir,* pp. 305–6.

49. Tumulty to Wilson, June 29, 1920, *Tumulty Mss.*

50. Tumulty to Cox, August 16; Tumulty to Cochran, October 1;

Tumulty to Wilson, October 18, 1920, *Tumulty Mss.*

51. Tumulty to Wilson, July 12, 26, October 6, 1920, *Tumulty Mss.*

52. Tumulty to Cox, August 16, September 24, October 13, 1920, *Tumulty Mss.*

53. Tumulty to Cox, September 6, 1920; Moore to Tumulty, October 21, 1920, *Tumulty Mss.*

54. Tumulty to Cox, September 9, 1920; Campbell to Tumulty, April 24, 1928, *Tumulty Mss.* Election expenses of both parties were reported in the New York *Times,* March 2, 1921.

55. Memorandum, *ca.* August 1, 1920, *Tumulty Mss.* See also Tumulty to E. B. Wilson, August 2, 1920; Tumulty to Wilson, August 3, 1920; Tumulty to Cummings, August 4, 1920, *Tumulty Mss.*

56. Tumulty to Cox, September 16, 1920, *Tumulty Mss.*

57. Tumulty to Cox, September 17, 20, 26, 29, 30, 1920; October 11, 12, 18, 26, 1920; Tumulty to Wilson, October 6, 1920; Tumulty to Mrs. G. Bass, Guffey, Moore, Cummings, Harrison, and McAdoo, September 16, 1920; Cox to Tumulty, October 9, 20, 1920, *Tumulty Mss.*; New York *Times,* November 1, 1920.

58. Moore to Cox, September 16, 1920; Cox to Moore, September 17, 1920, *Tumulty Mss.*

59. Tumulty to Wilson, September 16, 1920; Harrison to Wilson, September 25, 1920; White to Wilson, September 25, 1920, *Tumulty Mss.*

60. Tumulty to Wilson, September 26, 1920, with enclosure; Wilson to Tumulty, undated, *ca.* September 27, 1920, *Tumulty Mss.*

61. Tumulty to Cox, September 28, October 1, 1920; Tumulty to Wilson, October 19, 20, 1920; Cox to Tumulty, October 9, 1920; Morris

to Tumulty, September 30, 1920, *Tumulty Mss.*

62. New York *Times*, October 5–12, 1920; Tumulty to Spencer, October 4, 1920; Tumulty to Wilson, October 4, 1920; Wilson to Spencer, October 5, 6, 1920, *Tumulty Mss.*

63. New York *Times*, October 28, 1920.

64. *Ibid.*, October 4, 1920.

65. Tumulty to Wilson, October 1, 1920, *Tumulty Mss.*

66. Pencil notation in Wilson's hand on Tumulty's letter of October 1, cited above.

67. Tumulty to Baruch, October 25, 1920, *Tumulty Mss.*

68. The speech called for votes for Cox, but it was primarily a tribute to Wilson, see New York *Times*, October 29, 1920. It was later privately printed, with a few changes, as a pamphlet: "The Tribute of a Friend." Many of Wilson's friends, moved by the speech, wrote Tumulty congratulatory letters: Louis Wiley, October 28; E. N. Hurley, October 29; Jesse Jones, October 29; Carter Glass, October 29; G. F. Peabody, October 29; L. Seibold, October 31; Jouett Shouse, November 15, 1920, and others, *Tumulty Mss.*

69. Tumulty to E. B. Wilson, November 1, 1920; Tumulty to Cox, November 3, 1920, *Tumulty Mss.*; Bailey, *op. cit.*, p. 334.

70. Axson to Tumulty, March 21, 1922, *Tumulty Mss.*

71. Tumulty to E. B. Wilson, December 17, 1920; Wilson to Tumulty, February 25, 1921, *Tumulty Mss.*; New York *Times*, November 12, 13, 29, 30, December 5, 18, 1920; February 24, March 4, 1921.

72. Tumulty to Wilson, November 6, 1920; Tumulty recommended Hull in letters to Wilson of November 9, 1920, and February 4, 1921, *Tumulty Mss.*

73. Tumulty to E. B. Wilson, February 22, 1921; Tumulty to Hague, February 26, 1921; Tumulty to Grayson, March 3, 1921, *Tumulty Mss.*

74. Tumulty to Kerney, March 2, 1921; see also Tumulty to Colby, W. B. Wilson, Daniels, Burleson, Meredith, N. D. Baker, Payne, Palmer, Alexander, Houston, and McAdoo, all dated March 1, 1920; Tumulty to Bender, March 3; to Lawrence, March 3; to Logan, February 26; to Messenger, March 2; to Norton, February 26; to Seibold, February 26; to Sinnott, March 2; to Wiley, February 26, 1920, *Tumulty Mss.*

75. Tumulty to Philip Tumulty, Jr., March 3, 1920, *Tumulty Mss.*

Chapter XIV

EPILOGUE

Covering as it does a large number of topics over many years, this chapter rests primarily on manuscript materials cited below and the secondary works listed in each case with them.

1. House to Tumulty, November 24, December 4, 1921, *House Mss.*; Lawrence, *Wilson*, p. 335.

2. Interview with Joseph P. Tumulty, Jr.; New York *Times*, September 24, 1924.

3. Woolley to Tumulty, February 12, 1921; Baruch to Tumulty, Au-

gust 31, September 2, 1921; Tumulty to Baruch, September 1, 3, 1921; Hull to Tumulty, November 29, 1922; April 16, 1923; Tumulty to Hull, January 17, 1924, *Tumulty Mss.*; Glass to White, August 23, 1921; Glass to J. R. Bolling, September 14, 1921; Baruch to Wilson, August 10, 1921, *Wilson Mss.*

4. Wilson's S Street file in the *Wilson Mss.* contains all the documents on his post-presidential years. They reveal him in an unfortunate light. There was no correspondence with McAdoo. Wilson and his friends frequently criticized Cox and his associates. Wilson was not an avowed candidate for the Presidency, but his letters suggest that he was thinking along that line. On these topics, see particularly Wilson's correspondence in the S Street file, arranged alphabetically, with Glass, Baruch, Colby, N. H. Davis, and Cobb; worth special attention is Wilson's letter to Cobb of November 15, 1922. See also an excellent memorandum by Katharine Brand, in *Ray Stannard Baker Accessions* (Library of Congress, Washington, D.C.), on Wilson in the post-presidential years.

5. "Confidential Document," *Wilson Mss.* See also correspondence between Wilson and the men listed in the text, above; and K. Brand, Memorandum, *Baker Accession.*

6. Essary to J. R. Bolling, March 24, 1921, with Bolling's comment on the letter; Tumulty to Wilson, July 7, 1921, with Wilson's comment on the letter, *Wilson Mss.*

7. Tumulty to Wilson, January 25, 1922, *Wilson Mss.*

8. New York *Times,* January 26, 1922.

9. Tumulty to Wilson, April 5, 1922;

Wilson to Tumulty, April 6, 1922; see also Colby to Wilson, April 6, 1922, and Bolling to Colby, April 7, 1922, *Wilson Mss.*

10. New York *Times,* April 9, 1922.

11. New York *Times,* April 12, 1922; Tumulty to Wilson, April 12, 1922, *Tumulty Mss.* There are several accounts of the Wilson-Tumulty break, two of which contain the important correspondence. Tumulty's letters to Wilson and Mrs. Wilson are published, with insignificant omissions, in William A. White, *Woodrow Wilson* (Cambridge, 1924), pp. 504–11. Wilson's letters to Tumulty are in Edith B. Wilson, *My Memoir,* pp. 332–35. Edith Wilson's account is entirely from her point of view. White gives Tumulty's point of view in the pages cited above and in pages 472–82. The long quotation White published from a conversation with Tumulty is accurate as to fact but inaccurate in vocabulary and tone. Other good accounts of the episode, all more or less favorable to Tumulty, are in Lawrence, *op. cit.,* pp. 334–35; Baker, *American Chronicle,* p. 480; Cox, *Journey Through My Years,* pp. 406–7; and Kerney, *Wilson,* pp. 473–75, 479–80.

12. Tumulty to Wilson, April 13, 1922, *Tumulty Mss.*

13. New York *Times,* April 14, 1922.

14. Tumulty to E. B. Wilson, April 14, 1922, *Tumulty Mss.*

15. Axson to Tumulty, April 23, 1922; Helen Woodrow Bones to Tumulty, April 27, 1939; see also Fitz Woodrow to Tumulty, February 25, 1939; Cordell Hull to Tumulty, February 28, 1939; James F. Byrnes to Tumulty, September 19, 1924, *Tumulty Mss.* The press also took Tumulty's side; see especially the New York

Times, April 17, 1922; Charles G. Ross in the St. Louis *Post-Dispatch,* April 16, 1922; J. F. Essary in the Richmond *Times-Dispatch,* April 17, 1922; David Lawrence in the Chicago *Daily News,* April 16, 1922; Charles Michelson in the New York *World,* April 15, 1922; Cleveland *Plain Dealer,* April 15, 1922; New York *Tribune,* April 15, 1922; and Pearson and Allen in the Washington *Times-Herald,* March 4, 1939.

16. Kerney to Tumulty, March 7, 1924; Tumulty to the Editor of the *Saturday Evening Post,* February 23, 1939, *Tumulty Mss.* See also the *Saturday Evening Post,* April 8, 1939.

17. The paper was named the *National Democrat.* Of the large correspondence pertaining to it in the *Tumulty Mss.,* the most important letters are: Tumulty to Guffey, October 28, 1925; to Chadbourne, October 31, November 7, 1925; to Cummings, November 2, 1925; to Roper, November 10, 1925; Cummings to Tumulty, November 4, 1925; N. H. Davis to Tumulty, November 6, 1925; Cox to Tumulty, December 15, 1925; and Chadbourne to Tumulty, December 18, 1925. Among those who contributed funds to the project were Franklin D. Roosevelt, Norman H. Davis, Daniel C. Roper, Thomas L. Chadbourne, Joseph E. Guffey, Cordell Hull, Thomas Fortune Ryan, Owen D. Young, Bernard M. Baruch and Tumulty.

18. Tumulty's political activity was so sporadic and, from a national point of view, so unimportant after 1922 that detailed references to his letters and to newspaper accounts are unnecessary. His office file, arranged by correspondent, contains the letters to public men in which he articulated his views. Most important are his letters to Cox, Davis, Smith, Raskob, Roosevelt, Garner, Farley, and Harrison. The New York *Times* contains accounts of his work at national conventions and during national campaigns. The Boston *Herald, Globe,* and *Post* covered his New England speeches; the Newark *News* his New Jersey speeches.

19. Tumulty to J. W. Davis, July 12, 1924, *Tumulty Mss.*

20. See Tumulty's testimony and letters published in "Hearings Before a Special Committee to Investigate Lobbying Activities, United States Senate, Pursuant to Senate Resolution 165, a Resolution Providing for an Investigation of Lobbying Activities in Connection with the so-called 'Holding Company Bill' (S. 2796)," Part 2 (Washington, 1935), pp. 857-71; also the New York *Times,* August 11, 1935; also Tumulty's statements on Insull and on his work for Insull, privately printed and distributed, *Tumulty Mss.* Tumulty's correspondence with House and McAdoo shows their reconciliation in the late twenties and early thirties.

21. New York *Times,* October 25, 1925; February 5, 6, 7, 18, 1932; January 23, 1938; Tumulty to the Editor, *Liberty Magazine,* February 20, 1932, *Tumulty Mss.* See also Tumulty to Baruch, February 19, 1932, and enclosures, *Tumulty Mss.*

22. New York *Times,* February 5, 1924. The *Tumulty Mss.* contain copies of many other similar speeches by Tumulty.

INDEX